D1134610

The Therapeutic Relationship in the Cognitive Behavioral Psychotherapies

Although the therapeutic relationship is a major contributor to therapeutic outcomes, the cognitive behavioral psychotherapies have not explored this aspect in any detail. This book addresses this shortfall and explores the therapeutic relationship from a range of different perspectives within cognitive behavioral and emotion focused therapy traditions.

The Therapeutic Relationship in the Cognitive Behavioral Psychotherapies covers new research on basic models of the process of the therapeutic relationship, and explores key issues related to developing emotional sensitivity, empathic understanding, mindfulness, compassion and validation within the therapeutic relationship. The contributors draw on their extensive experience in different schools of cognitive behavioral therapy to address their understanding and use of the therapeutic relationship. Subjects covered include:

- The process and changing nature of the therapeutic relationship over time.
- Recognizing and resolving ruptures in the therapeutic alliance.
- The role of evolved social needs and compassion in the therapeutic relationship.
- The therapeutic relationship with difficult-to-engage clients.
- Self and self-reflection in the therapeutic relationship.

This book will be of great interest to all psychotherapists who want to deepen their understanding of the therapeutic relationship, especially those who wish to follow cognitive behavioral approaches.

Paul Gilbert is Professor of Clinical Psychology at the Mental Health Research Unit at Kingsway Hospital, University of Derby and Derbyshire Mental Health Services NHS Trust.

Robert L. Leahy is Clinical Professor of Psychology in Psychiatry at the Weill-Cornell University Medical College. He is the founder and director of the American Institute for Cognitive Therapy and President of the International Association for Cognitive Psychotherapy.

The Therapeutic Relationship in the Cognitive Behavioral Psychotherapies

Edited by Paul Gilbert and
Robert L. Leahy

Routledge
Taylor & Francis Group

LONDON AND NEW YORK

First published 2007
by Routledge
27 Church Road, Hove, East Sussex BN3 2FA

Simultaneously published in the USA and Canada
by Routledge
270 Madison Avenue, New York NY 10016

Reprinted 2008

Routledge is an imprint of the Taylor & Francis Group, an Informa business

Copyright © 2007 selection and editorial matter, Paul Gilbert &
Robert L. Leahy; individual chapters, the contributors

Typeset in Times by Garfield Morgan, Swansea, West Glamorgan
Printed and bound in Great Britain by TJ International Ltd, Padstow, Cornwall
Cover design by Sandra Heath

This publication has been produced with paper manufactured to strict
environmental standards and with pulp derived from sustainable forests.

British Library Cataloguing in Publication Data
A catalogue record for this book is available from the British Library

Library of Congress Cataloging-in-Publication Data
The therapeutic relationship in the cognitive behavioral psychotherapies /
edited by Paul Gilbert and Robert L. Leahy.
    p. cm.
  Includes bibliographical references and index.
  ISBN-13: 978-0-415-38437-7 (hbk)
  ISBN-10: 0-415-38437-0 (hbk)
  1. Psychotherapist and patient. I. Gilbert, Paul. II. Leahy, Robert L.
  RC480.8.T46 2007
  616.89'14–dc22
                                                        2006014580

ISBN: 978-0-415-38437-7 (hbk)

Contents

Contributors

Susan M. Andersen is Professor of Psychology and director of the doctoral program in social psychology at New York University (NYU). Trained in both clinical and social-personality psychology, she was on the faculty in the clinical program at NYU for over a decade, where she also served as Director of Clinical Training. She is Associate Editor of the journal *Self and Identity*, and former Associate Editor of *Psychological Review*, *Journal of Personality and Social Psychology*, *Social Cognition*, and *Journal of Social and Clinical Psychology*.

Michael Barkham is Professor of Clinical & Counselling Psychology and Director of the Psychological Therapies Research Centre at the University of Leeds. He is also a Visiting Professor at the Universities of Sheffield and Newcastle at Northumbria as well as Joint Editor of *British Journal of Clinical Psychology*.

James Bennett-Levy PhD is Consultant Clinical Psychologist at Oxford Cognitive Therapy Centre. He has developed and evaluated a training strategy for cognitive therapists known as self-practice/self-reflection (SP/SR), which highlights the value of personal experiential work in cognitive therapy training. Recently he has published a model of therapist skill development which sheds new light on the way that therapists acquire and refine therapy skills.

Jane Cahill is an experienced project researcher in systematic and scoping reviews in mental health services and organisational research. She also has an interest in outcome research and measure development.

Paul Gilbert is Professor of Clinical Psychology at the University of Derby and Director of the Mental Health Research Unit. He is a Past President of the British Association for Behavioural and Cognitive Psychotherapies and a Fellow of the British Psychological Society. He has written and researched in the area of mood disorders, shame and compassion focused therapy, and conducts training in compassion focused therapy.

Leslie S. Greenberg is Professor, Department of Psychology, York University and Director of the Psychotherapy Research Clinic. He is Past President of the Society for Psychotherapy Research and received the distinguished research career award of that society. He has published extensively on the role of emotion in psychotherapy. His most recent book is entitled *Emotion-focused Therapy of Depression* and he conducts training and practice in emotion-focused therapy for both individuals and couples.

Gillian Hardy is Professor of Clinical Psychology at the University of Sheffield and is Joint Editor of *British Journal of Clinical Psychology*. She has published widely in the area of psychotherapy process research.

Steven C. Hayes PhD is Nevada Foundation Professor at the Department of Psychology at the University of Nevada. An author of 27 books and 360 scientific articles. His career has focused on an analysis of the nature of human language and cognition and the application of this to the understanding and alleviation of human suffering.

Heidi L. Heard PhD is a Senior Trainer for Behavioral Tech in Seattle, WA. She has written numerous theoretical and empirical articles about borderline personality disorder and dialectical behavior therapy. While working at the University of Wales, she founded British Isles DBT Training and has served as its Senior Consultant since returning to the United States. She also serves as a clinical instructor at the University of Washington. Her current research focus is on the cost-effectiveness of DBT.

Adrienne W. Katzow MA is a doctoral student in Clinical Psychology at The New School for Social Research. Her research interests are in the area of attachment processes and the internal representation of the therapist.

Robert L. Leahy PhD is the President of the International Association of Cognitive Psychotherapy, President-Elect of the Academy of Cognitive Therapy and Professor of Psychology in Psychiatry at Weill-Cornell University Medical School. He is Associate Editor of *Journal of Cognitive Psychotherapy* and the editor and author of 14 books, including *Overcoming Resistance in Cognitive Therapy*, *Roadblocks in Cognitive-Behavioral Therapy*, and *Cognitive Therapy Techniques*. He recently published the critically acclaimed popular audience book, *The Worry Cure*.

Giovanni Liotti MD is a psychiatrist and psychotherapist, President of the Italian Association for Behavioral and Cognitive Therapies (SITCC), and founder and Past President of the Roman Association for Research on the Psychopathology of the Attachment System. He teaches at a number of postgraduate Schools of Psychotherapy in Italy on the clinical applications of attachment theory. He co-authored (with V.F. Guidano) *Cognitive Processes and Emotional Disorders* (1983), which was one of the first works integrating attachment theory and cognitive therapy. Since then he has focused on the links between dissociative psychopathology and disorganization of attachment, a theme explored in a number of journal papers and book chapters, in Italian, English, Spanish and German.

Regina Miranda is an Assistant Professor of Psychology at Hunter College of the City University of New York, where she directs the Experimental Psychopathology and Mood Disorders Lab. She is also an Adjunct Assistant Professor of Medical Psychology in Psychiatry in the Division of Child and Adolescent Psychiatry at Columbia University, College of Physicians and Surgeons. She received her training in clinical psychology at New York University, and her research focuses on elucidating the nature of social-cognitive processes relevant to the onset and maintenance of depression, along with assessing cognitive processes that increase vulnerability to suicidal thinking and behavior.

Cory F. Newman PhD, ABPP is Director of the Center for Cognitive Therapy, and Associate Professor of Psychology, in Psychiatry at the University of Pennsylvania School of Medicine. Dr Newman is a Diplomate of the American Board of Professional Psychology, with a specialty in Behavioral Psychology, and a Founding Fellow of the Academy of Cognitive Therapy. Dr Newman is an international lecturer and the author of dozens of articles and chapters, as well as four books on cognitive therapy for a wide range of disorders.

Heather Pierson MA is a psychology doctoral student at the University of Nevada, Reno and a full-time researcher with the Program Evaluation and Resource Center at the VA Palo Alto Health Care System.

Jeremy D. Safran PhD is Professor and Director of Clinical Psychology at the New School for Social Research in New York City. He is also Senior Research Scientist at Beth Israel Medical Center. He has published several books, including *Emotion in Psychotherapy*, *Interpersonal Process in Cognitive Therapy*, *Widening the Scope of Cognitive Therapy*, *Negotiating the Therapeutic Alliance: A Relational Treatment Guide*, and *Psychoanalysis and Buddhism: An Unfolding Dialogue*.

Michaela A. Swales PhD is a Consultant Clinical Psychologist at the North Wales Adolescent Service, Conwy & Denbighshire NHS Trust and a Lecturer-Practitioner in Clinical Psychology at the School of Psychology, University of Wales Bangor. She is currently the Director of DBT Training in the UK.

Richard Thwaites DClinPsy is a Clinical Psychologist within the NHS and Lecturer in CBT at St Martin's College, Carlisle. He has had a long-term interest in both the therapeutic relationship and interpersonal process in CBT. His current research interests include the effects of self-practice/ self-reflection programmes (SP/SR) on trainee cognitive behavioural therapists' levels of empathy.

Preface

We have been organizing symposia at Cognitive Behavioural Conferences on the therapeutic relationship for the past few years. What became apparent was that participants in the audience were eager to learn more about "how to relate to patients" so that therapy could work more effectively. Although we both recognize the importance of techniques and "empirically validated treatments", we also recognize that you won't get very far with techniques and treatments if patients are dropping out of treatment.

It has been noted in various schools of therapy that some therapists are adept at connecting with patients, reducing premature dropout and being open and explorative at times of difficulty, while other therapists, equally intelligent, conscientious and well-trained in techniques, seem to have a hard time keeping patients engaged or "being in tune" with their patients. In our experience of training therapists we have noticed this too, which has led us to consider whether at times "microskills" and the "wisdom-skills" of therapy are overlooked or assumed, or are touched on only in passing in some treatment manuals. Although we all appreciate that therapy is not simply a matter of "applying techniques" – it involves a human relationship that can either help or hinder the effectiveness of the therapy – we are also aware that clinicians outside the CBT tradition criticize CBT for not giving enough attention to the complexities and the importance of the therapeutic relationship. While we believe these criticisms are exaggerated, there may be a grain of truth in the observation that many of us who utilize CBT could do a better job of understanding and working with the therapeutic relationship to benefit the patient. Since CBT prides itself on its scientific approach, it is important that as we learn more about how our minds are influenced through relationships this will need to be taught during training and influence practice.

With these thoughts in mind, we had communicated on the idea for a book on the therapeutic relationship in CBT for some time and then at the annual British Association of Behavioural and Cognitive Psychotherapy conference at the University of York (UK) in July 2003 we decided to get on with it. Paul had been developing his work on the role of compassion in therapy and Bob had been focusing on validation, and from discussion with other attendees it was clear to us that there was a lot of interest and thinking going on in CBT about the therapeutic relationship. We also recognized that concepts like "transference" and "countertransference" had always been around in CBT but primarily seen through the lens of core beliefs and schemata, open to evidence-testing like any other belief. Recent research, however, was bringing to light new processes and issues important to therapeutic relationships – the importance of non-conscious processing, emotional awareness and socialization, attachment processes, shame and compassion, mindfulness, schematic processes, and interpersonal strategies. Each of these has implications for the therapeutic relationship and how to integrate such insights into practice.

In an effort to help articulate new thinking on the therapeutic relationship in CBT we decided to invite our colleagues to address a series of questions. Some invitations were declined and others did not come through, but the authors of this volume approached the project with great enthusiasm, sharing with us many interesting ideas and insights, and also sharing the view that a focus on the therapeutic relationship, and the diversity of views in CBT, was perhaps overdue. So we thought about some key questions to put to our authors, though we stressed that these were only guides and they might wish to address other issues. The issues we suggested included:

1   The importance of how you relate to your patient in the early stages, such that (for example) the patient feels safe and is motivated to return. We think that the issue of *safeness* may be crucial to a patient's preparedness to engage and begin the journey of change. What, for example, do you think of the role of non-verbal communication and cues, voice tone, forms of Socratic questioning, type of 'conversation', the difference between an invitation to explore and a formulation process?

2   How does the therapeutic relationship in CBT deal with therapeutic ruptures, sticking points, boundary setting and suchlike?

3   Psychotherapy involves moment-to-moment interactions between two people and we are interested in how you conceptualise this dynamic process of transference/counter-transference. To what extent might you use thoughts and feelings triggered in you by the patient to guide your therapeutic interventions and process?

4   How do you view the ending of therapy and the discussion of ending of the relationship? How might you deal with termination issues, such as dependency or apparent narcissistic indifference?

This collection of chapters provides an opportunity to see how the relationship can be considered in complex ways, reflected on, enriched, and utilized more effectively in CBT. Because of space limitations we were not able to include every important model, but we hope the reader will come away with an experience of the richness and vitality of these issues. We also hope that the scientific foundations for CBT and the active nature of CBT will provide new interventions, strategies and conceptualizations for addressing the core issue of the relationship in therapy.

We would like to thank all the authors of this volume for making our job as editors the enjoyable and educational one it has been.

Paul Gilbert and Robert L. Leahy
March 2006

Acknowledgements

Paul Gilbert: I would like to thank the Derbyshire Mental Health Trust and the University of Derby for their continuing support of the Mental Health Research Unit. Set up in 1996 as a joint venture, we are pleased to have been able to develop a research programme on shame and the treatment of shame. Special thanks go to Chris Irons for all his help with compassionate mind research. Chris Gillespie as head of psychology has not only been supportive for many years but has impressed on me the importance of micro-skills training in the therapeutic relationship. My colleague Tom Schroder has run the psychodynamic therapy course at Derby University and has recently taken up Head of Clinical Psychology training in Nottingham. Over many years we have had many illuminating discussions and peer supervisions, and I am indebted to him for his openness, range of experience, and education. Tom and I are now engaged in a qualitative study of shame in psychotherapists. The British Association for Behavioural and Cognitive Psychotherapy has been immensely supportive of work in a range of new CBT approaches including mindfulness and compassion training. Not only one of the friendliest of associations, it provided the conference platform for us to offer symposia on the therapeutic relationship, and we are indebted to its support. This book would have been more difficult without the help of my long-suffering secretary, Diane Woollands, and her great patience in reading and checking references.

Robert Leahy: I would like to acknowledge the support from the Foundation for the Advancement of Cognitive Therapy and, in particular, grants from the George F. Baker Trust and the Robert Wood Johnson IV Charitable Trust. I also wish to thank both Beth Elliot and Rena Shulsky for their generous support of my work. I would like to thank my colleagues at the American Institute for Cognitive Therapy for their support, ideas and critical insights. In particular, thanks go to Danielle Kaplan, Lisa Napolitano and Dennis Tirch for their valuable ideas about the nature of relationships and emotion. Special thanks goes to my research assistant, David Fazzari, who has been an essential part of our research programme. I also want to thank Philip Tata of the BABCP for being an enthusiastic and caring friend.

Of course there can be little knowledge or insight on these things without the support and guidance of patients, and we both wish to acknowledge our debt to their effort to educate us on the value of the therapeutic relationship, especially during their times of struggle. You can only understand relationships by living them; both of us have been fortunate to have found partners with whom we have been able to grow and we appreciate the love, patience and support of our wives. Bob is grateful to Helen, who has had to endure his obsessive preoccupation with his work as well as the "over-the-top" nature of his often infectious humour. Paul is grateful to Jean for all her love, deep friendship and encouragement over many years, and for smiling sweetly while listening to yet another (dreadful) CD of his guitar playing. The advice of "don't give up the day job" is probably wise.

For these and other reasons we dedicate this book to our beloved and long-suffering wives, Jean and Helen.

Part I

Key issues

Chapter 1

Introduction and overview
Basic issues in the therapeutic relationship

Paul Gilbert and Robert L. Leahy

Background

Efforts to heal people of a variety of aliments, via the nature of the relationship created between a "healer" and "sufferer", have been part of human culture for hundreds of years (Ellenberger, 1970). Over two thousand years ago the early Greek physician Hippocrates suggested that the relationship between a physician and patient was key to the process of healing. In other societies Csordas (1996, 2002) suggests that healing often involves "ritual events" including public behaviours, a focus for healing (e.g. mind, body and/or spirit), performative acts (e.g. laying on of hands, speaking in tongues) and *rhetoric* that creates a world of meaning in which healing takes place. He argues that "the rhetoric of transformation achieves its therapeutic purpose by creating a disposition to be healed, invoking experience of the sacred, elaborating previously unrecognised alternatives, and actualising change in incremental steps" (Csordas, 1996, p. 94). In these contexts the socially constructed powers invested in the healer, the emotional and relational experiences shared by sufferer and healer, and the agreed steps for change, are seen as key to success.

Although Franz Anton Mesmer (1734–1815) thought he had found a new form of energy that he could manipulate to heal his patients, others thought his results were more to do with his charisma, the type of patients attracted to him and his ability to alter patients' beliefs (Ellenberger, 1970). From Mesmer grew the new ideas of hypnosis by which a hypnotist could alter the states of mind of another. Even in its earliest days it was recognised that some patients are easier to hypnotise and some hypnotists are better at inducing certain states.

By the nineteenth century Western societies were under the influence of science, positivism and evolutionary ideas that our minds had evolved from earlier life forms (Ellenberger, 1970). Psychological disorders were seen no longer as sourced by supernatural forces but by processes operating from within the sufferer's own mind, especially the inner conflicts between (evolved) desires and impulses, and social acceptance. A new profession of psychotherapist was born where the role of the therapist was to create a relationship that could help a patient become conscious of unconscious conflicts and repressed memories and in so doing restore balance and health (Ellenberger, 1970). Whereas shamanic healers could act as a bridge to a supernatural world, the psychoanalyst could act a bridge to the unconscious world. During the 1940s and 1950s Carl Rogers (1965) suggested a major alternative to psychoanalytic views. He argued that the therapist's role was not to interpret or explore transferences but to create the conditions (via empathy, positive regard and warmth) such that the patients could find their own ways to heal themselves – that is, the therapy relationship stimulates the patient's movement to health and growth.

We offer this brief background to highlight the fact that the notion that relationships have healing properties is an old one, and shared in many cultures. How a healing relationship is contextualised and given meaning, how it unfolds, and the activities, tasks and goals embedded in that relationship, are socially constructed. Thus, how a therapeutic relationship is constructed is dependent on the shared meanings and beliefs of the sources of the difficulty and what is necessary to bring relief. Our Western concepts of the therapeutic relationship, how it should be construed, the skills and knowledge a therapist brings to that relationship, and how it should be used, are therefore deeply embedded in what we believe about the nature of the world we inhabit, our human psychologies, and the causes of suffering.

Cognitive therapy

The origins of the cognitive therapies can be traced back over 50 years. They emerged from a hybrid of historical influences that came together in the 1950 and 1960s. First were the ego analytic theorists, who 20 years earlier had broken away from Freud's drive theory and focused on attitudes, beliefs and the tyranny of the "shoulds" (e.g., Bibring, 1953). The 1950s saw new developments in the cognitive and social psychology of attitudes and beliefs (Festinger, 1954). With the rise of computer metaphors and science began the age of "information processing systems" and evidence testing. Kelly (1955) suggested humans construct "theories" about the world and then seek evidence to confirm them. These personal theories, and the constructs from which they are derived, give rise to vulnerabilities to psychopathology. Helping people examine and change these constructs could produce therapeutic change. In a similar vein, Ellis (1962) developed his ideas that psychological problems and emotions could be regulated with the use of reason – as the ancient Greeks had argued two thousand years earlier. Although trained as an analyst, Beck (1967, 1976) suggested that patients' emotions and moods were less influenced by non-conscious conflicts than by current ongoing, automatic thoughts and interpretations of events. Directing therapeutic attention specifically to these cognitive processes produced significant change. Although these ideas were based primarily on observation, it was not long before hypothesised constructs such as "core beliefs", "assumptions" and "schemata" were seen as sources for biases in automatic thoughts (see Padesky (2004) for a historical overview). So the ego analysts, Kelly (1955), Ellis (1962) and Beck (1967) shifted the therapeutic process from one of interpretation of unconscious material to one of education with the use of Socratic questions and evidence testing. This was obviously going to affect the therapeutic relationship, not least because unconscious material and how it played out in the mind of the therapist (central to psychodynamic formations) was considered less relevant.

The therapeutic relationship was always considered important in Beck's therapy but by this time the impact of Rogers (1965) on the key ingredients of a helping relationship (careful listening, positive regard and empathy) had permeated a range of therapeutic approaches (Kirschenbaum & Jourdan, 2005). So people training in cognitive therapy were assumed to have basic micro-skills and counselling skills from their core professional training. The focus of cognitive therapy was on using these skills to develop collaboration and facilitate guided discovery, a cognitive formulation and an invitation to explore alternative thoughts and ideas. Although transference and counter-transference were recognised in early cognitive therapy, they were not a focus for therapeutic engagement apart from being examples of the activation of core beliefs and assumptions – and subject to reality testing. Specific problems in forming, maintaining, understanding and dealing with ruptures in the therapeutic relationship were rarely addressed (Safran & Muran, 2000), at least until the advent of cognitive therapies' exploration of personality disorders.

Behaviour therapy

The origins of behavioural therapy stretched back further, to the work of the Russian physiologist Pavlov, famous for his salivating dogs, Thorndike's operant laws of learning, and Watson's application of beha-vioural principles of the "laws of effect to humans" (Reisman, 1991). The key focus of behaviourism was on inputs and outputs of systems, be these physiological systems (e.g., salivation), motor systems (e.g., avoidance, running away) or emotions. In a way, therefore, behaviourism refers to the "science of the behaviour and learning of living systems" and should not be overly identified with any particular system (Timberlake, 1994). From the days of Pavlov it was clear that many basic physiological systems could be *conditioned* simply via association of stimuli, and this became known as classical conditioning (Gray, 1980). Conditioning is possible without any cognitive awareness (Hassin, Uleman & Bargh, 2005). Moreover, if two stimuli, one associated with reward and one associated with punishment, are presented together, this produces approach–avoidance conflicts, and at times severe disorganisation ("experimental neurosis"), with bizarre and stereotypic behaviours (Gray, 1980). We suspect that approach–avoidance conflicts are more common in the therapeutic relationship than is sometimes recognised and may produce confusion in the patient and therapist.

In a different paradigm Thorndike had shown that animals learn to behave in ways that influence consequences and outcomes (for example, increase certain behaviours for rewards and reduce them to avoid punishment). This became known as operant or instrumental learning. Subsequent research has shown that learning is somewhat more complex but these "laws" still hold good as a basic science for how animals and humans adapt to their environments (Timberlake, 1994; Rescorla, 1988).

The therapeutic implications of behaviourism were radically different from those of the psychoanalysts. For behaviourists the focus is on retraining the mind via direct experiences – that is, "exposure", utilising concepts such as desensitisation and reciprocal inhibition – or emphasis on increasing rewards through behavioural activation and assertion. Interestingly, the value of guided exposure to replace avoidance and encouragement has been recognised in many cultures for hundreds of years. For example, in Buddhist practice, if you have a fear of death you might be encouraged to meditate on a corpse and to focus on the thought that all things decay! Even Freud understood the value of exposure for some people (Yalom, 1980). More recently attention has focused on the importance of safety behaviours/strategies as short-term efforts to defend self from harm or aversive experiences. These are seen as key in the process of accentuating and maintaining disorders (Mineka & Zinbarg, 2006; Salkovskis, 1996). These strategies may also involve efforts to avoid internal events such as emotions, thoughts or memories, and external events, and problematic aspects of the therapeutic relationship.

Behaviour therapy got something of a bad reputation when it flirted with aversion therapies, particularly for people with homosexual preferences. This was unfortunate because most behaviourists were well aware that punishment was a bad way of trying to change behaviour, not least because people will learn to avoid their punishment rather than the behaviour you are wanting to reinforce. Books and films like *Clockwork Orange* painted behavioural control in a very frightening way. However, for the most part the research on the therapeutic relationship in behaviour therapy tells a very different story. In fact, behavioural therapists are often rated as the warmest of all the schools of therapy. Schaap, Bennun, Schindler & Hoogduin (1993) reviewed a number of studies including some using videotaped interactions of therapists and patients. Their conclusion was:

> behaviour therapy has a characteristic style, which is different from other schools. Somewhat surprisingly studies indicate that behaviour

therapists are rated higher on relationship variables such as empathy, unconditional positive regard and congruence than are Gestalt therapists and psychodynamic psychotherapists. These results clearly contradict the traditional stereotype of the 'cold' and mechanistic behaviour therapist.

(p. 21)

A scientifically focused therapy

The union of cognitive and behavioural therapies in the 1970s was not originally a happy one, but today most cognitive therapists involve key behavioural aspects such as exposure to "the feared and avoided". It is also recognised that people's beliefs about the consequences of their behaviour (e.g., if I don't act assertively or I don't get over-aroused when my heart rate goes up, I will stay safe) can be key to maintaining unhelpful behaviours. However, one of the great strengths of cognitive behavioural therapy (CBT), which was certainly fuelled by the evidence-focused and experimental research of the behaviourists, is that its practitioners have always been very concerned to ally themselves strongly to a scientific understanding of psychological and psychopathological process. Behaviour therapy has been informed by animal and human research on learning, while the cognitive model has been continually influenced by research on the complexities and processes underpinning cognition and decision making. These are not without controversies (Haidt, 2001). Salkovskis (2002), among others, has pointed out that evidence-based treatments evolve partly through good linkage between theory, experimental research studies and outcome research. Indeed, CBT has become so wedded to psychological science (and increasingly neuroscience) that there is some argument that it is ceasing to be "a school" and is simply evidence-based psychological therapy.

In terms not only of process but also of efficacy, CBT has been at the forefront of efforts to develop *demonstrably* effective treatments. This is no easy task, and is not free of the numerous debates over methodologies in psychotherapy research. Concerns with the methods, findings and implications of psychotherapy research were aired in two journals in the late 1990s (*Journal of Consulting and Clinical Psychology*, 1998, volume 66; *Psychotherapy Research*, 1998, volume 8). Persons and Silberschatz (1998) debated the value of randomised controlled trials (RCTs) to clinicians. Persons viewed them as essential and Silberschatz argued that they are potentially artificial and limiting for clinical practice. Elliott (1998) outlined over 13 major concerns with developing guidelines prematurely from RCT evidence, including the concern that the need to standardise treatments via manualisation may introduce unhelpful artificialities to the treatment and affect the therapeutic relationship. Elliott also notes some concern as to how therapies will continue to develop in the future if they become over-identified with manual-based approaches, developed for RCTs. Nonetheless, CBT has now been developed and has proved helpful for many (but by no means all) individuals with a variety of defined disorders; it is often recommended as a treatment of choice (see www.NICE.org.uk).

In addition there has been a focus on *trans-diagnostic* cognitive processes such as memory, attention and rumination (Harvey, Watkins, Mansell & Shafran, 2004); behavioural process of avoidance (Hayes, Wilson, Gifford, Follette & Strosahl, 1996); safety behaviours (Mineka & Zinbarg, 2006; Salkovskis, 1996), shame (Gilbert, 1998, 2003), and resistance (Leahy, 2001, 2004). This is moving psychological therapy to a much more psychological as opposed to a medical-centred model of human difficulties. Unfortunately, academic journals are very wedded to medical diagnoses. When shame, resistance, safety behaviours and difficulties in articulating thoughts and feelings dominate the clinical picture, this may pose particular challenges to the therapeutic relationship.

Why focus on the therapeutic relationship?

Psychodynamic theories have focused on drive reduction, defence mechanisms, character structure or relationship formation. In these types of approach the therapeutic relationship both is a means for gaining insight and has therapeutic effects itself (Greenberg & Mitchell, 1983; Clarkin, Yeomans & Kernberg, 2006). As noted above, CBT has taken a very different approach to the therapeutic relationship. There is probably some agreement, however, between most therapies that the therapeutic relationship should be a "containing" relationship which enables the patient to feel safe with the therapist (Holmes, 2001). Given the intense interest in the scientific and research-focused approach to CBT it is time to recognise how the therapeutic relationship influences outcomes, and this means a greater awareness of the power of interpersonal relationships to affect a variety of physiological and psychological processes (Cacioppo, Berston, Sheridan, & McClintock, 2000). For example, early relationships, especially neglect and trauma, affect the maturation of the brain and that clearly has implications for therapy (Gerhardt, 2004; Schore, 2001). Interpersonal processing occurs at both conscious and non-conscious levels, and can be rapid and conditioned (Baldwin & Dandeneau, 2005; Hassin, Uleman & Bargh 2005; Miranda & Andersen, Chapter 4, this volume).

Social processing

We can look at this in a different way. Psychotherapy is, of course, an interpersonal relationship where the mind of one person seeks to impact on the mind of the other in an interactive dance. The interactional sequences, co-constructions and interpersonal dances of therapy are choreographed through specific psychological abilities of participants and what they are seeking to achieve. One such ability is "theory of mind", which relates to the way we make inferences about the internal causes of other people's behaviours, and assess what "is going on in their minds" – what they are thinking (Baron-Cohen, 1995; Byrne, 1995; Flavell, 2004). We are aware that we can be an object for other people's judgements – that is to say, each person is an object of observation and judgement for the other. This ability to "think about thinking" and to think about the relationship has been a focus in earlier work in developmental social cognition (see Selman, 1980, 2004). We cannot assume that these complex evaluative processes can be understood like any other cognitive or evaluative process with single notions of "beliefs" or "schemata". They are more complex than this – and they are interactive (Decety & Jackson, 2004; Malle & Hodges, 2005). Some people have major difficulties in being able to "read" others' minds or have empathy for others – as the work of Baron-Cohen, Selman and others demonstrates.

Theory of mind is a specific skill that is open to various forms of distortion (Nickerson, 1999). Theory of mind may well be a key quality in our capacity to create fantasy relationships – for example, with God – and to create and engage with fictions (Bering, 2002). Theory of mind, however, differs from empathy. Empathy is more related to an intuitive sense of what's going on in the mind – especially the emotions – of the other person. It requires ability not just "to think about" the mind of the other but to resonated emotionally with the feelings of another. New research in neuroscience is beginning to explore how the brain engages in theory of mind and empathic activities (Decety & Jackson, 2004; Völlm et al., 2006). Empathy and theory of mind provide opportunities to understand that others do not feel and think exactly as we do. Clearly, the way the therapist and patient relate to each other will be influenced by these processes.

The above touches on some of the psychological competencies that we (innately) have that allow us to engage in complex social interactions. In addition to these there are a host of other processes that clearly bear on the therapeutic relationship (Freeman & McCloskey, 2003; Klein et al., 2003).

Patient characteristics are an important component of the therapeutic relationship. These include expectations of being helped and symptom severity (Constantino, Arnow, Blasey & Agras, 2005), abilities to trust others and the therapist (Berretta, de Roten, Stigler, Drapeau, Fischer & Despland, 2005), history of relationships, especially those related to attachment experiences (Holmes, 2001; Leahy, 2005; Liotti, Chapter 7, this volume), self–other schemata (Leahy, Chapter 11, this volume), motivation to change (Miller & Rollnick, 2002) and homework engagement (Burns & Nolen-Hoeksema, 1992; Burns & Spangler, 2000). Also important are *therapist characteristics* such as basic microskills (Ivey & Ivey, 2003), abilities to connect emotionally and express empathy and warmth (Kirschenbaum & Jourdan, 2005), the ability to deal with therapeutic ruptures (Safran & Muran, 2000), skill in the therapeutic modality (Burns & Nolen-Hoeksema, 1992), and personality matches and clashes (Leahy, Chapter 11, this volume).

The nature of the therapeutic modality is also important. This includes the focus or tasks of the therapy – for example, specific symptoms vs inter-personal problem-focused issues (Constantino *et al.*, 2005; Klein *et al.*, 2003); activation of specific processing systems (Harvey, Watkins, Mansell & Shafran, 2004) such as specific memory and attentional systems in post-traumatic stress disorder (Dalgleish, 2004; Lee, 2005); use of imagery (Holmes & Hackmann, 2004), and use of homework (Burns & Nolen-Hoeksema, 1992). The interaction of these various factors is increasingly becoming a key focus for research (e.g., see Castonguay & Beutler, 2006). They are all involved in the co-construction of a relationship and thus in the transference/counter-transference process (Miranda & Anderson, Chapter 4, this volume).

Developing the therapeutic relationship

There is now general agreement that therapy involves three core elements, *bonds, tasks and goals* (see Hardy, Cahill & Barkham, Chapter 2, this volume). These are not mutually exclusive, however, because the way therapists form and develop their bonds (therapeutic relationships) will have an impact on task selection, task engagement and goals. As noted above, tasks/activities that bring improvement will aid the therapeutic relationship. The therapeutic relationship can be key during difficult times. Working and confronting painful experiences tends to run counter to traditional Western medicine, which has developed technologies to remove pain and suffering via medications or surgeries. Putting the patient back at the centre of the recovery process, with the therapist as guide, is key to the cognitive behavioural therapies. However, this does not obviate the need for the therapist to be in some measure "expert, knowledgeable and agenda guiding". The concept of collaboration becomes hazy in the shadow of the power dynamics. The assumption of collaboration does not mean that the skills in being able to contain, guide, and control the pace of therapy, and suggest ideas, are not important, or that in some sense patients have to "heal themselves".

Microskills

As noted above, therapists should be competent in a range of microskills and there is empirical support to show that these have a major impact on outcome (Ivey & Ivey, 2003; Feltham & Horton, 2006). The therapeutic relationship will be supported by the recognition that the therapist will be navigating through various stages. Their microskills therefore will be designed to facilitate these various stages and the transition from one stage to another. For example, Gilbert (2000) suggested ten stages:

1 Developing rapport.
2 Exploring possible fears, concerns and expectations of coming for counselling.
3 Shared understanding and meaning.
4 Exploring the story and eliciting key themes and cognitive emotive styles: (a) taking a historical perspective; (b) working in the here and now.
5 Sharing therapeutic goals.
6 Explaining the therapy rationale.
7 Increasing awareness of the relationship among thoughts, feelings and social behaviour.
8 Moving to alternative conceptualisations.
9 Monitoring internal feelings and cognitions, and role enactments.
10 Homework and alternative role enactments.

These stages can be classified into different groups of processes, as Hardy *et al.* (Chapter 2, this volume) outline as a more macro set of stages. Microskills facilitate each stage and smooth transition between stages. Microskills involve a mixture of (usually open) questions that invite the patient to discuss, explore and narrate their story; non-verbal communications that help the patient feel safe and non-threatened; and explanations of the processes that will unfold.

Attentiveness

There are two types – externally focused and internally focused. External attentiveness involves a variety of attending behaviours, such as appropriate eye contact. This means that the therapist is able to observe the non-verbal behaviour of the patient, such as subtle changes as the story unfolds (for example, shame patients may begin to look down and curl their head into their chest or go blank/shut down when narrating shame-filled experience). Other non-verbal pointers can be clenching the fist or jaw when discussing events. Careful attention to "the person as a whole" (not just verbal content but body postures and voice tones) gives a fuller picture of possible internal processes. Clearly, however, the eye contact of the therapist should not be staring or threatening. Research into non-verbal communication from both the patient and the therapist reveals complex interactions that can affect outcome (e.g., see Dreher, Mengele, Krause & Kämmerer (2001).

Therapist attentive behaviour is also expressed via *body posture*, which should be relaxed but show clear interest and focus. Another form of attentive behaviour is verbally following the client's stories with minimal prompts – for example, "hmm . . . I see . . . could you say more on that?" – rather than changing the subject or engaging in closed questions. Greenberg (Chapter 3, this volume) writes in terms of "presence" where the sense of self is suspended and the attention is purely on the patient. The therapist is absorbed in and curious about the patient's experience. Internal attentiveness involves a form of mindfulness. Katzow & Safran (Chapter 5, this volume) suggest that mindfulness involves learning to direct one's attention in a nonjudgemental fashion to one's own internal processes. This enables the therapist to become aware of his/her thoughts, feelings, and actions *as they emerge* in the present moment. It involves cultivating an attitude of open curiosity about one's inner experience as it unfolds, with an ability to let go of one's preconceptions as they arise when sitting with a patient. The therapist should be non-judgemental and certainly non-critical of thoughts and feelings that emerge from within themselves. Equally they should have sufficient internal capacity to "hold onto" and "contain" those thoughts and feelings without acting them out.

Thus, attention can move back and forth. Ideally therapists are able to move easily between external and internal attentiveness and be aware of their own reactions, thereby facilitating their choices of other microskills and questions. Psychodynamic writers have written far more on the importance of noting and understanding our reactions to patients, and their impacts in therapy, than have cognitive therapists (Greenberg & Mitchell, 1983). This may be partly because cognitive behavioural therapists have focused more on psycho-education with supportive warm encouragement to engage in key therapy tasks such as exposure (Schaap *et al.*, 1993). However, this is changing and Katzow & Safran (Chapter 5, this volume) develop this theme in important ways, while Bennett-Levy and Thwaites (Chapter 12, this volume) explore this aspect from a training point of view. As the story unfolds, three further microskills come into play. Content aspects or factual events in the story are *paraphrased*, aspects of feeling and emotion should be accurately *reflected*, and *summaries* build towards joint understanding and eventual formulation.

Reflections and empathic connecting

Accurately reflecting a patient's feelings is a skill that enables the therapist to keep in touch with, and form an empathic bridge to, the patient. The patients can hear the reflection and know that the therapist is "with him/her". It also gives direct feedback on "what is in the mind of the therapist" and thus aids "theory of mind" understanding. Here are some examples from Gilbert (2000):

Patient: When Jane invited me in for a coffee after the dance I just had to turn her down. At that point I wanted to get home as quickly as possible.
Therapist: Sounds as if her offer made you pretty anxious.
Client: Absolutely. I found my stomach turn over in case she wanted me to stay the night and all.

However, the same statement given in a different way, with voice tone and body language, and in a different context may prompt a different reflection of feelings:

Patient: When Jane invited me in for a coffee after the dance I just had to turn her down. At that point I wanted to get home as quickly as possible.
Therapist: Sounds as if her offer made you irritated.
Patient: Absolutely. She knew I had a busy day the next day and that I was really tired and there she was making more demands on me.

Here we are not exploring in depth the nature of, or underlying beliefs of, the anxiety or anger. We are simply reflecting on feelings. Reflecting feelings enables the therapist to convey his/her understanding and awareness of the client's internal experience and build an empathic bridge. It is a step towards acknowledgement and validation. Of course, the cognitive therapist might also choose to follow this up with Socratic questions of what was underneath that irritation – what was going through their mind? The point is that, if the therapist moves too quickly to help the patient focus on their thoughts and interpretations without reflecting on feelings, this can be felt to be unempathic. Here is an extreme example:

Patient: I don't want to live any more. You see, my baby was knocked over by the Number 42 Bus from Derby.
Therapist: So what goes through your mind when you think of your baby being knocked over by the Number 42 Bus from Derby?

Gilbert (Chapter 6, this volume) therefore suggests that therapists need to be compassionately engaged with their patients and sensitive to their distress, able to reflect it, and moved by their distress. When used well, reflecting feelings aids guided discovery, and enables people to recognise their safety behaviours and biases and gradually find the courage to confront them. This is a therapist skill that avoids telling the patient that their thinking is distorted or biased – an experience often accompanied by shame and self-criticism.

Paraphrasing and summarising

Paraphrasing, and at some stage tentatively *summarising*, gives an opportunity for the patient to hear their story placed in context and to correct
any misunderstanding, vagueness or lack of emphasis. These are the building blocks to formulation. Done skilfully, the formulation *emerges* because
the therapist has been building the blocks for the formulation via their
mini-summaries based on the patient's narrative. In CBT formulation it is a
collaborative building process, not an interpretive one.

Linking

A therapist might help patients link things together in ways they may not
have noticed before. For example, the therapist may offer the observation –
"Listening to your story, I notice that the fear of upsetting people is
something you mention often. I wonder if this is a key theme for you?" or
"Given what we have been saying so far, I wonder if it is possible to see how
these thoughts (feelings/behaviours/experiences) might be linked to earlier
events you told me about in your life?" It is sometimes said that CBT is not
interested in the past or in helping people understand the origins of their
difficulties as emerging from their personal histories. A lot depends on the
case, but for many of the more complex cases (especially where abuse and
trauma are involved in the background), it would be inappropriate to ignore
history. Indeed, working with traumatic memory is now commonplace in
CBT (Dalgleish, 2004; Hackmann, 2005; Lee, 2005).

Socratic questions

Socratic questions can be seen as "advanced" open questions that enable
and encourage the patient to discover connections in their meaning-making.
Socratic questions are designed to help patients explore in more detail their
meanings and the implications of what they are saying. So, for example,
they will include questions such as "What did that mean to you? What did
you make of that? What do you think will happen next?" or "What is your
worst fear in this situation?" Socratic questions are often used to help
patients to "ladder" or inference chain their thoughts. For example,
patients may discuss the fact that they find it difficult to be assertive. The
therapist may then ask "What is it about this difficulty with assertiveness
that most distresses you?" or "What do you think will happen if you are
assertive?" or "What do you think will happen as a result of your lack of
assertiveness?" These explorations are not integrations and thus again
nonverbal communication, voice tone and pacing are crucial here. A
question such as "What is it about this difficulty with assertiveness that
most distresses you?" can be asked in a dismissive or inquisitorial way (like

"Why do you get so upset about this – you wimp!"), or in a gentle way ("Let's explore this fear together"). Like a good joke, it is not what you say but how you say it.

It is important that the therapist show understanding for the patient's distress and gently acknowledge that, "I can see that thinking like that is very distressing and frightening for you", or "Those images/intrusions/ thoughts/feelings are terrifying for you". Here the therapist is connecting not to the source of the problems (which comes later) but with the experi- ence of the problem. When Tom's son broke his leg the physician held the son's hand and acknowledged how painful it must be while at the same time straightening the leg and plastering it.

Validation

Psychotherapists have long recognised the importance of empathy, valida- tion and unconditional positive regard (Rogers, 1965), with many studies indicating the importance of the perceived therapeutic relationship in pre- dicting outcome, regardless of therapeutic modality (Martin, Garske & Davis, 2000). Although it is commonly believed that validation and empathy contribute to successful outcome, it has also been argued that improvement in symptoms leads the patient to perceive greater empathy or care in the therapist (Feeley, DeRubeis & Gelf, 1999).

Leahy (2005) has offered the following distinction between empathy, validation and compassion:

> Validation – finding the truth in what we feel and think – stands as the fulcrum between empathy – where we recognize the feeling that another person has – and *compassion* – whereby we feel *with* and *for* another person and care about the suffering of that person. For example, empathy is recognizing what the other person feels ("It sounds like you are feeling sad"), validation adds on "finding the validity in the other's feelings" (e.g., "I can understand why you feel sad, since you believe that she was the only person that you might love"), and compassion (assumes empathy and validation) but goes further to assure the individual, "I care very much about how you are feeling and how hard it is for you and I want you to know I am here for you during this difficult time".

Empathy, validation and compassion are social–emotional experiences that are grounded in early attachment. As Gilbert (Chapter 6, this volume), Greenberg (Chapter 3, this volume) and Liotti (Chapter 7, this volume) indicate, the attachment bond during infancy and throughout childhood (and later life) is predicated on these experiences. Leahy (2005) has proposed that the willingness of parents to validate and empathise is related to Gottman's "emotional philosophies" – that is, parents who believe that their child's painful emotions provide an opportunity to get closer, to know and to help are more likely to validate and show compassion, whereas parents holding the view that the child's emotions are overwhelming, threatening or self-indulgent are less likely to validate (Gottman *et al.*, 1996; Leahy, 2002). As a result of these different emotional-coaching strategies, the child may come to learn that their emotions are a reason for embarrassment or that their emotions do not "make sense". Leahy (2002, 2005) has proposed a model of emotional schemata that reflect how individuals respond to their own emotions. Thus, negative emotional schemata are reflected by beliefs that one's emotions do not make sense, are shameful, are overwhelming, are out of control, will last indefinitely, are dangerous, are different from others and cannot be expressed.

Thus, one's beliefs about emotion are linked to the reflective empathising, validating, and emotional coaching that have occurred in early and later attachment relationships. Of course, the therapeutic relationship is another relationship that is viewed, from this perspective, as eliciting these earlier experiences of emotional socialisation. Therapy – even within the CBT model – is not simply eliciting and testing problematic thoughts; it also involves the elicitation of emotions, in what cognitive therapists have come to call "hot cognitions". Emotional experience is an essential part of this model, but therapists need to be attuned to how individual patients may experience the "opportunity" to share their emotions. For some it is a welcome experience, but for others it may resurrect old fears of shame, humiliation, confusion and loss of control.

Indeed, validation may be such a "problem" for some patients that they have developed their own "rules for being validated" (Leahy, 2001). For example, some patients may demand perfect validation – to the point of believing that unless the therapist has suffered exactly the same problems and intensity of despair, the therapist is incapable of validating. Moreover, some patients may engage strategies to elicit validation – such as escalating, catastrophising, creating emergencies, ruminating, and focusing on physical ailments – that may be intended to elicit validation from the therapist or from others, but which usually backfire. Leahy (2001) indicated that these specific rules and strategies for validation in therapy can provide an excellent opportunity to understand and, eventually, modify the patient's apparently "self-defeating" style of interaction in relationships outside therapy. Thus, "roadblocks" in therapy become opportunities for trans-forming change outside therapy.

While it is important to provide a warm and supportive emotional environment in therapy, it is also important to recognise that some patients – seeking out personal emotional goals or engaging in old habits – will violate the boundaries of the therapeutic relationship. Once again, these impediments to change, or "therapy interfering behaviours", can provide an opportunity for growth, if handled skilfully. The therapist can use a "dialectical" strategy of firmly and compassionately setting boundaries, while exploring with the patient the meaning of the boundary. It is often the case that patients who utilise coercive strategies in therapy have found that this may be the only way to be "heard" in earlier relationships.

Summary

We can see that there is a range of key therapy skills that advances the therapeutic relationship in creating a safe place where "work" can occur, courage to engage the process of change can be nurtured and new self-knowledge gained. CBT has a range of techniques at its disposal for helping people change and these are increasingly evidence-based, but this in no way means that we become psychological mechanics (Leahy, 2005).

Overview

We started this chapter by noting that the importance of the qualities of a relationship have been seen as central to the therapeutic process for a long time and in many different cultures. What occurs within the relationship, however, is linked to cultural meanings on the sources and cures for suffering. We live in a time where we have come to a particular set of views and beliefs on the sources and cures for suffering, and these beliefs texture the construction of the therapeutic relationship. Given the growing awareness of the complexities in developing a therapeutic working alliance or relationship, this book brings together a variety of clinicians representing different CBT orientations to address key issues of the therapeutic relationship. What emerges from these writings is a rich tapestry of thinking, conceptualisation and research focused on the therapeutic relationship and how this can impact on our therapeutic work. We have tried not to offer a single view but to reflect diversity of thinking within CBT.

The book is divided into two parts. The first part, "Key issues", examines the key elements that are involved in developing and maintaining the therapeutic relationship and bringing it to an end. The second part explores the therapeutic relationship in more specific types of CBT. That section also includes chapters on issues of training and therapist development.

Following this introductory chapter, Hardy, Cahill & Barkham (Chapter 2) give an overview of research on patient–therapist interactions. From their systematic review of the literature they develop a process model of the therapeutic relationship as it unfolds over time. Greenberg (Chapter 3) uses an emotion-focused approach to reflect on key microskills, such as empathy and "presence" within the therapeutic context – that is, how therapists listen, attend and respond to the emotional textures of patient communication and how these behaviours affect the process and outcome. Miranda and Andersen (Chapter 4) address the important issue of transference and counter-transference from a social-cognitive approach. They review a wealth of data on the importance of recognising relationships as co-constructions such that what the therapist brings and what the patient brings are important to the relationship pattern. In Chapter 5 Katzow & Safran discuss the therapeutic relationship in the light of major developments in the use of mindfulness within cognitive therapy. Mindfulness points to a specific set of microskills, which is the ability to attune to one's own inner processes "mindfully". They explore how this can be essential for understanding and resolving therapeutic ruptures. In Chapter 6, Gilbert contextualises the therapeutic relationship against the background of humans as evolved social beings with important social needs. Recent research suggests that we have special processing systems that are sensitive to social safeness and threat. Thus the way a therapist is able to create experiences of safeness, often with the use of compassion, can be key to therapy progress, especially with high shame and self-critical people. Liotti, in Chapter 7, develops the evolutionary theme with the importance of attachment theory as a model for understanding the therapeutic relationship. As he notes, if therapists can understand and recognise different patterns of attachment, particularly disorganised attachment, and how these can emerge in therapy, this can be highly beneficial to therapeutic understanding and the therapeutic relationship.

Newman, in Chapter 8, begins the second part of the book, which focuses on the therapeutic relationship in specific CBT-focused approaches. Newman outlines the traditional cognitive therapy approach and discusses how the relationship is important not only for developing collaboration but at times when therapists are required to be more challenging and confrontative. Chapter 9, by Swales & Heard, offers a dialectical behavioural therapy (DBT) approach to the therapeutic relationship. DBT was designed to help people with suicidal behaviour and with borderline personality difficulties. These patients can be especially difficult to engage, set boundaries for and develop a therapeutic programme with. As DBT recognises, the therapeutic relationship is crucial here. Pierson & Hayes, in Chapter 10, explore the therapeutic relationship from the point of view of acceptance and commitment therapy (ACT). ACT sees the therapeutic relationship as playing a key role in the ability of patients to be accepting of their difficulties. However, as they point out, it is also essential that the therapist has the same competencies and capacities.

In Chapter 11, by Leahy, the therapeutic relationship is understood as an interactive game whereby the participants ("players") are the therapist and the patient – each following his or her own set of rules and anticipating "moves" by the other. Of specific interest in this chapter are the individual "schemas" about emotion, relationship and engagement. Thus, the therapist with demanding standards and negative schemas about emotions may inadvertently confirm negative beliefs about relationships and emotions endorsed by the avoidant or dependent patient. Viewing the transference and counter-transference in this manner provides the therapist with a conceptualisation and a strategy to avoid unnecessary pitfalls in the therapeutic relationship, and to utilise these roadblocks to better understand how the patient's interpersonal world outside of therapy may be reflected in the current relationship in the therapy.

Training is a major issue for all therapies, especially training people in microskills that new therapists coming into CBT may lack. In Chapter 12, Bennett-Levy & Thwaites explore training issues but with particular attention to how therapists can become more self-aware and insightful using the very techniques and approaches that they will apply in their work. Early psychodynamic therapists were very keen that therapists should have personal therapy to ensure they do not bring their own agendas and unresolved conflicts into the therapy. However, this was before the days of video and audio tape recordings that allow supervisors to hear and see what is going on between therapist and patient in supervision. It is important therefore to consider how supervisors work with and help trainee therapists who may be bringing personal issues, who may be easily threatened and become defensive, or who may be anxious about challenging patients. Since CBT is not an interpretive therapy, the problems encountered in psychodynamic therapy are less likely here.

Although there are of course various CBT approaches that are not reflected here, we hope this book stimulates interest in the therapeutic relationship within the CBT approach, and puts to rest the view that CBT does not regard the therapeutic relationship as important or worthy of research and focus. Because cognitive therapy is a non-interpretive therapy but focuses on guided discovery, opportunities to expose self to various fears and desensitise to feared outcomes, re-attend, re-evaluate, and in some cases mature new ways of experiencing self and others, this does not mean that the therapeutic relationship is unimportant or a side issue. Research consistently shows the therapeutic relationship to be a key ingredient of many forms of successful therapy. We hope that the contributors to this book have shown how and why CBT is also very keen to establish scientific ways of understanding the therapeutic relationship and bringing the best qualities to the teaching of therapy and the provision of therapy to our patients.

References

Baldwin, M.W. & Dandeneau, S.D. (2005). Understanding and modifying the relational schemas underlying insecurity. In M.W. Baldwin (ed.), *Interpersonal cognition* (pp. 33–61). New York: Guilford.

Baron-Cohen, S. (1995). *Mindblindness: An essay on autism and theory of mind.* Cambridge, MA: MIT Press.

Beck, A.T. (1967). *Depression: Clinical, experimental and theoretical aspects*. New York: Harper & Row.

Beck, A.T. (1976). *Cognitive therapy and the emotional disorders*. New York: International Universities Press.

Bering, J.M. (2002). The existential theory of mind. *Review of General Psychology*, 6, 3–34.

Berretta, V., de Roten, Y., Stigler, M., Drapeau, M., Fischer, M. & Despland, J. (2005). The influence of patients' interpersonal schemas on early alliance building. *Swiss Journal of Psychology*, 64, 13–20.

Bibring, E. (1953). The mechanism of depression. In P. Greenacre (ed.), *Affective disorders*. New York: International Universities Press.

Burns, D.D. & Nolen-Hoeksema, S. (1992). Therapeutic empathy and recovery from depression in cognitive-behavioral therapy: A structural equation model. *Journal of Consulting and Clinical Psychology*, 60, 441–449.

Burns, D.D. & Spangler, D.L. (2000). Does psychotherapy homework lead to improvements in depression in cognitive-behavioral therapy or does improvement lead to increased homework compliance? *Journal of Consulting and Clinical Psychology*, 68, 46–56.

Byrne, R.W. (1995). *The thinking ape: Evolutionary origins of intelligence*. Oxford: Oxford University Press.

Cacioppo, J.T., Berston, G.G., Sheridan, J.F. and McClintock, M.K. (2000). Multilevel integrative analysis of human behavior: Social neuroscience and the complementing nature of social and biological approaches. *Psychological Bulletin*, 126, 829–843.

Castonguay, L.G. & Beutler, L.R. (2006). *Principles of therapeutic change that work*. New York: Oxford University Press.

Clarkin, J., Yeomans, F.E. & Kernberg, O.F. (2006). *Psychotherapy for borderline personality: Focusing on object relations*. Washington, DC: American Psychiatric Press.

Constantino, M.J., Arnow, B.A., Blasey, C. & Agras, W.S. (2005). The association between patient characteristics and the therapeutic alliance in cognitive-behvioural and interpersonal therapy for bulimia nervosa. *Journal of Consulting and Clinical Psychology*, 83, 203–211.

Csordas, T.J. (1996). Imaginal performance and memory in ritual healing. In C. Laderman & M. Roseman (eds), *The performance of healing*. New York & London: Routledge.

Csordas, T.J. (2002). *Body/meaning/healing*. New York: Palgrave Macmillan.

Dalgleish, T. (2004). Cognitive approaches to posttraumatic stress disorder: The evolution of multirepresentation theorizing. *Psychological Bulletin*, 130, 228–260.

Decety, J. & Jackson, P.L. (2004). The functional architecture of human empathy. *Behavioral and Cognitive Neuroscience Reviews*, 3, 71–100.

Dreher, M., Mengele, U., Krause, R. & Kämmerer, A. (2001). Affective indicators of the psychotherapeutic process: An empirical case study. *Psychotherapy Research*, 11, 99–117.

Ellenberger, H. (1970). *The discovery of the unconscious*. New York: Basic Books.

Elliott, R. (1998). Editor's introduction: A guide to the empirically supported treatments controversy. *Psychotherapy Research*, 8, 115–125.

Ellis, A. (1962). *Reason and emotion in psychotherapy*. Secaucus, NJ: Citadel Press.

Feeley, M., DeRubeis, R.J. & Gelf, L.A. (1999). The temporal relation of adherence and alliance to symptom change in cognitive therapy for depression. *Journal of Consulting and Clinical Psychology*, 67, 578–582.

Feltham, C. & Horton, I. (2006). *The Sage handbook of counselling and psychotherapy*, 2nd edition. London: Sage.

Festinger, L. (1954). A theory of social comparison processes. *Human Relations*, 7, 117–140.

Flavell, J.H. (2004). Theory-of-mind development: Retrospect and prospect. *Merrill-Palmer Quarterly*, 50, 274–290.

Freeman, A. & McCloskey, R.D. (2003). Impediments to psychotherapy. In R.L. Leahy (ed.), *Roadblocks in cognitive-behavioral therapy: Transforming challenges into opportunities for change* (pp. 24–48). New York: Guilford.

Gerhardt, S. (2004). *Why love matters: How affection shapes a baby's brain*. Hove, UK: Brunner-Routledge.

Gilbert, P. (1989). *Human nature and suffering*. Hove, UK: Lawrence Erlbaum Associates.

Gilbert, P. (1992). *Depression: The evolution of powerlessness*. Hove, UK: Lawrence Erlbaum Associates.

Gilbert, P. (1998). What is shame? Some core issues and controversies. In P. Gilbert & B. Andrews (eds), *Shame: Interpersonal behavior, psychopathology and culture* (pp. 3–36). New York: Oxford University Press.

Gilbert, P. (2000). *Counselling for depression*, 2nd edition. London: Sage.

Gilbert, P. (2003). Evolution, social roles and the differences in shame and guilt. *Social Research*, 70, 401–426.

Gilbert, P. & Miles, J.N.V. (2000). Sensitivity to put-down: Its relationship to perceptions of shame, social anxiety, depression, anger and self–other blame. *Personality and Individual Differences*, 29, 757–774.

Gottman, J.M., Katz, L.F. & Hooven, C. (1996). Parental meta-emotion philosophy and the emotional life of families: Theoretical models and preliminary data. *Journal of Family Psychology*, 10, 243–268.

Gray, J.A. (1980). *Ivan Pavlov*. New York: Viking Press.

Greenberg, J.R. and Mitchell, S.A. (1983). *Object relations in psychoanalytic theory*. Cambridge, MA: Harvard University Press.

Hackmann, A. (2005). Compassionate imagery in the treatment of early memories in Axis I anxiety disorders. In P. Gilbert (ed.), *Compassion: Conceptualisations, research and use in psychotherapy*. Hove, UK: Routledge.

Haidt, J. (2001). The emotional dog and its rational tail: A social intuitionist approach to moral judgment. *Psychological Review*, 108, 814–834.

Harvey, A., Watkins, E., Mansell, W. & Shafran, R. (2004). *Cognitive behavioural processes across psychological disorders: A transdiagnostic approach to research and treatment*. Oxford: Oxford University Press.

Hassin, R.R., Uleman, J.S. & Bargh, J.A. (2005). *The new unconscious*. New York: Oxford University Press.

Hayes, S.C., Wilson, K.G., Gifford, E.V., Follette, V.M. & Strosahl, K. (1996). Experiential avoidance and behavioral disorders: A functional approach to diagnosis and treatment. *Journal of Consulting and Clinical Psychology*, 64, 1152–1168.

Holmes, E.A. & Hackmann, A. (eds) (2004). *Mental imagery and memory in psychopathology* (Special Edition: Memory, Volume 12, No. 4). Hove, UK: Psychology Press.

Holmes, J. (2001). *The search for the secure base: Attachment theory and psychotherapy*. Hove, UK: Brunner-Routledge.

Ivey, A.E. & Ivey, M.B. (2003). *Intentional interviewing and counselling: Facilitating client change in a multicultural society*, 5th edition. Pacific Grove, CA: Brooks/Cole.

Kelly, G. (1955). *The psychology of personal constructs*. New York: Norton & Co.

Kirschenbaum, H. & Jourdan, A. (2005). The current status of Carl Rogers and the person-centred approach. *Psychotherapy: Theory, Research, Practice, Training*, 42, 37–51.

Klein, D.N., Schwartz, J.E., Santiago, N.J., Vivan, D., Vocisano, C., Castonguay, L.G., Arrow, B., Blalock, J.A., Manber, R., Markowitz, J.C., Riso, L.P., Rothbaum, B., McCullough, J.P., Thase, M.E., Borian, F.E., Miller, I.W. & Keller, M.B. (2003). Therapeutic alliance in depression treatment: Controlling for prior change and patient characteristics. *Journal of Consulting and Clinical Psychology*, 6, 997–1006.

Leahy, R.L. (2001). *Overcoming resistance in cognitive therapy*. New York: Guilford.

Leahy, R.L. (2002). A model of emotional schemas. *Cognitive and Behavioral Practice*, 9, 177–190.

Leahy, R.L (ed.) (2004). *Roadblocks in cognitive-behavioral therapy: Transforming challenges into opportunities for change*. New York: Guilford.

Leahy, R.L. (2005). A social-cognitive model of validation. In P. Gilbert (ed.), *Compassion: Conceptualisations, research and use in psychotherapy* (pp. 195–217). Hove, UK: Routledge.

Lee, D.A. (2005). The perfect nurturer: A model to develop a compassionate mind within the context of cognitive therapy. In P. Gilbert (ed.), *Compassion: Conceptualisations, research and use in psychotherapy* (pp. 326–351). Hove, UK: Routledge.

Malle, B.F. & Hodges, S.D. (eds), (2005). *Other minds: How humans bridge the divide between self and others*. New York: Guilford.

Martin, D.J., Gorske, J.P. & Davis, M.K. (2000). Relation of the therapeutic alliance with outcome and other variables: A meta-analytic review. *Journal of Consulting and Clinical Psychology*, 68(3), 438–450.

Miller, W.R. & Rollnick, S. (2002). *Motivational interviewing: Preparing people for change*. New York: Guilford,

Mineka, S. & Zinbarg, R. (2006). A contemporary learning theory perspective on the etiology of anxiety disorders: It's not what you thought it was. *American Psychologist*, 61, 10–26.

Nickerson, R.S. (1999). How we know – and sometimes misjudge – what others know: Inputting one's own knowledge to others. *Psychological Bulletin*, 125, 737–759.

Norcross, J.C. (2002). *Psychotherapy relationships that work*. New York: Oxford University Press.

Padesky, C.A. (2004). Aaron T. Beck: Mind, man and mentor. In R.L. Leahy (ed.), *Contemporary cognitive therapy: Theory, research and practice* (pp. 3–24). New York: Guilford.

Persons, J.B. & Silberschatz, G. (1998). Are results of randomized controlled trials useful to psychotherapists? *Journal of Consulting and Clinical Psychology*, 66, 126–135.

Reisman, J.M. (1991). *A history of clinical psychology*, 2nd edition. New York: Hemisphere.

Rescorla, R.A. (1988). Pavlovian conditioning: It's not what you think it is. *American Psychologist*, 43, 151–160.

Rogers, C. (1965). *Client centered therapy: Its current practice, implications and theory*. Boston: Houghton-Mifflin.

Safran, J.D. & Muran, J.C. (2000). *Negotiating the therapeutic alliance: A relational treatment guide*. New York: Guilford Press.

Salkovskis, P. (1996). The cognitive approach to anxiety: Threat beliefs, safety-seeking behavior, and the special case of health anxiety and obsessions. In P.M. Salkovskis (ed.), *Frontiers of cognitive therapy* (pp. 48–74). New York: Guilford.

Salkovskis, P. (2002). Empirically grounded clinical interventions: Cognitive-behavioural therapy progresses through a multi-dimensional approach to clinical science. *Behavioural and Cognitive Psychotherapy*, 30, 3–9.

Schaap, C., Bennun, I., Schindler, L. & Hoogduin, K. (1993). *The therapeutic relationship in behavioural psychotherapy*. Chichester, UK: Wiley.

Schore, A.N. (2001). The effects of early relational trauma on right brain development, affect regulation, and infant mental health. *Infant Mental Health Journal*, 22, 201–269.

Selman, R.L. (1980). *The growth of interpersonal understanding: Developmental and clinical analyses*. New York: Academic Press.

Selman, R.L. (2004). *The promotion of social awareness: Powerful lessons from the partnership of developmental theory and classroom practice*. New York: Russell Sage Foundation.

Teasdale, J.D. (1999). Emotional processing: Three modes of mind and the prevention of relapse in depression. *Behaviour Research and Therapy*, 37, 29–52.

Timberlake, W. (1994). Behavior systems, associationism, and pavlovian conditioning. *Psychonomic Bulletin and Review*, 1, 405–420.

Völlm, B.A., Taylor, A.N.W., Richardson, P., Corcoran, R., Stirling, J., McKie, S., Deakin, J.F.W. & Elliott, R. (2006). Neuronal correlates of theory of mind and empathy: A functional magnetic resonance imaging study in a nonverbal task. *NeuroImaging*, 29, 90–98.

Yalom, I.D. (1980). *Existential psychotherapy*. New York: Basic Books.

Zilboorg, G. & Henry, G.W. (1941). *History of medical psychology*. New York: W.W. Norton & Co.

Chapter 2

Active ingredients of the therapeutic relationship that promote client change

A research perspective

Gillian Hardy, Jane Cahill and Michael Barkham

Introduction

A good relationship between client and therapist is, at the very least, considered to be the base from which all therapeutic work takes place. This
circumscribed view of the therapeutic relationship is often taken by cognitive
and behavioural therapists and is described as "professional skills" in the
most widely used instrument for assessing therapist competence in cognitive
and behavioural therapy (CBT) (Cognitive Therapy Scale; Young & Beck,
1988). For other psychotherapy schools, the therapeutic relationship is seen
as one of the main therapeutic tools for achieving client change (Luborsky,
1994; Klerman, Weissman, Rounsville, & Chevron, 1984). Whatever therapeutic processes are involved in the client–therapist relationship, research
has consistently shown a significant association between this relationship
and outcome. For example, Norcross (2002) summarised the literature on
predictors of outcome in psychotherapy and stated that 15% of outcome is
due to expectancy effects, 15% to techniques, 30% to "common factors"
which primarily involve the therapeutic relationship, and 40% to extra-
therapeutic change.

Against this background, in this chapter we set out three overarching
objectives. First, we briefly explore the differing views drawn from diverse
theoretical models of what is understood by the term "therapeutic relationship". Second, we consider why the therapeutic relationship is important. A key component of this relates to the reported relationship with
treatment outcome. The role of "common factors" in achieving good
treatment outcome will be also outlined. And third, in the substantive part
of the chapter we consider the extent of our understanding of the therapeutic relationship and the active ingredients that promote client change. In
so doing, we draw on a systematic review we conducted. We provide a map
of the development of the relationship between the client and therapist and
highlight elements that contribute to the relationship at different stages

in the therapy process. Throughout the chapter we refer to the general literature on the therapeutic relationship, not only findings in relation to CBT.

What is the therapeutic relationship?

Freud was the first to consider the importance of the relationship between the therapist and patient in the therapeutic process, and labelled this "positive transference" (Freud, 1940). Greenson (1965) developed the idea that the relationship is central to enabling client change and made the distinction between the working alliance (task focused) and the therapeutic alliance (personal bond). Luborsky (1976) and Bordin (1979, 1994) broadened the concept so that it would be relevant to other types of therapy. The former described two phases of the relationship: the initial relationship being characterised by the client's belief in the ability of the therapist to help him or her and the therapist's requirement to provide a secure environment for the client; this later developing into a mutual relationship of working on the tasks of therapy.

Most current conceptualisations of the therapeutic alliance are based on Bordin's (1979) definition of: "three features: an agreement on goals, an assignment of task or series of tasks, and the development of bonds" (p. 253). Bordin's definition moved our understanding of the relationship from primarily a psychodynamic to a pan-theoretical concept. This arose as empirical studies to find the ingredients of successful therapy identified factors that are common to most psychotherapies as being responsible for a large part of therapeutic gain. These will be discussed in the next section. In CBT a positive relationship is seen as necessary, though not sufficient, for change to occur. For some therapists interpersonal processes are central to promoting change, and these include using the client–therapist relationship (Safran & Segal, 1990; Whisman, 1993).

However, what this definition of the relationship lacks is a consideration of what the client and therapist bring through their experiences of their past relationships (see Leahy, Chapter 11, this volume). These influence the nature of the relationship that the client and therapist form (Holmes, 1996; Mace & Margison, 1997). There is some evidence that assessing clients' and therapists' relationship styles, and acknowledging and working with these styles in therapy and supervision, can improve the therapeutic relationship (Meyer & Pilkonis, 2002). This will be discussed in more detail later in the chapter.

So, to summarise, the main components that contribute to the quality and strength of the therapeutic relationship are: the affective bond and partnership; the cognitive consensus on goals and tasks; and the relationship history of the participants. Finally, a variety of terms have been used to conceptualise the therapeutic relationship. In this chapter we use these terms interchangeably: they include therapeutic relationship, working relationship, alliance, therapeutic alliance, and therapeutic bond.

Why study the therapeutic relationship?

The context for studying the therapeutic relationship is the interest in the more general question of why psychological therapies work. The therapeutic relationship has consistently been associated with treatment outcome, with correlations ranging from .21 to .29. This association is higher than associations between specific therapy techniques and outcome. Clients' assessments of the relationship tend to be better predictors of outcome than therapist or observer ratings of the relationship, and measures of the relationship taken early in therapy are better predictors of outcome than measures taken later in therapy. Aspects of the therapeutic relationship that appear to be important in achieving good outcomes form the basis of a book titled *Psychotherapy Relationships that Work* (Norcross, 2002), and are discussed later.

The current challenges facing alliance researchers include trying to understand better how relationship factors work with other "common" and "specific" factors to help clients change. For example, there is a debate in the literature about the nature and importance of "non-specific" or "common" factors (see DeRubeis, Brotman, & Gibbons, 2005; Kazdin, 2005; and Wampold, 2005). These factors are so-called because they are thought to be common across most therapies. They include a treatment rationale, expectations of improvement, a treatment ritual and the therapeutic relationship (Frank, 1961; Lambert & Ogles, 2004). As stated above, these factors have been consistently associated with outcome, are assumed by many to be important in helping clients change, and importantly, would lead to non-significant differences between treatments (Stiles, Shapiro, & Elliott, 1986). However, there is some debate about this. DeRubeis *et al.* (2005) argue that psychotherapies, particularly CBT, work, to a greater extent than the supporters of common factors claim, through techniques specific to a therapy. A good therapeutic alliance, they suggest, may be a product of good outcome rather than the other way round.

In an attempt to bring together this discussion, Castonguay & Holtforth (2005) make a number of points. First, within each of the broad categories of factors, such as alliance or technique, there are many variables, which may vary in their usage with different therapies. It is in some sense artificial to separate out these factors, as techniques always happen within a relationship. It is perhaps then more useful to see components of the therapeutic relationship as elements of the set of skills a therapist has to be used, when appropriate, to help clients change.

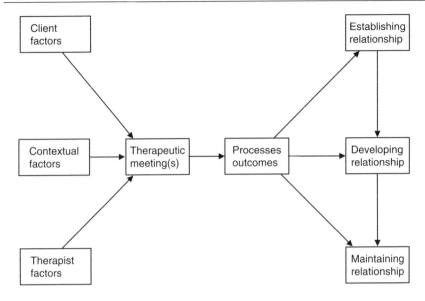

Figure 2.1 Conceptual map.

How does the therapeutic relationship work?

In this third section, which constitutes the substantive portion of this chapter, we report on the findings of a systematic search of the literature for review articles pertaining to the client–therapist relationship that were then used to map out the domains and concepts of the therapeutic relationship. The electronic search was conducted on PsycINFO. Two research workers sifted all identified references and the final list of references was rated for their degree of relevance on a five-point scale. All (45) top and (67) next rated articles were summarised (details of the search strategy and findings can be found in Cahill (2003)), and from these summaries the "map" of the therapeutic relationship was formulated. This map is described below and summarised in Figure 2.1.

Three main stages of the relationship are used to organise the research findings. These are: *establishing a relationship*, *developing a relationship*, and *maintaining a relationship*. We have listed key *processes* involved in establishing what might be called "mini outcomes" or *objectives* for each of the three stages. It is assumed that although these stages develop across therapy, there will also be a cycling through these stages within a therapeutic meeting, or over a number of weeks or months. For example, a therapeutic relationship may be well developed but a break in treatment may result in client-reported dissatisfaction. The therapist will work to repair this rupture in the relationship and may also return to the use of engagement skills

Table 2.1 Establishing the relationship

Engagement processes	Engagement objectives
Empathy, warmth and genuineness	Expectancies
Negotiation of goals	Intentions
Collaborative framework	Motivation
Support	Hope
Guidance	
Affirmation	

described in *establishing a relationship*. In addition to describing stages in the development of the therapeutic relationship, we will briefly consider broader *therapist, client* and *contextual* factors within which the therapeutic interactions take place.

Establishing a relationship

There is clear evidence that the early development of a good relationship between therapist and client predicts better outcome and helps clients to remain in therapy (Martin, Garske, & Davis, 2000). Client engagement in therapy is the primary aim at the beginning of therapy and can be divided into the following objectives: *expectancies, intentions, motivation* and *hope* (Table 2.1). It is important to build clients' positive *expectations* of therapy, both role (what is expected of the client and therapist) and outcomes (Garfield, 1974; Arnkoff, Glass, & Shapiro, 2002). For example, higher client expectations of therapy predicted outcome in CBT group therapy for social phobia (Safren, Heimberg, & Juster, 1997). It is also important to develop clients' *intentions* and *motivation* for change (Whiston & Coker, 2000). In an interesting study looking at client and therapist microprocesses during the first therapy session, the earlier that emotional involvement and meaningful connection (independently rated) were established, the better the alliance was as rated by clients (Sexton, Littauer, Sexton, & Tommeras, 2005).

There have been a number of studies looking at what therapists find important in enabling early client involvement in therapy. For example, two studies have found that therapists rate clients as more attractive if they are seen to be motivated to change and such clients are likely to become better engaged in therapy (Davis, Cook, Jennings, & Heck, 1977; Tryon, 1990). Further studies have found that good relationship ratings in early therapy sessions were associated with high levels of client working and of client involvement (Reandeau & Wampold, 1991).

Finally, developing clients' sense of hope is associated with remaining in therapy and with better outcomes. Kuyken (2004), for example, found that clients who expressed high levels of hopelessness at the beginning of therapy, which did not reduce over the first few sessions, had significantly worse outcomes than clients whose hopelessness reduced in this initial period.

Also, therapists' expressed hope for the usefulness of therapy is important in engaging clients in therapy (Russell & Shirk, 1998). This links to client expectancies (Garfield, 1974; Winston & Muran, 1996), which in turn increases therapists' abilities to influence clients (Puskar & Hess, 1986). Nathan (1999) examined hope in relation to difficult clients, and found that therapists often lack hope with such clients, which leads to impoverished therapeutic relationships. The importance of openly addressing hope or the lack of it with clients is discussed by Bordin (1979). For example, improvements in the client–therapist relationship were evidenced when the early building of a sense of hope with clients was achieved (Everly, 2001).

Therapist behaviours that are associated with the above objectives of intentions, expectancies, motivation and hope include the three elements of Rogers' therapeutic conditions: warmth, genuineness or respect, and empathy (Bachelor & Horvath, 1999; Rogers, 1957). Empathy is particularly linked to good engagement and is described as the ability of the therapist to enter and understand, both affectively and cognitively, the client's world (Bohart, Elliott, Greenberg, & Watson, 2002). In a meta-analysis on available research, empathy accounted for between 7% and 10% of the variance in outcome (Bohart *et al.*, 2002). Unexpectedly, this meta-analysis also found some evidence for empathy being more important in the outcome of CBT than of other therapies. Why this might be is still an open question.

Engagement also involves the therapist discussing and agreeing the aims of therapy with the client. There is evidence that it is important to reach consensus early in therapy. For example, early session information gathering and later session sharing and negotiation of problem formulation and treatment plans have been found to improve engagement and return for further sessions of therapy (Tryon, 2002). In an earlier study, Tracy (1977) compared two types of initial interview, one where therapists gathered information but did not share their understandings and one where therapists shared their understandings of the client's problems and negotiated treatment goals. Clients were significantly more likely to return for therapy if they had attended the latter interviews. The early agreement on goals, however, is not so strongly linked with overall treatment outcome. For example, Gaston, Marmar, Gallagher, & Thompson (1991) did not find a significant association between early goal consensus and outcome.

There is evidence that mutual involvement in the helping relationship is even more important than goal consensus for engaging clients in therapy and in gaining positive treatment outcome. Therapist behaviours that are associated with this development of a collaborative framework include: talking rather than remaining silent; encouraging client experiencing so that sessions are reported as being "deep"; and avoiding conflict within the

Table 2.2 Developing the relationship

Processes	Objectives
Exploration	Openness
Reflection	Trust
Feedback	Commitment
Relational interpretations	
Nonverbal communications	

sessions (Tryon & Winograd, 2001, 2002). Mutual involvement has also been assessed through homework completion, with a number of studies showing that clients who are better at attempting to do their homework between sessions have fewer symptoms at the end of therapy (Worthington, 1986; Schmidt & Woolaway-Bickel, 2000).

Over half of the reviews considered discuss the importance of offering support to clients. Aspects of support that are described as being important within cognitive and behavioural therapies include tolerance (Mallinckrodt, 2000) and guidance (Luborsky, 1990). Therapist affirmation and positive regard are other aspects of support. Farber and Lane (2002) reviewed the research in this area and conclude that there is a positive but modest association between positive regard and outcome. Other techniques that improve client engagement include providing early clarifications in the here and now (Waldinger, 1987) and using client preparatory techniques, such as information sheets and educational sessions (Heitler, 1976).

Developing a relationship

At the second stage we consider therapists' techniques and objectives that are helpful in progressing therapy and developing the client–therapist relationship (see Table 2.2). Once clients are hopeful that therapy may help and are motivated to change, it is important that they are able to turn to the tasks of the developing of the therapeutic relationship. To do this they need to have *trust* in the therapist, *openness* to the process of therapy and a *commitment* to working with their therapist. These, then, provide the objectives of this second stage of therapy. Therapist engagement and relationship development behaviours described in the previous section of course continue to be important. Clients who show good engagement in therapy are more likely to follow through therapeutic tasks (Corrigan, Dell, Lewis, & Schmidt, 1980; Ross, 1977). In contrast, defensiveness and hostility have been negatively linked to the quality of the client's working relationship (Binder & Strupp, 1997).

Important techniques at this stage include exploration and reflection of aspects of the client–therapist relationship. These methods are generally emphasised by psychodynamic, interpersonal and humanistic therapies

(Blagys & Hilsenroth, 2000; Blos, 1972; Dozier & Tyrrell, 1998; Enns, Campbell, & Courtois, 1997; Ogrodniczuk & Piper, 1999). There is some evidence to show that therapists who do not manage their counter-transference issues have less good alliances than therapists who successfully manage such issues (Ligiero & Gelso, 2002). Countertransference here is defined as "internal and external reactions in which unresolved conflicts of the therapist, usually but not always unconscious, are implicated" (Gelso & Hayes, 2002, p. 269). Management of countertransference issues consists of five interrelated factors: self-insight, self-integration, empathy, anxiety management, and conceptualising ability (Van Wagoner, Gelso, Hayes, & Diemer, 1991).

"Mutual affirmation" is seen as important therapist activity (Kolden, Howard, & Maling, 1994). Positive feedback also helps establish and strengthen the relationship (Claiborn, Goodyear, & Horner, 2001; Schaap, Bennun, Schindler, & Hoogduin, 1993). Feedback is usefully conceptualised as an influence process where the therapist changes the client's behaviour through the delivery of discrepant, change-promoting messages or positive reinforcement of aspects of the client's behaviour or self-beliefs. The feedback message can be descriptive or inferential. Research evidence indicates that descriptive feedback is more useful and positive feedback is generally more acceptable (although negative feedback can be useful if preceded by positive feedback). Ogrodniczuk & Piper (1999) discuss the fact that, when working with clients with personality disorders, therapists must balance transference work with supportive work, such as reassurance and praise.

Finally, relational interpretations are a therapy technique where the therapist makes an intervention that addresses interpersonal links, connections or themes within clients' stories. A number of studies have linked the use of relational interpretations, particularly those that address the central interpersonal theme of the client, to positive outcome and to the quality of the alliance (for example, see review by Crits-Christoph & Connolly, 1999).

Maintaining a relationship

The objectives or outcomes of the client–therapist interactions at the third stage of our model include: client continued *satisfaction* with the relationship; a productive and positive *working alliance*; increased ability for clients to *express their emotions* and to experience a *changing view of self with others* (see Table 2.3).

The first objective includes general satisfaction with and positive appraisal of the relationship (Hill & Williams, 2000; McGuire, McCabe, & Priebe, 2001). Clients' relationship satisfaction is associated with their satisfaction with therapy in general (Reis & Brown, 1999). It is an experiential rather than a behavioural phenomenon. Clients tend to be less discriminating than therapists about the quality of their relationship, forming

Table 2.3 Maintaining the relationship

Threats	Processes	Objectives

Therapist behaviour
  Intrusive
  Defensive
  Negative feelings
  Self-disclosure
	Self-reflection
	Metacommunication	

Client behaviour
  Resistance
  Hostility
  Negative feelings
	Flexibility
	Responsiveness
		Satisfaction
		Alliance
		Emotional expression
		Changing view of self

Relationship challenges
  Ruptures (confrontations
    or withdrawal)
  Misunderstandings
	Repair	

a global positive or negative impression of the relationship (Bachelor & Horvath, 1999). Dissatisfaction with the relationship is the most frequent reason given for leaving therapy and for non-compliance (Reis & Brown, 1999).

The second objective is referred to as the alliance (working, therapeutic, etc.). We discussed some aspects of the alliance at the beginning of the chapter. Although there are important differences in the definitions of the alliance (Horvath & Bedi, 2002), a major controversy exists as to whether the alliance arises from the interpersonal process or is an intrapsychic phenomenon (Saketopoulou, 1999), with different therapies emphasising different aspects of the alliance. However, it does appear that it is the quality and strength of the collaborative relationship between client and therapist that is the most important (Winston & Muran, 1996).

The third objective is emotional expression and emotional acceptance (see Greenberg, Chapter 3; Swales and Heard, Chapter 9; Pierson and Hayes, Chapter 10, this volume). For some therapies the relationship is the vehicle for emotions to be supported and expressed. The emotional relationship is seen as a cathartic experience (Garfield, 1974; Truax, 1967), although for some the emotional experience leads to change in cognitions and self-understanding and for others experiential insight is the key to change (Warwar & Greenberg, 2000; Winston & Muran, 1996). The final objective, which has been described in a number of reviews, is to enable the client to explore alternative views of themselves. These are sometimes referred to as narrative truths: social constructionists describe the processes in therapy as the client and therapist constructing the relationship together, where old problems are deconstructed and new narratives arise (Crits-Christoph, 1998; McGuire *et al.*, 2001; Stiles, Honos-Webb, & Surko, 1998).

As therapy progresses it is likely that difficulties in the relationship will arise (Katzow and Safran, Chapter 5, this volume; Safran, Muran, Samstag, & Stevens, 2001). Although these are common, therapy may be impeded if the problems are not resolved. Indeed resolution appears to lead to a deeper and better relationship and better treatment outcome (Safran *et al.*, 2001). Kivlighan and Shaughnessy (2000) and Stiles *et al.* (2004) found that the pattern of alliance ratings that went from high to low and back to high had the best association with good outcome.

Possible threats to the relationship have been grouped into: *therapist behaviours*, *client behaviours* and *relationship challenges*. The therapist actions needed to avoid or resolve these threats are grouped as *self-reflection*, *metacommunication*, *flexibility* and *repair*. These threats and therapist actions are discussed below.

Therapists may have negative feelings about their clients that are not spoken about but can still have a detrimental impact on the alliance (Gelso & Carter, 1985; Safran *et al.*, 2002). If these feelings are recognised, owned and explored, therapists report positive consequences (Greenberg, Chapter 3, this volume; Harris, 1999). Other therapist behaviours that clients have described as intrusive and defensive and as having a negative impact on the relationship include therapists imposing their own values, making irrelevant comments, and being critical, rigid, bored, blaming, moralistic, or uncertain (Ackerman & Hilsenroth, 2001). Poor use of therapeutic techniques, such as continued application of a technique when not accepted or found helpful by the client or poor use of silence, is linked with a poor therapeutic relationship (Binder & Strupp, 1997; McLennan, 1996).

Clients also tend to hide their negative feelings (such as fear, hostility, and anger) and often the therapist is unaware of what the client is feeling. Such client deference to the therapist has been linked with poor outcome (Binder & Strupp, 1997; Beutler, Clarkin, & Bongar, 2000; Warwar & Greenberg, 2000). This type of behaviour has sometimes been termed "client resistance". Resistance was originally developed as a psychoanalytic concept of the client's unconscious avoidance of the analytic work. It was later developed in social psychology as a theory of psychological reactance that was seen as a normal reaction to a perceived threat. Social influence theory defined the concept of resistance as a product of incongruence between the therapist's behaviour and the power or legitimacy ascribed to the therapist. In their review of the literature, Beutler, Moleiro, and Talebi (2002) conclude that therapy is most effective if therapists "can avoid stimulating the patient's level of resistance" (p. 139) through adjusting how directive they are in their interventions.

Relationship challenges often occur when there are misunderstandings between clients and therapists on the goals and tasks of therapy. Such disagreements may result in confrontations and client withdrawal (Bachelor & Horvath, 1999; Safran *et al.*, 2001). Such ruptures in therapy are common and should be an expected part of treatment (Ackerman & Hilsenroth, 2001; Bachelor & Horvath, 1999; Binder & Strupp, 1997; Hill & Williams, 2000; Katzow & Safran, Chapter 5, this volume). Therapist recognition of a rupture in the relationship is an important first step towards resolution. This involves therapists being able to reflect on their own position in therapy and their feelings about the client and how therapy is progressing (Binder & Strupp, 1997).

The importance of repairing ruptures has been mentioned above. Safran and Muran (1996) have developed a model of rupture resolution, which provides four stages: attending to the rupture marker, exploring the rupture experience, exploring avoidance and emergence of a wish or need. Evidence for this model has been found in a number of studies (see Safran *et al.* (2001) for a review). Aspland, Llewelyn, Hardy, Barkham, and Stiles (2006) looked at rupture repair sequences in CBT and found that, contrary to Safran's model, therapists did not openly discuss the rupture with clients.

Of paramount importance in maintaining the relationship is the therapist's ability to tailor therapy to the individual needs and characteristics of clients. This involves therapists responding appropriately to relational fluctuations so that negative reactions are contained and managed. For example, therapists' inflexible adherence to treatment strategies (either cognitive or interpretations) is associated with poor relationships (Stiles *et al.*, 1998). Appropriate responsiveness and flexibility are seen as important in maintaining the therapeutic relationship (Davis, 1991; Stiles *et al.*, 1998).

Contextual factors

There are also broader client, therapist and contextual factors that impact on the quality of the therapeutic relationship. Two of the main client characteristics found to moderate treatment outcome and poor therapeutic relationships are functional impairment and coping style (Beutler, Harwood, Alimohamed, & Malik, 2002). Functional impairment includes problems in work, social and intimate relationships. The more difficulties clients have in these areas, the less likely they are to benefit from therapy. Problem complexity has also been associated with poor relationship development (Kilmann, Scovern, & Moreault, 1979). For such clients to be able to benefit from therapy, treatment often needs to be of more than six months in length to give time for the therapeutic relationship to develop.

Therapist characteristics that are associated with negative aspects of the client–therapist relationship include being rigid, uncertain, distant, tense, and distracted, and level of experience (Ackerman & Hilsenroth, 2001). A further significant therapist factor related to negative outcome is therapists' underestimating the seriousness of clients' problems (Beutler & Clarkin, 1990). As has been stated, therapists who stick rigidly to therapy techniques when there are relationship ruptures rather than exploring the nature of the relationship problem are less likely to achieve satisfactory client outcomes.

Clients' and therapists' attachment style has been found to influence the quality of the therapeutic relationship, with clients who have insecure attachment styles less able to form satisfactory alliances (Eames & Roth, 2000). Hardy, Cahill, Shapiro, Barkham, Rees, & Macaskill (2001) found that clients with an underinvolved interpersonal style (avoidant) did less well in CBT, and that this relationship between interpersonal style and outcome was mediated by the therapeutic alliance. There is also some evidence that therapists' attachment style impacts on the quality of the relationship formed with clients. For example, therapists who have an insecure, overinvolved attachment style tend to respond less empathically to clients than secure therapists (Rubino, Barker, Roth, & Fearon, 2000).

At the broader level, cultural and demographic variables have been found to have an impact on the therapy relationship. Although the evidence is limited, clients from minority groups are less likely to remain in therapy and tend to drop out prematurely (Bernstein, 2001; Draguns, 1997; Heitler, 1976; Margolese, 1998; Peltzer, 2001; Spector, 2001; Reis & Brown, 1999). Again there is little research on whether clients should be matched with therapists from the same ethnic background, social class, religion, etc. Sue and Lam (2002) report a number of studies that suggest that matching of therapist and client in terms of cultural background may improve outcome and decrease premature termination of therapy. There is some evidence that perceived similarity with one's therapist results in greater satisfaction (Bernstein, 2001). For example, similarity in social class between therapist and clients has been linked with the formation of a better therapeutic relationship (Gardner, 1964), although two further reviews concluded that social class did not impact on the quality of the relationship (Harrison, 1975). There is also some evidence that perspective and attitude convergence and positive complementarity are associated with higher ratings of the relationship and better outcome (Bachelor & Horvath, 1999; Whiston & Coker, 2000; Crastnopol, 2001; Reis & Brown, 1999). Positive complementarity involves both reciprocity in terms of control and correspondence in terms of affiliation (Hill & Williams, 2000).

Finally, many of the reviews mention the importance of influence in the therapeutic relationship. Keijsers, Schaap, & Hoogduin (2000) describe effective behaviour therapists as being influential. This process is linked to social influence theory or the ability of the therapist to influence the client on the basis of social power. Influence is also linked to the credibility of the therapist (McGuire et al., 2001; Corrigan et al., 1980). In addition, power has been described as the vital force in therapy (Puskar & Hess, 1986). Power in this context includes that offered through the role and status of the therapist, and the negotiated power through agreement of the therapy contract and through the therapist's interaction. Clients, through their engagement in and compliance with their role and respect they offer to therapists, legitimise the power then given to the therapist. From a different perspective, therapists working within a social constructionist framework aim to empower (or enable) clients (Sexton & Whiston, 1994). It is this social influence aspect of the therapist's role that is put forward as being the route through which computer/internet therapies achieve success (Binik *et al.*, 1997).

It is also possible to link the concept of power to ruptures in the relationship. Gilbert (1993, 2000) describes how our interactions with others are influenced by our perceived social status or rank. Clients are likely to feel inferior to their therapist. If they experience a difficulty in their therapeutic relationship this may result in feelings of shame and humiliation, which may be hidden for fear of losing status in the relationship.

Conclusion

The establishment of a good relationship is necessary from the first stages of therapy. An exploration of the research on the therapeutic relationship suggests that clients tend to emphasise the importance of therapist warmth and emotional involvement, while therapists judge the quality of the relationship in terms of clients' active participation and collaboration. Together, these make the primary components of the initial objectives for the first stage in the relationship: expectancies, intentions and hope. As therapy continues, the second stage of the relationship develops into one in which therapeutic activity is carried out. This leads to a deepening of the therapist–client relationship, but also, as the relationship shifts into the third stage, leads to misunderstandings, conflicts, activation of defences, negative reactions and ruptures. Maintaining the quality of the relationship through the various stages of therapy involves therapists ensuring they are appropriately responsive to their clients, able to recognise and seek to repair ruptures in the relationship. Maintaining this complex developing and changing relationship requires therapists to individualise their responses to specific aspects of clients' needs and relating styles. Therapist understanding and appreciation of contextual factors are also important for developing and maintaining the therapeutic relationship. Research suggests that it is the blending of these various skills that makes for a good therapeutic relationship, which in turn will influence the outcome for the client. These findings are pertinent to all psychotherapies, including cognitive-behavioural-focused therapies.

References

Ackerman, S.J. & Hilsenroth, M.J. (2001). A review of therapist characteristics and techniques negatively impacting the therapeutic alliance. *Psychotherapy*, 38, 171–185.

Arnkoff, D.B., Glass, C.R. & Shapiro, S.J. (2002). Expectations and preferences. In J. Norcross (ed.), *Psychotherapy relationships that work: Therapist contributions and responsiveness to patients* (pp. 335–356). Oxford: Oxford University Press.

Aspland, H., Llewelyn, S., Hardy, G.E., Barkham, B. & Stiles, W.B. (2006). Alliance ruptures and resolution in CBT: A task analysis. Submitted for publication.

Bachelor, A. & Horvath, A. (1999). The therapeutic relationship. In M.A. Hubble & B.L. Duncan (eds), *The heart and soul of change: What works in therapy* (pp. 133–178). Washington, DC: American Psychiatric Association.

Bernstein, D.M. (2001). Therapist–patient relations and ethnic transference. In W.S. Tseng & J. Streltzer (eds), *Culture and psychotherapy: A guide to clinical practice* (pp. 103–121). New York: Brunner-Routledge.

Beutler, L.E. & Clarkin, J.F. (1990). *Systematic treatment selection: Toward targeted therapeutic interventions.* New York: Oxford University Press.

Beutler, L.E., Clarkin, J.F. & Bongar, B. (2000). *Guidelines for the systematic treatment of the depressed patient.* New York: Oxford University Press.

Beutler, L.E., Harwood, T.M., Alimohamed, S. & Malik, M. (2002). Functional impairment and coping style. In J. Norcross (ed.), *Psychotherapy relationships that work: Therapist contributions and responsiveness to patients* (pp. 145–176). Oxford: Oxford University Press.

Beutler, L.E., Moleiro, C. & Talebi, H. (2002). Resistance. In J. Norcross (ed.), *Psychotherapy relationships that work: Therapist contributions and responsiveness to patients* (pp. 129–144). Oxford: Oxford University Press.

Binder, J.L. & Strupp, H.H. (1997). "Negative process": A recurrently discovered and underestimated facet of therapeutic process and outcome in the individual psychotherapy of adults. *Clinical Psychology – Science & Practice, 4*, 121–139.

Binik, Y.M., Cantor, J., Ochs, E. & Meana, M. (1997). From the couch to the keyboard: Psychotherapy in cyberspace. In S. Kiesler (ed.), *Culture of the Internet* (pp. 71–100). Mahwah, NJ: Lawrence Erlbaum Associates.

Blagys, M.D. & Hilsenroth, M.J. (2000). Distinctive feature of short-term psychodynamic–interpersonal psychotherapy: A review of the comparative psychotherapy process literature. *Clinical Psychology – Science & Practice, 7*, 167–188.

Blos, P., Jr (1972). Silence: A clinical exploration. *Psychoanalytic Quarterly, 41*, 348–363.

Bohart, A.C., Elliott, R.E., Greenberg, L.S. & Watson, J.C. (2002). Empathy. In J. Norcross (ed.), *Psychotherapy relationships that work: Therapist contributions and responsiveness to patients* (pp. 89–108). Oxford: Oxford University Press.

Bordin, E.S. (1979). The generalizability of the psychoanalytic concept of the working alliance. *Psychotherapy: Theory, Research & Practice, 16*, 252–260.

Bordin, E.S. (1994).Theory and research in the therapeutic working alliance: New directions. In O. Horvath & L.S. Greenberg (eds), *The working alliance.* New York: Wiley.

Cahill, J. (2003). *A review and critical appraisal of measures of therapist–patient interactions in mental health settings.* National Co-ordinating Centre for Research Methodology, Birmingham, Final Report.

Castonguay, L.G. & Holtforth, M.G. (2005). Change in psychotherapy: A plea for no more "nonspecific" and false dichotomies. *Clinical Psychology: Science and Practice*, 12, 198–201.

Claiborn, C.D., Goodyear, R.K. & Horner, P.A. (2001). Feedback. *Psychotherapy: Theory, Research, Practice, Training*, 38, 401–405.

Corrigan, J.D., Dell, D.M., Lewis, K.N. & Schmidt, L.D. (1980). Counseling as a social influence process: A review. *Journal of Counseling Psychology*, 27, 395–441.

Crastnopol, M. (2001). Convergence and divergence in the characters of analyst and patient: Fairbairn treating Guntrip. *Psychoanalytic Psychology*, 18, 120–136.

Crits-Christoph, P. (1998). The interpersonal interior of psychotherapy. *Psychotherapy Research*, 8, 1–16.

Crits-Christoph, P. & Connolly, M.B. (1999). Alliance and technique in short-term dynamic therapy. *Clinical Psychology Review*, 19, 687–704.

Davis, D.M. (1991). Review of the psychoanalytic literature on countertransference. *International Journal of Short-Term Psychotherapy*, 6, 143–151.

Davis, C.S., Cook, D.A., Jennings, R.L. & Heck, E.J. (1977). Differential attractiveness to a counseling analogue. *Journal of Consulting Psychology*, 24, 472–476.

DeRubeis, R.J., Brotman, M.A. & Gibbons, C.A. (2005). *Clinical Psychology: Science and Practice*, 12, 174–183.

Dozier, M. & Tyrrell, C. (1998). The role of attachment in therapeutic relationships. In J.A. Simpson & W.S. Rholes (eds), *Attachment theory and close relationship* (pp. 221–248). New York: Guilford Press.

Draguns, J.G. (1997). Abnormal behavior patterns across cultures: Implications for counseling and psychotherapy. *International Journal of Intercultural Relations*, 21, 213–248.

Eames, V. & Roth, A. (2000). Patient attachment orientation and the early working alliance: A study of patient and therapist reports of alliance qualtiy and ruptures. *Psychotherapy Research*, 10, 421–434.

Enns, C.Z., Campbell, J. & Courtois, C.A. (1997). Recommendations for working with domestic violence survivors, with special attention to memory issues and posttraumatic processes. *Psychotherapy*, 34, 459–477.

Everly, G., Jr (2001). Personologic alignment and the treatment of posttraumatic distress. *International Journal of Emergency Mental Health*, 3, 171–177.

Farber, B.A. & Lane, J.S. (2002). Positive regard. In J. Norcross (ed.), *Psychotherapy relationships that work: Therapist contributions and responsiveness to patients* (pp. 175–194). Oxford: Oxford University Press.

Frank, J.D. (1961). *Persuasion and healing*. Baltimore, MD: Johns Hopkins University Press.

Freud, S. (1940). The dynamics of transference. In J. Strachey (ed.), *The standard edition of the complete psychological works of Sigmund Freud*, Vol. 12 (pp. 122–144). London: Hogarth.

Gardner, G.G. (1964). The psychotherapeutic relationship. *Psychological Bulletin*, 61, 426–439.

Garfield, S.L. (1974). What are the therapeutic variables in psychotherapy? *Psychotherapy & Psychosomatics*, 24, 372–378.

Gaston, L., Marmar, C.R., Gallagher, D. & Thompson, L.W. (1991). Alliance prediction of outcome: Beyond in-treatment symptomatic change as psychotherapy progress. *Psychotherapy Research*, 1, 104–112.

Gelso, C.J. & Carter, J.A. (1985). The relationship in counseling and psychotherapy:

Components, consequences, and theoretical antecedents. *Counseling Psychologist*, 13, 155–243.

Gelso, C.J. & Hayes, J.A. (2002). The management of countertransference. In J. Norcross (ed.), *Psychotherapy relationships that work: Therapist contributions and responsiveness to patients* (pp. 267–284). Oxford: Oxford University Press.

Gilbert, P. (1993). Defence and safety: Their function in social behaviour and psychopathology. *British Journal of Clinical Psychology*, 32, 131–153.

Gilbert, P. (2000). The relationship of shame, social anxiety and depression: The role of the evaluation of social rank. *Clinical Psychology and Psychotherapy*, 7, 174–189.

Greenson, R.R. (1965). The working alliance and the transference neurosis. *Psychoanalytic Quarterly*, 34, 155–181.

Hardy, G.E., Cahill, J., Shapiro, D.A., Barkham, M., Rees, A. & Macaskill, N. (2001). Client interpersonal and cognitive style as predictors of response to time limited cognitive therapy for depression. *Journal of Consulting and Clinical Psychology*, 68, 841–845.

Harris, A.H.S. (1999). Incidence and impacts of psychotherapists' feelings toward their clients: A review of the empirical literature. *Counselling Psychology Quarterly*, 12, 363–375.

Harrison, D.K. (1975). Race as a counselor–client variable in counseling and psychotherapy: A review of the research. *Counseling Psychologist*, 5, 124–133.

Heitler, J.B. (1976). Preparatory techniques in initiating expressive psychotherapy with lower-class, unsophisticated patients. *Psychological Bulletin*, 83, 339–352.

Hill, C.E. & Williams, E.N. (2000). The process of individual therapy. In S.D. Brown & R.W. Lent (eds), *Handbook of counseling psychology*, 3rd edition (pp. 670–710). New York: John Wiley & Sons.

Holmes, J. (1996). *Attachment, intimacy and autonomy: Using attachment theory in adult psychotherapy*. Northvale, NJ: Arison.

Horvath, A. & Bedi, R. (2002). The alliance. In J. Norcross (ed.), *Psychotherapy relationships that work: Therapist contributions and responsiveness to patients* (pp. 37–70). Oxford: Oxford University Press.

Horvath, A.O. (1995). The therapeutic relationship: From transference to alliance. *In Session – Psychotherapy in Practice*, 1, 7–17.

Kazdin, A.E. (2005). Treatment outcomes, common factors, and continued neglect of mechanisms of change. *Clinical Psychology: Science and Practice*, 12, 164–188.

Keijsers, G.P.J., Schaap, C.P.D.R. & Hoogduin, C.A.L. (2000). The impact of interpersonal patient and therapist behavior on outcome in cognitive-behavioral therapy: A review of empirical studies. *Behavior Modification*, 24, 264–297.

Kilmann, P.R., Scovern, A.W. & Moreault, D. (1979). Factors in the patient–therapist interaction and outcome: A review of the literature. *Comprehensive Psychiatry*, 20, 132–146.

Kivlighan, D.M. & Shaughnessy, P. (2000). Patterns of the working alliance development: A typology of clients' working alliance ratings. *Journal of Counseling Psychology*, 47, 362–371.

Klerman, G.L., Weissman, M.M., Rounsville, B.J. & Chevron, E.S. (1984). *Interpersonal therapy of depression*. New York: Basic Books.

Kolden, G.G., Howard, K.I. & Maling, M.S. (1994). The counseling relationship and treatment process and outcome. *Counseling Psychologist*, 22, 82–89.

Kuyken, W. (2004). Cognitive therapy outcome: The effects of hopelessness in a naturalistic study. *Behaviour Research and Therapy*, 42, 631–646.

Lambert, M.J. (1989). The individual therapist's contribution to psychotherapy process and outcome. *Clinical Psychology Review*, 9, 469–485.

Lambert, M.J. & Ogles, B.M. (2004). The efficacy and effectiveness of psychotherapy. In M. Lambert (ed.), *Bergin and Grafield's handbook of psychotherapy and behaviour change*, 5th edition (pp. 139–193). New York: John Wiley and Sons.

Ligiero, D.P. & Gelso, C.J. (2002). Countertransference, attachment and the working alliance: The therapists' contribution. *Psychotherapy: Theory, Research, Practice, and Training*, 39, 3–11.

Luborsky, L. (1976). Helping alliance in psychotherapy. In J.L. Cleghorn (ed.), *Successful psychotherapy* (pp. 92–116). New York: Brunner/Mazel.

Luborsky, L. (1990). Theory and technique in dynamic psychotherapy: Curative factors and training therapists to maximize them. *Psychotherapy & Psychosomatics*, 53, 50–57.

Luborsky, L.B. (1994). Therapeutic alliances as predictors of psychotherapy outcomes. In O.A. Horvath & L.S. Greenberg (eds), *The working alliance: Theory, research and practice*. New York: Wiley.

Mace, C. & Margison, F. (1997). Attachment and psychotherapy: An overview. *British Journal of Medical Psychology*, 70, 576–617.

McGuire, R., McCabe, R. & Priebe, S. (2001). Theoretical frameworks for understanding and investigating the therapeutic relationship in psychiatry. *Social Psychiatry & Psychiatric Epidemiology*, 36, 557–564.

McLennan, J. (1996). Improving our understanding of therapeutic failure: A review. *Counselling Psychology Quarterly*, 9, 391–379.

Mallinckrodt, B. (2000). Attachment, social competencies, social support, and interpersonal process in psychotherapy. *Psychotherapy Research*, 10, 239–266.

Margolese, H.C. (1998). Engaging in psychotherapy with the Orthodox Jew: A critical review. *American Journal of Psychotherapy*, 52, 37–53.

Martin, D.J., Garske, J.P. & Davis, M.K. (2000). Relation of the therapeutic alliance with outcome and other variables: A meta-analytic review. *Journal of Consulting and Clinical Psychology*, 68, 438–450.

Meyer, B. & Pilkonis, P.A. (2002). Attachment style. In J. Norcross (ed.), *Psychotherapy relationships that work: Therapist contributions and responsiveness to patients* (pp. 367–383). Oxford: Oxford University Press.

Nathan, R. (1999). Scientific attitude to 'difficult' patients. *British Journal of Psychiatry*, 175, 87.

Norcross, J. (2002). *Psychotherapy relationships that work: Therapist contributions and responsiveness to patients*. Oxford: Oxford University Press.

Ogrodniczuk, J.S. & Piper, W.E. (1999). Use of transference interpretations in dynamically oriented individual psychotherapy for patients with personality disorders. *Journal of Personality Disorders*, 13, 297–311.

Peltzer, K. (2001). An integrative model for ethnocultural counseling and psychotherapy of victims of organized violence. *Journal of Psychotherapy Integration*, 11, 241–262.

Puskar, K.R. & Hess, M.R. (1986). Considerations of power by graduate student nurse psychotherapists: A pilot study. *Issues in Mental Health Nursing*, 8, 51–61.

Reandeau, S.G. & Wampold, B.E. (1991). Relationship of power and involvement to the working alliance: A multiple-case sequential analysis of brief therapy. *Journal of Counseling Psychology*, 38, 107–114.

Reis, B.F. & Brown, L.G. (1999). Reducing psychotherapy dropouts: Maximizing perspective convergence in the psychotherapy dyad. *Psychotherapy*, 36, 123–136.

Ross, M.B. (1977). Discussion of similarity of client and therapist. *Psychological Reports*, 40, 699–704.

Rogers, C.R. (1957). The necessary and sufficient conditions of therapeutic personality change. *Journal of Consulting Psychology*, 22, 95–103.

Rubino, G., Barker, C., Roth, T. & Fearon, P. (2000). Therapist empathy and depth of interpretation in response to potential alliance ruptures: The role of therapist and patient attachment styles. *Psychotherapy Research*, 10, 408–420.

Russell, R.L. & Shirk, S.R. (1998). Child psychotherapy process research. *Advances in Clinical Child Psychology*, 20, 93–124.

Safran, J.D. & Muran, J.C. (1996). The resolution of ruptures in the therapeutic alliance. *Journal of Consulting and Clinical Psychology*, 64, 447–458.

Safran, J.D., Muran, J.C., Samstag, L.W. & Stevens, C. (2001). Repairing alliance ruptures. *Psychotherapy: Theory, Research, Practice, Training*, 38, 406–412.

Safran, J.D. & Segal, Z. (1990). *Interpersonal processes in cognitive therapy*. New York: Basic Books.

Safren, S.A., Heimberg, R.G. & Juster, H.R. (1997). Clients' expectancies and their relationship to pretreatment symptomatology and outcome in cognitive-behavioral group treatment for social phobia. *Journal of Consulting and Clinical Psychology*, 65, 694–698.

Saketopoulou, A. (1999). The therapeutic alliance in psychodynamic psychotherapy: Theoretical conceptualizations and research findings. *Psychotherapy*, 36, 329–343.

Schaap, C., Bennun, I., Schindler, L. & Hoogduin, K. (1993). *The therapeutic relationship in behavioural psychotherapy*. Chichester, UK: Wiley.

Schmidt, N.B. & Woolaway-Bickel, K. (2000). The effects of treatment compliance on outcome in cognitive-behavioral therapy for panic disorder. *Counseling and Clinical Psychology*, 68, 13–18.

Sexton, H., Littauer, H., Sexton, A. & Tommeras, E. (2005). Building the alliance: Early process and the client–therapist connection. *Psychotherapy Research*, 15, 103–116.

Sexton, T.L. & Whiston, S.C. (1994). The status of the counseling relationship: An empirical review, theoretical implications, and research directions. *Counseling Psychologist*, 22, 6–78.

Spector, R. (2001). Is there a racial bias in clinicians' perceptions of the dangerousness of psychiatric patients? A review of the literature. *Journal of Mental Health*, 10, 5–15.

Stiles, W.B., Glick, M.J., Osatuke, K., Hardy, G.E., Shapiro, D.A., Agnew-Davies, R., Recs, A. & Barkham, M. (2004). Patterns of alliance development and the rupture-repair hypothesis: Are productive relationships U-shaped or V-shaped? *Journal of Counseling Psychology*, 51, 81–91.

Stiles, W.B., Honos-Webb, L. & Surko, M. (1998). Responsiveness in psycho-therapy. *Clinical Psychology – Science & Practice*, 5, 439–458.

Stiles, W.B., Shapiro, D.A. & Elliott, R. (1986). Are all psychotherapies equivalent? *American Psychologist*, 41, 165–180.

Sue, S. & Lam, A. (2002). Cultural and demographic diversity. In J. Norcross (ed.), *Psychotherapy relationships that work: Therapist contributions and responsiveness to patients* (pp. 401–422). Oxford: Oxford University Press.

Sweet, A.A. (1984). The therapeutic relationship in behavior therapy. *Clinical Psychology Review*, 4, 253–272.

Truax, C.B. & Carkhuff, R.R. (1967). *Toward effective counseling and psychotherapy*. Chicago: Aldine.

Tryon, G.S. (1990). Session depth and smoothness in relation to the concept of engagement in counseling. *Journal of Counseling Psychology*, 37, 248–253.

Tryon, G.S. (2002). Engagement in counseling. In G.S. Tryon (ed.), *Counseling based on process research: Applying what we know* (pp. 1–26). Boston: Allyn & Bacon.

Tryon, G.S. & Winograd, G. (2001). Goal consensus and collaboration. *Psychotherapy: Theory, Research, Practice, Training*, 38, 385–389.

Tryon, G.S. & Winograd, G. (2002). Goal consensus and collaboration. In J. Norcross (ed.), *Psychotherapy relationships that work: Therapist contributions and responsiveness to patients* (pp. 109–125). Oxford: Oxford University Press.

Van Wagoner, S.L., Gelso, C.J., Hayes, J.A. & Diemer, R. (1991). Countertransference and the reputedly excellent psychotherapist. *Psychotherapy: Theory, Research and Practice*, 28, 411–421.

Waldinger, R.J. (1987). Intensive psychodynamic therapy with borderline patients: An overview. *American Journal of Psychiatry*, 144, 267–274.

Wampold, B.E. (2005). Establishing specificity in psychotherapy scientifically: Design and evidence issues. *Clinical Psychology: Science and Practice*, 12, 194–197.

Warwar, S. & Greenberg, L.S. (2000). Advances in theories of change and counseling. In S.D. Brown & R.W. Lent (eds), *Handbook of counseling psychology*, 3rd edition (pp. 571–600). New York: Wiley.

Whisman, M.A. (1993). Mediators and moderators of change in cognitive therapy of depression. *Psychological Bulletin*, 114, 248–265.

Whiston, S.C. & Coker, J.K. (2000). Reconstructing clinical training: Implications from research. *Counselor Education & Supervision*, 39, 228–253.

Wilson, G.T. (1984). Clinical issues and strategies in the practice of behavior therapy. *Annual Review of Behavior Therapy: Theory & Practice*, 10, 291–320.

Winston, A. & Muran, J.C. (1996). Common factors in the time-limited psychotherapies. *American Psychiatric Press Review of Psychiatry*, 15, 43–68.

Worthington, E.L. (1986). Client compliance with homework directives during counseling. *Journal of Counseling Psychology*, 33, 124–130.

Young, J.E. & Beck, A.T. (1988). *Revision of the Cognitive Therapy Scale*. Unpublished manuscript, University of Pennsylvania, Philadelphia.

Chapter 3

Emotion in the therapeutic relationship in emotion-focused therapy

Leslie S. Greenberg

Introduction

Emotion-focused therapy (EFT: Greenberg, 2002; Greenberg & Watson, 2006) views the relationship, characterized by the therapist's presence and the provision of empathy, acceptance and congruence, as an affect-regulating bond. It also posits that this type of bond provides an optimal therapeutic environment for the facilitation of deeper emotional processing and experiencing. Empathy, acceptance and congruence not only create an optimal therapeutic environment in which clients feel safe to engage fully in the process of self-exploration and new learning, but also contribute to clients' affect regulation by providing interpersonal soothing. Over time this interpersonal regulation of affect is internalized into self-soothing and enhances the capacity to regulate inner states. In this view, the therapist's overall attitude, not only his/her techniques, are seen as influencing the client's well-being. This chapter will discuss elements such as pacing and facial, tonal and postural communication of affect that create a therapeutic emotional climate. In addition to the climate's role in promoting enhanced affect regulation, its role in providing the optimal environment for facilitating emotional processing will be discussed.

In our view the relationship serves a dual purpose in psychotherapy (Greenberg & Watson, 2006). First, the relationship is therapeutic in and of itself by serving an affect regulation function which is internalized over time. This function is accomplished by offering a soothing, affect-attuned bond characterized by the therapist's presence and empathic attunement to affect as well as acceptance and congruence. Second, the relationship functions as a means to an end. The relationship offers the optimal environment for facilitating specific modes of emotional processing. Affect is much more likely to be approached, tolerated and accepted in the context of a safe relationship. The combination of functions results in a style of relating that involves a combination of both, following and leading, responding and guiding.

In the most general terms, EFT is built on a genuinely prizing (a term used in client-centred therapy in place of unconditional positive regard) empathic relationship and on the therapist being highly present, respectful and responsive to the client's experience. At the same time, EFT therapists also assume that it is useful to guide the client's emotional processing in different ways at different times. The optimal situation in this approach is an active collaboration between client and therapist, with each feeling neither led nor simply followed by the other. Instead, the ideal is an easy sense of co-exploration. Nevertheless, when disjunction or disagreement occurs, the client is viewed as the expert on his or her own experience, and the therapist always defers to the client's experience. Thus, therapist interventions are offered in a *non-imposing*, *tentative* manner, as conjectures, perspectives, "experiments" or offers, rather than as pronouncements, lectures or statements of truth.

In this relational framework we have come to view a therapist who works in this way as an emotion coach (Greenberg, 2002). Coaching in this view entails both acceptance and change (Linehan, 1993). The therapist both promotes and validates awareness and acceptance of emotional experience and coaches clients in new ways of processing emotion. The non-directive following style provides change towards acceptance of what is while the more leading style provides guidance and introduces novelty and the possibility of change towards something new. In our view an EFT relationship differs from a CBT relationship in relying on empathic attunement and exploratory empathy as its main tool rather than creation of rapport and Socratic dialogue. Questions are not used much by therapists and the relational style in EFT is far less educative, challenging, disputational or change-oriented. In addition, believing that clients cannot leave a place before they have arrived at it, the focus in the relational dialogue is on acceptance and validation of emotion rather than on modification of cognition. It is only after validation of what is being experienced, as shown in the transcript below, that transformation via accessing new affect and creation of new meaning comes into play. The relational emphasis is more on facilitation of strength than on correction of error.

An example of a therapist responding to a depressed client's sense of isolation after a divorce is given below to exemplify the type of empathic attunement and exploration characteristic of the relational style in EFT.

T53: Do you think you could put your sister in the chair and talk to her?

C54: No. [Pause]

T54: It's really a hard one for you. [Pause] What are you feeling right now?

C55: [Small voice:] Scared. [=Vulnerability begins to emerge]

T55: [Gently:] Scared. [Pause] Uh-huh. Just so scared about . . .

C56:   What will happen to the little [rueful laugh:] relationship that we have.

T56:   Uh-huh, scared that if you assert yourself here, you could lose her.

C57:   What change will it bring in her, towards me? I don't think I could handle it. (T: mhm)

T57:   "If I assert my feelings or if I express my true feelings of jealousy towards her, will it ruin the shred of a relationship that we *do* have? (C: mhm) Will it ruin the little bit of e-mail I *do* get?" It might destroy even those little threads, and it's so scary to think about not having that relationship. (C: mhmm mhm)

C58:   Yeah. It is such a risk. I don't know if I can bear the loss. Without her it's like I would have nothing.

T58:   Just a feeling that, "Without that connection I will be left totally alone."

C59:   Yes, that's how I would feel, totally alone, not anything to anybody.

T59:   Uh-huh, without any value to anyone.

C60:   Yes, it's like feeling that I could die without anyone knowing.

T60:   No one would even know.

C61:   Yes. I feel tight in my throat. (T: mhm) My stomach hurts.

In the above segment, the therapist responds empathically to the client's vulnerability in a prizing and congruent manner. This helps the client's vulnerability emerge at C55, when she reports feeling scared. The therapist validates the scared feelings, and in C59 the client begins to articulate the unbearable sense of loss. This leads her towards focusing on a bodily felt sense of pain and the therapist, as shown below, guides her to regulate the feeling and to explore it to access the implicit meanings.

T64:   That's good. [Pause] Good calming breaths. [Pause] [Whispers:] Take a minute, just to relax. Quiet down inside [long pause]. So there's this feeling inside. What's it like?

C65:   Sometimes it's just like I want to go crawl in my bed and just stay in there and nobody bother me. [=Vulnerability emerges further]

T65:   Mhm, mhm. "I just want to shut my eyes and shut all the pain shut out (C: mhm, mhm) And shut all the people out. Yeah. (C: mhm) I just want to make all the pain go away."

After a deepening to get to core vulnerability, the acceptance and validation by the therapist helps the client stay with the painful, vulnerable feelings, while the therapist listens for what is worst or most painful about the whole thing.

T68:   What hurts the most right now? I know it's really hard. [Pause] What part of it is hardest?

C69:   It's like I'm drowning, (T: [whispers:] drowning) and I keep reaching up, and I've been struggling since I was a kid.

T69:   [Whispering:] Like you're drowning, and a little piece of you, one hand, one arm just keeps reaching up.

At the same time as witnessing and receiving the helpless aspects of her experience and making vivid the depths of the client's despair, the therapist is listening for the genuine emergence of adaptive emotions and for the wants and needs in the personality. This begins to emerge above in the image of reaching up and is developed below, through exploring feelings tied to an episodic memory of a time in her childhood when she nearly drowned; her reorganization into a more resilient state is recognizable below in her reaching out for comfort and safety from others:

C74:   [Stronger:] And, and you know, reaching, and just keep reaching (T: mhm, hm) and I think it was one of my brothers who [rueful laughter:] realized I was drowning [laughs], you know, pulled me up, and uh, um, I don't even know how old I was, but, but very traumatized by that.

T74:   And right now, it's like you're saying, "Is there anyone that can reach me and pull me up out of this?" (C: mhm)

The client then goes on to self-challenge her expectations:

C77:   Mhm, And I'm reaching for something, somebody. (T: mhm, mhm) [large sigh] You know, thinking back, I think, OK, I did have an unrealistic expectation of getting married to Dave, and moving away. And that was just so exciting to me. [Self-reorganization taking place]

The end of this segment below reveals the significance of the relationship in helping her reorganize in a more resilient manner.

T88:   What are you experiencing right now?

C89:   I guess that's why therapy is so important to me. I really need someone to help me find my way. And so it feels good in a way for me to be able to tell someone about these things.

T89:   I'm pleased to be here with you and that telling me about it is helping.

C90:   Uh-huh. And I don't feel so desperately in need of someone in my family like my brother or sister to rescue me, or so angry when they're too tied up in their own lives. But still I would like to hold onto my relationships with them. There are moments when I know I can make it. It's just sometimes it feels so overwhelming and I go to that drowning place again.

T90:   So in spite of everything, you feel you can manage at times?

The relationship and affect regulation

Deficits in empathy and emotional connection between infants and their caretakers have been found to affect areas of right brain development involved in empathy and compassion (Schore, 2003). When an empathic connection is made with the therapist, affect processing centres in the brain are effected and new possibilities open up for the client. This creates an optimal therapeutic environment in which clients feel safe to engage fully in the process of self-exploration and new learning, but also contributes to clients' affect regulation by providing interpersonal soothing. Over time this interpersonal regulation of affect is internalized into self-soothing or the capacity to regulate inner states. These optimal therapeutic relational qualities thus facilitate the dyadic regulation of emotion through provision of safety, security and connection. This breaks the client's sense of isolation, confirms self-experience, and promotes both self-empathy and self-exploration.

Emotion self-regulation

In experimental psychology the regulation of emotion is usually defined in terms of the conscious or volitional self-regulation of emotion. Emotion regulation refers here to the set of control processes by which people voluntarily control their experience of their emotions. Emotion regulation, for example, is defined as the process by which individuals influence which emotions they have, when they have them and how they experience and express them (Gross, 1999). This view of emotion regulation generally sees appraisals as resulting in emotion and suggests that people have emotion, which they then need to regulate. This is a two-factor view of emotion regulation, in which one system is seen as generating emotion and another is seen as subsequently regulating emotion. This is a self-control view of emotion regulation.

A broader, one-factor view sees emotion regulation as intrinsic in the experience of generating emotion. In this broader view, regulation, rather than self-control, is seen as *an integral aspect of the generation of emotion* and coterminous with it (Campos, Frankel, & Camras, 2004), and appraisal and emotion are seen as occurring simultaneously to generate emotional meanings. Affective neuroscience supports this broader view of emotion regulation rather than the narrower two-factor, conscious control, view (Cozolino, 2002). Evidence shows that although the prefrontal cortex is connected to and can influence the amygdala, the amygdala is highly connected to many parts of the brain and to the prefrontal cortex and influences decisions (Le Doux, 1996; Damasio, 1999). Evidence from affective neuroscience also indicates the possibility that there is both implicit (right hemispheric) and explicit (left hemispheric) affect regulation (Schore, 2003). Emotion in this broader view thus is both inherently regulated and regulatory. The cognitive system is seen as *receiving information* from the emotion system as well as influencing it, and as *guided* by emotion, as well as making sense of emotion. Emotion systems thus can be transformed or regulated by processes other than cognition, such as by other emotions and by attachment (Greenberg, 2002).

Essential affective self-regulatory processes thus are involved in self-maintenance, rather than self-control, and these occur largely below conscious awareness. This probably occurs in the orbitofrontal cortex which takes over amygdala and lower level right hemispheric functioning in more complex processing (Schore, 2003; Lane & Nadel, 2000). Implicit affect regulation that occurs through right hemispheric processes is not verbally mediated, is highly relational, and is most directly affected by such things as relational and emotional communication, facial expression, vocal quality and eye contact.

In clinical work, regulation is not easily achieved through the cognitive system alone. A validating relationship is crucial to affect regulation. People with under-regulated affect have been shown to benefit from interpersonal validation as much as from the learning of emotion regulation and distress tolerance skills (Linehan, 1993; Linehan et al., 2002). Problems in vulnerable personalities arise most from deficits in the more implicit forms of regulation of emotion and emotional intensity. Although deliberate behavioural and cognitive forms of regulation – more left hemispheric process – are useful for people who feel out of control, over time it is the building of implicit or automatic emotion regulation capacities that is important for highly fragile personality disordered clients. Implicit forms of regulation often cannot be trained or learned as a volitional skill. Directly experiencing aroused affect being soothed by relational or non-verbal means – a more right hemispheric process (Schore, 2003) – is one of the best ways to build the implicit capacity for self-soothing. Being able to soothe the self develops initially by internalization of the soothing functions of the protective other (Stern, 1985). Soothing then most centrally comes interpersonally in the form of empathic attunement and responsiveness to one's affect and through acceptance and validation by another person. The provision of a safe, validating, supportive and empathic environment in therapy helps soothe automatically generated under-regulated distress. Internalizing the soothing of the therapist is one of the best ways of developing implicit soothing. Empathy from the other over time is internalized and becomes empathy for the self, and this leads to a strengthening of the self (Bohart & Greenberg, 1997). Implicit soothing of distressing emotion can be developed. Often it is a relationship with an attuned other that is essential in developing this form of emotion regulation.

The nature of an emotion-regulating relationship

Therapists first create a warm, safe and validating climate by their way of being with the client. One of the central elements of this way of being is the affective climate created by facial, vocal, gestural and postural cues. The emotional climate has to do with the total attitude of the therapist: being perceptive and attuned to the client is communicated by means of therapists' verbal expressions as well as body posture and vocal and facial expression. Clearly, the therapist's overall attitude, not only his/her techniques, influences the client's responses and the way the client's feelings are experienced and expressed in the therapeutic relationship. Martin Buber (1958) wrote that a compassionate human face, when unadorned by pretence, role or assumption of superiority, offers more hope to another than the most sophisticated psychological techniques. In working with emotion, although the therapist may be an expert in the possible therapeutic steps that might be facilitative, it is made clear that the therapist is a compassionate human being who is a facilitator of client experience.

The therapist who conveys genuine interest, acceptance, caring, compassion and joy, and no anger, contempt, disgust and fear, creates the environment for a secure emotional bond. A recent analysis of the classic film *Gloria: The Three Psychotherapies* by Rogers, Perls & Ellis (Magai & Haviland-Jones (2002)) studied the emotional climate created by the therapists. This analysis revealed that each of these therapists, in their behaviour in the film, in their theories, and more generally in their personalities and personal lives, expressed and focused on very different emotions. Rogers showed interest, joy and shame. Perls showed contempt and fear, and Ellis anger and fear. Anyone who has seen these films can see that they created very different therapeutic environments.

The therapists' facial, postural and vocal expressions of emotion clearly set very different emotional climates and are aspects of their ways of being. Clients' right hemispheres respond to therapists' micro affective communication as well as to their explicit words, and all these influence clients' processes of dynamic self-organization. The categorical emotions, such as interest, anger, sadness, fear and shame, expressed by the therapist are important and strongly influence the relational environment. The vitality aspects of the therapist's emotional expression, such as rhythm, cadence and energy, are also important in affective attunement.

Therapists' facial communication of emotion is one of the central aspects of the emotional climate. As Levinas (1998) has argued, seeing the face of the other evokes experience in us. The face is a powerful if ambiguous text, from which much is read. Facial expression thus is a central aspect of relational attunement. People have been shown to read facial affect automatically at incredibly high speed, especially those affects, such as anger and fear, that are crucial to survival. Childhood abuse has been shown to affect the accuracy of interpretation of facial cues and to lead to the over-attribution of hostility to others' facial expressions. Clients see their experience reflected in the therapist's face and manner of response. If clients are having feelings, and they see that their therapist understands and validates what they are feeling, this gives credibility to their feelings and has an impact on clients. Clients thus learn some of who they are and how acceptable they are from the facial expressions of their therapists, which evoke in them certain feelings. Clients thereby are helped to acknowledge that they themselves do experience and that they communicate their feelings. Put more simply, a client feels "Oh, you get it, you get me, and I get that you get me too!"

For example when clients are experiencing grief or sadness, therapists respond to clients' pain in different ways. Therapists' faces register pain, maybe their eyes even fill with a tear, they lean in, listen closely (all of these are right brain to right brain communications; cf. Schore (2003)). Then to bring this experience into the room even further, and help solidify it with the client, therapists might ask clients what it's like to share these feelings with them, how they experience the therapist or what their sense of the therapist is in the moment. The therapist also might ask what the client sees in his or her face, and how this makes the client feel. Therapists may also share with their clients their own sense of feeling close to them as clients share their feelings. This validates the client's ability to be with these feelings, and to let them into the experience. In this way therapists deepen the dyadic experience (Fosha, 2004).

Therapists' pacing is another of the more crucial ways of influencing the type of emotional climate. A slow pace, for example, is essential for working with sad emotions. The tone, energy, rhythm and cadence need to be appropriate to the emotion being worked with. A slow, soothing tone and manner are crucial in accessing core vulnerable emotions. An encouraging, more energetic tone is helpful in supporting the more boundary-setting emotions of anger and disgust.

The therapeutic alliance

Numerous studies have shown that a positive therapeutic alliance is associated with good outcome. The alliance reflects three important aspects of therapeutic work: the bond or the feelings the participants have towards each other, the level of agreement that exists between them about the goals of therapy, and the ways in which they will go about meeting those goals (Bordin, 1979). The development of collaboration has been established as an important, empirically supported aspect of the therapeutic relationship. Thus, as well as creating the emotional climate that secures a warm trusting bond, it is important to foster a collaborative alliance through the course of therapy, one to work with emotions: both avoided emotions and under- or over-regulated emotions.

We have identified a number of ways to assist in the development and maintenance of the therapeutic alliance to work with emotions. The first of these involves conveying that the primary focus of treatment is the client's concerns and underlying painful feelings. The therapist conveys that a central intention of therapy is to help clients to open up and reveal their inner feelings, meanings and fears – to risk being vulnerable with their therapists in the hope that together they can come to a better understanding of the clients' inner and outer worlds and effect meaningful change that will ameliorate clients' sense of despair. Without this exploratory goal being adequately negotiated between the parties the therapy will likely end prematurely or not progress. From the start the client is implicitly being trained, by the therapist's consistent empathic focus on the client's internal experience, to attend to this internal experience.

Therapists in the early phase of therapy convey understanding, acknowledge the client's pain, validate their struggles, and focus on the emotional impact of events in the client's life. By the therapist's attentive listening, presence and caring and by the attitude conveyed by the therapist's face, body, hands and eyes that validates the client's specialness, the client comes to feel seen, valued and respected and is thereby more inclined to trust and be open. By attending to clients' core humanness and expressing unconditional confidence in clients' strengths and capacities for growth, the therapist helps reveal clients' uniqueness and strength. It is by seeing the possibility of growth in another being that this possibility is stimulated.

The deeply held therapeutic attitude of empathy and positive regard or prizing of the client and a focus on strengths and resources help create an emotional bond of trust and respect and help develop the safe environment and a secure base for the exploration that will take place as the therapy progresses. In addition to creating a bond, a rationale is provided, right from the start, that the goal of treatment is for the person to access and become aware of underlying feelings and needs involved in their difficulties. If, however, their emotions are under-regulated, the goal is set of finding better ways of coping with feelings that seem overwhelming. People are told that their feelings provide important information about how they are reacting to situations and that it is important to get clear on what their emotions are telling them. There is a strong emphasis from the start on validating and accepting the pain that people feel. When people come to therapy they do so because they are suffering and feel some form of pain – it feels like something in their life or inside of them is broken. It is with the quickness and sureness with which the therapist can grasp the nature of the client's chronic enduring pain that an emotional bond and collaboration to work on it will be created. Once the chronic enduring pain has been articulated, the person's sense of isolation is broken. There is a sense of relief that it has been spoken, that someone understands and that the person now is not so alone in the struggle. Hope is created and agreeing to work on resolving the chronic enduring pain creates an alliance, spurred by this hope. Resolving the articulated enduring pain becomes the goal of treatment and the basis for the working alliance.

Sharing a rationale

It is necessary, in the early phase of therapy, to provide a rationale as to how working with emotion will help achieve goals. For some clients the importance of focusing on emotion is self-evident as they recognize that their emotions are the source of their distress; for others it is a totally new way of viewing problems. First, a general rationale is given that emotions provide information about one's reactions to situations and about central concerns and that awareness of these, the ability to deal with them and their message is central to healthy functioning. People are informed, in a respectful, conversational way, that lack of awareness, suppression and dysregulation can lead to distress, and the relationship between depressive symptoms such as hopelessness and rumination and avoidance of under-lying emotions is highlighted.

As treatment progresses, more specific aspects of a rationale are pro-vided. When, for example, it is judged necessary to explicitly direct clients to attend to internal experience, it can be explained that their body is telling them something about how they reacted and it is important to receive that message. When a feeling is interrupted in the moment, the client's attention is brought to the interruption and the difficulties produced by the person's fear and avoidance of emotion are discussed. Rationales are offered in as individualized a form as possible, relevant to the shared understandings of the client's unique problems. The general rationale, however, is that feelings are adaptive guides to action, provide information about reactions, need to be acknowledged and reflected on, and, if dysfunctional, need to be transformed. As the treatment proceeds, the therapist also needs to obtain the client's agreement to engage in more evocative processing tasks like chair work and imagery that best fit with the client's state, the focus of treatment and the agreed-upon goals in therapy.

Therapists thus, right from the first session, work to acknowledge the depths of clients' pain and provide validation rather than trying to talk them out of their feelings. This provides hope and begins the process of alliance formation. Therapists strive to create an environment in which their clients can express their pain and vulnerability without fear of being evaluated. The opportunity for clients to share the full intensity of their feelings of despair in therapy and to feel recognized and validated can be experienced as a tremendous relief, as they no longer have to put up a front and cover up how badly they feel.

Developing the bond

Bond creation is the major task in the first three to five sessions. It is an important part of building the initial alliance and continues to be important throughout treatment. The emotional climate set by the therapist in the early sessions strongly influences what will follow. Creating an emotion-friendly environment is important to help clients access and focus on their painful feelings. At the beginning of treatment therapists accept clients' experiences as they are presented. They do not attempt to challenge their clients' views, nor do they suggest alternative responses. Instead, as therapists convey their understanding and concern for their clients they begin to build their understanding of their clients' functioning and ways of processing their experience.

Throughout therapy it is important to help clients feel validated so that they can reveal the depth and extent of their feelings without fear of criticism or of being shamed. Empathy and compassion are antidotes to shame, and a genuine acceptance ensures that the therapist does not shame the client (see Gilbert, Chapter 6, this volume; Greenberg & Paivio, 1997a, 1997b; Wheeler, 1996). Most importantly, EFT therapists do not convey the message that clients' feelings have to change, or that their feelings are invalid or mistaken. The primary objectives, especially initially, thus are to help the client feel safe and understood and to facilitate the client's self-disclosure. If clients are to reveal vulnerable aspects of their subjective selves they need to feel safe knowing that they will be understood. The trust and support that develop between the participants help the client to share painful aspects of their experience that may be difficult to talk about and share with another. The process of revealing self to an understanding and supportive other contributes to the development of a therapeutic bond, which in turn facilitates and enhances the emotion-work that follows. The bond is strengthened as clients begin to become more aware and experience the relief and benefits of exploring their experience.

In addition to providing a safe and responsive emotional climate, attuned to clients' feelings, therapists facilitate different types of processing and also utilize specific interventions that have been found to help clients resolve particular cognitive–affective problems: for example, directing attention inwards when the client is external, promoting dialogues between parts of self to facilitate integration, facilitating a broader view of a significant other with empty chair work, focusing on an unclear felt sense and evocatively unfolding to promote an understanding of problematic reactions (Greenberg, Rice & Elliott, 1993).

Therapeutic presence

In order to establish a positive alliance it is important for therapists first to be present to their clients. A question often asked by trainees is: what does one need to do to help a constricted client access feeling? But this implies that it something one needs to *do to the client*. My answer is that the ability to access emotions depends first and foremost on the type of *relationship* created. It is the therapist's ability to be present that will help the client access emotion. A qualitative analysis of therapists' experience of presence revealed that therapeutic presence involves being receptively open and sensitive to one's own moment-by-moment, changing experience; being fully immersed in the moment; feeling a sense of expansion and spaciousness; and being with and for the client (Geller & Greenberg, 2002). It is these qualities that will help create the climate that will lead clients to attend to their moment-by-moment affective experience. It is important that therapists are able to be receptive and open to their clients' emotional experiences. The kind of "presence" that seems to be therapeutic is the state of mind in which there is an awareness of moment-by-moment emotional reactions as well as thoughts and perceptions occurring in the client, in the therapist and between them in the therapeutic relationship. This means that therapists need to let go of their own specific concerns, the quarrel with their spouse this morning, the falling value of the dollar or an upcoming vacation, and truly show up in the session. To be present for clients is to empty oneself, to clear a space inside so as to be able to listen clearly in the moment to the narratives and problems that clients bring. Therapists need to see their clients' faces and hear their voices. It is through the therapist's undivided and focused attention that clients feel valued and are able to clearly discern their own concerns and difficulties. By giving clients their full attention therapists are able to resonate more fully with their clients' feelings and their experience of events and provide the level of empathic responding that will be most optimal at different points during the session.

Dialogue of this type often leads to heightened moments of meeting or what Buber (1958) referred to as I–Thou contact. In these moments people share living through an emotional experience together. Here an intersubjective experience is lived while it is occurring: it is a shared experience of attending to and experiencing the same thing at the same time and knowing that the other is co-experiencing the same thing. Each person experiences something of the other's experience and knows that this is occurring. This creates a strong bond, a sense of togetherness that breaks any sense of existential isolation and promotes trust and openness. It also is a lived moment of experience that remains indelibly stamped in memory. These moments produce therapeutic change both in the people's sense of self and their way of relating.

We see the Rogerian conditions of empathy, positive regard or accept-ance, and congruence (Rogers, 1957) as part of a single therapeutic way, that of being *fully present* with the other. Empathy has been established as one of the three empirically supported aspects of the relationship, one that correlates highly (e.g., $r = .32$) with outcome (Bohart *et al.*, 2002). Thus, I will briefly discuss below each of the client-centred attitudes. However, while we talk about each as if it were distinct from the others, as we have said, it is more accurate to see them as part of a single therapeutic way of trying to be *fully present* with and understand another (Geller & Greenberg, 2002). Without being fully present it is not possible to communicate affect-regulating empathy. While it is possible to empathize with another without necessarily feeling accepting, this would be cold, clinical empathy. Simi-larly, while it is possible to convey intentionally that you understand another and care for them, if this is without sincerity one risks appearing artificial and not someone to be trusted with the most precious and vul-nerable aspects of the client's psyche. As Rogers highlighted, empathy without positive regard and genuineness can be used in the service of manipulation and thus it is important to distinguish between compassionate and non-compassionate forms of empathy (Gilbert, 1989; Bohart & Greenberg, 1997).

A recent study looked at clients who were being treated for depression in cognitive-behavioral and process experiential psychotherapy. It found that clients' perceptions of the Rogerian relationship conditions were highly correlated with clients' ratings of the therapeutic alliance in both approaches (Watson & Geller, 2005) and were associated with changes in clients' level of self-esteem, and their self-report of interpersonal difficulties, while therapists' acceptance of their clients was predictive of changes in depression.

Empathy

It is clear that unless therapists are empathically attuned to clients' feelings and meanings they will not be able to perceive their clients' goals nor work with them to identify the tasks that might be helpful in their realization. Some of the essential steps in affect regulation are awareness, labelling and differentiation of emotions, followed by modulation and evaluation of the response. Empathic responding by therapists helps clients become aware of their emotional experience, label it in awareness and modulate it so that it is not overwhelming or excessively muted so that its message is lost. Empathic understanding responses and empathic affirmations amplify the client's experience so that it can be apprehended more clearly, while evocative reflections and empathic conjectures facilitate its differentiation, modula-tion and evaluation (Greenberg, Rice & Elliott, 1993). Empathic explora-tion facilitates the client turning inwards to explore and unpack their inner subjective world views and feelings about events (Elliott, Watson, Goldman, & Greenberg, 2003). At the same time as empathy and validation provide support and understanding, they also highlight the subjectivity of clients' perceptions and experience. EFT therapists highlight the constructed nature of events by emphasizing the subjectivity of the clients' perceptions and construals of reality. For example, the use of the word "seems" in phrases like "It seems so hopeless" suggests that a depressogenic construal is a subjective state that is open to reformulation, and may be time-limited.

Acceptance

Humans have evolved to be highly influenced by the minds of those they interact with, and the experience of acceptance in the mind of a valued person can have profound effects on physiological processes (Gilbert, Chapter 6, this volume). Warmth, compassion, openness and respect towards the client and his/her experience, caring for the client as a separate person, with permission to have his or her own feelings and experiences, is a crucial aspect of therapy. The sense that another is accepting and can be trusted, to the extent that one perceives the other as congruent and sincere, is very important to the sense that one is valued and liked by the other. Acceptance by another affirms one's existence and fosters a sense of belonging and participation as it simultaneously allows one to accept one's own experience. Acceptance of experience does not mean that the therapist evaluates it as good; rather it is a type of acknowledgement that this is what the client is experiencing in the moment; the experience is what it is. Acceptance also involves unconditional confidence in the inner core of possibility in the client. Through sensing the therapist's unconditional acceptance of their experience, clients lose their preoccupation with their therapists and their energy becomes available to turn inwards and contact their own experience. Reduction of interpersonal anxiety leads to capacity for tolerance of more intrapersonal anxiety. Clients are able to face and accept more of their experience with the unconditional acceptance of another.

Congruence

The positive real relationship is a very important aspect of therapy and enhances the alliance and client progress (Gelso & Hayes, 1998). Congruence or authenticity can at an initial level of analysis be broken into two separate components (Lietaer, 1993): (1) awareness of one's own internal experience, and (2) transparency, the willingness to communicate to the other person what is going on within. The deeper level intentions include, in addition to valuing and understanding the other, the intentions to facilitate the other's development, to be accepting and non-critical of the other, to confirm the other's experience, to focus on their strengths, and above all to do the other no harm. These intentions, and more, are what determine whether congruence is therapeutic. If one had a genuine desire to harm, being congruent would not be therapeutic.

The case of transparency or the communication component of congruence is much more complicated than the self-awareness component. It seems that being facilitatively transparent involves many interpersonal skills (Greenberg & Geller, 2001). This component involves the ability not only to express what one truly feels but to express it *in a way that* is facilitative. Transparency thus is a global concept for a complex set of interpersonal skills embedded within a set of therapeutic attitudes. These skills depend on three factors: first, on therapist attitudes; second, on certain processes such as facilitativeness, discipline and comprehensiveness; and third, on the interpersonal stance of the therapist.

The set of skills involved in facilitative congruent communication is best explicated by looking at congruent interaction in terms of the interactional stance taken by therapists as described by a circumplex grid of interpersonal interactions (Benjamin, 1996). This grid is based on the two major dimensions of autonomy/control and closeness/affiliation. Consistent with interpersonal theory, this grid outlines a set of complementary responses that fit each other and that interactionally "pull" for each other. Thus attack pulls for defensiveness or withdrawal, and affirmation pulls for disclosure and revelation. The skill of congruent responding involves not reacting in a complementary fashion to a negative interpersonal "pull" of the client, like recoiling when attacked, but rather to act in such a way as to "pull" for a more therapeutically productive response from one's client, such as clear expression. This would be achieved by an empathic understanding response to an attack rather than by recoiling.

What to do when the therapist is not feeling affirming but is feeling angry, critical and rejecting, and can't get past this feeling to something more affiliative? As we have said, an interactional response in order to be faciltatively congruent involves first connecting with the fundamental attitudes or intentions of trying to be helpful, understanding, valuing, respecting and non-intrusive or non-dominant. This will lead to these feelings being expressed as disclosures. If the interpersonal stance of *disclosing* the difficult feeling is adopted, rather than the complementary stances of expressing it by attacking, or rejecting, or seducing, then this congruent response is more likely to be facilitative. It is not the content of the disclosure that is the central issue in being facilitative; rather it is *the interpersonal stance of disclosure in a facilitative way* that is important. What is congruent is the feeling of wanting to disclose in the service of facilitating, and the action of disclosing. The different ways of being facilitatively congruent in dealing with different classes of difficult feeling thus are to some degree specifiable. They all involve adopting a position of disclosing.

Expressing a feeling that could be perceived as negative, in a *stance that is disclosing*, rather than expressing it in the stance that usually accompanies that feeling, will help make it facilitative because disclosing is an affiliative and non-dominant form of interaction whereas being angry is clearly non-affiliative and may be dominant. Disclosure implicitly or explicitly involves willingness to explore, or an interest in exploring, with the other what one is disclosing. For example, when attacked or feeling angry therapists do not attack the other but rather *disclose* that they are feeling angry. They do not use blaming, "you" language. Rather they take responsibility for their feelings and use "I" language that helps disclose what they are feeling. Above all they do not go into one up, escalatory, positions in this communication, but openly disclose feelings of fear, anger or hurt. When the problem is one of the therapist's experiencing non-affiliative, rejecting feelings or loss of interest in their clients' experience, the interactional skill involves being able to disclose this in the context of communicating congruently that the therapist does not wish to feel this. Or therapists disclose these feelings as problems getting in the way and that they are trying to repair so that they will be able to feel more understanding and closer. The key in communicating what could be perceived as negative feelings in a congruently facilitative way is to communicate them in a non-dominant, affiliative disclosing way with appropriate non-verbals. Both timing and type of client need to be considered in deciding whether or not to disclose.

Coaching as an aspect of the relationship

In addition to presence and being with the client, EFT therapists also lead and guide client processing – an activity that we have termed "coaching". Emotion coaching involves a partnership of co-exploration in a growth-promoting process aimed at helping people achieve goals of emotional awareness, regulation, reflection and transformation (Greenberg, 2002). It involves facilitating awareness of emotions, and new ways of processing the emotion, and provides guidance in ways of soothing or regulating the emotion. Awareness in turn involves helping clients verbally label emotions while they are being felt, helping them accept the emotion and talking with clients about what it is like to experience an emotion. In addition, coaching clients involves facilitating the utilization of adaptive emotions, usually anger and sadness, to guide action and transform maladaptive emotions, usually fear, shame or anger. It is important to note that people often cannot simply be taught new strategies conceptually for dealing with difficult emotions, but rather have to be facilitated experientially to engage in the new process and only later explicitly taught what to do. For example, accessing anger or getting to an emotionally experienced need or goal may be very helpful in overcoming a sense of depressive hopelessness or defeat.

However, explicitly teaching people that this is what they should do is not nearly as helpful as interpersonally facilitating this by asking them at the right time in the right way what it is they feel or need.

Some clients, however, are extremely externally focused and helping them contact their feelings can be challenging. A persistent gentle pressure to focus on current internal experience is required by means, first, of empathic responding and emotion enquiries, and later, by process directives that focus the client's attention on internal experience. The client is encouraged to become aware of internal experience and to develop mindfulness (Perls, Hefferline & Goodman, 1951; Kabat-Zinn, 1990; Katzow & Safran, Chapter 5, this volume). Later process directives, such as suggesting the client repeat key phrases that stimulate emotion in the session, can be used to intensify experience and make it more vivid. A balance needs to be struck between allowing clients to tell their story and tracking their reactions, and explicitly directing their attention internally. Questions that are used in this phase and throughout therapy are: What are you aware of as you say this? What is happening in your body? What is it like inside right now?

Using empathic exploratory responses and emotion awareness questions, the therapist therefore works to help clients approach, tolerate, regulate and accept their emotional experience. Acceptance of emotional experience as opposed to its avoidance is the first step in emotion awareness work. Having facilitated the acceptance of emotion rather than its avoidance, the therapist then helps the client in the utilization of emotion. Here clients are helped to make sense of what their emotion is telling them and to identify the goal/need/concern that it is organizing them to attain. Emotion is used both to inform and to move.

Helping people arrive at, accept and regulate their feelings involves helping them do the following (Greenberg, 2002):

- become mindfully aware of their emotions
- accept, tolerate and allow their emotional experience when emotion is over-regulated (this does not necessarily mean they must express everything they feel to other people, but rather that they acknowledge it themselves) or develop emotion regulation skills to allow the person to tolerate emotion that is under-regulated
- label and describe their feelings in words in order to aid them in their problem-solving and lower arousal levels
- identify their primary (core) feelings in a situation.

Conclusion

The relationship is first and foremost an affect-regulating bond that is, in and of itself, facilitative of psychological change conducive to growth and well-being. Second, the therapeutic relationship, characterized by presence, empathy, acceptance and congruence, helps clients to feel safe enough to face dreaded feelings and painful memories. Once an alliance has been consolidated the therapist guides clients towards new ways of processing emotion, coaching them to become aware of, regulate, reflect on and transform their emotions. It is in the blending of these various elements that successful therapy emerges. EFT suggests that people's experiences and meanings are not easily subdivided into cognitive and emotional domains, indeed there is little evidence that the brain processes data in such ways, rather emotions are part and parcel of appraisal processes and therefore need to be open to introspection and opportunities for new learning. Working with emotion processes directly through the relationship is central to EFT rather than approaching them only through a cognitive route. As this volume shows, many therapists are now beginning to recognize the importance of this domain, especially with the therapeutic relationship acting as an emotional regulator, validator and educator.

References

Benjamin, L.S. (1996). Introduction to the special section on structural analysis of social behavior. *Journal of Consulting and Clinical Psychology*, 64, 1203–1212.

Bohart, A.C., Elliott, R., Greenberg, L.S. & Watson, J.C. (2002). Empathy. In J. Norcross (ed.), *Psychotherapy relationships that work* (pp. 89–108). New York: Oxford University Press.

Bohart, A.C. & Greenberg, L.S. (eds) (1997). *Empathy reconsidered: New directions in psychotherapy*. Washington, DC: American Psychological Association.

Bordin, E.S. (1979). The generalizability of the psychoanalytic concept of the working alliance. *Psychotherapy*, 16, 252–260.

Buber, M. (1958). *I and thou*, 2nd edition. New York: Charles Scribner's Sons.

Campos, J., Frankel, K. & Camras, L. (2004). On the nature of emotion regulation. *Child Development*, 75, 377–394.

Cozolino, L. (2002). *The neuroscience of psychotherapy: Building and rebuilding the human brain*. New York: Norton.

Damasio, A. (1999). *The feeling of what happens*. New York: Harcourt-Brace.

Elliott, R., Watson, J.C., Goldman, R.N. & Greenberg, L.S. (2003). *Learning emotion-focused therapy: The process-experiential approach to change*. Washington, DC: American Psychological Association.

Fosha, D. (2000). *The transforming power of affect: A model of accelerated change*. New York: Basic Books.

Fosha, D. (2004). "Nothing that feels bad is ever the last step:" The role of positive emotions in experiential work with difficult emotional experiences. Special issue on Emotion, L. Greenberg (ed.), *Clinical Psychology and Psychotherapy*, 11, 30–43.

Geller, S. & Greenberg, L. (2002). Therapeutic presence: Therapists experience of presence in the psychotherapy encounter in psychotherapy. *Person Centered & Experiential Psychotherapies*, 1, 71–86.

Gelso, C. & Hayes, J. (1998). *The psychotherapy relationship: Theory, research and practice.* New York: Wiley

Gilbert, P. (1989). *Human nature and suffering.* Hove, UK: Lawrence Erlbaum Associates.

Greenberg, L. & Geller, S. (2001). Congruence and therapeutic presence. In G. Wyatt & P. Saunders (eds), *Rogers' therapeutic conditions: Evolution, theory and practice.* Vol. 1: *Congruence*, pp. 131–149. Ross-on Wye, UK: PCCS Books.

Greenberg, L. & Paivio, S. (1997a). Varieties of shame experience in psychotherapy. *Gestalt Review*, 1(3), 205–220.

Greenberg, L. & Paivio, S. (1997b). Integrating "being" and "doing" in working with shame. *Gestalt Review*, 1(3), 271–274.

Greenberg, L. & Watson, J. (2006). *Emotion-focused therapy of depression.* Washington, DC: APA Press.

Greenberg, L.S. (2002). *Emotion-focused therapy: Coaching clients to work through their feelings.* Washington, DC: American Psychological Association.

Greenberg, L.S., Rice, L.N. & Elliot, R. (1993). *Facilitating emotional change: The moment by moment process.* New York: Guilford Press.

Gross, J.J. (1999). Emotion and emotion regulation. In L.A. Pervin & O.P. John (eds), *Handbook of personality theory and research* (pp. 525–552). New York: Guilford Press.

Gross, J.J. (2002). Emotion regulation: Affective, cognitive, and social consequences. *Psychophysiology*, 39, 281–291.

Kabat-Zinn, J. (1990). *Full catastrophe living.* New York: Delta.

Lane, R. & Nadel, L. (2000). *Cognitive neuroscience of emotion.* New York: Oxford University Press.

Le Doux, J. (1996). *The emotional brain: The mysterious underpinnings of emotional life.* New York: Simon & Schuster.

Levinas, E. (1998). *Otherwise than being; or Beyond essence.* Pittsburgh: Duquesne University Press.

Lietaer, G. (1993). Authenticity, congruence and transparency. In D. Brazier (ed.), *Beyond Carl Rogers: Towards a psychotherapy for the 21st century* (pp. 17–46). London: Constable.

Linehan, M.M. (1993). *Cognitive-behavioral treatment of borderline personality disorder.* New York: Guilford Press.

Linehan, M.M., Dimeff, L.A., Reynolds, S.K., Comtois, K.A., Shaw Welch, S., Heagerty, P. & Kivlahan, D.R. (2002). Dialectical behavior therapy versus comprehensive validation plus 12 steps for the treatment of opioid dependent women meeting criteria for borderline personality disorder. *Drug and Alcohol Dependence*, 67, 13–26.

Magai, C. & Haviland-Jones, J. (2002). *The hidden genius of emotion.* Cambridge: Cambridge University Press.

Perls, F., Hefferline, R.F. & Goodman, P. (1951). *Gestalt therapy.* New York: Dell.

Rogers, C.R. (1957). The necessary and sufficient conditions of therapeutic personality change. *Journal of Consulting Psychology*, 21, 95–103.

Schore, A.N. (2003). *Affect dysregulation and disorders of the self.* New York: Norton.

Stern, D. (1985). *The interpersonal world of the infant.* New York: Basic Books.

Watson, J.C. & Geller, S.M. (2005). The relation among the relationship conditions, working alliance, and outcome in both process-experiencial and cognitive-behavioral psychotherapy. *Psychotherapy Research*, Special Issue, *The Therapeutic Relationship*, 15(1–2), 25–33.

Wheeler, G. (1996). Self and shame. In R. Lee & G. Wheeler (eds), *The voice of shame: Silence and connection in psychotherapy*. San Francisco: Jossey Bass.

Chapter 4

The therapeutic relationship

Implications from social cognition and transference

Regina Miranda and Susan M. Andersen

Introduction

Numerous studies have demonstrated that the therapeutic alliance that develops early in treatment predicts psychotherapeutic outcome (see Martin, Garske, & Davis, 2000). There remains limited research, however, on what factors influence the therapeutic alliance. Although we have not focused on therapeutic processes *per se* in our own research, we have focused on psychological processes in everyday interpersonal relations thought central to psychotherapy. In some form or another, classical theories have long suggested that the mental representations an individual holds about significant others are often influential in psychotherapy and that this may either facilitate or impede progress. Considering the process of transference may be helpful to understanding the formation of a therapeutic alliance.

In our work, we directly examine the ways in which a new person can be experienced as friend, not foe, or vice versa, in a matter of moments. Quite automatically, based on the social-cognitive process, this occurs in the process of transference. We examine this process in an experimental paradigm using the techniques of social cognition research. Even very early work on psychotherapy suggested that the therapeutic alliance might be important in psychotherapy outcome. Clients who are satisfied with treatment tend to like their therapist more and believe he or she is more friendly and involved, and by contrast, therapists with few (vs. many) premature terminations in their case histories are deemed more adept in understanding the client's own issues, more accepting, secure and affectionate, and easy to get along with (see Beutler, Crago, & Arizmendi, 1986). Early researchers argued, as well, that a client's "subjective feeling of change" may well be the best predictor of therapy outcome, associated as it appears to be with the client's own involvement or engagement (Garfield, 1986). It is to this issue of establishing an effective working relationship, a therapeutic alliance, and what facilitates or disrupts this that we now turn our attention.

Our model of transference (and the evidence we have collected) is rooted in social cognition. The focus is on mental representations of significant others and on the relationship one has with those others. "Significant others" are family members, romantic partners, friends, or others whom individuals consider important and who have had an impact on their lives. This may include people whom they like or love (i.e., whom they regard positively), along with those whom they regard negatively, whether currently or no longer in their lives. We argue that transference occurs in everyday life, when such representations of significant others are triggered, and that it is thus a process by which people re-experience past relationships in their everyday social relationships and interactions. The research is conducted in laboratory settings and has amassed considerable evidence in support of this view, thus offering the first experimental demonstration of transference (Andersen & Cole, 1990; Andersen & Baum, 1994; Andersen, Glassman, Chen, & Cole, 1995). We believe this evidence has implications for the therapeutic relationship in a variety of therapeutic modalities – including cognitive-behavioral and psychodynamic psychotherapy.

The social-cognitive model of transference

Historical backdrop

Originally conceived by Freud (1912/1958), transference is regarded as an important part of the therapeutic relationship; indeed, perhaps the bedrock of psychoanalytic treatment (Greenberg & Mitchell, 1983). There could hardly be a more central psychological phenomenon in Freudian treatment. Transference was conceptualized by Freud as a process by which an individual displaced childhood fantasies and psychosexual conflicts onto an analyst (Freud, 1912/1958), and the process of psychoanalysis involved interpreting transference to bring to light the unconscious conflicts. Freud's model of transference was based on drive-structure assumptions (Greenberg & Mitchell, 1983) with id, ego, and superego, and thus made no use of other kinds of mental structures, let alone mental "representations," though he did mention the "imago" as a repository of parental material (he did not integrate it closely into his model, which was about the tripartite drive) (Freud, 1912/1958). Harry Stack Sullivan, by contrast, argued that "personifications" of the self and other (similar to mental representations) and "dynamisms" (i.e., the dynamics linking the self and other) play out in relationships with other people. He viewed transference as *parataxic distortion*, which involves relational patterns re-experienced with new people. Unlike Freud, Sullivan viewed transference, i.e., parataxic distortion, as rooted not in psychosexual conflicts, but rather in basic needs for satisfaction and security. Satisfaction needs are best met when developing one's own talents and expressing one's emotions while remaining connected with (or "integrated" with) others, and experiencing tenderness with them (Sullivan, 1953). This departure from the Freudian assumptions exemplifies the distinction between psychodynamic, drive reduction and relational theorists (see Greenberg & Mitchell, 1983). Our own conceptualization more closely resembles that of Sullivan (1953).

Another body of work relevant to our conceptualization of the relational self is the attachment literature, which grew out of behavioral, evolutionary, and psychodynamic theory, and focuses on the importance of internal working models of significant others and how they may be shaped through early relationships with primary caregivers (Ainsworth *et al.*, 1978; Bowlby, 1969). Thus, there is interest in how attachment styles may influence current relationships (see Simpson & Rholes, 1998, for a review; see Liotti, Chapter 7, this volume). Our research is compatible (see Andersen & Berk, 1998; Andersen, Reznik, & Chen, 1997) but social cognitive in nature. Most work on the clinical notion of transference has been restricted to the client–therapist relationship. Transference has been regarded as interfering with, but perhaps also being essential to, the therapeutic relationship. The aim is to make it conscious and resolve it in order to move the therapy forward (see Westen, 1988).

Our social-cognitive model

Our social-cognitive model of transference presupposes that mental representations of significant others exist in memory, and such representations can readily be triggered by relevant cues in any context, which then leads people to view new others through the lens of pre-existing significant others (Andersen & Cole, 1990; Andersen & Baum, 1994; Andersen & Glassman, 1996). We further assume that the self and significant others are linked in memory as an inherent consequence of (or representation of) their significance (Andersen *et al.*, 1997). These linkages in memory obviously imply concurrent activation, such that when one is activated, the other will be activated too (see also Baldwin, 1992). Our model of the relational self lays out the ways in which this is particularly relevant to the self.

Given the link between representations of the self and significant others, individuals develop unique representations of themselves as they are with each of their significant others. Thus, when relevant contextual cues are encountered – particularly cues coming from a new person – that are similar (even minimally) to the representation, this will activate the representation. This representation may then be applied in interpersonal perception in the process we have termed transference. Moreover, triggering a significant-other representation in this way can also shift one's view of the self in the direction of the self-when-with-the-significant-other, while at the same time activating a host of affects, expectancies, motivations, and behaviors typically experienced in relation to the significant other. This is, in short, what this research has demonstrated in the process of transference. Hence, the emotional and motivational significance of the significant other is what enables the experience of transference, which is not dispassionate.

Our model is consistent with other social-cognitive models of the relational self and their associated empirical paradigms. For example, Baldwin's (1992) model of *relational schemas* suggests that people represent relationships in memory via *interpersonal scripts*, or stereotyped relationship patterns, and a self-schema that defines the self within that interaction. Recent research on this model suggests that these relationship schemas can be activated and can impact the way people evaluate themselves even by cues that are not initially associated with the representation but that come to be associated through conditioning (see Baldwin, Granzberg, & Pritchard, 2003). Hence, there can be rapid, automatic responses to people that can begin before a person is even aware of them. Whereas Baldwin's model emphasizes stereotyped and generic representations of relationships, however, our model emphasizes the unique and idiosyncratic aspects of the relationship and of the self within that relationship (see Andersen & Chen, 2002).

Why our model suggests that transference is not just cognitive

We suggest, then, that transference is not only cognitive, but also deeply intertwined with affect and motivation. Elsewhere we have argued that people may have a fundamental need for human connection (Andersen & Chen, 2002) – that is, for attachment, belonging, and relatedness (see also Baumeister & Leary, 1995). This assumption is drawn not only from classical theories (e.g., Horney, 1939; Sullivan, 1953), but also from more contemporary theory (e.g., Bowlby, 1969; Deci, 1995; Safran, 1990). It is relevant to attachment research (e.g., Hazan & Shaver, 1994; Thompson, 1998) and to models of relational schemas (e.g., Baldwin, 1992), both of which share assumptions with our model.

Paradigm and evidence for the transference process

The paradigm: Assessing transference

Our paradigm for triggering transference involves a laboratory setting and a two-session research design with college-student participants (for recent reviews, see Andersen & Berenson, 2001; Andersen & Chen, 2002; Andersen & Miranda, 2006; Andersen, Reznik, & Glassman, 2005; Andersen & Saribay, 2005). In an initial session, participants are asked to describe positive and negative characteristics of two significant others using a series of freely generated phrases (as sentence-completions). The second session of the study is conducted at least two weeks later. In this session, participants arrive at a different lab for an allegedly separate study and are led to expect that they will interact with someone whom they have never met for a "getting-acquainted" conversation. They are told that an interviewer is next door with this person collecting some information about this other participant, and the experimenter goes next door to retrieve it. They are then asked to read a series of descriptions about the new person – presumably provided by the "interviewer" – and are asked to imagine interacting with the person.

Individuals are randomly assigned either to a transference condition or to a yoked control condition. In the transference condition, the descriptions of the new person that participants read consist of some of the statements that these participants provided in the first session to describe their own significant other. In the yoked control condition, each participant is yoked with one participant (at random) from the transference condition, and is then exposed to features of that person's significant other. We perfectly control content across the two main conditions.

In addition, the descriptions provided about the new person contain both positive and negative features, regardless of how loved or disliked the significant other is, so that this overall valence of the description is not identical to the valence of the features. Filler items the participant had previously classified as irrelevant to their significant other are also included in the description of the new person to make the crucial statements less obvious. As noted, because each participant in the transference condition is paired with another person (a yoked control participant) who views exactly the same descriptions about the new person, resemblance (or not) to the participant's own significant other is what accounts for any effects, not differences in stimulus content.

After participants learn about the new person, they are asked to rate such things as the degree to which they remember learning particular things about the new person (i.e., their recognition memory) and how they feel about (i.e., evaluate) the new person. They are also asked to indicate whether they are motivated to approach or avoid the new person and their expectations of being accepted or rejected by the person, as well as their various emotional responses. Beyond this, they may also offer self-assessments, by providing self-descriptive sentences about themselves at the moment – i.e., their working self-concept.

Our main index of whether or not transference occurs involves assessing the degree to which individuals "go beyond the information given" (Bruner, 1957), that is, assign characteristics of their significant other to the new person that were not actually presented when learning about the person. Differences between the significant-other-resemblance condition and the control condition show greater inferences and memory of this kind – colored by the significant-other representation when there is such resemblance. A difference in how participants evaluate the new person also arises, as does an overall difference in positive affect, in expectancies for acceptance vs. rejection, in motivation to approach or avoid the new person, and in behaviors elicited from this new person. Changes in how an individual views herself or himself arise as well, and are associated with a wide variety of emotional consequences, depending on the nature of the significant-other relationship.

The evidence demonstrating transference

Inferences and memory: Going beyond the information given

The earliest research using this paradigm suggests that significant-other representations can be activated and applied to a new person, as revealed in biases in inferences and memory. For example, when participants are in a transference condition of an experiment (in which a new person is portrayed in a way that resembles their own significant other), they later show more biased memory in what they learned about this new person – relative to a control group exposed to no such resemblance. That is, when indicating how confident they are that certain phrases were presented to describe the new person, they report higher levels of confidence in having seen the features derived from their significant other but not actually presented about the new person. This is the case both when they learn about fictional characters (Andersen & Cole, 1990; Andersen, Glassman, Chen & Cole, 1995; Chen, Andersen, & Hinkley, 1999; Glassman & Andersen, 1999b) and when they learn about a new person with whom they expect to interact (e.g., Andersen & Baum, 1994; Andersen, Reznik, & Manzella, 1996; Baum & Andersen, 1999; Berenson & Andersen, in press; Berk & Andersen, 2000; Hinkley & Andersen, 1996; Reznik & Andersen, in revision). In the latter case, the effect occurs regardless of whether the representation is positive or negative. In the former, it was possible to rule out that just any cues that had been self-generated earlier by the participants themselves would produce the effect, or that just any activated mental representation would lead to the same level of the effect. While other representations (e.g., stereotypes and other social categories) function similarly, the effect is more pronounced for significant-other representations, which are chronically accessible (i.e., have a low-level tendency to be used willy-nilly) and are also readily triggered by cues in a new person.

Indeed, it has also been shown that the effect will clearly arise even when stimulus cues are presented entirely outside of conscious awareness. That is, the effect has been shown to occur non-consciously and automatically. For example, in one study, features of an individual's own or of another person's significant other were presented subliminally (in parafoveal vision for less than 90 ms and then pattern masked). Even under these conditions, participants who where presented with the relevant contextual cues subliminally were more likely to infer that a new person (with whom participants were presumably playing a computer game) had features of their significant other that were never presented, not even subliminally (Glassman & Andersen, 1999a). Clearly, then, the transference process can occur without awareness.

Using another measure altogether, a recent study (Miranda, Andersen, & Edwards, in preparation) assessed *activation* of the significant-other representation using a response latency index. Participants who learned about a new person in a transference paradigm showed faster reaction times to decide whether or not a given moderately positive adjective was a word – if it was highly descriptive of their significant other (vs. less so), and this did not occur in the non-transference control condition (see Andersen & Miranda, 2006).

Thus, the evidence demonstrates transference as a cognitive process, and is evoked by immediate cues in a situation, i.e., in another person (e.g., another person's behavior, style or qualities), which become all the more probable because these representations also have a chronic tendency to be used. Moreover, the evidence shows that transference occurs automatically in that it is activated without intention or effort and also without consciousness (on automaticity, see Bargh, 1997), leading relevant inferences to be made about the new person (see Andersen, Reznik, & Glassman, 2005).

Incorrect assumptions a client makes about a therapist may thus derive from this process. For example, an individual may make a snap judgment about whether or not he likes, versus dislikes, or feels safe, versus threatened, in a new therapeutic encounter, depending on cues that trigger a particular significant-other representation. At the same time, this is unlikely to occur in a vacuum. The therapist's own qualities (e.g., appearance, style of interaction, tone of voice, or other cue associated with the significant other) may trigger the process by activating the representation. Moreover, the therapist's own inferences and mis-memories of a client may derive from the therapist's own representations, again provoked in part by momentary shifts in what the person is saying and doing, and how (in addition to more stable characteristics). This process is automatic and largely unconscious, and we have no reason to believe it is different when it occurs in a therapist – commonly called counter-transference. This is de-pathologizing and may be illuminating for therapists.

More broadly, transference may be ubiquitous in people's everyday interpersonal encounters and important relationships, in part as a function of contextual and expressive shifts in the other's behavior in new situations. The implication is that it is just as possible to engage with a client about interpersonal encounters in his or her regular life and the ways in which prior relationships may be playing out in these present encounters – quite independently of what is going on in the therapeutic relationship. While some therapists find such work tangential to the immediate experience of the therapeutic relationship, it has the advantage of being "about" the client's real life – his or her ongoing, regular experience outside of the therapeutic hour that brought him or her to treatment in the first place. Nevertheless, whether a patient feels safe in therapy may have implications for the type of information he or she may be willing to explore in treatment, particularly if the individual has a history of relationships in which he or she was made to feel unsafe (e.g., trauma history).

Automatic evaluation and affect

Our assumption has been that the overall evaluation associated with a significant other will come to be associated with a new person who is seen through this lens. That is, activation of a significant-other representation should lead to positive evaluation of a new person if the significant other is positive and to negative evaluation if the significant other is negative (in accord with the process of schema-triggered affect; Fiske & Pavelchak, 1987). In fact, the evidence shows precisely this. When a new person resembles a positive (vs. a negative) significant other, people come to like them considerably more, and this does not occur in a control condition (Andersen & Baum, 1994; Andersen et al., 1996; Baum & Andersen, 1999; Berk & Andersen, 2000).

Because the processes presumed to underlie this effect (activation, application of social knowledge) occur automatically (Bargh, 1997) and because evidence shows that *automatic evaluation* arises in response to *any* encountered stimuli (Duckworth, Bargh, Garcia, & Chaiken, 2002), we assume that our effects reflect automatic evaluations as well. This is further substantiated by research examining participants' immediate facial expressions. Depending on whether they are learning about someone who resembles a positive versus negative significant other, the facial affect shown in immediate facial expression reflects the evaluation of the significant other, and no such effect occurs in the control condition. Individuals who read about a new person and are recorded by a hidden camera are assessed by independent raters as showing more positive facial affect when a new person resembles a positive versus a negative significant other (Andersen et al., 1996).

At the very least, these data provide further evidence that transference occurs and occurs automatically, while also showing its profound emotional quality. Thus, an initial encounter may set the tone of a relationship depending on which significant-other representation is activated. We also assume that relevant momentary responses may also be evoked midway in a relationship, depending on whether or not a particular significant-other representation is activated at that moment. An individual's encounter with a clinician, whether an initial interview or a later session, will thus quite likely result in automatic evaluation of the therapist, depending on features the therapist exemplifies that trigger a significant-other representation. Likewise, the therapist may well have an automatic positive or negative evaluation of the client based on cues from that person that trigger his or her own significant-other representations. We thus assume that it can facilitate or interfere with a positive working alliance.

If and when a problematic transference occurs in the therapeutic relationship, it may interfere with effectively working with outside-of-treatment material. Of course, such a negative transference in therapy can also become pronounced enough to destroy the therapeutic relationship, leading the client to quit, and it is thus important to watch for this impediment to nip it in the bud, though obviously not all negative responses from a client are transference. In some instances, anyone would respond that way to the actions or expressions of the therapist.

Expectations for acceptance and rejection

We also assume that the love, acceptance, dislike, or rejection experienced with a significant other translates in transference into expectancies about how the new person will respond, i.e., with acceptance or rejection. Indeed, when individuals encounter someone who resembles their own positive (vs. negative) significant other, they report expecting this new person to be accepting of them and not rejecting, and this differential expectation does not occur in the control condition (Andersen et al., 1996; Berk & Andersen, 2000). Other research has also suggested that expectancies for rejection can have profound consequences in their own right (Downey & Feldman, 1996) and may be stored in memory as part of relationships with significant others or, more broadly, relational schemas (Baldwin & Sinclair, 1996). Research on relational schemas has also shown unconscious activation of significant-other representations using a priming methodology, and it does so in part through effects on self-evaluation (e.g., Baldwin, Carrell, & Lopez, 1990).

The evidence again demonstrates transference while also showing that it includes assumptions about the significant other's presumed feelings. That is, what is stored in memory contains not only how one feels about the significant other, but how one believes one is evaluated by that other.

In therapy, this might be reflected in the client feeling liked or well-regarded by the clinician, or disliked/rejected, or alternatively as the client disliking and rejecting the therapist. Likewise, if the therapist views the client as especially liking or adoring him or her, or as being rejecting of him or her, this may also be a reflection of the therapist's own transference of a prior relationship(s) that is now experienced with the client. Indeed, such expectancies as they arise in the client's everyday life may have this same source, and the corrosive effect of rejection expectancies on interpersonal relations in everyday life is well understood.

Motivation to approach or avoid a new person

Our model of the relational self assumes that people have a basic need to be close to or connected with others and, as such, that this motive should be triggered when a significant-other representation is activated, because motives and goals are associated with significant-other representations in memory (Andersen *et al.*, 1996) and are stored in memory as cognitive representations (Bargh, 1990; Bargh & Barndollar, 1996). All things being equal, people are motivated to approach those they like or love and to avoid those they dislike, and are more disclosing with the former than with the latter. Our evidence has shown that when a new person resembles a positive versus a negative significant other, individuals report greater motivation to approach and to be close to this new person (versus wanting to avoid and be emotionally distant from him or her; Andersen *et al.*, 1996; Berk & Andersen, 2000). This does not occur in a control condition. Other research has also shown that activating a significant-other representation activates goals automatically (Fitzsimons & Bargh, 2003; Shah, 2003).

In psychotherapy this may involve the degree to which a client wants to come to therapy sessions and to disclose about deeply personal matters. Motives to reveal hopes, dreads, and fears can be evoked in a client based on a positive transference, which can facilitate therapeutic work, even if it is, in a sense, illusory. This evidence also suggests that a negative transference can (if unaddressed or resolved) be an impediment, perhaps even bringing authentic disclosure to an abrupt halt. In a therapist, the desire to be "closer" to the client, to enable the client to "know" the therapist better, to fully grasp the therapist's own feelings and perceptions, may arise in the same way. The process may occur as well in the desire to be distant and withholding with a client.

Triggering behavioral patterns consistent with significant-other relationships

We have also examined affectively-laden processes in overt behavior in an interpersonal encounter with a stranger. We focused on the interactional behavior with the new person in transference – by focusing on the new person – to see if the effects of transference could be observed in a self-fulfilling prophecy (also known as "behavioral confirmation;" Snyder, Tanke, & Berscheid, 1977). Participants learned about a new person, as usual, who did or did not resemble a positive or negative significant other and then engaged in a brief telephone interaction with a naïve participant who had been randomly assigned to be paired with this perceiver (Berk & Andersen, 2000). The results showed that independent judges rated the conversational behavior elicited from the new individual as more positive in the context of a positive vs. a negative transference (i.e., when a positive vs.

negative significant-other representation had been triggered in the perceiver). Thus, participants actually elicited the same behavior from the
naïve individual – expressed in this new person's behavior – as was typical
of the significant other.

The evidence showing the relational self in transference

Views of the self in transference: Shifts in working self-concept and self-evaluation

Given our proposition that one's views of the self are constructed in the
midst of important relationships, and that self-representations are thus
"entangled" with significant-other representations (Andersen & Chen,
2002), it stands to reason that triggering a particular significant-other representation should lead to changes in how a person views the self – as the
self-when-with-the-significant-other. One becomes a particular version of
oneself, depending on the significant-other relationship that is active. This is
what our research has shown. In one study (Hinkley & Andersen, 1996),
participants not only described a positive and negative significant other in
advance of the experiment but also characterized how they viewed themselves when with each significant other. In a later session, when they learned
about a new person resembling either their positive or negative significant
other, they were also asked to list phrases characterizing their working self-
concept – i.e., how they viewed themselves at that moment.

As expected, the working self-concept of individuals in the transference
condition shifted to reflect the self-when-with-the-significant-other, even
after adjusting for baseline self-concept descriptions. Their self-concept
features listed after learning about the new person showed a greater degree
of overlap with how they described themselves as they were when with that
significant other (compared to the non-transference condition) – for both
positive and negative significant others. In addition, participants classified
the newly overlapping features (with the self-when-with-the-significant-
other) more positively in the positive transference condition than in the
negative transference condition, and this did not occur in the control
condition. Both effects have also been found when only positive significant-
other representations are activated – and these involve an individual with
whom one experiences a desired self or a dreaded sense of self (Reznik &
Andersen, 2004). Thus, significant others with whom people have positive
self-views appear to lead people to view themselves in positive ways in
transference, while significant others with whom people hold more negative
views of themselves lead to corresponding negative shifts in the self-concept
in transference. Such shifts in self-views in transference may have implications for the experience of a variety of self-conscious emotions, such as
shame (see Gilbert, 2003), in new interpersonal encounters. For example, if

one experiences a negative, "shame-self" with one's father, then another man who may resemble one's father could reactivate that shame-self representation or experience. Not only may one tend to think/feel that a new person will look down on the self but also one's own experience of the self-when-with-the-significant-other is affected. The experience of self and of other are woven together. It may be valuable in therapy to know it is entirely "normal" for a client's sense of self to shift as a function of which significant-other representation is activated. Self-evaluation and one's sense of worth may vary in tow. That this happens for the therapist, as well as in the context of daily life, can also be illuminating.

Self-regulation in transference

SELF-PROTECTIVE SELF-REGULATION

We have found that in addition to shifting their views of themselves in transference, individuals also shift their self-regulatory responses. When significant-other representations are triggered, this leads people to *regulate* their views both of themselves and of loved ones accordingly. Despite negative shifts in the self-concept involving the self-when-with-the-significant-other, in a negative transference, people also show an overall shift in their self-views that is far more positive when with their negative significant other. Individuals thus appear to show compensatory self-inflation or self-enhancement (see Greenberg & Pyszczynski, 1985), a kind of defense, in a negative transference. This is *self-protective self-regulation* and does not occur in a positive transference, or in the control condition (Hinkley & Andersen, 1996).

OTHER-PROTECTIVE SELF-REGULATION

In addition, people show regulatory responses indicative of a desire to protect their views of their significant others in transference. When reading positive and negative descriptions of a new person who resembles a positively-toned significant other, individuals demonstrate especially positive facial affect when exposed to negative features of a positive significant other as descriptions of a new person. The effect does not occur in negative transference, nor in the control condition. Thus, individuals appear to exhibit what we have termed *other-protective self-regulation* in positive transference, and they may use regulatory strategies to maintain a positive view of an important other who is liked or loved (Andersen *et al.*, 1996). Such self- and other-protective regulatory responses may be adaptive in enabling people to maintain an overall positive view of themselves despite a threat to self-esteem and to maintain positive views of important others, and relationships of trust. Clearly, if a client expresses "puffed up" views of the self in treatment, this may be due to an insult to the self through the self-when-with-the-significant-other activated in the transference. This may also make the client less willing to address (or face) directly the experienced insult. Protecting the self from experienced insult may likewise render a therapist less fully self-reflective or self-honest. The process may be off-putting to others, in everyday life as well as in therapy, although this is speculative. It may also be highly adaptive self-regulation (reflected in affect), and this is known to sustain relationships and yet may bind one to problematic relationships as well.

The self and affect: Disruptions in positive affect in positive transference

We now turn to the ways some positive experiences may break down even in a "positive transference" and may thus become problematic – potentially leading to disruptions in positive mood states and even to the induction or exacerbation of negative moods. We have found three conditions under which pleasant mood is disrupted in a positive transference: when a new person violates the interpersonal role associated with the significant other (Baum & Andersen, 1999); when there is a chronically unsatisfied goal associated with the significant other (Berk & Andersen, 2004); and when the significant-other representation triggered is that of a person around whom one tends to become a dreaded version of the self (Reznik & Andersen, 2004).

CONTEXTUAL ROLE VIOLATION

Given that knowledge about significant others is stored in memory, information about the relational role the other person usually takes in relation to the self should also be stored with the significant-other representation. There is evidence that the violation of roles is disruptive to interpersonal relationships (e.g., Sheldon & Elliot, 2000). We thus expected (and found) that when a representation of an important other who held a particular type of role was activated in the context of an anticipated interaction with a new person, individuals would experience mood disruptions when they learned that the new person somehow violated this interpersonal role. In our research, we found that when transference involved a representation of a positive authority figure, the positive mood that participants would usually experience in a positive transference was disrupted if the participant also learned that the new person whom they expected to meet was a novice (i.e., thus unable to fulfill the interpersonal role associated with the significant-other representation; Baum & Andersen, 1999).

CHRONICALLY UNSATISFIED GOALS

Our work has also demonstrated that positive mood is disrupted and hostility increased when one has experienced chronically unsatisfied (vs.

satisfied) goals for acceptance and affection with a positive significant other (Berk & Andersen, 2004), and this significant-other representation is triggered in relation to a new person. The activation of this representation is even associated with overt behaviors designed to solicit acceptance from the new person under the circumstance that the significant other is a family member.

THE DREADED SELF

Disrupted positive mood also occurs in relation to a positive significant-other representation with whom one tends to experience a dreaded sense of self. When individuals expect to meet a new person who resembles such a significant other (i.e., one associated with experiencing a dreaded self), they also come to experience a decrease in positive mood and an increase in negative mood relative to when they expect to meet a new person who resembles a positive significant other with whom one tends to experience a desired sense of self, which results in positive affect (Reznik & Andersen, 2004).

PHYSICAL AND PSYCHOLOGICAL ABUSE

The experience of physical, sexual, or psychological abuse at the hands of loved caregivers should sensibly disrupt positive feelings in a positive transference, and perhaps lead to distinctive affective experiences. Empirical evidence suggests that a history of childhood maltreatment (Shields, Ryan, & Cicchetti, 2001) and sexual abuse is associated with greater interpersonal problems in both childhood (Shields et al., 2001) and adulthood (Classen, Field, Koopman, Nevill-Manning, & Spiegel, 2001), and also with holding more maladaptive parental representations (Cloitre, Cohen, & Scarvalone, 2002; Shields et al., 2001). Research examining the mood states evoked by triggering representations of abusive family members in transference among females with a history of such physical and psychological abuse by this attachment object is revealing (Berenson & Andersen, in press). It suggests that when women with an abuse history expect to meet someone who resembles the relevant parent and are also told that this new person is becoming increasingly tense and irritable, they report disliking the person, mistrusting him or her, and expecting to be rejected by him or her (relative to non-abused participants). They also reported being more indifferent toward this new person, suggesting disengagement.

Indeed, in terms of mood, abused individuals actually report decreases in dysphoric mood in transference after being told that this person is becoming irritable, while the latter cue spiked their dysphoric mood in the control condition, and no such differences arise among non-abused participants (Berenson & Andersen, in press). Thus, despite *explicit* dislike and mistrust of the new person, women with an abuse history showed damp-ened negative mood in transference based on the target-irritability cue, which may be a kind of "emotional numbing." In fact, the affective responses among these individuals are even more complex in that they display the same immediate positive facial affect in transference as do non-abused participants (compared to the control condition) when first reading descriptions of a new person resembling their parent and when encountering the irritability cue, revealing very mixed emotional reactions in *implicit* vs. *explicit* affect. In short, a client's varying mood states may result from far more nuanced processes than immediately meet the eye.

Evoking specific emotions in transference based on the relational self

We now turn to considering the conditions under which discrete negative affects might be triggered in transference.

SELF-DISCREPANCIES

Early relational models of psychopathology and psychotherapy emphasized the importance of the ideal self as contrasted with what is true of the self (Horney, 1939) or measured self-reported ideal and actual selves (see Rogers, 1951). These constructs have been reconceptualized in social cognition within a theoretical framework that makes predictions about discrete emotional states. That is, self-discrepancy theory (Higgins, 1987) suggests that a discrepancy between a standard held in memory and one's actual self creates emotional vulnerability. Such a discrepancy can be held from one's own viewpoint or from that of a significant other. For example, discrepancies between one's ideals (hopes and aspirations) and one's actual self lead to dysphoric affect while discrepancies between the actual self and one's duties and obligations ("oughts") result in anxiety. In our exami-nation of self-discrepancies in transference (Reznik & Andersen, in press), we found that people who have an ideal self-discrepancy from a parent's standpoint show increases in dysphoric mood when the parental repre-sentation is triggered. Similarly, when a representation of a parent from whose viewpoint one has an "ought" self-discrepancy is triggered, more agitation-related affect arises, along with decreased relaxation and increased resentful, hostile mood (Reznik & Andersen, in revision).

ATTACHMENT STYLES

Attachment theory assumes that early interactions with caregivers shape the mental models of the self and other that a person develops (Ainsworth *et al.*, 1978; Bowlby, 1969). The assumptions of our theory are thus quite compatible with attachment theory (see Andersen & Berk, 1998; Andersen *et al.*, 1997). In fact, we have evidence that individuals experience specific emotional reactions in transference that involve the particular attachment style they have with their significant other. Recent evidence suggests that people can differ in the attachment styles they hold with different people (Pierce & Lydon, 2001), and that attachment styles can be triggered by contextual cues (Mikulincer, Gillath, & Shaver, 2002). Research on transference has examined differences in emotional states evoked by the activation of representations of parents with whom the individual has a secure, anxious-ambivalent, avoidant, or fearful attachment.

Differing affective states are triggered in transference involving a parent, depending on the attachment style held with that parent, as assessed by self-reported mood (Andersen, Bartz, Berenson, & Keczkemethy, 2003). Transference involving a parent with whom one has a secure-attachment relationship results in increases in positive affect (relative to the control condition), but this did not occur for anxious-ambivalent, avoidant, or fearful attachment. In addition, transference involving a parent with whom an individual has an anxious-ambivalent attachment is associated with more anxiety (relative to the control condition), and this was not the case for secure, avoidant, or fearful participants. Finally, transference involving a parent with whom one has an avoidant attachment style results in decreases in self-reported levels of hostility (compared to the control condition), which does not occur for other individuals, suggesting a lack of emotional expression, and even suppressed hostility, as one might expect. Given the purported importance of internal working models of primary caregivers to the attachment system, this work contributes to the literature by providing evidence that transference may be one mechanism by which attachment styles are triggered in everyday living (see Liotti, Chapter 7, this volume).

Increases in dysphoric mood and self-concept shifts among depressed persons

There is increasing evidence that depression is associated with impairment in interpersonal relationships (Hammen, 2000). In our work we thus assume that depressed individuals may have experienced more problematic interpersonal relationships than non-depressed individuals (Davila, Hammen, Burge, Paley, & Daley, 1995). Triggering a significant-other representation associated with a problematic relationship may lead mood regulatory capacity to break down (see Nolen-Hoeksema & Corte, 2004).

For example, encountering a new person who is similar to a loved one with whom one has experienced rejection may lead to increases in dysphoric mood. We examined this hypothesis in a recent study using a college-student sample of individuals pre-selected for high versus low symptoms of depression on the Beck Depression Inventory (Beck, Rush, Shaw, & Emery,

1979). Participants learned about a new person who resembled or did not resemble a positive or negative significant other with whom they had not experienced the level of acceptance that they would have preferred in the past (or, viewed differently, with whom they had experienced rejection) (Miranda *et al.*, in preparation; see also Andersen & Miranda, 2006).

As such, depressed individuals show increases in dysphoric mood (adjusting for baseline levels of dysphoria) in the positive transference condition (that is, where the representation triggered was of a family member who was liked or loved by the individual), compared to the control condition, i.e., when the significant other was positive and still rejecting. Their freely listed self-descriptors, moreover, are rated by independent judges (adjusting for baseline self-concept) as characterized by a feeling of being rejected, while those of non-depressed individuals are not. These findings suggest that depressed persons are more vulnerable to a transference involving a positive but rejecting significant other than are non-depressed individuals. Depressed individuals may thus be particularly pained by rejection in their relationships with people whom they like or love a great deal, and this emerges in a relevant transference.

Implications for the therapeutic relationship

This body of work has important implications for treatment. It underscores the importance of the relational self both for facilitating the therapeutic encounter and relationship in emotional terms, and for disrupting it. The individual's current emotional and interpersonal functioning in any relationship will depend very specifically on what particular cues are perceived and experienced in the encounter, which shifts their own mental state. Our research tracks this and thus offers a precise, cue-based way of seeing the texture of an encounter, through its evoked relational meaning for the person, rather than merely identifying abstract differences in trait predispositions or generalized cognitions, such as dysfunctional attitudes about the self. Understanding transference in these terms thus provides useful information to the therapist.

We do not mean to suggest, however, that transference should necessarily be a central and explicit focus of therapy in the therapeutic encounter, as is often the case in psychodynamic treatment. Instead, we argue that the focus of attention in therapy should be on the client's meaning-making in his or her life across varying contextual cues. This may best be accomplished by being directed to the client's daily life, ongoing relationships, and interpersonal encounters. At the same time, our data suggest that understanding a person's relationship history – not only the "here and now" – might be important when working with someone who presents with interpersonal difficulties. This offers a window on the transference processes occurring there – if one knows something about the content of the individual's significant-other representations and his or her relationship with each one. Since much human suffering is located in the relational nexus of people's lives, we argue that this can be invaluable.

Modifying interpersonal schemas and relationship patterns in treatment

Over the past two decades, interpersonal relationships have received increasing attention in models of psychotherapy. Interpersonal psychotherapy for depression (Klerman, Weissman, Rounsaville, & Chevron, 1984), for example, which draws on the theories of Harry Stack Sullivan (1953) and John Bowlby (1969), is a time-limited treatment that addresses the interpersonal context of depression. A major part of this treatment, which has been shown to be efficacious for both adolescent and adult depression (Mufson, Weissman, Moreau, & Garfinkel, 1999; Weissman, Klerman, Prusoff, Sholomskas, & Padian, 1981; see Markowitz & Weissman, 1995), is the identification of interpersonal problem areas that may exacerbate or maintain symptoms of depression and then helping clients develop strategies to address these problem areas.

To take another example, Cloitre and colleagues (Cloitre, Koenen, Cohen, & Han, 2002) developed a cognitive-behavioral treatment for post-traumatic stress disorder (PTSD) that involves skills training in affective and interpersonal regulation prior to an exposure component in which the individual is exposed to components of a trauma narrative. The skills training component of the treatment includes identification of maladaptive interpersonal schemas and patterns of interaction and identifying ways to modify these interpersonal patterns. This treatment has been shown to be effective in reducing symptoms of PTSD and in maintaining symptom improvement as long as 9 months after treatment (Cloitre et al., 2002).

In our view, interpersonal perception and relations are profoundly influenced by the mental representations of (and relationships with) significant others that one brings to a situation. In considering what is "maladaptive" about the otherwise normal, nonpathological process of transference, it is useful to distinguish *process* and *content* (see Andersen & Berk, 1998). The process of transference appears to be quite general. The basic process is that once a significant-other representation is triggered, it is likely to lead to certain thoughts, feelings, motivations, and behaviors. What is distinctive to the person and more relevant to human suffering and dysfunction is the content of an individual's significant-other representations and relationships. And this is what can be assessed in psychotherapy. A first step in our own research is to ask participants to name and describe important others in their lives using free-form sentence completions. By having individuals in psychotherapy describe important others in their lives, including the person's qualities, quirks, preferences, interests, ways of relating, as well as the nature of the relationship, much can be learned about the individual, especially as experience varies across significant others. This is analogous to the initial phases of existing treatment models that focus on the interpersonal relationship as the unit of analysis (see, e.g., Weissman, Markowitz, & Klerman, 2000). The emotions evoked by these others in these relationships, as well as the motives and expectancies with these others, may be experienced anew in new contexts with new people (both you, the therapist, and other people in the individual's daily life).

Once these representations are identified, the therapist may be able to see when they have been activated (or infer when they may have been activated) by looking for comparable patterns of response to you (or to another person) as experienced in the pre-existing significant-other relationship. The therapist may also be able to ask the client if these seem to be the same responses that the individual had in the other relationship (see Leahy, 2001). This can provoke a dialogue about whether or not there were aspects of your response (or a new person's response) that reminded the client of dealing with the significant other. Presumably, such experience can help the client to identify relevant triggering cues himself or herself – potentially learning over time to expand the "moment of freedom" between the occurrence of these cues and having the typical response, perhaps permitting a choice as to how to respond, instead. That is, therapy can thus be directed, in part, to helping the individual modify old patterns in new relationships as instigated by activation of significant-other representations and relationships. This may help the individual to process information about new people in more conscious and effortful ways – and in more diverse terms rather than in the simpler automatic ways that otherwise occur, allowing alternate ways of responding to be considered, tried out and practiced over time in changing patterns in small ways, step by step.

Significant-other representations and the therapeutic alliance

While transference has been the crucible of psychodynamic thinking, and there has been much discussion of the therapeutic alliance in most thinking about psychotherapy, there has been less research on the actual relationship between therapist and client in psychotherapy than would be valuable. On the one hand, research has certainly begun to suggest that the matching of client and therapist on a variety of dimensions of preference and expectancy and style facilitates a therapeutic alliance (Beutler et al., 1986). On the other hand, very little research examines the process of client–therapist interaction in precise terms, perhaps because it is so labor-intensive to conduct.

One exception is research on therapeutic relationships showing that positive therapeutic relationships contribute to positive treatment outcomes (see Horvath & Luborsky, 1993). The ability to engage a client in treatment and to maintain that bond and the trust it usually requires will be affected by the response a client has toward the therapist – and this is likely to manifest itself relatively early in treatment. It is also likely to have an impact on the client's ability to acquire new skills in cognitive-behavioral therapy. For example, in PTSD treatment among women with a history of childhood physical or sexual abuse, the client's rating of the therapeutic relationship in the first few sessions of treatment predicts improvement in symptoms through changes in the client's perceptions of her own ability to regulate her emotions (Cloitre, Stovall-McClough, Miranda, & Chemtob, 2004). Such findings argue for the need for a richer, more comprehensive understanding of relational processes in psychotherapy, and we believe our work on interpersonal perception and interpersonal relations can inform this development.

Whether a client has an initially positive or negative response to the therapist matters, and is likely to be determined, in part, by the mental representations triggered in therapeutic interactions with the therapist. For instance, an individual who experiences mistrust of the therapist and a motivation to avoid engaging openly may well experience this based partly on cues that the therapist himself or herself gives off that happen to trigger a prior significant-other representation and relationship. Approach motivation can be diminished and anxious or dysphoric mood can also be evoked, as the client perceives that she or he has failed to meet the therapist's expectations. This can occur based on a positive significant-other representation, not only a negative one, and so can be relevant even when the apparent alliance is strong. Furthermore, even attempts by the therapist to act in role-specific ways (e.g., trying to be understanding and getting to know the client, to be empathic, or to place boundaries and act as a containing authority) may be alarming to a client, particularly when this behavior violates role expectancies – as when in a client's history, closeness is associated with abuse (see Gilbert, Chapter 6, this volume). Indeed, it is likely that even a relapse in symptoms can be evoked by the transference process. Moreover, if the client is experiencing other difficulties or there happens to be a relapse for other reasons, such a transference involving rejection expectancies can then interrupt secondarily the very trust and bond needed to help the individual through the difficult times.

Our data suggest that an individual's initial response to a new person can be gauged non-verbally – in fleeting facial expressions (Andersen et al., 1996). A client's initial non-verbal expressions of affect during early therapeutic encounters may thus be informative about his or her reaction to the therapist. Just as positive facial affect may reflect a positive transference, the opposite – when observed in a client – may reflect a negative transference. Our work suggests, then, that clinicians should remain attentive to clients' facial expressions and other non-verbal expressions of affect (body posture, etc.), particularly during early phases of treatment, as these may help predict how well the individual will engage in treatment over time. It is also worth noting that beyond the initial sessions, it is quite likely that subtle variations in what the therapist is giving off and communicating can trigger variability in the kind of transference evoked, even if these happen not to have been observed in early sessions, as they can perhaps be an indicator of such processes during any stage of therapy.

The evidence we have presented showing that disruptions in mood and self-regulatory responses occur in transference offers both a warning to clinicians about the potential deleterious impacts of the process of transference and some encouragement about when it can work well for therapy. It perhaps offers some grist for humility both about the well-organized and well-practiced (automatic) aspects of what clients bring to psychotherapy and the fateful question of effective or problematic match with a therapist at a given time.

Concluding comments

We have presented a model of the social-cognitive process of transference and of the relational self. We have suggested that one's sense of self is constructed through significant-other relationships. Mental representations of the self, held in memory, are tied to representations of significant others. Transference is the process by which such mental representations are triggered by social contextual cues and applied to new individuals. These are often responses that arise automatically in a variety of domains – in cognitive inferences, biases and retrieval; core affective responses (e.g., like/dislike, positive/negative); evaluative responses and expectations (of being accepted/rejected); motivations (to approach or avoid), and the feelings, thoughts and behaviors evoked in the recipient of the transference. Even views of the self, held in relation to each unique significant other, will come to define the self, depending on whether or not that significant-other representation is activated. This line of research is the first experimental evidence of transference, and it demonstrates it in everyday interpersonal life.

While our research has been restricted to settings outside the therapeutic encounter, and to non-clinical samples, even Freud assumed that transference occurred both inside and outside of analysis, and Sullivan and most other early theorists concurred. Our work has clinical relevance for what transpires in psychotherapy in a variety of ways. Using basic behavioral science research in the field of social cognition, it shows that the long-standing clinical assumption that "transference" occurs in psychotherapy is correct. Our research does not address how a therapist should (or should not) deal with transference in therapy, but illuminates how it *can* occur – in the client and from the client's point of view.

We also suggest that the same processes can be applied to the understanding of transference and counter-transference experiences in the therapist. We show how this normal process operates in everyday inter-actions among "ordinary" people and how it can lead to emotionally painful consequences or, conversely, to feeling connected, bonded, and comfortable. The key message is therefore that in deepening our understanding of "normal" social psychology we can throw light on therapeutic relationships. There is no reason to assume that the evolved conscious and non-conscious social processing systems that make our complex social life possible are not also key to psychotherapy.

Acknowledgment

This research was funded in part by a grant from the National Institute of Mental Health (#R01-MH48789).

References

Ainsworth, M.D.S., Blehar, M.C., Walters, E. & Wall, S. (1978). *Patterns of attachment: A psychological study of the strange situation.* Hillsdale, NJ: Lawrence Erlbaum Associates.

Andersen, S.M., Bartz, J., Berenson, K. & Keczkemethy, C. (2003). Triggering the attachment system in transference: Evoking specific emotions through transiently activating a parental representation. Unpublished manuscript, New York University.

Andersen, S.M. & Baum, A. (1994). Transference in interpersonal relations: Infer-ences and affect based on significant-other representations. *Journal of Personality,* 62, 459–498.

Andersen, S.M. & Berenson, K. (2001). Perceiving, feeling, and wanting: Motivation and affect based on significant-other representations. In J.P. Forgas, K.D. Williams & L. Wheeler (eds), *The social mind: Cognitive and motivational aspects of interpersonal behavior* (pp. 231–256). New York: Cambridge University Press.

Andersen, S.M. & Berk, M.S. (1998). Transference in everyday experience: Implications of experimental research for relevant clinical phenomena. *Review of General Psychology,* 2, 81–120.

Andersen, S.M. & Chen, S. (2002). The relational self: An interpersonal social-cognitive theory. *Psychological Review,* 109, 619–645.

Andersen, S.M. & Cole, S.W. (1990). "Do I know you?": The role of significant others in general social perception. *Journal of Personality and Social Psychology,* 59, 383–399.

Andersen, S.M. & Glassman, N.S. (1996). Responding to significant others when they are not there: Effects on interpersonal inference, motivation and affect. In R.M. Sorrentino & E.T. Higgins (eds), *Handbook of motivation and cognition* (Vol. 3, pp. 262–321). New York: Guilford.

Andersen, S.M., Glassman, N.S., Chen, S. & Cole, S.W. (1995). Transference in social perception: The role of chronic accessibility in significant-other representations. *Journal of Personality and Social Psychology,* 69, 41–57.

Andersen, S.M. & Miranda, R. (2006). Through the lens of the relational self:

Triggering emotional suffering in the social-cognitive process of transference. In R. Kreuger & J. Tackett (eds), *Personality and psychopathology* (pp. 292–334). New York: Guilford Press.

Andersen, S.M., Reznik, I. & Chen, S. (1997). The self in relation to others: Motivational and cognitive underpinnings. In J.G. Snodgrass & R.L. Thompson (eds), *The self across psychology: Self-recognition, self awareness, and the self-concept.* New York: New York Academy of Science.

Andersen, S.M., Reznik, I. & Glassman, N.S. (2005). The unconscious relational self. In R. Hassin, J.S. Uleman & J.A. Bargh (eds), *The new unconscious.* New York: Oxford University Press.

Andersen, S.M., Reznik, I. & Manzella, L.M. (1996). Eliciting facial affect, motivation, and expectancies in transference: Significant-other representations in social relations. *Journal of Personality and Social Psychology*, 71, 1108–1129.

Andersen, S.M. & Saribay, S.A. (2005). The relational self and transference: Evoking motives, self-regulation, and emotions through activation of mental representations of significant others. In M.W. Baldwin (ed.), *Interpersonal cognition* (pp. 1–32). New York: Guilford Press.

Baldwin, M.W. (1992). Relational schemas and the processing of information. *Psychological Bulletin*, 112, 461–484.

Baldwin, M.W., Carrell, S.E. & Lopez, D.F. (1990). Priming relationship schemas: My advisor and the Pope are watching me from the back of my mind. *Journal of Experimental Social Psychology*, 26, 435–454.

Baldwin, M.W., Granzberg, A. & Pritchard, E.T. (2003). Cued activation of relational schemas: Self-evaluation and gender effects. *Canadian Journal of Behavioural Science*, 35, 153–163.

Baldwin, M.W. & Sinclair, L. (1996). Self-esteem and "if . . . then" contingencies of interpersonal acceptance. *Journal of Personality and Social Psychology*, 71, 1130–1141.

Bargh, J.A. (1990). Auto-motives: Preconscious determinants of social interaction. In E.T. Higgins & R.M. Sorrentino (eds), *Handbook of motivation and cognition: Foundations of social behavior* (Vol. 2, pp. 93–130). New York: Guilford Press.

Bargh, J.A. (1997). The automaticity of everyday life. *Advances in Social Cognition*, 10, 1–61.

Bargh, J.A. & Barndollar, K. (1996). Automaticity in action: The unconscious as repository of chronic goals and motives. In P.M. Gollwitzer & J.A. Bargh (eds), *The psychology of action: Linking cognition and motivation to behavior* (pp. 457–481). New York: Guildford Press.

Baum, A. & Andersen, S.M. (1999). Interpersonal roles in transference: Transient mood states under the condition of significant-other activation. *Social Cognition*, 17, 161–185.

Baumeister, R.F. & Leary, M.R. (1995). The need to belong: Desire for interpersonal attachments as a fundamental human motivation. *Psychological Bulletin*, 117, 497–529.

Beck, A.T., Rush, A.J., Shaw, B.F. & Emery, G. (1979). *Cognitive therapy of depression.* New York: Guilford Press.

Berenson, K. & Andersen, S.M. (in press). Childhood physical and emotional abuse by a parent: Transference effects in adult interpersonal relationships. *Personality and Social Psychology Bulletin.*

Berk, M.S. & Andersen, S.M. (2000). The impact of past relationships on interpersonal behavior: Behavioral confirmation in the social-cognitive process of transference. *Journal of Personality and Social Psychology*, 79, 546–562.

Berk, M.S. & Andersen, S.M. (2004). Chronically unsatisfied goals with significant others: Triggering unfulfilled needs for love and acceptance in transference. Unpublished manuscript, New York University.

Beutler, L.E., Crago, M. & Arizmendi, T.G. (1986). Therapist variables in psychotherapy process and outcome. In S. Garfield & A. Bergin (eds), *Psychotherapy and behavior change* (3rd edition, pp. 257–310). New York: Wiley.

Bowlby, J. (1969). *Attachment and loss: Vol. 1. Attachment*. New York: Basic Books.

Bruner, J. (1957). Going beyond the information given. In H.E. Gruber, K.R. Hammond & R. Jessor (eds), *Contemporary approaches to cognition* (pp. 41–69). Cambridge, MA: Harvard University Press.

Chen, M. & Bargh, J.A. (1997). Nonconscious behavioral confirmation processes: The self-fulfilling consequences of automatic stereotype activation. *Journal of Experimental Social Psychology*, 33, 541–560.

Chen, S. & Andersen, S.M. (1999). Relationships from the past in the present: Significant-other representations and transference in interpersonal life. In M.P. Zanna (ed.), *Advances in experimental social psychology* (Vol. 31, pp. 123–190). San Diego, CA: Academic Press.

Chen, S., Andersen, S.M. & Hinkley, K. (1999). Triggering transference: Examining the role of applicability and use of significant-other representations in social perception. *Social Cognition*, 17, 332–365.

Classen, C., Field, N.P., Koopman, C., Nevill-Manning, K. & Spiegel, D. (2001). Interpersonal problems and their relationship to sexual revictimization among women sexually abused in childhood. *Journal of Interpersonal Violence*, 16, 495–509.

Cloitre, M., Cohen, L.R. & Scarvalone, P. (2002). Understanding revictimization among childhood sexual abuse survivors: An interpersonal schema approach. *Journal of Cognitive Psychotherapy*, 16, 91–112.

Cloitre, M., Koenen, K.C., Cohen, L.R. & Han, H. (2002). Skills training in affective and interpersonal regulation followed by exposure: A phase-based treatment for PTSD related to childhood abuse. *Journal of Consulting & Clinical Psychology*, 70, 1067–1074.

Cloitre, M., Stovall-McClough, K.C., Miranda, R. & Chemtob, C.M. (2004). Therapeutic alliance, negative mood regulation, and treatment outcome in child abuse-related posttraumatic stress disorder. *Journal of Consulting & Clinical Psychology*, 72, 411–416.

Davila, J., Hammen, C., Burge, D., Paley, B. & Daley, S. (1995). Poor interpersonal problem-solving as a mechanism of stress generation in depression among adolescent women. *Journal of Abnormal Psychology*, 104, 592–600.

Deci, E.L. (1995). *Why we do what we do*. New York: Putnam.

Downey, G. & Feldman, S. (1996). Implications of rejection sensitivity for intimate relationships. *Journal of Personality and Social Psychology*, 70, 1327–1343.

Duckworth, K.L., Bargh, J.A., Garcia, M. & Chaiken, S. (2002). The automatic evaluation of novel stimuli. *Psychological Science*, 13, 513–519.

Fiske, S.T. & Pavelchak, M.A. (1986). Category-based versus piecemeal-based affective responses: Developments in schema-triggered affect. In R.M. Sorrentino

& E.T. Higgins (eds), *Handbook of motivation and cognition: Foundations of social behavior* (pp. 167–203). New York: Guilford Press.

Fitzsimons, G.M. & Bargh, J.A. (2003). Thinking of you: Nonconscious pursuit of interpersonal goals associated with relationship partners. *Journal of Personality and Social Psychology*, 84, 148–164.

Freud, S. (1958). The dynamics of transference. In J. Strachey (ed. & trans.), *The standard edition of the complete psychological works of Sigmund Freud* (Vol. 12, pp. 97–108). London: Hogarth. (Original work published 1912).

Garfield, S.L. (1986). Research on client variables in psychotherapy. In S. Garfield & A. Bergin (eds), *Psychotherapy and behavior change* (3rd edition, pp. 213–256). New York: Wiley. (Original work published 1971).

Gilbert, P. (2003). Evolution, social roles, and the differences in shame and guilt. *Social Research*, 70, 401–426.

Glassman, N.S. & Andersen, S.M. (1999a). Activating transference without consciousness: Using significant-other representations to go beyond what is subliminally given. *Journal of Personality and Social Psychology*, 77, 1146–1162.

Glassman, N.S. & Andersen, S.M. (1999b). Transference in social cognition: Persistence and exacerbation of significant-other based inferences over time. *Cognitive Therapy and Research*, 23, 75–91.

Greenberg, J.R. & Mitchell, S.A. (1983). *Object relations in psychoanalytic theory.* Cambridge, MA: Harvard University Press.

Greenberg, J. & Pyszczynski, T. (1985). Compensatory self-inflation: A response to the threat to self-regard of public failure. *Journal of Personality and Social Psychology*, 49, 273–280.

Hammen, C. (2000). Interpersonal factors in an emerging developmental model of depression. In S.L. Johnson & A.M. Hayes (eds), *Stress, coping, and depression* (pp. 71–88). Mahwah, NJ: Lawrence Erlbaum Associates.

Hazan, C. & Shaver, P. (1994). Attachment as an organizational framework for research on close relationships. *Psychological Inquiry*, 5, 1–22.

Higgins, E.T. (1987). Self discrepancy: A theory relating self and affect. *Psychological Review*, 94, 319–340.

Higgins, E.T. (1989). Knowledge accessibility and activation: Subjectivity and suffering from unconscious sources. In J.S. Uleman & J.A. Bargh (eds), *Unintended thought* (pp. 75–123). New York: Guilford.

Higgins, E.T. (1991). Development of self-regulatory and self-evaluative processes: Costs, benefits, and tradeoffs. In M.R. Gunnar & L.A. Stroufe (eds), *Self processes and development: The Minnesota Symposia on Child Development* (Vol. 23, pp. 125–165). Hillsdale, NJ: Lawrence Erlbaum Associates.

Higgins, E.T. (1998). Promotion and prevention: Regulatory focus as a motivational principle. In M.P. Zanna (ed.), *Advances in experimental social psychology* (Vol. 30, pp. 1–46). New York: Academic Press.

Hinkley, K. & Andersen, S.M. (1996). The working self-concept in transference: Significant-other activation and self change. *Journal of Personality and Social Psychology*, 71, 1279–1295.

Horney, K. (1939). *New ways in psychoanalysis.* New York: Norton.

Horvath, A.O. & Luborsky, L. (1993). The role of the therapeutic alliance in psychotherapy. *Journal of Consulting and Clinical Psychology*, 61, 561–573.

Klerman, G.L., Weissman, M.M., Rounsaville, B.J. & Chevron, E.S. (1984). *Interpersonal psychotherapy of depression.* New York: Basic Books.

Leahy, R.L. (2001). *Overcoming resistance in cognitive therapy.* New York: Guilford Press.

Markowitz, J.C. & Weissman, M.M. (1995). Interpersonal psychotherapy. In E.E. Beckham & W.R. Leber (eds), *Handbook of depression* (2nd edition, pp. 376–390). New York: Guilford Press.

Martin, D.J., Garske, J.P. & Davis, M.K. (2000). Relation of the therapeutic alliance with outcome and other variables: A meta-analytic review. *Journal of Consulting and Clinical Psychology,* 68, 438–450.

Mikulincer, M., Gillath, O. & Shaver, P.R. (2002). Activation of the attachment system in adulthood: Threat-related primes increase the accessibility of mental representations of attachment figures. *Journal of Personality and Social Psychology,* 83, 881–895.

Miranda, R., Andersen, S.M. & Edwards, T. (in preparation). Worsening dysphoria among depressed individuals through indirect activation of rejection expectancies in the social-cognitive process of transference. Manuscript in preparation.

Mufson, L., Weissman, M.M., Moreau, D. & Garfinkel, R. (1999). Efficacy of interpersonal psychotherapy for depressed adolescents. *Archives of General Psychiatry,* 56, 573–579.

Nolen-Hoeksema, S. & Corte, C. (2004). Gender and self-regulation. In R.F. Baumeister & K.D. Vohs (eds), *Handbook of self-regulation: Research, theory, and applications* (pp. 411–421). New York: Guilford Press.

Pierce, T. & Lydon, J. (2001). Global and specific relational models in the experience of social interactions. *Journal of Personality and Social Psychology,* 80, 613–631.

Reznik, I. & Andersen, S.M. (2004). Becoming the dreaded self: Diminished self-worth with positive significant others in transference. Unpublished manuscript, New York University.

Reznik, I. & Andersen, S.M. (in revision). Agitation and despair evoked in transference: Indirect triggering of self-discrepancies and self-regulatory focus through significant-other representations. Manuscript in revision.

Rogers, C. (1951). *Client-centered therapy.* Boston: Houghton-Mifflin.

Russell, J.A. (2003). Core affect and the psychological construction of emotion. *Psychological Review,* 110, 145–172.

Safran, J.D. (1990). Toward a refinement of cognitive therapy in light of interpersonal theory: I. Theory. *Clinical Psychology Review,* 10, 87–105.

Shah, J. (2003). Automatic for the people: How representations of significant others implicitly affect goal pursuit. *Journal of Personality and Social Psychology,* 84, 661–681.

Sheldon, K.M. & Elliot, A.J. (2000). Personal goals in social roles: Divergences and convergences across roles and levels of analysis. *Journal of Personality,* 68, 51–84.

Shields, A., Ryan, R.M. & Cicchetti, D. (2001). Narrative representations of caregivers and emotion dysregulation as predictors of maltreated children's rejection by peers. *Developmental Psychology,* 37, 321–337.

Simpson, J.A. & Rholes, W.S. (1998). *Attachment theory and close relationships.* New York: Guilford Press.

Snyder, M., Tanke, E.D. & Berscheid, E. (1977). Social perception and interpersonal behavior: On the self-fulfilling nature of social stereotypes. *Journal of Personality and Social Psychology*, 35, 656–666.

Sullivan, H.S. (1953). *The interpersonal theory of psychiatry*. New York: Norton.

Thompson, R.A. (1998). Early sociopersonality development. In W. Damon (series ed.) & N. Eisenberg (vol. ed.), *Handbook of child psychology: Vol. 3. Social, emotional, and personality development* (5th edition, pp. 25–104). New York: Wiley.

Weissman, M.M., Klerman, G.L., Prusoff, B.A., Sholomskas, D. & Padian, N. (1981). Depressed outpatients: Results one year after treatment with drugs and/or interpersonal psychotherapy. *Archives of General Psychiatry*, 38, 52–55.

Weissman, M.M., Markowitz, J.C. & Klerman, G.L. (2000). *Comprehensive guide to interpersonal psychotherapy*. New York: Basic Books.

Westen, D. (1988). Transference and information processing. *Clinical Psychology Review*, 8, 161–179.

Chapter 5

Recognizing and resolving ruptures in the therapeutic alliance

Adrienne W. Katzow and Jeremy D. Safran

Introduction

Although research has consistently demonstrated that cognitive therapy is an effective treatment for numerous disorders, studies have also shown that many patients fail to benefit from this modality. One of the most consistent findings in psychotherapy research is that the quality of the therapeutic alliance is one of the strongest predictors of successful outcome as evident across a variety of treatment modalities (Horvath & Symonds, 1991; Martin, Garske, & Davis, 2000) including cognitive therapy.

Another important finding is that good outcome cases demonstrate less negative interpersonal process (i.e., hostile interactions between patient and therapist) than bad outcome cases. Psychotherapy research results such as these are highlighting the inevitability of negative process or ruptures in the therapeutic alliance and the importance (for therapists) of handling negative process and repairing ruptures in the therapeutic alliance (Binder & Strupp, 1997; Bordin, 1994; Henry & Strupp, 1994; Henry, Strupp, Butler, Schacht, & Binder, 1993; Horvath, 1995; Rhodes, Hill, Thompson, & Elliot, 1994; Strupp, 1993). We see the working through of negative process and the negotiation of ruptures as integral to the change process in therapy.

Although cognitive behavior therapy (CBT) has traditionally deemphasized the therapeutic alliance, a shift has occurred in which many are now placing increasing emphasis on the alliance and the therapeutic relationship (Gilbert, 2000; Leahy, 2001; Liotti, 1987; Safran, 1998; Safran & Muran, 2000; Safran & Segal, 1990; Young, Klosko, & Weishaar, 2003). In this chapter we will look at the model advanced by Safran and his colleagues (e.g., Safran, 1998; Safran & Muran, 2000; Safran & Segal, 1990) which focuses on the therapeutic relationship in CBT and the different ways that ruptures can be identified and resolved. We will also discuss the vital importance of the therapist's subjective experience and the use of mindfulness practice in working with patients at impasse moments.

The alliance in general

In recent years, many researchers and theorists from various traditions have begun to explore the potential value of the therapeutic alliance as a general psychotherapy construct. The concept of the therapeutic alliance has its origins in the psychoanalytic literature, with Freud arguing that the patient and analyst must band together against the patient's symptoms in an "analytic pact" grounded in the patient's exploration and the analyst's understanding (Freud, 1937, 1940). Although the construct of the therapeutic alliance had existed in the psychoanalytic literature for quite some time, it was not until the late 1970s that it received attention from psychotherapy researchers and theorists. This shift was influenced, in part, by Edward Bordin's (1979) reformulation of the alliance in transtheoretical terms. Almost 30 years later, the alliance construct has increasingly spread to a variety of different psychotherapy schools and has garnered further interest as many search to understand common mechanisms of change, given that no particular treatment has been shown to be consistently more effective than any other (Smith, Glass, & Miller, 1980).

The alliance in cognitive behavioral psychotherapy

Psychotherapy research has traditionally distinguished between "specific" and "nonspecific" factors. "Specific factors" are technical factors specific to a particular type of psychotherapy, whereas "nonspecific factors" are those factors common to all forms of psychotherapy. CBT has traditionally separated the "nonspecific" factors, such as the alliance, from technique, which has been seen as the central agent of change. This has sometimes led to a deemphasis of the therapeutic alliance. Today many cognitive behavioral therapists (Leahy, 1993; Safran, 1998; Safran & Segal, 1990; Young et al., 2003) conceptualize the alliance as an integral part of the treatment that can be used in conjunction with technique to drive change.

In terms of the alliance, CBT has always stressed the importance of establishing a strong collaborative relationship between patient and therapist where the therapist plays an active role. Beck, Rush, Shaw & Emery (1979) suggested that therapists be genuinely warm, empathic, and open so as to foster a strong therapeutic relationship whereby they can collaboratively develop therapeutic goals and homework assignments. Additionally, therapists are encouraged to give regular feedback as well as rationales to the patient, which further strengthens the relationship.

When faced with resistance at impasse moments, CBT therapists traditionally were advised to continue to apply standard CBT techniques such as challenging cognitive distortions, rather than directly discussing the alliance. Today, it is more common to emphasize interventions such as joining the resistance of patients at impasse moments rather than challenging it (e.g., Leahy, 2001). Many approaches to CBT still emphasize empiricism as a tool for therapists to help patients modify their cognitions to be more in line with reality. But there has been a shift towards more explicitly and consistently emphasizing the importance of focusing on therapeutic impasses. For example, Young and his colleagues (2003) emphasize "empathic confrontation" at impasse moments. This involves empathizing and validating patients' reactions toward the therapist as understandable considering their life histories and then, subsequently, helping them to challenge some of the inaccuracies in their beliefs. Thus standard and specific cognitive techniques continue to be utilized in helping patients change their behaviors in treatment, but the importance of the therapeutic relationship and of dealing with problems in the therapeutic relationship has become increasingly highlighted.

Our approach focuses specifically on the alliance as a process of ongoing negotiation (Safran & Muran, 2000). Elaborating upon Bordin's trans-theoretical reformulation of the alliance (1979), we have come to see the alliance as an intrinsic part of the change process and resolving ruptures as a critical component of the treatment (Safran, 1998; Safran & Muran, 1996, 1998, 2000; 2006; Safran, Muran, Samstag, & Stevens, 2002; Safran & Segal, 1990). This reconceptualization of the alliance allows us to see how traditional CBT interventions and assumptions function to promote change through the alliance as well as to examine ways in which they may hinder treatment under some circumstances.

The alliance as negotiation

According to Bordin (1979, 1994), collaboration between patients and therapists is at the heart of the therapeutic alliance. He argued that all schools of psychotherapy have some form of the therapeutic alliance but the type of alliance varies depending on the psychotherapeutic modality and the demands placed on both individuals. Yet regardless of the therapy practiced, the alliance consists of three interdependent components: tasks, goals, and the bond. The strength of the therapeutic alliance depends on the degree of agreement between patient and therapist about the tasks and goals of psychotherapy as well as the strength of the relational bond between them.

In short, the tasks of psychotherapy consist of certain activities the patient is asked to engage in to benefit from the treatment, such as completing behavioral assignments between sessions. The goals of psychotherapy are the general objectives toward which the treatment is directed such as eliminating symptoms. The bond component of the alliance refers to the affective quality of the relationship between patient and therapist. These three components, the tasks, goals, and bond, influence one another in an ongoing fashion so an agreement about the tasks or goals will likely strengthen the quality of the bond and, alternatively, when there are disagreements, the existence of an adequate bond will facilitate the negotiation of tasks and goals.

Extending Bordin's conceptualization of the alliance, our approach has come to view the ongoing *negotiation* between patient and therapist as central to the change process (Safran & Muran, 2000). Both the patient and therapist bring preexisting expectations, beliefs, and needs into therapy which inevitably shape their interactions and relationship. Therefore a strong working alliance depends on the ability of both parties to negotiate a good fit between these two sets of expectations and needs without compromising themselves. Inherent in this perspective on the alliance is the assumption that technique is inextricably linked to the particular interpersonal context to which it is applied. Any intervention may have a positive or negative impact on the quality of the bond between therapist and patient depending on its meaning to each of them. It is important to remember that both therapist and patient are always participating in a relational configuration shaped by each of their unique subjectivities. It is important for therapists to be guided by an understanding of what a particular therapeutic task means to a particular patient in a given moment. It is also important to bear in mind that the impact of an intervention will be mediated by the meaning of that intervention to the therapist. For example, challenging a patient's automatic thoughts will have a different impact if the therapist is feeling supportive than it will if the therapist is feeling critical.

Both the therapist and patient bring into therapy their own expectations, attitudes, and unique characteristics. Thus for both parties, the development of a working relationship will mean an ongoing negotiation between the needs of the self and the needs of the other. This negotiation often will occur at least partially out of awareness when things are running smoothly, but when there is an overt rupture in the alliance this negotiation becomes the central focus.

Humans are constantly struggling with how to negotiate the needs of the self versus the needs of others, but some grapple more with this conflict than others. Often patients bring problems into therapy that reflect their difficulty in negotiating this tension. With these patients, ruptures in the alliance can be conceptualized as breaches in relatedness (Safran, 1998). Impasse moments, in turn, can provide the therapist with an opportunity to work with the patient's characteristic way of construing relationships and the problematic patterns of interpersonal behavior that emerge from this construal. The exploration of a rupture can lead to the elucidation of a dysfunctional cognitive–interpersonal cycle that the patient might be enacting with the therapist and possibly in his or her everyday interactions (Safran, 1984b, 1998; Safran & Segal, 1990). It is important for therapists to be able to use their own subjective reactions to understand their patient's interpersonal difficulties more deeply. As Safran and Segal (1990) point out: "By analyzing problems in the therapeutic alliance through the interaction of the patient's typical construal styles and the therapist's behavior, a possibility of 'unpacking' the concept of the therapeutic alliance emerges, one that can potentially provide new insights into facilitating the alliance and resolving impasses in the therapeutic relationship that impede treatment" (p. 39).

Relational schemas and cognitive–interpersonal cycles

Many developmental and relational theorists have argued that our need to maintain relationships is a basic human instinct (Bowlby, 1969, 1973, 1980; Stern, 1985; Sullivan, 1953). Over time, we learn from our interactions with important attachment figures which behaviors and emotions lead to maintaining proximity to attachment figures and which tend to jeopardize relatedness. These learning experiences lead to the development of schematic representations of self and other interactions which we refer to as "interpersonal" or "relational schemas" (Safran, 1998; Safran & Muran, 2000; Safran & Segal, 1990).

Psychologically healthy people have developed interpersonal schemas that predict interpersonal relatedness as reasonably attainable and that allow them to feel and act in a wide range of ways. In contrast, people who are less psychologically healthy expect interpersonal relatedness to be difficult to achieve and maintain, and believe that a wide range of feelings and actions present potential threats to interpersonal relatedness. Such people disown large parts of their internal experience and have a highly restrictive sense of how they must "be" in order to maintain relatedness. For example, a man who learns that feeling "needy" is a sign of weakness that leads to rejection may have difficulty experiencing and expressing vulnerable feelings. This can lead to his own emotional detachment which can cause others to react distantly, thus confirming his dysfunctional beliefs about self and others.

A central tenet of interpersonal theory is that interpersonal exchanges are shaped by the principle of *complementarity* (Kiesler, 1996). This principle states that specific, interpersonal behaviors tend to pull for other specific, interpersonal behaviors. Thus a person acting in a dominant manner will likely define a relationship in a certain way, that is, the self as dominant and the other as submissive.

In many ways, Kiesler's (1996) theory provides a lens through which to better understand how a patient's maladjusted interpersonal schemas become self-reinforcing. First, maladaptive interpersonal schemas can greatly restrict an individual's life in that they often may choose to avoid situations that evoke their problematic relational tendencies. Their avoidance, in turn, deprives them of the opportunity to disconfirm their beliefs and expectancies. Conversely, these people will tend to seek out or "pull" for others who are comfortable with their interpersonal style, although they often are unaware of this tendency. While this approach enables them to avoid uncomfortable ways of relating, it also perpetuates the problematic cycles that create anxiety in the first place.

A patient's maladaptive interpersonal schema can also cause him to act proactively to protect himself from what he believes to be the dangerous responses of others. For example, a woman who learns that acts of self-assertion disrupt interpersonal relatedness may have difficulty processing angry feelings and consistently behave submissively. Because she expects others to reject her if she asserts herself, she tends to construe their behavior in a schema-consistent way, which amplifies her attempts to behave submissively. This, in turn, pulls for dominant behavior from others, which reinforces her sense of self as submissive and others as dominant.

Another way that maladaptive cognitive–interpersonal cycles are self-reinforcing is that people often attempt to control or conceal emotions they have come to believe are threatening to their relationships. Yet these attempts are often not completely successful. A feeling of anger, while denied and concealed, can unconsciously be expressed in subtle, nonverbal ways, such as through very direct eye contact or a clenching of the jaw. Due to the subtlety of nonverbal communication, people are often unaware of what they are responding to when someone pulls them to act in a complementary way. This can make it difficult, if not impossible, for them to give feedback even if they were so inclined (Safran & Muran, 2000; Safran & Segal, 1990).

For all of these reasons, those who are psychologically maladjusted experience a much greater redundancy in characteristic interpersonal patterns than psychologically healthy individuals. They live in an interpersonal world of their own making and rarely have the opportunity to encounter an interpersonal experience that can provide schema-disconfirming evidence. Moreover, even in situations where they are exposed to disconfirming information, they will tend to assimilate the new information into the old schema.

Working with ruptures and cognitive–interpersonal cycles

Ruptures in the alliance often occur when a maladaptive relational schema has been triggered in the therapeutic situation. These moments of breakdown in the negotiation process provide unique opportunities for viewing and clarifying the nature of patients' interpersonal beliefs, expectations, and appraisal processes that play a central role in perpetuating their dysfunctional cognitive–interpersonal cycle (Safran & Segal, 1990).

Overt ruptures in the alliance, such as the patient blaming the therapist, might seem confusing or excessive to the therapist but these responses can be seen as the patient reacting fearfully to what might happen if he acts in a certain way. Other ruptures might be more subtle and more difficult to notice such as when a patient tries to ward off their own feelings or defers, rather than acting in an overtly aggressive fashion. Here the therapist may have difficulty identifying the rupture or pinpointing the source of this breakdown in communication. The patient might have difficulty accessing and expressing certain feelings or needs due to the rigidity of his inter-personal schema. This can make it more difficult for him to communicate these feelings or needs directly. The subtlety of this interaction might result in therapists only becoming aware of their embeddedness in an inter-personal cycle after some time has passed. Thus the only way that therapists can start to identify and disembed from these more subtle cycles is by tracking their own subjective experience with the patient. For example, a therapist might become aware that her attention has been drifting over the course of the session with the patient. If the therapist is able to become cognizant of this shift and then explore it with the patient, they might discover that the patient has been withdrawing by dissociating threatening feelings about the therapist. This discussion can lead then to further exploration of a cycle that the patient might be enacting with others unbeknown to himself.

In many ways, the CBT approach to the alliance facilitates ongoing negotiation between patients and therapists and promotes the alliance as an agent of positive change. Yet at certain times when the negotiating process breaks down, empathizing with the patient's beliefs and then challenging the accuracy of these beliefs (Young *et al.*, 2003) can exacerbate rather than resolve ruptures. For example, a patient who is particularly concerned about being invalidated may perceive a challenging intervention as invali-dating. In this kind of situation, the therapist should stop in the midst of the intervention and explore precisely what is going on for the patient *at that moment*. Having done this, the therapist may discover that the patient feels criticized and invalidated. Here it is essential that the therapist unhook or disembed from the enactment and empathically explore the patient's feelings rather than continue to confront or challenge the accuracy of the patient's beliefs. If the therapist is unable to disembed from the enactment and continues to challenge, he or she may confirm the patient's dysfunc-tional belief that he or she is not respected by others. The therapist responds to the patient's interpersonal pull like others, yet is able to monitor his or her own feelings and response tendencies and to use them to generate hypotheses about the patient's dysfunctional interpersonal style.

Leahy (2001) has discussed the importance of CBT therapists learning how to validate patients' needs at impasse moments. He argues that therapists can use "validation resistance", i.e., the patient's demand for empathy and understanding to foster exploration into the patient's current problems and past invalidating environments. He advises CBT therapists not only to accept the patient's need for validation, but also to acknowledge that tasks involving the changing of thoughts and behaviors sometimes can feel invalidating. Further, therapists should welcome patients to give feedback when they are feeling invalidated in-session so that discussion around this topic can continue. Leahy also suggests that therapists recognize and identify their own thoughts and feelings regarding the patient's need for validation; by gaining further self-awareness, the therapist will be able to better validate and empathize with the patient.

Our approach views the therapist's subjective reactions and internal experience as vital sources of information and as important therapeutic instruments (Safran & Muran, 2000; Safran & Segal, 1990). We emphasize the need for therapists to cultivate a stance of ongoing awareness that better enables them to collaboratively explore the patient's construal patterns with them in the moment. We see supervision as a means to facilitate the development of this skill. The therapist's ability to take the stance of the participant–observer (Sullivan, 1953), who simultaneously participates in the interaction while observing his participation, helps him to understand the patient's interpersonal patterns and schemas more deeply.

In training we emphasize the importance of mindfulness practice for therapists as a tool for cultivating this ability (Safran & Muran, 2000). The discipline of mindfulness practice can help therapists to approach the therapeutic encounter with a "beginner's mind." As Zen master Suzuki (1970) wrote: "If your mind is empty, it is always ready for anything; it is open to everything. In the beginner's mind, there are many possibilities; in the expert's mind, there are few" (p. 21). Mindfulness involves learning to direct one's attention in a nonjudgmental fashion in order to become aware of one's thoughts, feelings, and actions as they emerge in the present moment. It involves cultivating an attitude of intense curiosity about one's inner experience as it unfolds (Safran, 1998; 2003; Safran & Muran, 2000; Safran & Segal, 1996) and an ability to let go of one's preconceptions as they arise when sitting with a patient. The emphasis on mindfulness is not just on the observation of one's internal experience but also on one's own and one's patient's contributions to the interactions (Safran & Muran, 2000).

There are important similarities between the type of observational stance facilitated through mindfulness and what Schon (1983) refers to as "reflection-in-action." According to Schon, skilled psychotherapists, like experts across a range of different domains, possess the ability to engage in an ongoing reflective conversation with the situation, which allows them to modify their understanding and reactions in response to relevant feedback.

The concept of mindfulness, however, incorporates an additional important dimension. As indicated previously, this dimension consists of *nonjudgmental* awareness. The reason this dimension is so important is that as therapists it is often our own negative judgments about our own internal reactions that keeps us embedded in maladaptive cycles. For example, a therapist who judges her own feelings of anger harshly will have difficulty becoming aware of how her own unconscious aggression contributes to the rupture.

To work with ruptures, therapists must first recognize that they are involved in a maladaptive cycle. They must begin to reflect on their own contributions to the cycle and begin the process of *disembedding* from it. A useful tool for facilitating this is therapeutic *metacommunication*, which is the practice of focusing on and communicating about the therapist–patient interaction *as it occurs* in session (see Safran & Muran, 2000; Safran & Segal, 1990). We think of metacommunication as a type of mindfulness-in-action. Through this process therapists become aware of their own feelings and actions, and make use of that awareness as they engage with the patient in a collaborative inquiry into what is going on in the therapeutic relationship. By exploring the patient's construal of events rather than continuing to react in a way that is consistent with the patient's beliefs and past experience, the therapist is able to begin to *disconfirm* those beliefs and offer the patient a new relational experience. This process of *disembedding* and *disconfirmation* through metacommunication is central to working with ruptures. Some of the fundamental principles of the metacommunication process are: focusing on the immediate details of experience and behavior, establishing a sense of collaboration in the exploration, and being open to exploring and acknowledging one's own subjectivity and contribution to the interaction (Safran, 1998; Safran & Muran, 2000; Safran & Segal, 1990).

A model for rupture resolution

The goal of working with ruptures is not simply to repair them so that therapy can continue with a strengthened alliance but rather to help patients understand how they construe events and how that construal impacts their interaction with others. These moments can also provide crucial opportunities for patients to have new relational experiences that disconfirm their beliefs about themselves.

We have found it useful in our research to distinguish between *withdrawal ruptures* and *confrontation ruptures* and have developed specific resolution models for each one. Here we will outline a more simplified model that can be used to conceptualize the resolution process for both withdrawal and confrontation ruptures. This model consists of five stages, each of which describes a dyadic interaction between therapist and patient. The various stages can be conceptualized as different tasks that are critical for the patient to engage in at different points in the resolution process, and as therapist interventions that can be facilitative (for more detailed model, see Safran & Muran, 2000). We will present a consecutive series of stages but keep in mind that, in practice, the process of ruptures resolution typically cycles back and forth through different stages. It is crucial that therapists remain aware of and respond to shifts in the moment with the patient rather than relying on these prescribed stages (Safran & Muran, 2000).

Stage 1: The cognitive–interpersonal cycle and rupture markers

Ruptures often occur when the patient perceives the therapist's action as confirming his or her negative, dysfunctional beliefs about relationships. For example, a patient quickly complies with or defers to the therapist by agreeing with her interpretation in an acquiescent fashion. The therapist might miss the subtle indications that the patient is frustrated and, in turn, the patient's overly submissive behavior might pull for the therapist to take a more controlling stance in the treatment, which then reinforces the patient's beliefs that they need to be accommodating and that attempts to be more assertive will be ignored or met with rejection. This moment is part of an ongoing enactment in which the therapist has become embedded in the patient's cognitive interpersonal cycle. Therapists need to remember that regardless of whether the patient's initial expectations are realistic or distorted, at this point, the therapist and patient are *both* engaged in a cycle of reaction and counter-reaction.

Stage 2: Recognizing and disembedding from the cognitive–interpersonal cycle

In this stage, therapists begin drawing attention to the rupture and establishing a focus on the here-and-now of the therapeutic relationship. Some rupture markers, such as openly attacking the therapist, are obvious opportunities for negotiation while others are more subtle, such as a patient trying to conceal their anger. In these moments, the therapist's awareness of his or her own subjective experience having shifted, for example through boredom or annoyance, might be the best indicator of a strain in the relationship.

Since ruptures reflecting a patient's maladaptive interpersonal schemas can happen at any time in treatment, a therapist needs to maintain an ongoing awareness of her subjective states as the interactive process unfolds (Safran, 1998; Safran & Muran, 2000). Therapists can better detect impasses in the relationship by tracking their own emotional responses to patients that will help them identify what patient behaviors are pulling for a specific complementary response. The therapist can then use her own reactions to begin to disembed from the enactment.

Once the therapist has realized that she and the patient are embedded in a cycle, she can begin the disembedding process in which both the therapist and patient try to communicate about what is happening between them in the moment. Here the therapist metacommunicates his or her observations about the cycle. For example, the therapist might bring the patient's attention to how her own attention has been drifting and then probe for the patient's experience. The therapist might say: "I'm aware of my attention wandering. I'm not sure what's going on, but I think it may have something to do with a kind of distant sound in your voice. Any sense of what's going on for you right now?" This presents an opportunity for the patient to acknowledge that he is withdrawing because he feels hurt by something the therapist said. It is essential during this stage that the therapist direct the patient's focus to the here-and-now of the therapeutic relationship.

Therapists, when metacommunicating, should maintain a curious, empathic, and noncontrolling stance toward the patient and be open to any negative feelings that emerge. It is common at this point for patients to speak about negative feelings in general terms, rather than directly confronting the therapist. For example, a patient may complain about the mental health field in general and, in response, the therapist might find it helpful to explore those feelings in terms of the present situation. For example, the therapist might say: "If you're willing, I'd like to ask you to experiment with personalizing what you're saying. Do these concerns apply to me as well?"

It is crucial that therapists respect any decision on the patient's part not to discuss negative feelings toward the therapist. This is particularly important with patients who tend to be compliant because to push for something that the patient is not ready to explore simply invites more compliance and can contribute to a new variation of an enactment (Safran & Segal, 1990).

Stage 3: Exploring the patient's construal patterns

This stage involves a collaborative exploration into the patient's construal of events. The focus should remain on the therapeutic interaction *in the moment*. The purpose here is not only to provide the patient with a deeper understanding of the cycles that they get caught in, but to provide them with *the experience* of working their way out of those cycles with another person. To achieve this end, the therapist needs to help the patient figure out what precipitated the rupture. The focus here is not on identifying or correcting cognitive distortions but, rather, on collaboratively coming to a better understanding of the patient's response and what led up to it. For example, if a patient angrily tells a therapist that his intervention was cold and unsympathetic, the therapist might acknowledge the patient's feelings and ask what specifically had felt cold or hostile. Again, it is critical that the therapist maintain a curious and empathic stance at this point and be receptive to any of the patient's negative feelings. Similarly, the therapist needs to be willing to acknowledge his or her own contribution to the rupture. The aim here is to use the rupture as an opportunity for exploration that can help the patient more deeply understand their construal patterns as they have just occurred in the session with the therapist.

Stage 4: Avoidance of vulnerability/aggression

Although the exploration of the patient's experience of the rupture may lead to resolution, the exploration in itself may cause anxiety and trigger avoidance of underlying feelings (Safran & Muran, 2000). In a typical resolution process, the exploration of the rupture proceeds to a certain point and then becomes blocked by a patient's coping strategies that function to avoid the emotions associated with the rupture experience. For example, the patient who believes that expressions of vulnerability and need will result in abandonment will have difficulty expressing such feelings. A therapist's use of exploration and sustained empathy for the patient might be the most useful interventions in this context. For example, a patient may ask his therapist to be more helpful but qualify this request by saying: "It's not a big deal." The therapist might respond: "I'm aware of you qualifying your request. Any sense of what makes it difficult to ask without qualifying?"

Throughout this discussion, it is very important that the therapist track subtle shifts in the patient's experience as he explores his construal of events. When the therapist realizes that the patient is becoming more angry, the focus needs to shift to the anger arising in the moment. The therapist's words should be phrased in a way that encourages patients to discover their experience in the moment (e.g., "I'm afraid of offending you"), rather than to engage in intellectually distant speculation (e.g., "It relates to my fear of authority figures"). At this point, it is critical that the therapist maintain an empathic stance and avoid challenging the accuracy of the patient's fears since this will only make it more difficult for him or her to articulate them more fully.

Typically, patients will alternate between expressing and avoiding their feelings, with the exploration of both these experiences helping them to better understand, and more comfortably articulate, a wider range of feeling states.

Step 5: Expressing the underlying wish or need (self-assertion)

In this stage, the patient comes to access and *express underlying needs or wishes* to the therapist. The preliminary expression of these feelings continues to be associated with beliefs that they are unacceptable or that needs will go unmet and, thus, a patient's initial expressions of a wish or need may be expressed in a qualified or indirect way. As with any other stage in the process, the danger here is that if the therapist is not aware of his or her own feelings and responses, the complementary responses pulled for by this qualified presentation can perpetuate a new enactment of the cycle. If the therapist can continue to be aware of her own reactions then continued work can lead to the examination of the underlying wish or need.

As the exploration continues with the therapist empathically validating the patient's emotional responses, the patient can gradually become more comfortable expressing underlying feelings and needs directly. Patients can begin to articulate a wider range of emotions and needs without feeling that this endangers interpersonal relatedness. They will also begin to understand that all of their wants and needs cannot be met and that any consequent disappointment can be tolerated and accepted. At this stage, patients may be able to express disappointment that therapy cannot solve all of their problems or sadness at a recent loss without feeling that the therapist must make these feelings go away.

Summary: Some basic principles of therapeutic metacommunciation

Metacommunication is an attempt to disembed from the relational configuration by collaboratively exploring and communicating about the current interaction between therapist and patient. It is a type of mindfulness in action. We have elaborated in greater detail on the various principles that therapists can follow in other sources (Safran, 1998, 2002; Safran & Muran, 2000; Safran & Segal, 1990). In this chapter, we have tried to show how some of these ideas can be used to work with ruptures in a CBT treatment. We have focused especially on the following.

1   *Awareness:* The therapist should be open to exploring and acknowledging his or her own subjective feelings and experience as well as those of the patient.
2   *A collaborative focus:* We advocate a collaborative approach whereby the therapist accepts responsibility for his or her own contribution to the relationship and the enactment occurring. Establishing a sense of "we-ness" frames the impasse as a shared experience that can be worked on together.
3   *A present, specific focus:* The focus should constantly be on the here-and-now of the therapeutic relationship, with special attention given to moment-to-moment shifts.
4   *An emphasis on understanding and awareness rather than change:* The goal of the exploration is to understand the patient's construal of events and to accept and validate the patient's emotional responses and needs. It is the experience of having the therapist react in a different way than had been expected, while simultaneously recognizing and validating the patient's experience, that leads to growth.

Conclusion

Our approach to working with ruptures conceptualizes the therapeutic alliance as an ideal arena for facilitating change. When the alliance process breaks down, the ability to understand and work through the rupture can provide therapists with a unique opportunity to explore and help the patient to expand the range of their cognitive-affective and interpersonal patterns by closely tracking the negotiation process as well as their own subjective reactions. Here we summarize some of the principles most central to our model.

1 The alliance should be understood as an ongoing negotiation process that is constantly in flux.
2 Ruptures in the alliance need to be viewed as windows into the patient's interpersonal belief system which provide opportunities for growth.
3 Therapists need to develop an awareness of their own subjective feelings and use their responses to assess what is happening with the patient.
4 Therapists need to be able to explore the patient's construal of events and be willing to take responsibility for their contribution to rupture moments.
5 Therapists need to be aware that any intervention takes on a specific meaning depending on the interpersonal context and they need to be willing to explore that meaning in context with their patients.
6 Therapists' ability to maintain an ongoing awareness of their own subjective experiences from moment to moment can be strengthened by the cultivation of a more mindful and *accepting* stance which can be further developed in supervision, and via formal mindfulness practice.

References

Beck, J.S. (1995). *Cognitive therapy: Basics and beyond.* New York: Guilford Press.
Beck, J.S., Rush, J., Shaw, B. & Emery, G. (1979). *Cognitive therapy of depression.* New York: Guilford Press.
Binder, J.L. & Strupp, H.H. (1997). "Negative process:" A recurrently discovered and underestimated facet of therapeutic process and outcome in the individual psychotherapy of adults. *Clinical Psychology: Science and Practice*, 4, 121–139.
Bordin, E.S. (1979). The generalizability of the psychoanalytic concept of the working alliance. *Psychotherapy: Theory, Research and Practice*, 16, 252–260.
Bordin, E.S. (1994). Theory and research on the therapeutic alliance: New directions. In A.O. Horvath & L.S. Greenberg (eds), *The working alliance: Theory, research and practice* (pp. 13–37). New York: John Wiley & Sons.
Bowlby, E. (1969). *Attachment and loss: Vol. 1. Attachment.* New York: Basic Books.

Bowlby, E. (1973). *Attachment and loss: Vol. 2. Separation, anxiety and anger*. New York: Basic Books.

Bowlby, E. (1980). *Attachment and loss: Vol. 3. Loss: Sadness and depression*. New York: Basic Books.

Freud, S. (1937/1964). Analysis terminal and interminable. In *Standard edition* (Vol. 23, pp. 209–253). London: Hogarth Press.

Freud, S. (1940/1964). An outline of psycho-analysis. In *Standard edition* (Vol. 23, pp. 139–207). London: Hogarth Press.

Gilbert, P. (2000). *Counselling for depression* (2nd edition). London: Sage.

Henry, W.P. & Strupp, H.H. (1994). The therapeutic alliance as interpersonal process. In A.O. Horvath & L.S. Greenberg (eds), *The working alliance: Theory, research, and practice* (pp. 51–84). New York: Wiley.

Henry, W.P., Strupp, H.H., Butler, S.F., Schacht, T.E. & Binder, J.L. (1993). Effects of training in time-limited psychotherapy: Changes in therapist behavior. *Journal of Consulting and Clinical Psychology*, 61, 434–440.

Horney, K. (1950). *Neurosis and human growth: The struggle towards self-realization*. New York: Norcross.

Horvath, A.O. (1995). The therapeutic relationship: From transference to alliance. *In Session: Psychotherapy in Practice*, 1, 7–18.

Horvath, A.O. & Symonds, B.D. (1991). Relation between working alliance and outcome in psychotherapy: A meta-analysis. *Journal of Counseling Psychology*, 38, 139–149.

Kiesler, D.J. (1996). *Contemporary interpersonal theory and research*. New York: Wiley.

Leahy, R. (1993). *Overcoming resistance in cognitive therapy*. New York: Guilford.

Liotti, G. (1987). The resistance to change of cognitive structures: A counter-proposal to psychoanalytic metapsychology. *Journal of Cognitive Psychotherapy*, 2, 87–104.

Martin, D., Garske, J. & Davis, K. (2000). Relation of the therapeutic alliance with outcome and other variables: A meta-analytic review. *Journal of Consulting and Clinical Psychology*, 68(3), 438–450.

Rhodes, R.H., Hill, C.E., Thompson, B.J. & Elliot, R. (1994). Client retrospective recall of resolved and unresolved misunderstanding events. *Journal of Counseling Psychology*, 41(4), 473–483.

Safran, J.D. (1984a). Assessing the cognitive–interpersonal cycle. *Cognitive Therapy and Research*, 8, 333–348.

Safran, J.D. (1984b). Some implications of Sullivan's interpersonal theory for cognitive therapy. In M.A. Reda & M.J. Mahoney (eds), *Cognitive psycho-therapies: Recent developments in theory, research and practice*. Cambridge, MA: Ballinger.

Safran, J.D. (1993a). Breaches in the therapeutic alliance: An arena for negotiating authentic relatedness. *Psychotherapy*, 30, 11–24.

Safran, J.D. (1993b). The therapeutic alliance as a transtheoretical phenomenon: Definitional and conceptual issues. *Journal of Psychotherapy Integration*, 3, 33–49.

Safran, J.D. (1998). *Widening the scope of cognitive therapy*. Northvale, NJ: Aronson.

Safran, J.D. (1999). Faith, despair, will, and the paradox of acceptance. *Contemporary Psychoanalysis*, 35, 5–24.

Safran, J.D. (2002). Brief relational psychoanalytic treatment. *Psychoanalytic Dialogues*, 12, 171–196.

Safran, J.D. (2003). The relational turn, the therapeutic alliance and psychotherapy research: Strange bedfellows or postmodern marriage? *Contemporary Psychoanalysis*, 39, 449–475.

Safran, J.D., Crocker, P., McMain, S. & Murray, P. (1990). Therapeutic alliance rupture as a therapy event for empirical investigation. *Psychotherapy*, 27, 154–165.

Safran, J.D. & Muran, J.C. (1994). Towards a working alliance between research and practice. In P.F. Talley, H.H. Strupp & S.F. Butler (eds), *Psychotherapy research and practice: Bridging the gap* (pp. 206–226). New York: Basic Books.

Safran, J.D. & Muran, J.C. (1996). The resolution of ruptures in the therapeutic alliance. *Journal of Consulting and Clinical Psychology*, 64, 447–458.

Safran, J.D. & Muran, J.C. (1998). *The therapeutic alliance in brief psychotherapy*. Washington, DC: American Psychological Association.

Safran, J.D. & Muran, J.C. (2000). *Negotiating the therapeutic alliance: A relational treatment guide*. New York: Guilford Press.

Safran, J.D. & Muran, J.C. (2006). *Resolving therapeutic impasses*. DVD, Customflix.com.

Safran, J.D., Muran, J.C. & Samstag, L.W. (1994). Resolving therapeutic alliance ruptures: A task-analytic investigation. In A.O. Horvath & L.S. Greenberg (eds), *The working alliance: Theory, research and practice* (pp. 225–255). New York: John Wiley & Sons.

Safran, J.D., Muran, J.C., Samstag, L.W. & Stevens, C. (2002). Repairing alliance ruptures. In J.C. Norcross (ed.), *Psychotherapy relationships that work* (pp. 235–254). New York: Oxford University Press.

Safran, J.D. & Segal, Z.V. (1996). *Interpersonal process in cognitive therapy*. New York: Basic Books; 2nd edition, Northvale, NJ: Aronson.

Schon, D. (1983). *The reflexive practitioner*. New York: Basic Books.

Smith, M.L., Glass, G.V. & Miller, M.I. (1980). *The benefits of psychotherapy*. Baltimore: Johns Hopkins University Press.

Stern, D.B. (1985). *The interpersonal world of the infant*. New York: Norton.

Strupp, H.H. (1993). The Vanderbilt Psychotherapy Studies: Synopsis. *Journal of Consulting and Clinical Psychology*, 61, 431–433.

Sullivan, H.S. (1953). *The interpersonal theory of psychiatry*. New York: Norton.

Suzuki, S. (1970). *Zen mind, beginner's mind*. New York: Weatherhill.

Wachtel, P.L. (1993). *Therapeutic communication: Knowing what to say when*. New York: Guilford Press.

Young, J.E., Klosko, J.S. & Weishaar, M.E. (2003). *Schema therapy: A practitioner's guide*. New York: Guilford Press.

Chapter 6

Evolved minds and compassion in the therapeutic relationship

Paul Gilbert

The therapeutic relationship and working alliance emerge from what patients and therapist bring to the interaction. This co-constructed relationship impacts on outcomes (Freeman & McCloskey, 2003; Norcross, 2002). Part of the therapist's role is to guide and support a patient into, and through, domains of experience that he/she may be fearful of or find distressing, or that he/she has erected a range of (disorder maintaining) safety strategies to cope with. Moreover, the prospect of change may involve risks (e.g., to a relationship), fears of change to a self-identity, fear of loss of control, and for some people, terrors. Indeed, for nearly all patient difficulties the therapist is confronted by the patient's experience of threat (and lack of safeness) in specific domains (Gilbert, 1993). In this context of confronting threats, the therapist can be called on to enact a multitude of roles – as educator, mentor, coach, validator, boundary setter, soother–reassurer, morale-enhancer, inspirer, container, safe base, encourager – as well as being simply a fellow human being to share the painful with. The fact that all of these functions may be crucial for some patients points to a need to reflect on how and why these interpersonal domains exert the power they do; how is it that the mind of one person can have such a powerful impact on the mind of another?

Part of the answer becomes clear when we lift our eyes beyond the therapeutic relationship and contextualise humans in their evolutionary and social contexts. Humans are an exquisitely social species, who from the first moments of conception, and then throughout life, are physiologically influenced and regulated via social relationships. The exact patterns of genes we inherit depend on the choices our parents make with regard to whom they reproduce with and timing of conception. The environment of the womb, for example whether a mother is well fed or stressed, and her hormone levels, impacts on the maturation of the foetus and possibly on modes of inheritance (Harper, 2005). When we are born, social relationships influence the way our brain matures (Gerhardt, 2004; Schore, 1994, 2001; Siegel, 2001), the regulation of stress and immune functions throughout life (Cacioppo, Berston, Sheridan & McClintock, 2000), joy and happiness

(Argyle, 1987), depression and anxiety (Gilbert 1992), our resilience to life stressors (Masten, 2001), self-evaluations (Baldwin & Dandeneau, 2005) and even the way we confront our own death (Aldridge, 2000). Briefly, when we experience the minds of others as loving, caring, forgiving, supportive and friendly (that is to say, compassionate), we are psychologically and physiologically regulated in different ways than when we experience the minds of others as condemning, rejecting, critical and withdrawing (Gilbert 2005a; Porges, 2001; Wang, 2005). It is not just that in the former case we are more likely to experience positive affect, and in the latter case to experience negative affect, but also that compassion from another creates internal conditions for feelings of safeness and soothing, can help deactivate threat and self-protective strategies, and facilitates internal conditions conducive to growth, maturation, change, healing and well-being (Gilbert, 2005a; Wang, 2005).

As we increasingly recognise the power of social relationships as psychophysiological regulators we are able to move away from the idea that we are autonomous, self-centred beings, to a greater appreciation of our social nature *and needs*. So this chapter will contextualise the psychotherapy relationship in an evolutionary context that considers how our minds have evolved to *co-regulate each other*. We will also explore various components of compassion as therapeutic agents in their own right, and as processes that help patients engage with the various tasks of cognitive behavioural interventions.

The evolved mind

The basic infrastructures of our brains have emerged from millions of years of evolution. Over this time they have acquired capacities for a varied array of motivations, emotions and passions. More recently our hominid evolution has equipped us with abilities for language, symbolic reasoning and meta-cognitions – capabilities that can influence, dampen or inflame more basic affect systems (Wells, 2000). Cognitive therapists have been well aware that many of our problematic emotions and motives, especially those that lead to the seeking of psychotherapy, are routed in evolved systems and strategies (Beck, 1987, 1996, 1999). Gilbert (1984, 1989, 1992, 2005a, 2005b) focused on innate systems underpinning attachment, cooperation, and dispositions to form social ranks and hierarchies. In fact, various therapists have focused on evolved attachment and other interpersonal processes as central to the psychotherapy process (Holmes, 2001; Knox, 2003). In cognitive therapy Guidano & Liotti (1983) offered the first major integration of attachment theory into cognitive therapy, and Safran (1998) extended the interpersonal dimension in cognitive therapy following traditions from Cooley, Mead and Sullivan. More recently new approaches emphasise that our minds are organised *around multiple and parallel processing systems*, e.g., forms of attention, memory and emotions (Harvey, Watkins, Mansell & Shafran, 2004) that do not always work well together (Dalgleish, 2004). For example, our threat-systems, that evolved millions of years ago, can easily override more recently evolved competencies for rational thoughts; we can have powerful distressing intrusions at times when we wish to concentrate; we have memory lapses when we need to remember; our sensory and verbal memories may not cohere; we can experience negative emotional shifts when we want to be happy. There is much in evolutionary psychology that has focused on the fact that our minds are rather full of conflicting motives, thoughts and processing systems (Gilbert, 1989, 2000; MacLean, 1985).

Although concepts of schemas, core beliefs and assumptions are central to cognitive models, they can be problematic if they become tautological (Hammen, 1992) or if therapists are overly reliant on (only) consciously accessible thoughts (Baldwin, 2005; Hassin, Uleman & Bargh, 2005). We know, for example, that people's verbal reports of reasons for their feelings and values may not be accurate (Haidt, 2001; Hassin *et al.*, 2005). There is also evidence that we can process self-relevant and self-esteem information in non-conscious (implicit) and conscious (explicit) ways, and that these may not be congruent (Jordan, Spencer, Zanna, Hoshino-Browne & Correll, 2003). New work, using implicit self-esteem measures, suggests that depressed people may have *positive* implicit self-esteem (Raedt, Schacht, Franck & Houwer, 2006). Gilbert (1984, 2005a; Gilbert & Irons, 2005) suggested that some forms of low self-esteem and self-blame can reflect implicit, defensive strategies in the face of more powerful others where externalisation of blame is dangerous. The focus in therapy then may be on the fear of others and the patient's own (avoided) retaliatory (aggressive) strategies. The therapeutic relationship will obviously differ according to whether therapists consider self-blame as a cognitive distortion or as a (functional) safety strategy.

Increasingly, cognitive therapists are developing therapies that target sub-components of our processing systems, such as types of memory, attention and rumination (Dalgleish, 2004; Harvey *et al.*, 2004; Lee, 2005). Evolution-focused psychologists explore our innate relationship-building systems such as a kin-attachment, mating, or alliance formation (Buss, 2003), while others are beginning to explore the processing components (or modules) that enable complex social behaviours such as empathy (Decety & Jackson, 2004). The therapeutic relationship is clearly a form of relationship that involves helping and altruism and thus can be considered in the light of what we know about (innate and learned aspects of) relationship building. Bailey (2002), for example, suggests that in order to feel safe some patients will try to build certain types of kinship relationship with their therapist. It is the accessing of these processing systems that enables the patient to be oriented to new learning within the relationship. My own efforts to link psychotherapeutic processes with evolved psychological systems, especially those associated with social behaviour, considers the evolved nature of four domains of functioning (Gilbert, 1984, 1989, 1993, 1995, 2005a):

1   basic threat and safeness processing
2   role-seeking and role-forming
3   symbolic and meta-cognitive abilities
4   identity-forming that depends on abilities for certain types of self awareness, and that gives rise to a sense of self "who is", "who can", and "who wants to be".

Our "sense of self" emerges from the choreographies of the other aspects of our minds and is shaped via social relationships in which the self is embedded. Since each of these four domains impacts on the emergence of the therapeutic relationship, we can briefly explore them.

Threat and safeness

All living things must be able to make decisions in their domain of existence that pertain to whether stimuli impinging on them are threats or are safe (Gilbert, 1989; Porges, 2001). Very primitive defences might be to move away, take flight and avoid. Defences become more complex with evolution (Marks, 1987). Hence, over many millions of years there have evolved a range of specific behaviours (fight, flight, submission, camouflage, help-seeking), specific emotion-potentials (anger, anxiety, and disgust), and attentional–cognitive "better safe than sorry" processing heuristics for detecting and evaluating threats (Gilbert, 1993, 1998a, 2001; Marks, 1987). The defensive strategies are routed in earlier evolved brain structures (LeDoux, 1998), extended into the peripheral and autonomic nervous system (Porges, 2001), and can be triggered fast and directly by unconditioned stimuli, and by conditioned stimuli. As a result of learning, interacting with genetic sensitivity, these defensive processes can become easily triggered and frequent, with accentuated intensity and duration of negative emotional states (Gilbert, 2001; Rosen & Schulkin, 1998).

A key distinction here is between safety-seeking and safeness (Gilbert, 1989, 2005a). *Safety-seeking* pertains to defensive behaviours such as fight, flight, avoidance, immobilisation, submission and returns to a "safe base" that are triggered by specific stimuli or events. Planned safety behaviours may be carrying tranquillisers in one's pocket or deliberate avoidance, and are associated with beliefs of the value of safety behaviours (Salkovskis, 1996). These directly regulate activity in threat systems in that if they are successfully enacted a person may feel relatively safe. However, any block to the safety strategies can reactivate the threat system. In contrast, when desensitised to fear/threat certain stimuli no longer trigger the same threat response because the person is processing *the threat itself* in a different way. Thus the network of safety strategies, such as remaining vigilant to the possible threat, and being ready with defensive safety behaviours, is deactivated. In this context one can feel relatively safe even in the presence of (what were) threatening stimuli. One may even come to enjoy them (e.g., an agoraphobic may come to enjoy going out). In childhood the transition from (natural) fear and safety behaviours to those of feeling "safe with", and exploration and engaging, depend crucially on parental soothing and social referencing (Schore, 1994). The therapeutic relationship may play a similar key role in how a patient makes the journey from threat evaluations and safety behaviours to explorations, coping and coming to feel "safe with" (Gilbert, 1989; Holmes, 2001).

Leahy (2001, 2005) has pointed out that people can develop a range of negative threat reactions to their own internal stimuli of emotions/motives/desires and fantasies – that is, these internal experiences constitute threats. These threats are linked to beliefs that certain emotions/desires/fantasies might be overwhelming, confusing, that they would be shamed by others, and by beliefs in thought–action fusion (if I think or feel it, it is as bad as doing it). Safety behaviours here can involve trying not to think about certain things, avoidance of situations that elicit certain feelings, hiding feelings from others, denial or dissociation. Leahy makes it clear that the therapist's role here involves containment and psycho-education on the complexities of our evolved and socially shaped emotional lives; that we can have multiple and conflicting feelings/desires (because of parallel processing systems) to the same event (for example, we can be angry with someone we love), normalising (i.e., "it is understandable that you feel threatened by this because . . ."), exposure and validation. Therapist empathy and warmth is crucial here so as not to activate shame ("I am stupid to think like this; my therapist thinks I am immature with my emotions"). This requires the therapist to be empathically attuned with the patient, have an appropriate understanding of emotions and feared material (for example, a patient can have sadistic revenge fantasies that are feared), and feel safe enough with their own emotions and "shadow material" to act as a *soothing* agent. The therapist helps patients (re)code their inner world as safe to the extent that, while some emotions/fantasies are unpleasant or strange, they are normal to our humanity, and are manageable once we accept them, no longer fight to suppress or deny them, or label ourselves negatively as a consequence of having them. They can in fact be important sources of information that need to be addressed (Greenberg, Chapter 3, this volume). Carl Jung believed that "shadow material" could be a source of vitality and creativity if approached in certain ways and integrated in the mind.

We can look at these difficulties in another way based on conditioning. For some patients, therapists will be aware that some emotions/desires are under conditioned inhibitory control (Ferster, 1973; Gilbert, 1992). Ferster (1973) pointed out that if a child's expression of anger or affection-seeking is constantly punished this will generate anxiety and fear of punishment. Thus the inner stimuli/feelings of anger or affection-seeking will be associated with fear, until the arousal of anger or affection-seeking automatically elicits a conditioned fear/anxiety response. In this context the child may gradually become unaware of feelings of anger or affection-seeking, in the context where these could be useful. Instead they are only aware of the secondary conditioned anxiety to stimuli, and not anger feelings or affection-seeking. This can have serious consequences for the child's abilities to recognise certain emotions and mature them in helpful ways. Consider Jane, who saw her mother as powerful, critical but also "always right/clever". Jane idealised her and relied on her for help. Jane felt that she herself was physically unattractive. Jane was able to recall how her mother would often tell that she had an awkward body, and that "everything you wear looks like a rag on you". Although these "put downs" were clearly a source of shame (and she internalised these judgements), Jane was at first unaware and then very fearful of acknowledging anger to her mother for shaming her, or that her mother could be wrong. To begin to consider these alternative possibilities can be intensely threatening, especially if "the other" is more powerful and can inflict harm on us for rebellion or defiance (Gilbert & Irons, 2005). Her healing of shame emerged with seeing her mother as *not* always right, acknowledging and processing her anger at her mother, fear of the mother's counter-attack or punishment (like a dominant on a subordinate), letting go of her dependency, and learning to cope with the changed dynamic of the daughter–mother bond. Healing shame often requires changes in our inner representation of others, processing feared and conditioned emotions, revisiting and working with shame–trauma memories, reducing submissive defences and becoming more able to defend/maintain a sense of self from external and internal (memory-linked) "attacks". These may be key to alterations in *self*-evaluations.

Safeness

Some therapists work with threats via processes of desensitisation, re-evaluation and negative arousal reduction. Compassionate mind work, however, suggests another important process. Over 30 years ago Bowlby (1969, 1973; Cassidy & Shaver, 1999) noted that a crucial element of parental care is that it provides a *safe base* for the infant. Not only does access to a parent offer protection, but parent–child interactions can soothe and calm an infant. For an infant to be calmed and feel secure, via interactions with others, implies the evolution of mental mechanisms that are sensitive and responsive to such care-providing behaviours (MacLean, 1985). Hence, what has evolved in mammals, and especially humans, is a

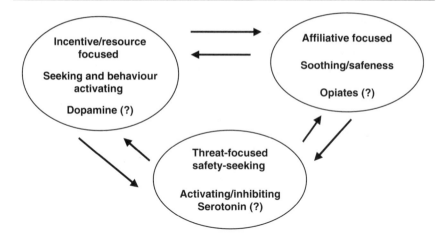

Figure 6.1 Types of affect-regulating system (from Gilbert, 2005a).

social safeness system that is specifically attuned to certain social cues (e.g., touch, voice tone, facial expressions, access to care) from others (Gilbert, 1989, 1993, 2005a). There is now evidence that these signals impact on various and different aspects of mammalian physiological systems (Hofer, 1994). Such cues are not just signals of an absence of threat. We now know that the way the nervous system has evolved is hierarchical and the social safeness system, or what Porges (2001) calls a social engagement system, actually inhibits activity in threat systems, and deactivated fight/flight responses. Moreover, new research has shown that social safeness, which comes through certain types of relationships, is linked to a specific type of positive affect system.

This can be clarified by noting the growing evidence that, in addition to a range of threat/stress processing systems, there are at least *two different types of positive affect* systems, mediated by different physiological systems. Depue & Morrone-Strupinsky (2005) distinguish the appetitive/seeking aspects of motivation, related to dopaminergic systems, and consumatory contentment and soothing aspects related to oxytocin and opiate activity. Different drugs can affect these systems, with (for example) amphetamines tending to increase positive affect associated with drive, but opiate drugs producing a more calm, non-striving and "contented/laid-back" form of positive affect. By way of a simplification we can depict three types of affect-related system as shown in Figure 6.1.

Depue & Morrone-Strupinsky (2005) link the two positive affect systems to types of social behaviour. They distinguish affiliation from agency and sociability. Agency and sociability are linked to control, achievement-seeking, social dominance and the (threat focused) avoidance of rejection and isolation. Affiliation and affiliative interactions, however, are linked to feelings of connectedness to others, and have a more calming effect on participants. They can alter pain thresholds, the immune and digestive systems, and they operate via an oxytocin–opiate system. A number of researchers suggest that the beneficial effects of affiliation are mediated via oxytocin (Carter, 1998; Depue & Morrone-Strupinsky, 2005; Uväns-Morberg, 1998). Thus, of special importance for psychotherapy is the safeness-affiliative positive affect system that appears to be linked to a pattern of neuro-hormones (e.g., oxytocin and endorphins) that mediates *affiliative and affectionate* behaviour and provides a neural basis for soothing, and feeling soothed and safe (Carter, 1998; Depue & Morrone-Strupinsky 2005; Uväns-Morberg, 1998; Wang, 2005). The powerful role of oxytocin in social behaviour and stress regulation evolved in part as the physiological substrate for attachment (Carter, 1998; Uväns-Morberg, 1998). Recent research has shown that oxytocin and social support interact, and both have inhibiting effects on the stress/threat system as measured by cortisol, especially in evaluative and stressful situations (Heinrichs, Baumgartner, Kirschbaum & Ehlert, 2003). So experiences of safeness are not simply via the absence of threat but are *conferred* and stimulated by others. Moreover, these systems actively inhibit threat based systems and open up new cognitive and emotional processing options that can be incorporated into schemas of self and other (Porges, 2001). New ongoing work in our department suggests that feeling safe and content may differ from feeling relaxed–calm.

For the young child the specific unconditioned signals/stimuli that stimulate the safeness, soothing system include: the care-giving signals of touching, stroking, and holding (Field, 2000), voice tone, the "musicality" of the way a mother speaks to her child, facial expressions, feeding and mutually rewarding interchanges that form the basis for the emergence of an attachment *bond* (Trevarthen & Aitken, 2001). Depressed mothers who may not directly threaten their infants can nevertheless have detrimental effects on their infant's maturation because of the relative *absence* of (positive) forms of communication such as eye gaze, smiling, positive facial expressions, holding, talking to and stroking that stimulate positive affects in the infant, and create experiences of safeness and soothing and exploration/engagement with the world (Murray & Cooper, 1997). Given the power of non-verbal signals, it is clear why the non-verbal behaviour of the therapist may be important in how safe a patient feels with their therapist. This is especially important as we now know that we monitor the non-verbal behaviour of others both consciously and non-consciously (Decety & Jackson, 2004).

Distinguishing safeness from threat systems is thus very important for psychotherapy because it implies that the warmth a patient may feel emanating from the therapist could stimulate the safeness–oxytocin–opiate system that regulates cortisol and stress experiences (Heinrichs *et al.*, 2003).

Under the influence of the safeness–oxytocin–opiate system (which probably also involves the frontal cortex (Schore, 1994, 2001)), stressors may be recoded as "safe". If this is so then we are not simply lowering threat tone to a stressor (e.g., by repeated exposure) but also attempting to increase activity in the safeness systems. This has clear conditioning implications, especially with working on threatening imagery. For example, it is possible to stimulate compassionate images when having to confront threatening images/memories (Lee, 2005).

Interaction between safeness and threat

There is now general agreement that our threat systems are set up to be oriented to "better safe than sorry", assume the worst and engage in protective actions (Baumeister, Bratslavsky, Finkenauer & Vohs, 2001; Gilbert, 1989, 1998a). What is required to regulate them is (among other things) development of the frontal and prefrontal cortex (Schore, 1994, 2001). These areas modulate the excitations in the threat systems and are important for coding stimuli as safe. The maturation of these areas is highly influenced by early care and empathic and affectionate interactions (Gerhardt, 2004). Abusive and neglectful parenting has a detrimental impact on the frontal cortex and can over-stimulate the threat system (Perry, Pollard, Blakley, Baker & Vigilante 1995; Rothschild, 2000; Teicher, 2002). These kinds of insights are important because they help us understand that some of what we are doing as psychotherapists is activating and deactivating key physiological systems (Cozolino, 2002; Lee, 2005; Schwarts & Begley, 2002). They are also important because many of the key social competencies that make us a highly sociable being, sensitive to the minds of others and empathic, depend on appropriate maturation and functioning of various structures of the frontal cortex (Decety & Jackson, 2004; Schore, 1994, 2001)

The emergence of the social self

The human mind has evolved a range of complex competencies to be emotionally regulated, cognitively oriented and perceptive to the minds of others. These competencies include abilities to emotionally resonate with, and simulate, the feelings of others, intersubjectivity, theory of mind, and perspective taking (Decety & Jackson, 2004). All these competencies play key roles in the therapeutic relationship.

Emotional resonance

A key component of empathy is to be able to represent the feelings of others in oneself (Decety & Jackson, 2004). Recent research has shown that we can understand the feelings of others because their emotion cues stimulate similar patterns of neuronal firing in ourselves – as if we were experiencing the emotion. One way this occurs has become clear with the discovery of mirror neurons (Borenstein & Ruppin 2005; Brass & Heyes, 2005; Decety & Jackson, 2004). Mirror neurons are neurons that fire when we observe emotional expressions or actions by others. For example, when we watch things happening to others, such as watching a sad or exciting film, we can feel sad or excited ourselves. The anterior insula is an important area of the brain for processing disgust. Wicker, Keysers, Plailly, Royet, Gallese & Rizzolatti (2003) found that observing others experiencing disgust (smelling noxious odours) stimulated the anterior insula in observers. Wicker *et al.* (2003) and Decety & Chaminade (2003) suggest that this empathic resonance (which mirror neurons facilitate) enables us to understand others by (automatically) simulating internal models of feelings and actions that others are feeling or doing. Based on these new findings of mirror neurons, Preston & de Waal (2002) present the *perception action-model* of empathic learning with a review of neurophysiological data that shows that signals expressed by one person can directly stimulate corresponding systems in recipients. Presumably empathic resonance can go both ways in therapy. It is the automatic simulation of affect in the mind of a therapist that enables the therapist to tune into and understand the feelings of his/her patients. Equally a patient's attention to the emotion displays, expressions and voice tones of the therapist can influence the internal simulations of the patient.

Intersubjectivity

This direct capacity for mirroring affect states in others forms the basis for what has been called intersubjectivity. This forms the earliest basis for social communication (Trevarthen & Aitken, 2001). From the first days of life the mental state and motives of a mother (what is going on in her mind) are translated into a range of behaviours such as how she talks/sings; looks at, strokes and holds her infant; stimulates positive affect of affection/joy; and her ability to empathically reflect and resonate with her infant's feelings and mental states. The infant is innately responsive to these communications (Trevarthen & Aitken, 2001). A mother's smile may induce the motor programs for smiling in her infant (Decety & Chaminade, 2003). The process by which the mind of the mother is able to influence the mind (and physiological state) of the infant, through a process of empathic resonance, is called "intersubjectivity" (Trevarthen & Aitken, 2001) – that is, intersubjectivity is related to the moment-by-moment co-regulation of participants as they experience the feelings of others directed at them and emerging from the interaction (Gilbert, 2005a; Stern, 2004). These co-regulating "dances" of mother and infant have important effects on the infant's mind/brain, helping to choreograph the infant's brain maturation as it forms new neuronal connections at a rate of many thousand a day (Gerhardt, 2004; Schore, 1994; Siegel, 2001). Later, the way others, as socialising agents (especially the primary carer), understand and empathise with the child's emotions and behaviours has major impacts on the child's ability to understand and regulate their own emotions, behaviours and personal characteristics. In essence emotions can be coded as safe and manageable (the child has experienced soothing when distressed) or threatening (the child has experienced hostility or withdrawal of love when distressed) (see Ferster (1973) and Gilbert (1992) for a conditioning view). Over time these experiences form the basis for self-processing and self-defining systems (Leahy, 2005; Siegel, 2001). The key point is that social relationships regulate how (internal and external) stimuli are processed by a child and whether they become coded as manageable/safe (coded into the safeness systems) or as threats requiring safety strategies. Clearly, these issues are important in the therapeutic relationship especially for people who, as a result of abuse, may suffer difficulties with their affect regulation systems.

Social cognition

With maturation comes a host of evolved cognitive competencies which are specifically focused on understanding the mind of others and our relation to other minds. These include: theory of mind (Byrne, 1995; Suddendorf & Whitten, 2001); symbolic self–other representations (Sedikides & Skowronski, 1997); mentalisation (Bateman & Fonagy, 2004); metacognition (Bjorklund, 1997; Wells, 2000) and perspective taking (see Decety & Jackson (2004) for a review). These abilities play a crucial role in social interactions and self-regulation (Suddendorf & Whitten, 2001). With theory of mind abilities one can think about the mind of someone else; that is, we understand that minds give rise to agents with intentions, desires and knowledge. Thus we can think about what motivates *their* behaviour, what they might value, what they know and what they don't know, whom they may like and why, and we can *think* how to manipulate them to like us or be wary of us. Whiten (1999) argues that: "Reading others' minds makes minds deeply social in that those minds *interpenetrate* each other" (p. 177; emphasis in original).

If theory of mind relates to how we reason and think about the mental states of others, then clearly attributions are important for this ability. Holmes (2005) notes, for example, that some cognitive techniques of reattribution training may have a direct impact on theory of mind abilities. However, the way we make attributions when interacting with sentient beings is different from how we reason when interacting with non-sentient things. Not only can we attribute motives and intentions to sentient beings but we can also derive beliefs about how they judge and think about us. Suppose someone is angry with us. If we just respond to the external behaviour then we might feel attacked and attack back. However, with theory of mind we might think they are attacking us because they feel threatened or are depressed – we go beyond external appearances and may change our behaviour accordingly. The ability to think about and reflect on what is going on in the mind of the other is key to therapy, of course. Lacking this ability to "mentalise" other people's states of mind may be part of the borderline problem (Bateman & Fonagy, 2004) and may inhibit compassion (Gilbert, 2005a).

However, how we use theory of mind (and how we reason about other people's mental states and behaviours) can be influenced by our own mental state. Holmes (2005) notes that when we feel stressed or threatened our responses can be more automatic and defensive to the threat rather than reflective on the mind of the other. That is to say, when we are stressed we tend to revert to threat processing and self-defence. One implication of this is that the ability to develop complex reasoning about other people's minds and not to be automatically on the defensive requires some modicum of feeling safe. Individuals who have had a secure attachment may find theory of mind easier than those who come from abusive backgrounds. Hence, once again we see the importance of threat and safeness interacting with other evolved competencies.

Another implication of this is that if therapists are working with threatening patients (for example, they may feel out of their depth, overwhelmed, burnt out or pressurised to get a quick result) or if (say) they are worried about external persecution if a patient kills themselves or makes sexual advances, this will impact on their therapeutic stance and abilities. Many implications flow from this, including the therapist having good insight into his or her own areas of threat. In addition therapists will need support from others who can convey safeness – a point well understood in dialectical behavior therapy's (Linehan, 1993) recommendation that therapists need to work in supportive teams when working with complex cases. Thus the issue of threat and safeness impacts on our capacities to use our social cognitive competencies therapeutically. Furthermore, therapeutic relationships should not be decontextualised from the wider social arenas in which therapists operate.

The attracting/attractive self

Social threats either from patients or from external agencies who may judge our work, or our own negative self-evaluations of our abilities, are central to therapeutic safeness. In fact this is linked to a wider issue of why we have evolved some of these complex abilities, to read and be so in tune with the feelings of others. One reason is that we have evolved to be highly dependent on others for our survival and maturation. Over our evolution, unless one could court good relationships and reputations with others, survival, maturation and reproduction would be compromised. In fact there is a long history to the idea that humans are highly motivated to try to create positive feelings and impressions in the eyes of others (Buss, 2003; Gilbert, 1992, 1998b). We want to be cared for by our parents, desired by our lovers, liked by our friends, valued by our bosses and accepted in our groups. So humans have evolved social motivation systems to be valued and wanted by others with mental mechanisms for tracking and estimating the thoughts and feelings that we create in the mind of others, technically called *social attention holding power* (Gilbert, 1989, 1997, 2003). Experiencing our impact on the mind of the other as positive makes the world *safe* and increases the chances that we will be able to influence others in our favour. In contrast, experiencing the mind of the other as having hostile or contemptuous feelings and thoughts about us makes the world threatening and sets in motion various defensive strategies – with shame or humiliation being the most common (Gilbert, 1998b). The motive to create positive affects and thoughts in the mind of the other begins from the first days of life (Trevarthen & Aitken, 2001) and textures many subsequent relationships. Shame then is a major social threat because it is an indication that others are potentially rejecting or hostile (Gilbert, 2003).

Meta-representations

Emotional resonance is linked to the way emotion systems (especially those in the limbic system) are stimulated in interactions. The evolution of the frontal cortex in humans, however, has been key to many of our social cognitive competencies such as theory of mind and other aspects of empathy (Decety & Jackson, 2004). Psychopaths, for example, may have intact theory of mind abilities but lack empathic resonance due to disturbance in the limbic system – they are not emotionally affected by others' distress (Decety & Jackson, 2004). Various aspects of the frontal cortical structures also support abilities to meta-represent self as an object for introspection (Wells, 2000). *Symbolic* self-awareness comes with language and the ability to symbolise "the self", to "imagine" the self as an object and to judge and give value to the self; to have self-esteem, to think about the meaning of one's appearance to others and other implications (Sedikides & Skowronski, 1997). This gives rise to a range of self-conscious emotions such as pride, shame and guilt. Self-identities and self-presentations emerge from both emotional experiences of how others treat the self in certain roles, and our introspective reasoning and thinking about such experiences.

Thus consider early experiences of how a child experiences *the emotions of others* in an interaction and how these become the foundations for self-beliefs. A positive belief of, "I am a lovable competent person" can be shorthand for, "in my memory systems are many emotionally textured experiences of *having elicited positive emotions in others* and being treated in a loving way; therefore I am lovable". Suppose parents often express anger to a child. This child may develop beliefs that others do not see her positively, which is shorthand for, "in my memory systems are emotionally textured experiences of *having elicited anger in others* and being treated as inadequate – therefore I am vulnerable". Consider the child who is sexually abused. This can become, "in my memory systems are emotionally textured experiences of fear and disgust – therefore I am, disgusting and bad". Tomkins (1987) argued that shame (and other self-conscious emotions) are laid down in memory as scenes and fragments of images of *self in relationships*. These encoded scenes can then become "mini coordinators" of attention, thinking, feeling and behaviour.

The importance of the internalised safe and soothing other

The importance and power of "how we experience and exist in the mind of the other" has been shown in a number of studies. Both conscious and non-conscious information processing can follow an "if–then" rule based on appraisals of how we exist in the mind of others (Baldwin & Dandeneau, 2005). For example, a rule can be: *if* others express disapproval *then* respond with withdrawal or shame/submissive defences. Such automatic rules and safety strategies have been explored in a research programme by Baldwin and colleagues (for reviews see Baldwin & Dandeneau, 2005). In one early study students were asked to generate research ideas and then subliminally primed (outside conscious awareness) with either the approving or the disapproving face of the department professor. Those primed with the disapproving face rated their ideas more unfavourably than those primed with the approval face. *Self*-evaluation was non-consciously linked to approval/disapproval from another (see Baldwin & Dandeneau, 2005). Once again we see that the reasons people may give for certain types of feelings are not necessarily accurate (Haidt, 2001), and that there is a possible role for mirror neurons in these evaluations.

Consciously priming people with feelings of being cared for also impacts on shame-related processes. For example, Baldwin & Holmes (1987) found that people who were primed with a highly evaluative relationship, and who then failed at a laboratory task, showed depressive and shame-like responses of blaming themselves for their failure and drawing broad negative conclusions about their personality. Conversely, individuals who were instead primed with a warm, supportive relationship were much less upset by the failure and attributed the negative outcome to situational factors rather than personal shortcomings. People can cope better with failures if they have access to a schema of others as warm and supportive.

Kumashiro & Sedikides (2005) gave students a difficult intellectual test. They were then asked to visualise a close-negative, close-neutral, or close-positive relationship. Those who visualised the close-positive relationship had the highest interest in obtaining feedback on the test even when feedback reflected unfavourably on them. Baldwin and his colleagues (see Baldwin & Dandeneau, 2005 for reviews) have demonstrated that a key variable determining self-evaluative styles in certain contexts is the cognitive accessibility of other-to-self (others as critical or reassuring) and self-to-self (self-critical and self-reassuring) schemas. Attachment theorists have also shown that the way people respond to various interpersonal threats (i.e., the degree of anxiety and anger they may feel) is related to internal working models of attachment security (see Baldwin & Dandeneau, 2005; Mikulincer & Shaver, 2005 for reviews). These studies suggest that the degree to which people are able to access warm and supportive (in contrast to condemning and critical) other-to-self and self-to-self-scripts and memories has a central bearing on emotional and social responses to negative, self-defining events, and abilities to cope with (shame-linked) failures. The implications for psychotherapy are clear from this research.

We can take a conditioning approach to threat and soothing systems in relationship to a sense of self. As noted, soothing is stimulated by natural cues (e.g., voice tone, facial expressions, holding), especially for the infant. If an infant is distressed and the parent soothes and calms the infant using these cues, then this affect system will be linked to that of distress and thus offer internal regulators for distress. Memories of being comforted and helped by others will be laid in emotion memory systems ready for use when distress arises. In contrast, if feelings of distress go unanswered or are punished then an internal distress cue can become a conditioned stimulus for fear or the return of feelings of "there is no one there to help or soothe me". An unanswered question is the degree to which the empathic therapeutic relationship may also be a source for exploring and changing these conditioned responses.

Taking all the above together, we arrive at the view that humans are highly regulated by the minds of others, our abilities to create positive thoughts and feelings in the minds of others, our conscious and non-conscious appraisals of how others see us, and theory of mind. In fact psychotherapy would be a pointless task unless there were ways by which the mind of one person could impact on the mind of another. Although many animals are obviously oriented to social behaviour, and thus co-ordinate their behaviour for various functions (e.g., reproduction), it is only comparatively recently that we have begun to recognise the multiple, complex processes and mechanisms (for example, social motives to create positive affects in others about the self, empathic resonance, theory of mind, mentalising, meta-representations, non-conscious tracking of others' feelings about us) that underlie *human* social behaviour and self-regulation. In the years to come this "science of mind" will have profound implications for psychotherapy, especially with complex cases (Bateman & Fonagy, 2004; Decety & Jackson, 2004).

Role forming: Biosocial goals and social mentalities

There is, of course, far more to human social behaviour than trying to create positive impressions in the minds of others. We do this partly because there are various roles and social tasks to pursue (for example, forming attachments, belonging to groups, mating and caring for offspring). Hence evolution has provided a set of motivating and processing systems, which guide us towards particular *kinds* of role and relationship. These have been referred to as *biosocial goals* (Gilbert, 1989, 1995, 2005a). Humans, like other animals, have to be *motivated* to care for their young, seek out sexual partners, form alliances with other members of the group, avoid being ejected from groups, compete for resources within groups, and so forth.

Social mentalities refer to the information-processing competencies that keep goal-focused behaviours on track (Gilbert 1989, 2005a, 2005b). For example, in the attachment role the young (of many species) need to be able to attend to and process information relevant to the accessibility and availability of the parent (Bowlby, 1969). Threat systems are triggered if information arrives that the parent is (for example) too distant. In a competitive role, however, a different set of information-processing abilities are required, such as social comparison. The same signal, e.g., eye gaze, can have quite different meanings, and automatic effects on threat and safeness systems, according to whether it occurs in the role of love/affection or competition.

As noted elsewhere (Gilbert, 1989) there is no commonly agreed classification of basic social roles, but a brief classification is given in Table 6.1.

The enactment of a social role depends on a number of different psychological processes. For example, there are attentional and motivating systems that direct attention and create interest in different types of stimuli. Thus, for example, care-eliciting and care-giving would not exist unless infants were "interested" in stimuli associated with mother (e.g., face and skin contact), were seeking care, would recognise care when it was available, and would be physiologically responsive to those inputs (Hofer, 1994; Knox, 2003). On the other side of the relationship, care-seeking would be useless unless there were individuals who were motivated to provide care, would have a sense of reward by doing so, and would have various psychological abilities to process the needs of others (Gilbert, 1989, 2005a). This is shown in Table 6.1. Care-giving and care-seeking roles emerge from motivating systems in each participant and information-processing that monitors the exchange of signals and from this constructs self in a specific relationship to another.

For co-operation, individuals must be motivated to be a member of a dyad or group and have a sense of belonging on the basis of similarity, sharing and collaboration. Hence humans are motivated to form alliance-

Table 6.1 Link between biosocial goals (care-eliciting, care-giving, co-operation, rank/status) and social mentalities

	Self as	*Other as*	*Monitoring threat/safeness*
Care-seeking	Needing seeking	Providing alleviating	Availability access
Care-giving	Providing alleviating	Needing seeking	Distress in other empathy
Co-operating	Sharing belonging	Sharing belonging	Similarity cheating
Rank/status	Power comparing	Power comparing	Relative power talents, abilities
Sexual	Attracting attracted	Attracting attracted	Attractiveness

Innate motivational (seeking) systems with range of emotional and cognitive processing systems that link to a "sense of self". Adapted from Gilbert (1989).

type relationships and to have a sense of belonging and connectedness (Baumeister & Leary, 1995; Gilbert, 1992; Kohut, 1977). Of course, to feel accepted means we have to have a sense that we exist in the mind of the other(s) as acceptable, and thus we feel safe in the body of the group. Hence these experiences provide information on social support and mutuality and give us feelings of *safeness* with others (Gilbert, 1989, 2005a). For some patients a sense of belonging and connectedness may not have developed, leaving them feeling different from others – as an outsider, isolated and easily threatened. The focus on common humanity (Neff, 2003a, 2003b), and work on validating (Leahy, 2005) and de-shaming (Gilbert & Irons, 2005) can help some patients gain a sense of connection with (being just like) others. Indeed, this may be one of the key therapeutic aspects of group therapy (Bates, 2005).

Competitive behaviour can be used to enhance one's own standing and position, taking pleasure in success, without necessarily deriving self-evaluative conclusions. However, we can compete to be seen as more likable or desirable than others and thus be chosen for various roles (for example, wanted as a friend or sexual partner). We can feel depressed or anxious when we feel that our competition is going badly; we are not creating sufficiently positive feelings in others about us, and people will not choose in our favour, want to associate with us, or help us (Gilbert, 1992, 2003).

Competition also gives rise to conflicts over resources or interests and individuals will try to defend themselves, advance their own interests, and avoid inferiority and being marginalised, rejected or powerless. Threats to our abilities to exert control in social and other domains can involve more aggressive ways of exerting control. In these contexts we may be less interested in stimulating positive affect in others about the self, and more in stimulating fear or submissive behaviour (Gilbert 1997, 2003). The bully, for example, exerts his/her control by creating wariness in others via aggression or "putting down" others. In psychotherapy, aggression is not an uncommon defence to the experience of threat, and it can be stimulated quickly (because our threat systems are ready to respond to threats) even against people's conscious wishes. What also matters here is the post-event cognitions; while one person may feel guilt and remorse for having hurt somebody (able to switch to a care-focused mentality), the bully can be pleased they have hurt others, for it offers a sense of safety in their abilities to keep control and defend themselves (Gilbert, 2005c).

The activation of a mentality *patterns* motivations, emotions and cognitive processes. Hence, for example, in competitive behaviour, and especially if this is between enemies, the sub-components of the care-giving system, which focuses on distress, concern and helping others, *are turned off*. In care-giving, however, it is the desire to harm others that is turned off and we might feel guilt if we do cause harm. In other words, the activation of a mentality patterns components of our minds, turning on and off different motives, emotions and processing systems. Although this has some similarity to Beck's (1996) concept of modes, it is also different because social mentality theory is based on innate dispositions for *organising* the mind in certain ways (Wang, 2005). This is crucial for psychotherapy because it means that we are not just working with modes or schemas but actually with psychobiological patterns and organising *principles* in the mind.

Another aspect of social mentality theory is that children's abilities to understand themselves in relationship to others, to have feelings of empathy, concern for others, guilt and shame, to develop theory of mind, take an interest in peer relating and sexuality, are emergent through development; that is to say, they are part of our innate predispositions. Importantly, as the innate abilities for thinking about self and other unfold, motivational systems and social mentalities *can blend together* so that thoughts and feelings in one mentality (for example, caring) can come to influence those in another (for example, how one competes with others or treats one's friends). Although sexual motivations are common to humans, one person may treat a sexual partner as an object, there only for their own enjoyment, while another cares for, cherishes and loves their sexual partner. As outlined by Liotti (Chapter 7, this volume) these role-forming processes can emerge within the psychotherapy relationship. The therapist can have an attentive ear to *the kinds of* relationship that are being co-created (and those avoided) via the awareness of the transference–counter-transference interactions. Some roles may be avoided or excessively engaged (for example, becoming dependent on, or competing with or challenging the therapists). How a therapist attends to, understands, supports, feels threatened by or withdraws from these manoeuvres will impact on the co-creation of roles between them and the mentalities activated in each (see Leahy, Chapter 11, this volume; Liotti, Chapter 7, this volume; Katzow & Safran, Chapter 5, this volume). Cognitive therapists recognise that core beliefs are often important windows on these role-regulating systems.

Some implications of role forming

Focusing on these role-forming systems touches on the social aspects of psychopathology and therapy, which have been prominent in psychodynamic writings (Holmes, 2001) and implied rather than specifically stated in cognitive behavioural therapy (though see Safran, 1998). However, contextualising role-forming in evolutionary and social contexts allows us to consider aspects of our therapeutic interactions, such as transference and counter-transference, within basic social processing models (Marcus & Buffington-Vollum, 2005; Miranda & Andersen, Chapter 4, this volume).

Our social evolution has given rise to biosocial goals and mentalities, bringing with them the fact that we *use each other* for advancing certain goals and creating states of mind; our survival and reproduction depend on how we engage with others and how others engage with us. If people do not communicate with us we cannot develop language and modes of communication, which will have a major impact on our brain maturation and thinking abilities; without early care we die; without a sexual partner we cannot reproduce; without friends (at least in the evolutionary past) we would not have survived long. The implication of having evolved to be social animals is that we use others to obtain support and as soothing inputs when we are not able to do this for ourselves. Indeed, studies of the neurophysiological mechanisms underpinning relationships show just how powerful relationships are in regulating our physiological states (Cacioppo *et al.*, 2000). We need others to understand our emotions and develop a coherent sense of self (Bateman & Fonagy, 2004; Schore, 1994). Hence the story so far is that one cannot overstate the importance of the experience of the mind of another, in interaction with our own mind. This interaction is central to how our brain develops, and our abilities to understand and cope with our inner worlds of emotions, motivations, desires and fantasies. The mind of the other is key to the process of organising our inner potentials in becoming "a self".

Compassion-focused therapy and the therapeutic relationships

The above offers some background for a focus on the nature and value of compassion. Compassion is the context for the therapy and self-compassion is one of the key therapeutic tasks for patients who are highly self-critical and shame-prone. Compassion-focused therapy was developed for people who have severe shame and self-attacking problems. These individuals typically come from abusive backgrounds, have disturbed attachment systems, have poorly developed self-soothing abilities and can pick up all sorts of labels, particularly personality disorder. Having worked with people who have these difficulties for some years, what struck me was that they had little ability to be self-soothing, partly because they had few emotional memories of being soothed and validated. Cognitive interventions did not always work for them because although they could learn to do such tasks, they rarely *felt* soothed or reassured by them. It was as if the positive soothing affect system had atrophied. Indeed, as I began to try to develop their self-soothing and "compassion for the self" when things go wrong, it turned out that many were *frightened* of such feelings. A feeling of warmth and care from the therapist was alarming, as it was associated with memories of abuse, or of the parent who could be kind one minute but aggressive and withholding the next. Self-compassion and warmth were seen as a weakness, letting oneself off the hook, not deserved, or dangerous because one was letting one's guard down. Using a conditioning paradigm, I tended to see inner feelings of warmth as associated with affects of anxiety or disgust. The implication is that although we might be able to reduce negative emotions in traditional ways, one should not assume the positive affects will automatically come on line. Moreover, as I have stressed above, the soothing systems evolved as separate systems to regulate threat. Clearly, then, if the soothing systems are not available, this will have a major impact on the *internal organisation* of psychological processes. Yet if well-being is associated with abilities to access warmth, have emotional memories of others as warm, and turn to others for help (Baldwin, 2005; Masten, 2001) and be self-compassionate (Neff, 2003a, 2003b) then these affect systems need to be directly targeted. Thus, compassion-focused therapy was designed to try to stimulate the safeness–oyxtocin–opiate systems (Gilbert, 2000, 2005a). We are in the process of trying to develop studies to explore this.

In this section I am not going to focus on specific interventions that are designed to stimulate self-compassion (see Gilbert & Irons, 2005), but rather will focus on how the therapist can use an understanding of compassion to think about their own styles and forms of therapeutic engagement, and the co-construction of roles between them and their patient. If the arguments I have put forward so far have any value, then it may be in part via experiencing the mind of the therapist as compassionate (especially in nonverbal modes of communication), which can be internalised by the patient, which begins the road to self-compassion and healing.

What is compassion?

Compassion is a complex multi-faceted process and different therapies have slightly different views of it. There are a range of therapeutic models that articulate what are believed to be key healing ingredients in the therapeutic relationship, such as accurate empathy, positive regard, mirroring, and validation, which can form the basis for compassion (Gilbert, 1989; Kirschenbaum & Jourdan, 2005; Norcross, 2002; Gilbert & Leahy, Chapter 1, this volume). Some therapists, however, have specifically focused on compassion as a therapeutic process. For example, McKay & Fanning (1992), who develop a cognitive-based self-help programme for self-esteem, view compassion as involving understanding, acceptance and forgiveness. Neff (2003a, 2003b), from a social psychology and Buddhist tradition, sees *self-focused* compassion as consisting of bipolar constructs related to kindness, common humanity and mindfulness. *Kindness* involves understanding one's difficulties and being kind and warm in the face of failure or setbacks rather than harshly judgemental and self-critical. *Common humanity* involves seeing one's experiences as part of the human condition rather than as personal, isolating and shaming; *mindful acceptance* involves mindful awareness and acceptance of painful thoughts and feelings rather than over-identifying with them. Neff, Kirkpatrick & Rude (in press) have shown that self-compassion is different from self-esteem and is conducive to many indicators of well-being.

My approach to compassion is rooted in social mentality theory (Gilbert, 1989, 2000, 2005a, 2005b). The compassion model I use suggests that compassionate behaviour evolved out of the *care-giving mentality*. As such it utilises and *patterns* a variety of motivational, emotional and cognitive competencies that are care-focused. These are called the *compassion circle*, given in Figure 6.2.

Care and concern for the well-being of the patient

The evolved origins of compassion are to be found in the evolution of altruism and nurturance (Decety & Jackson, 2004; Gilbert, 1989, 2005a). Altruism makes possible a genuine desire to help others, alleviate suffering and engage with others to foster development and change conducive to their well-being. Fogel, Melson & Mistry (1986) define the core element of care–nurturance as: "the provision of guidance, protection and care for the purpose of fostering developmental change congruent with the expected potential for change of the object of nurturance" (p. 55).

They also suggest that nurturance involves awareness of the need to be nurturing, motivation to nurture, expression of nurturing feelings, understanding what is needed to nurture, and an ability to match nurturing with the feedback from the impact on the other of nurturing. Nurturing, then, needs to be skilfully enacted using various competencies that facilitate caring behaviour. Problems with any of these competencies can interfere with compassion in a (therapeutic) relationship. However, when a patient experiences these processes/motives occurring "in the mind of the therapist"

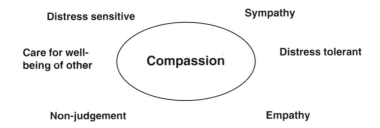

Distress sensitive   Sympathy

Care for well-   **Compassion**   Distress tolerant
being of other

Non-judgement   Empathy

**Create opportunities for growth and change
with warmth**

Figure 6.2 Components of compassion (from Gilbert, 2005a).

– that is, that the mind of the therapist is oriented towards them in a compassionate way – this may activate the social safeness system. As this system begins to come on line this may create opportunities for new learning and conditioning. This is clearly a research question, but it is obviously important for a patient to "feel safe enough" to engage in painful therapeutic work. Keep in mind, though, that for some patients compassion is frightening and associated with negative beliefs (for example, it is weak, it can't be trusted, or people are nice to you so they can exploit you).

Distress sensitivity

This requires micro-skills and refers to how a therapist notices, attends to and processes the patient's verbal and nonverbal behaviour (Gilbert & Leahy, Chapter 1, this volume). Therapists trained in different schools of therapy will attend their "listening ear" in different ways. Being sensitive to what is going on inside the patient requires the therapist to be skilful in engaging with the patient so that they can tell their stories of their distress, as they understand them. Therapists may hear things that are deeply distressing and patients may be upset in the telling. Therapists can have ways of steering patients away from things that are upsetting (Leahy, Chapter 11, this volume), especially if the patient is upset with the therapist (Dalenberg, 2004). If I feel myself becoming defensive or autocratic, chances are I have stopped hearing the patient, and am less sensitive to their distress, and I have slipped into a competitive, defensive or controlling mentality and style. Therapists need to be internally attentive to this possibility (Bennett-Levy & Thwaites, Chapter 12, this volume). Unresolved or feared issues in the therapist can impact on distress sensitivity. The way the therapist is sensitive to distress (for example, with empathic resonance) while engaging with (say) Socratic questioning, formulation, exposure work

Table 6.2 Comparing sympathy and empathy (from Gilbert, 1989)

Sympathy	Empathy
Involves a heightened awareness of the suffering or need of the other. Something to be alleviated. The focus is on the other person's well-being	Involves a heightened awareness of the experiences of the other (not necessarily suffering) as something to be understood
Behaviour is based on relating, acting to alleviate (or mediating responses)	Behaviour is based on knowing, conceptualising, understanding
Sympathy is relatively automatic	Empathy is effortful and depends on imaginal capabilities
In sympathy the self is moved by the other	The self reaches out to the other
The other is the vehicle for understanding and some loss of identity may occur	The self is the vehicle for understanding and never loses its identity

or helping resistant patients can be crucial for some patients (Katzow & Safran, Chapter 5, this volume). Therapy with high shame-prone patients, who may "hide" their true feelings from the therapist, cannot be engaged with as a technical or mechanical operation (Leahy, 2005). Shame-prone therapists who easily become defensive may be problematic for shame-prone patients.

Sympathy

Sympathy and empathy relate to different processes as depicted in Table 6.2.

Eisenberg's (1986, 2002) landmark work on the origins of prosocial behaviour drew attention to the fact that research has confounded different emotional constructs related to empathy, sympathy and personal distress. She articulates these as follows.

1   The situation in which an individual feels the same emotion as another or understands what is in the mind of another: this is neither self-centred nor other-directed, but rather is *true* empathy or emotional contagion.

2   The responses of one to the distress of the other, which need not match the other but are focused on the *well-being* of the other. This is labelled *sympathy*. Sympathy is closely associated with altruism. In social mentality theory it is a key emotion of the care-giving mentality and thus of compassion.

3   A self-centred response related to anxiety, worry, shame or guilt rather than sympathy: this is labelled *personal distress*. Personal distress is related to self-focused threat processing. Therapists who are worried about "doing therapy right", fearful of some external threat linked to failure (for example, persecution if a patient kills themselves), or who

have unresolved feelings in themselves, may suffer personal distress that sets in motion their own self-protection strategies.

In sympathy we are emotionally *drawn into* the suffering of the other with feelings created in the self. As noted above, mirror neurons may be involved in this process. The accuracy of *understanding* may be loose, however. The feelings and emotions ignited by sympathy may not always match those of the patient because we bring our own reactions to distress. In extreme cases, the therapist may feel more upset than the patient; this can be especially true for patients who are somewhat dissociated from their emotions. Sympathy moves by the elicitation of feelings within oneself and can be elicited by projection, whereas projection reduces accurate empathy (Gilbert, 1989).

Distress sensitivity and sympathy are often conveyed by the therapist's non-verbal communication of facial expressions, voice tone, postures, use of language and softness, and other micro-skills. The fact that the patient can experience a therapist as genuinely moved by their stories and distress helps the patient "know" they can have an emotional impact on the mind of the therapist. A non-sympathetic therapist is impassive and the patient may feel they are talking to a potato or a technocrat. This is complex, however. Suppose a patient tells of severe abuse and callousness by her father or husband. The therapist's emotion might be anger. The patient might see the therapist getting angry (albeit on her behalf), but stirring this emotion is alarming to the patient (especially if she has been abused) and the therapist is missing sympathy with the feelings of terror and power-lessness. Another patient may see anger on their behalf as a positive. Here the therapist may ponder how the patient ignites feelings in others, tells stories that make others angry on their behalf, and thus may avoid anger and assertion themselves. The point about distress sensitivity, and sympathy with it, is the way it conveys to the patient a feeling that "my therapist feels with me". This advances feelings of attunement.

There are times in therapy where the emotion exchanged is one of sadness and extreme grief that can move a therapist to tears too. New research suggests that processing sad affect may be key to recovery for some depressions (Rottenberg, Joormann, Brozovich & Gotlib, 2005). Gilbert & Irons (2005) suggested that for some patients, when the soothing affect systems are toned down, people may have problems in processing grief for self. From the therapist's point of view, however, he/she does not want to dissolve into tears but on the other hand does not want to sit impassively as if the shared moment has no emotional impact on him/her and he/she is indifferent or just technically focused on affect regulation. The way a therapist conveys how they are moved by the patient's feelings (e.g., sadness) is important. Therapists who have strong beliefs that they must not show emotion to their patients, who feel they must rush in as rescuer, or who themselves struggle with feelings such as grief, may struggle with "allow-ing" grief as a normal process that they have to simply "be with" and share in a validating way. Grief can be a sign that a patient is beginning to make real inroads into they pain they have felt. Not all grief, however, is helpful, so again the therapist's skill is to be sensitive to a grief process that is healing rather than one that is not. For example, repeatedly ruminating on one's sadness may not be helpful.

Distress tolerance

Although compassion is focused on the alleviation of suffering, this does not mean that one rushes in as a rescuer at painful points in the therapy to try to alleviate that distress. This can compromise the other important function of compassion, which is to "foster developmental change in the patient con-ducive to their well-being". Exposure of, working with, and learning to accept and tolerate painful emotions or memories and new appraisals and meaning may be crucial to developmental change (Greenberg, Chapter 3, this volume; Pierson & Hayes, Chapter 10, this volume; Swales & Heard, Chapter 9, this volume). Sometimes, in exposure work, the patient will feel worse for a while, and this can be openly discussed as the ability to tolerate discomfort in the service of growth and development (Leahy, 2001, 2005).

Therapists should be cautious of "filling the spaces" during silences because this can be intrusive and dominating and interferes with learning how to tolerate certain emotions and memories. In other words, therapy does require at times spaces and silences for reflection. However, with shame-prone people, who can simply close down, *not* filling the space can also be unhelpful. This is because the patient has become stuck in a shame-frozen state, feels highly scrutinised by the therapist, concerned with what is expected of them and their own frozen state. Attention has switched from working on a specific emotion or memory to a concern with what is in the mind of the therapist and their social presentation. To work collaboratively means to talk about silences: what they might mean, what is going through the mind of the patient when they occur, when they are useful because they offer space "to be with" and explore one's feelings, and when they are not because the patient has switched to ruminating about what the therapist is thinking and expecting of them and feeling under shame-linked scrutiny.

The importance of trying to change feelings vs. learning to tolerate and accept them is part of new therapies in dialectical behaviour therapy; acceptance therapy; and mindfulness therapies (Hayes, Follette & Linehan, 2004; Pierson & Hayes, Chapter 10, this volume; Katzow & Safran, Chapter 5, this volume; Swales & Heard, Chapter 9, this volume). The great strength of behaviour therapy has been the importance placed *on feelings* via exposure and desensitisation. Few cognitive-behavioural therapists would try to treat common anxiety problems without helping people activate anxiety and working with that emotion, and the thoughts and safety behaviours associated with it. Anxiety, however, is only one of a range of emotions that patients may avoid, are fearful of, or are dominated by. Whatever the troublesome emotion might be (e.g., fear, disgust, rage, sexuality) the same issues apply: learning to tolerate *and* give new meanings to experiences, and reduce safety behaviours.

Empathy

Empathy has long been linked to compassion but has a chequered history in psychotherapy. This is partly because empathy has been used to refer to different things, i.e., a cognitive skill, a feeling state and a personality disposition (Decety & Jackson, 2004; Duan & Hill, 1996; Eisenberg, 1986, 2002; Preston & de Waal, 2002). As noted above, it can be confused with sympathy (see Table 6.2) and has been subject to increasing research in neuroscience. Empathy involves a particular capacity to be emotionally resonant with the other, which may depend on mirror neurons. We are then able to process and think about those feelings that have been stimulated within us. So empathy involves both this emotional communication and abilities to think about our emotions. Emotions that are stimulated in us that frighten us may lead to defensive reactions that are very non-empathic. Also key to empathy is the ability to recognise that what one feels is a simulation, and not to confuse self-feelings with those in others (Decety & Jackson, 2004).

There can also be confusion in the distinctions between genuineness, unconditional positive regard and empathy. Consider two examples from Book (1988, p. 422).

Example 1

A first-year resident, when verbally assaulted by a paranoid client, responded, 'I'm glad to see you can get your anger out.' The client hesitated, looked perplexed, and then angrily roared, 'You bastard! To be so happy that I am this upset!' When asked about his comment, the resident stated, 'I was just trying to be empathic.'

In this example the therapist had confused a genuine desire to help and form an empathic bond to help the patient feel safe to express his anger, and empathy.

Example 2

A Holocaust survivor raged against the rudeness to which he felt subjected at work. His Jewish counsellor responded, 'It really makes me angry when I hear that. What the hell's the matter with them?' The client responded, 'That's what I'm telling you. They're all a bunch of butchers.'

In the second example the therapist was responding from his own frame of reference. Book (1988) gives many other examples, including hearing but not really believing that a client can mean what they say, or making subtle alterations in the client's statement that actually change the meaning. As Decety & Jackson (2004) point out, keeping a distinction between "what self feels" and "what the other feels" is a skill, and leakage is common.

In empathy, one listens and attends to both what is actually said and expressed, and what is not. Therapist empathy is not just about attentive listening but is effortful because the therapist is trying to use his/her own mind to understand the mind of the patient. One may note possible *hidden* shame and resentment, the fear of loss or the disappointment that lies behind a self-attack (Gilbert & Irons, 2005). As Kohut (1977) points out, a client's rage can often hide a deep sense of loss, a feeling of being devalued and marginalised. An empathic response helps the client make contact with those feelings behind the anger and their internal self-judgements.

Another misunderstanding of empathy is filling in the blanks or finishing a client's sentence for him/her. This can be experienced as an intrusion. Instead, the therapist enables the patient to fill in his/her own blanks. Thus, as Book (1988) says, empathy may be understanding what the client is going to say, but being empathic is not saying it. A good measure of empathy is whether or not it enables clients to deepen their understanding and continue with their narrative and exploration.

A genuine empathic response from the therapist is not necessarily perceived as such by the client, and therefore Miller (1989) refers to the "therapeutic empathic communication process". This is a multi-stage model involving a therapist's recognition of the client's internal experience (via the client's verbal and non-verbal cues); the sending of signals of recognition; and the client's ability to recognise and internalise such signals (i.e., I understand, I show you I understand, and you understand that I have understood). Problems may occur at any stage. Empathy is a way of being with, or an "intuneness to", the patient, not simply a skill to be "brought to bear". As Margulies (1984) pointed out, empathy requires a "sense of wonder", openness, and caring interest. Interest alone can appear detached. Caring alone can involve more sympathy and too vigorous an effort to "get the patient better".

Another aspect of compassionate empathy is being able to view each other and ourselves as all part of a common humanity (Neff, 2003a, 2003b). As such we all inherit a set of genes (many of which we share with other species), we are born with a set of motives and needs that unfold with maturation (for example, for attachment and affection, group belonging, and to find sexual partners and reproduce). We can understand each other precisely because we are all the same. If children were not able to assume that others think and feel much as they do, if we could not make assumptions about how the minds of others work, then everyone would appear unfathomable aliens (Nickerson, 1999). Without commonalities we could never have a psychological or biological science because everyone would be so individually different as to make the project pointless. Individual differences and variation matter of course, but not so much as to make us total strangers to each other. Indeed, psychotherapy begins from this position, that we are all the same, with more or less the same needs, emotions and vulnerabilities to suffering, but by virtue of (small) genetic variations, and life histories that shape us, these become patterned and choreographed in different ways. As therapists, then, we seek to explore the patterning and choreographies of our common human nature that give rise to different patterns of suffering. A compassion-focused therapy begins with the notion of our common humanity that sets us on a journey to explore these commonalties and archetypal roots to our "being in the world". Compassion-focused therapy is thus science-based, requiring knowledge of how the mind works, the processes underpinning altruistic motives, and competencies such as theory of mind and empathy. It is not just about being warm, kind or having positive regard – important as these are.

Non-judgement

This involves suspending one's own immediate reactions to what a patient is saying or doing. This can be tricky for some cognitive therapists, who may believe that they have to help people spot cognitive distortions. Unfortunately, the term "distortion" itself implies a judgement that can easily be heard by a patient as "I have got my thinking wrong". Shame-prone patients can be very black and white in their thinking and easily slip into such thoughts. Judgements can also interfere with "being-in-the-moment" and learning acceptance (Katzow & Safran, Chapter 5, this volume). For this reason, in compassion-focused therapy, we try to avoid the language of "cognitive distortion" or "maladaptive schemas" or even (more recently) "negative thoughts", but focus on depressive thoughts, anxious thoughts, "understandable safety strategies" and "better safe than sorry thinking". These more typically reflect actual processes in the brain. Moreover, patients find it easier to work with their thoughts and feelings once they construe them as threat-focused and the way our threat systems are just trying protect us, by accentuating warnings and worrying about catastrophes. As one recent patient noted, once I had helped construe his anxiety as an over-enthusiastic warning system that had been conditioned early in life (rather than as a distortion), he felt better able to be compassionate with the feelings of his own anxiety.

Salkovskis (1996) makes this point clear when he says that the aim of cognitive behavioural therapy:

> is *not* to persuade persons that their current way of looking at the situation is wrong, irrational, or too negative; instead it is to allow them to identify where they have become stuck in their way of thinking and allow them to discover other ways of looking at their situation.
>
> (p. 49; emphasis in original)

The therapeutic relationship is an important vehicle for this learning because the therapist pulls the patient into their own way of thinking; that is, the patient is pulled into how they exist in the mind of the therapist, the compassionate validating experiences that are occurring in the mind of the therapist *and* the beliefs of the therapist. Ideally the patient is able to begin to take the perspective of the therapist and see and judge himself or herself with the same compassion that the therapist has for him/her. These experiences make it more likely that the patient will move into those feared areas they have avoided, and openly consider alternatives because they believe that the therapist genuinely believes in those alternatives.

The importance of warmth

All these qualities of compassion are not segregated and isolated but flow and blend together in the mind of the therapist, and ideally they are infused with a quality that is often called *warmth*. Warmth is a difficult quality to define and is often associated with empathy, but is not empathy itself. For example, a sales person may appear "empathic" to a degree and know how to stimulate your interest and address your anxieties about a product (i.e., he/she is using theory of mind), but this is not necessarily with warmth and concern for you. The worst torturer to have is one who has some theory of mind abilities to the extent they can work out how best to hurt and frighten you. The non-theory of mind torturer puts the gun to your head; the theory of mind one puts the gun to the head of your child or spouse (Gilbert, 1989). So a patient may feel their therapist is understanding them and can see things from their point of view, but if this is not associated with warmth and *a feeling of being cared for*, it can also be experienced as deeply threatening. In work with a colleague (Sophie Mayhew) we have found that some paranoid patients may be frightened of being empathically understood if they believe that this could be used against them or they will reveal feared secrets. Warmth can be problematic because it implies closeness, and closeness can be experienced as a threat.

So warmth relates to a type of softness and gentleness that *conveys caring concern*, although not at the expense of avoiding the painful. It is related to affectionate relating, but is not affection as such. It is a quality that we intuitively sense when we encounter it, usually from a person's non-verbal communication and manner. The key element of warmth in my view is that it provides stimuli that are coded as safe, and it activates, and is recognised by, the soothing system as safe. Lightness, gentleness, humour, containment, non-verbal cues (such as voice tone and facial expressions, pacing) and styles of using language in self-expression may be key to it. Bedics, Henry & Atkins (2005) found that therapist warmth had an impact on reducing hostility and submissive behaviour and increased patient affiliative behaviour. Warmth may activate a patient's care-focused social mentality. Because a social mentality patterns and choreographs different elements of our minds, as this mentality is activated it may help reorganise various subcomponents of our minds that can ripple through the whole psychological system (Gilbert & Irons, 2005; Wang, 2005).

Putting the elements together

Cognitive behavioural therapies have developed a range of ways of engaging in therapy that vary significantly from some psychoanalytic traditions. These include forms of exploration called Socratic questioning, inference changing and guided discovery; ways to directly educate and train patients in how they can attend and evaluate internal and external stimuli in new ways; progressive exposure and behavioural experiments. More recently, processes of imagery, affect tolerance, grieving, mindfulness and meditation have been incorporated into the therapy. Where possible, cognitive behavioural therapists act like personal trainers, collaborating with their patients to engage in certain tasks to achieve certain goals that are conducive to healing and well-being. Recently there have been efforts to design psychological therapies to target specific neurophysiological systems and functions (Cozolino, 2002; Gilbert & Irons, 2005, Schwartz & Begley, 2002). The more the patient understands and collaborates in designing the steps for change, the more involved (and less threatened) they are likely to be. However, these are not technologies to be brought to bear relatively regardless of the quality of the therapeutic relationship. A poor relationship may lead to drop-out, concealment, avoidance, poor collaboration or submissive compliance; we are not thought mechanics (Leahy, 2005).

For over two thousand years Buddhism has suggested that all beings seek to reduce suffering. Our patients are struggling the best way they can to survive or cope with great distress and we remain deeply respectful of that. We focus on the suffering of a person and their desire to find their way through the evolved and constructed complexities of mind, in their search for well-being, not just their diagnosis. Finally we can address the question that was posed earlier: how can the mind of one person have such an impact on the mind of another? There is one reason only – that we have evolved minds that are highly sensitive to the relationships in which they are embedded. This is shown in our needs for attachment, for protection and nurturance, to our need for other minds to help our own mind mature. So important is our social embeddness that evolution has given rise to a range of abilities to understand other minds and be significantly influenced by them. It is against this backdrop of evolved design that psychotherapists can work in the way they do – to use their mind to heal and help the minds of their patients. In this context the compassion in the mind of the therapist may be a key healing process.

Conclusion

This chapter has tried to contextualise the therapeutic relationship within an evolutionary and social context. Of special interest to the psychotherapist is how the mind of one person can have an impact on the mind of another. It turns out that there is an extraordinarily complex psychology underpinning these interactional processes. For example, there are a range of detection/response systems for threats (fast and slow) and these can be contrasted with affect-processing systems for cues, signalling and safeness. The safeness system seems to have evolved in complex ways with the evolution of attachment and social affiliation, exerting inhibitory control over threat and defence system processing. Our minds therefore are extraordinarily sensitive to the emotions and images we are creating in the minds of those around us, and mirror neurons play a key role in this.

Humans are also goal-seeking and relationship-creating. Within this context, caring and being cared for have played a major role in our evolution and may well underpin mechanisms for compassion. Understanding the processing systems involved in compassion, and the experience of receiving compassion, and developing self-compassion, may point to new ways of understanding the therapeutic relationship and its potential to operate as a healing process. Cognitive behavioural therapy, no less than any other therapy, is highly invested in trying to ensure that the processes that facilitate people's ability to overcome their difficulties (for example, expose themselves to the feared and develop new ways of thinking) are adopted by patients. Teachers, coaches, mentors and therapists who engage in their crafts compassionately may be more likely to form collaborative relationships that increase the chances that patients will adopt healing practices and walk the sometimes difficult road of change.

References

Aldridge, D. (2000). *Spirituality, healing and medicine.* London: Jessica Kingsley.
Argyle, M. (1987). *The psychology of happiness.* London: Routledge.
Bailey, K.G. (2002). Recognizing, assessing and classifying others: Cognitive bases of evolutionary kinship therapy. *Journal of Cognitive Psychotherapy: An International Quarterly,* 16, 367–383.

Baldwin, M.W. (2005). *Interpersonal cognition*. New York: Guilford.

Baldwin, M.W. & Dandeneau, S.D. (2005). Understanding and modifying the relational schemas underlying insecurity. In M.W. Baldwin (ed.), *Interpersonal cognition* (pp. 33–61). New York: Guilford.

Baldwin, M.W. & Holmes, J.G. (1987). Salient private audiences and awareness of the self. *Journal of Personality and Social Psychology*, 52, 1087–1098.

Bateman, A. & Fonagy, P. (2004). *Psychotherapy for borderline personality disorder: Mentalization-based treatment*: Oxford: Oxford University Press.

Bates, T. (2005). The expression of compassion in group psychotherapy. In P. Gilbert (ed.), *Compassion: Conceptualisations, research and use in psychotherapy* (pp. 369–386). London: Routledge.

Baumeister, R.F., Bratslavsky, E., Finkenauer, C. & Vohs, K.D. (2001). Bad is stronger than good. *Review of General Psychology*, 5, 323–370.

Baumeister, R.F. & Leary, M.R. (1995). The need to belong: Desire for interpersonal attachments as a fundamental human motivation. *Psychological Bulletin*, 117, 497–529.

Beck, A.T. (1987). Cognitive models of depression. *Journal of Cognitive Psychotherapy: An International Quarterly*, 1, 5–38.

Beck, A.T. (1996). Beyond belief: A theory of modes, personality and psychopathology. In P. Salkovskis (ed.), *Frontiers of cognitive therapy* (pp. 1–25). New York: Oxford University Press.

Beck, A.T. (1999). Cognitive aspects of personality disorders and their relation to syndromal disorders: A psycho-evolutionary approach. In C.R. Cloninger (ed.), *Personality and psychopathology* (pp. 411–430). Washington, DC: American Psychiatric Association.

Bedics, J.D., Henry, W.P. & Atkins, D.C. (2005). The therapeutic process as a predictor of change in patients' important relationships during time-limited dynamic psychotherapy. *Psychotherapy: Theory, Research, Practice, Training*, 42, 279–284.

Bjorklund, D.F. (1997). The role of immaturity in human development. *Psychological Bulletin*, 122, 153–169.

Book, H.E. (1988). Empathy: Misconceptions and misuses in psychotherapy. *American Journal of Psychiatry*, 145, 420–424.

Borenstein, E. & Ruppin, E. (2005). The evolution of imitation and mirror neurons in adaptive agents. *Cognitive Systems Research*, 6, 229–242.

Bowlby, J. (1969). *Attachment. Attachment and Loss*, Vol. 1. London: Hogarth Press.

Bowlby, J. (1973). *Separation, Anxiety and Anger. Attachment and Loss*, Vol. 2. London: Hogarth Press.

Brass, M. & Heyes, C. (in press). Imitation: Is cognitive neuroscience solving the correspondence problem? *Trends in Cognitive Sciences*, 9, 489–495.

Buss, D.M. (2003). *Evolutionary psychology: The new science of mind*, 2nd edition. Boston: Allyn & Bacon.

Byrne, R.W. (1995). *The thinking ape*. Oxford: Oxford University Press.

Cacioppo, J.T., Berston, G.G., Sheridan, J.F. & McClintock, M.K. (2000). Multilevel integrative analysis of human behavior: Social neuroscience and the complementing nature of social and biological approaches. *Psychological Bulletin*, 126, 829–843.

Carter, C.S. (1998). Neuroendocrine perspectives on social attachment and love. *Psychoneuroendocrinology*, 23, 779–818.

Cassidy, J. & Shaver, P.R. (eds) (1999). *Handbook of attachment: Theory, research and clinical applications* (pp. 115–140). New York: Guilford Press.

Cozolino, L. (2002). *The neuroscience of psychotherapy: Building and rebuilding the human brain*. New York: Norton.

Dalenberg, C.J. (2004). Maintaining the safe and effective therapeutic relationship in the context of distrust and anger: Countertransference and complex trauma. *Psychotherapy: Theory, Research, Practice, Training*, 41, 438–447.

Dalgleish, T. (2004). Cognitive approaches to posttraumatic stress disorder: The evolution of multirepresentation theorizing. *Psychological Bulletin*, 130, 228–260.

Decety, J. & Chaminade, T. (2003). Neural correlates of feeling sympathy. *Neuropsychologia*, 41, 127–138.

Decety, J. & Jackson, P.L. (2004). The functional architecture of human empathy. *Behavioral and Cognitive Neuroscience Reviews*, 3, 71–100.

Depue, R.A. & Morrone-Strupinsky, J.V. (2005). A neurobehavioral model of affiliative bonding. *Behavioral and Brain Sciences*, 28, 313–395.

Duan, C. & Hill, C.E. (1996). The current state of empathy research. *Journal of Counselling*, 43, 261–274.

Eisenberg, N. (1986). *Altruistic emotion, cognition and behaviour: A new view*. Hillsdale, NJ: Lawrence Erlbaum Associates.

Eisenberg, N. (2002). Empathy-related emotional responses, altruism, and their socialization. In R. Davidson & A. Harrington (eds), *Visions of compassion: Western scientists and Tibetan Buddhists examine human nature* (pp. 131–164). New York: Oxford University Press.

Ferster, C.B. (1973). A functional analysis of depression. *American Psychologist*, 28, 857–870.

Field, T. (2000). *Touch therapy*. New York: Churchill Livingstone.

Fogel, A., Melson, G.F. & Mistry, J. (1986). Conceptualising the determinants of nurturance: A reassessment of sex differences. In A. Fogel & G.F. Melson (eds), *Origins of nurturance: Developmental, biological and cultural perspectives on caregiving*. Hillsdale, NJ: Lawrence Erlbaum Associates.

Freeman, A. & McCloskey, R.D. (2003). Impediments to psychotherapy. In R.L. Leahy (ed.), *Roadblocks in cognitive-behavioral therapy: Transforming challenges into opportunities for change* (pp. 24–48). New York: Guilford.

Gerhardt, S. (2004). *Why love matters: How affection shapes a baby's brain*. Hove, UK: Brunner-Routledge.

Gilbert, P. (1984). *Depression: From psychology to brain state*. London: Lawrence Erlbaum Associates.

Gilbert, P. (1989). *Human nature and suffering*. Hove, UK: Lawrence Erlbaum Associates.

Gilbert, P. (1992). *Depression: The evolution of powerlessness*. Hove, UK: Lawrence Erlbaum Associates; New York: Guilford.

Gilbert, P. (1993). Defence and safety: Their function in social behaviour and psychopathology. *British Journal of Clinical Psychology*, 32, 131–153.

Gilbert, P. (1995) Biopsychosocial approaches and evolutionary theory as aids to integration in clinical psychology and psychotherapy. *Clinical Psychology and Psychotherapy*, 2, 135–156.

Gilbert, P. (1997). The evolution of social attractiveness and its role in shame, humiliation, guilt and therapy. *British Journal of Medical Psychology*, 70, 113–147.

Gilbert, P. (1998a). The evolved basis and adaptive functions of cognitive distortions. *British Journal of Medical Psychology*, 71, 447–463.

Gilbert, P. (1998b). What is shame? Some core issues and controversies. In P. Gilbert & B. Andrews (eds), *Shame: Interpersonal behavior, psychopathology and culture* (pp. 3–36). New York: Oxford University Press.

Gilbert, P. (2000) Social mentalities: Internal 'social' conflicts and the role of inner warmth and compassion in cognitive therapy. In P. Gilbert & K.G. Bailey (eds), *Genes on the couch: Explorations in evolutionary psychotherapy* (pp. 118–150). Hove, UK: Brunner-Routledge.

Gilbert, P. (2001). Evolutionary approaches to psychopathology: The role of natural defences. *Australian and New Zealand Journal of Psychiatry*, 35, 17–27.

Gilbert, P. (2003). Evolution, social roles, and differences in shame and guilt. *Social Research: An International Quarterly of the Social Sciences*, 70, 1205–1230.

Gilbert, P. (2005a). Compassion and cruelty: A biopsychosocial approach. In P. Gilbert (ed.), *Compassion: Conceptualisations, research and use in psychotherapy* (pp. 9–74). Hove, UK: Routledge.

Gilbert, P. (2005b). Social mentalities: A biopsychosocial and evolutionary reflection on social relationships. In M.W. Baldwin (ed.), *Interpersonal cognition* (pp. 299–335). New York: Guilford.

Gilbert, P. (2005c). Bullying in prisons: An evolutionary and biopsychosocial approach. In J.L. Ireland (ed.), *Bullying in prisons: Innovations in theory and research* (pp. 176–190). Uffculme, UK: Willan.

Gilbert, P. & Irons, C. (2005). Focused therapies and compassionate mind training for shame and self-attacking. In P. Gilbert (ed.), *Compassion: Conceptualisations, research and use in psychotherapy* (pp. 263–325). Hove, UK: Routledge.

Guidano, V. & Liotti, G. (1983). *Cognitive processes and the emotional disorders*. New York: Guilford.

Haidt, J. (2001). The emotional dog and its rational tail: A social intuitionist approach to moral judgment. *Psychological Review*, 108, 814–834.

Hammen, C. (1992). Cognition and psychodynamics: A modest proposal. *Clinical Psychology and Psychotherapy*, 1, 15–19.

Harper, L.V. (2005). Epigenetic inheritance and the intergenerational transfer of experience. *Psychological Bulletin*, 131, 340–360.

Harvey, A., Watkins, E., Mansell, W. & Shafran, R. (2004). *Cognitive behavioural processes across psychological disorders: A transdiagnostic approach to research and treatment*. Oxford: Oxford University Press.

Hassin, R.R., Uleman, J.S. & Bargh, J.A. (2005). *The new unconscious*. New York: Oxford University Press.

Hayes, S.C., Follette, V.M. & Linehan, M.N. (2004). *Mindfulness and acceptance: Expanding the cognitive behavioral tradition*. New York: Guilford.

Heinrichs, M., Baumgartner, T., Kirschbaum, C. & Ehlert, U. (2003). Social support and oxytocin interact to suppress cortisol and subjective responses to psychosocial stress. *Biological Psychiatry*, 54, 1389–1398.

Hofer, M.A. (1994). Early relationships as regulators of infant physiology and behavior. *Acta Paediatrica Supplement*, 397, 9–18.

Holmes, E.A. & Hackmann, A. (eds) (2004). Mental imagery and memory in psychopathology (Special edition: *Memory*, Volume 12, No. 4). Hove, UK: Psychology Press.

Holmes, J. (2001). *The search for the secure base*. Hove, UK: Brunner-Routledge.

Holmes, J. (2005). Notes on mentalizing – Old hat or new wine? *British Journal of Psychotherapy*, 22, 179–197.

Jordan, C.H., Spencer, S.J., Zanna, M.P., Hoshino-Browne, E. & Correll, J. (2003). Secure and defensive high self-esteem. *Journal of Personality and Social Psychology*, 85, 969–978.

Kirschenbaum, H. & Jourdan, A. (2005). The current status of Carl Rogers and the person-centred approach. *Psychotherapy: Theory, Research, Practice, Training*, 42, 37–51.

Knox, J. (2003). *Archetype, attachment, analysis: Jungian psychology and the emergence of mind*. London: Brunner-Routledge.

Kohut, H. (1977). *The restoration of the self*. New York: International Universities Press.

Kumashiro, M. & Sedikides, C. (2005). Taking on board liability-focused information: Close positive relationship as a self-bolstering resource. *Psychological Science*, 16, 732–739.

Leahy, R.L. (2001). *Overcoming resistance in cognitive therapy*. New York: Guilford.

Leahy, R.L. (2002). A model of emotional schemas. *Cognitive and Behavioral Practice*, 9, 177–191.

Leahy, R.L. (ed.) (2004). *Roadblocks in cognitive-behavioral therapy: Transforming challenges into opportunities for change*. New York: Guilford.

Leahy, R.L. (2005). A social-cognitive model of validation. In P. Gilbert (ed.), *Compassion: Conceptualisations, research and use in psychotherapy* (pp. 195–217). Hove, UK: Routledge.

LeDoux, J. (1998). *The emotional brain*. London: Weidenfeld & Nicolson.

Lee, D.A. (2005). The perfect nurturer: A model to develop a compassionate mind within the context of cognitive therapy. In P. Gilbert (ed.), *Compassion: Conceptualisations, research and use in psychotherapy* (pp. 326–351). Hove, UK: Routledge.

Linehan, M.M. (1993). *Cognitive-behavioral treatment of borderline personality disorder*. New York: Guilford Press.

McKay, M. & Fanning, P. (1992). *Self-esteem: A proven program of cognitive techniques for assessing, improving, and maintaining your self-esteem*, 2nd edition. Oakland, CA: New Harbinger Publishers.

MacLean, P. (1985). Brain evolution relating to family, play and the separation call. *Archives of General Psychiatry*, 42, 405–417.

Marcus, D.K. & Buffington-Vollum, K. (2005). Countertransference: A social relations perspective. *Journal of Psychotherapy Integration*, 15, 254–283.

Margulies, A. (1984). Toward empathy: The uses of wonder. *American Journal of Psychiatry*, 141, 1025–1033.

Marks, I.M. (1987). *Fears, phobias and rituals: Panic, anxiety and their disorders*. Oxford: Oxford University Press.

Masten, A.S. (2001). Ordinary magic: Resilience processes in development. *American Psychologist*, 56, 227–238.

Mikulincer, M. & Shaver, P. (2005). Mental representations of attachment security:

Theoretical foundations for a positive social psychology. In M.W. Baldwin (ed.), *Interpersonal cognition* (pp. 233–266). New York: Guilford.

Miller, I.J. (1989). The therapeutic empathic communication (TEC) process. *American Journal of Psychotherapy*, 43, 531–545.

Murray, L. & Cooper, P.J. (1997). *Postpartum depression and child development*. New York: Guilford.

Neff, K.D. (2003a). Self-compassion: An alternative conceptualization of a healthy attitude toward oneself. *Self and Identity*, 2, 85–102.

Neff, K.D. (2003b). The development and validation of a scale to measure self-compassion. *Self and Identity*, 2, 223–250.

Neff, K.D., Kirkpatrick, K.L. & Rude, S.S. (in press). Accepting the human condition: Self-compassion and its links to adaptive psychological functioning.

Nickerson, R.S. (1999). How we know – and sometimes misjudge – what others know: Inputting one's own knowledge to others. *Psychological Bulletin*, 125, 737–759.

Norcross, J.C. (2002). *Psychotherapy relationships that work*. New York: Oxford University Press.

Perry, B.D., Pollard, R.A., Blakley, T.L., Baker, W.L. & Vigilante, D. (1995). Childhood trauma, the neurobiology of adaptation and "use-dependent" development of the brain: How "states" become "traits". *Infant Mental Health Journal*, 16, 271–291.

Porges, S.W. (2001). The polyvagal theory; phylogenetic substrates of a social nervous system. *International Journal of Psychophysiology*, 42, 123–146.

Preston, S.D. & de Waal, F.B.M. (2002). Empathy: Its ultimate and proximate bases. *Brain and Behavioural Sciences*, 25, 1–71 (including commentaries).

Raedt, R., Schacht, R., Franck, E. & Houwer, J. (2006). Self-esteem and depression revisited: Implicit positive self-esteem in depressed patients? *Behaviour Research and Therapy*, 44, 1017–1028.

Rohner, R.P. (1986). *The warmth dimension: Foundations of parental acceptance–rejection theory*. Beverly Hills, CA: Sage.

Rosen, J.B. & Schulkin, J. (1998) From normal fear to pathological anxiety. *Psychological Bulletin*, 105, 325–350.

Rothschild, B. (2000) *The body remembers: The psychophysiology of trauma and trauma treatment*. New York: W.W. Norton.

Rottenberg, J., Joorman, J., Brozovich, F. & Gotlib, I. (2005). Emotional intensity of idiographic sad memories in depression predicts symptom levels 1 year later. *Emotion*, 5, 238–242.

Safran, J.D. (1998). *Widening the scope of cognitive therapy: The therapeutic relationship, emotion and the process of change*. Northvale, NJ: Aronson.

Safran, J.D. & Muran, J.C. (2000). *Negotiating the therapeutic alliance: A relational treatment guide*. New York: Guilford.

Salkovskis, P.M. (1996). The cognitive approach to anxiety: Threat beliefs, safety-seeking behavior, and the special case of health anxiety and obsessions. In P.M. Salkovskis (ed.), *Frontiers of cognitive therapy* (pp. 48–74). New York: Guilford.

Schaap, C., Bennun, I., Schindler, L. & Hoogduin, K. (1993). *The therapeutic relationship in behavioural psychotherapy*. Chichester, UK: Wiley.

Schore, A.N. (1994). *Affect regulation and the origin of the self: The neurobiology of emotional development*. Hillsdale, NJ: Lawrence Erlbaum Associates.

Schore, A.N. (2001). The effects of early relational trauma on right brain development, affect regulation, and infant mental health. *Infant Mental Health Journal*, 22, 201–269.

Schwartz, J.M. & Begley, S. (2002). *The mind and the brain: Neuroplasticity and the power of mental force*. New York: Regan Books.

Sedikides, C. & Skowronski, J.J. (1997). The symbolic self in evolutionary context. *Personality and Social Psychology Review*, 1, 80–102.

Siegel, D.J. (2001). Toward an interpersonal neurobiology of the developing mind: Attachment relationships, "mindsight" and neural integration. *Infant Mental Health Journal*, 22, 67–94.

Stern, D.N. (2004). *The present moment in psychotherapy and everyday life*. New York: Norton.

Suddendorf, T. & Whitten, A. (2001). Mental evolutions and development: Evidence for secondary representation in children, great apes and other animals. *Psychological Bulletin*, 127, 629–650.

Teicher, M.H. (2002). Scars that won't heal: The neurobiology of the abused child. *Scientific American*, 286(3), 54–61.

Tomkins, S.S. (1987). Shame. In D.L. Nathanson (ed.), *The many faces of shame*. New York: Guilford.

Trevarthen, C. & Aitken, K. (2001). Infant intersubjectivity: Research, theory, and clinical applications. *Journal of Child Psychology and Psychiatry*, 42, 3–48.

Uväns-Morberg, K. (1998) Oxytocin may mediate the benefits of positive social interaction and emotions. *Psychoneuroendocrinology*, 23, 819–835.

Wang, S. (2005). A conceptual framework for integrating research related to the physiology of compassion and the wisdom of Buddhist teachings. In P. Gilbert (ed.), *Compassion: Conceptualisations, research and use in psychotherapy* (pp. 75–120). Hove, UK: Routledge.

Wells, A. (2000). *Emotional disorders and metacognition: Innovative cognitive therapy*. Chichester, UK: Wiley.

Whiten, A. (1999). The evolution of deep social mind in humans. In M.C. Corballis & S.E.G. Lea (eds), *The descent of mind: Psychological perspectives on humanoid evolution* (pp. 173–193). New York: Oxford University Press.

Wicker, B., Keysers, C., Plailly, J., Royet, R.P., Gallese, V. & Rizzolatti, G. (2003). Both of us disgusted in *my* insula: A common neural basis of seeing and feeling disgust. *Neurone*, 40, 655–664.

Chapter 7

Internal working models of attachment in the therapeutic relationship

Giovanni Liotti

Introduction

The therapeutic alliance is the best predictor of outcome across a range of treatment modalities. Repairing the ruptures in the therapeutic alliance should, therefore, be a major concern for any psychotherapist, including cognitive-behavioural therapists (Chapters 9 and 10, this volume). The aim of this chapter is to clarify the role of attachment theory and research in helping therapists to understand the motivational underpinnings of alliance ruptures and to devise ways of coping with them in the therapeutic relationship.

Attachment theory (Bowlby, 1982) is part of a multi-motivational view of human relatedness based on evolutionary thinking. According to this view, human beings are biologically adapted for participating in at least four different types of interpersonal exchanges: careseeking–caregiving, dominant–subordinate, sexual and cooperative exchanges (Gilbert, 1989, 2000, 2004; Liotti, 1994, 2000; Liotti & Intreccialagli, 2003). The attachment system is conceived as a control system regulating careseeking behaviour. It is based on an inborn, evolved disposition to actively search for help or soothing from a member of the social group, perceived as stronger and/or wiser than the self (Bowlby, 1979, p. 129), whenever one is distressed or vulnerable to any type of danger. The expression of this disposition depends on memory structures, called internal working models (IWMs), that convey learned expectations of how other people will react to one's requests for help and soothing (Bowlby, 1979, 1982, 1988).

The therapeutic alliance implies the prevailing activity, within the therapeutic relationship, of the cooperative motivational system in both partners of the clinical exchange. The cooperative system is based on the inborn tendency to share intentions, goals and action plans on equal grounds (Tomasello, 1999; Tomasello, Carpenter, Call, Behne & Moll, 2005). Ruptures of the therapeutic alliance become possible whenever the therapeutic relationship shifts from a mainly cooperative clinical dialogue to enduring patterns of careseeking–caregiving, dominant–subordinate (i.e., competitive) or sexual interactions between patients and therapists. Many ruptures in the therapeutic alliance, even when they involve competitive or sexual interactions, can be traced back to the operations of the patient's attachment system. This assertion implies that the effort of repairing ruptures of the therapeutic alliance often provides the opportunity for corrective experiences in the therapeutic relationship, that may lead to healthy changes in the patient's IWM of attachment.

In order to explore how dysfunctional mental operations linked to the attachment system may emerge within the therapeutic relationship and hamper the therapeutic process, this chapter deals first with the general reasons for the activation of the attachment system within the therapeutic relationship. A second section summarizes what is known about the main different types of IWM: activations of the attachment system within the therapeutic dialogue become counterproductive to the aim of the treatment only when they are governed by an insecure, and particularly by a dis-organized, IWM. The other sections of this chapter deal with the different types of insecure IWM that may interfere negatively with the therapeutic alliance and the process of psychotherapy, and with some ways of coping with them and achieving their correction towards greater attachment security within the therapeutic relationship. It should be emphasized that successful attempts at repairing ruptures in the therapeutic alliance involve, first, achieving attachment security within the therapeutic relationship, and only afterwards regaining a cooperative attitude towards a shared goal. In other words, regaining a collaborative relationship after a rupture of the therapeutic alliance is usually achieved through empathic (i.e., non-judgemental and non-defensive) explorations of the patient's motives and negative expectations that led to the crisis in the therapeutic relationship. The cooperative interactions that characterize the therapeutic alliance should convey a warm, empathic feeling tone, not a cold, task-focused one.

Activation of the attachment system during the psychotherapy process

Cognitive and behavioural psychotherapists usually strive to shape the therapeutic relationship, from the very first session, according to the ideal of collaborative empiricism (Beck & Emery, 1985). This is performed usually through the active search of an explicit agreement on goals and rules of the therapeutic work (Chapter 10, this volume). Even with difficult patients, who may be unable to provide a credible personal goal for the treatment, cognitive therapists try to construct mutual agreement on shared goals at the beginning of the treatment through carefully devised contracting procedures (e.g., Linehan, 1993; see also Chapter 11, this volume).

If the joint formulation of a shared goal for the treatment has been successful, the motivational system mediating cooperative behaviour is likely to become active both in the therapist and in the patient at the beginning of the treatment. However, other role-forming elements that extend beyond collaborative activity arise from the fact that, from the beginning of psychotherapy, patients are gradually disclosing their troubles, distress, feelings of shame and fear, with the hope that the therapist is benevolent, understanding, accepting, emotionally available and capable of providing efficient help (i.e., the therapist is hopefully perceived as "stronger and/or wiser" than themselves: Bowlby, 1979, p. 129). Disclosing one's suffering to an available person who is perceived as stronger and wiser than the self, normally and adaptively activates the attachment system, "from the cradle to the grave" (Bowlby, 1979, p. 129). Therefore, in the course of psychotherapy, the cooperative system will almost inevitably give way to the attachment system (Liotti, 1991, 2000). The activation of the care-seeking aspects of the attachment system within the therapeutic relationship is suggested by a variety of signs. For instance:

- the patient may straightforwardly display emotions of vulnerability (distress, fear, emotional pain) and the wish to be soothed by the therapist
- an analysis of the therapist's emotional reactions as assessed through self-observation may show that the therapist begins to feel protective towards the patient, losing in part the previously predominant orientation towards the shared therapeutic goal (see the concept of the therapist's emotions as "markers" of particular interpersonal cycles and schemata: Safran & Segal, 1990)
- the patient's representations of self and the therapist as they may appear during the therapeutic dialogue suggest that the patient begins to perceive the therapist as an almost omnipotent rescuer from present and past sufferings (i.e., the patient idealizes the therapist).

The shift from a cooperative reciprocal attitude (in which patient and therapist interact on equal grounds, both aiming at the shared therapeutic goal) to an attachment–caregiving type of interaction (in which the patient asks for soothing responses and the therapist signals safety via non-verbal communication from facial expressions to warm tone of voice) may not be a durable or serious challenge to the therapeutic alliance. Indeed, the ability to move into these "attachment-like" forms of relating can be helpful in that they provide information that the therapist creates a safe base and is able to be a source of validation and mirroring. In fact, if the patient does not experience a therapist as wiser/stronger and able to contain and help make sense of the material that emerges in the interaction, the patient may feel unsupportive and fearful – re-enacting traumas from the past (Liotti, 2000).

If the temporary attachment–caregiving interaction between patient and therapist is secure (i.e., if the therapist judiciously provides context-appropriate soothing, mirroring and validation responses without becoming *over*protective or violating the professional boundaries of psychotherapy, and the patient accepts the therapist's response by calming down quickly), then the therapeutic process usually resumes the cooperative atmosphere centred on the joint awareness of the therapeutic goal. If, however, the attachment–caregiving interaction between patient and therapist is insecure – i.e., the therapist becomes alarmed at the care-seeking behaviour of the patient, ignores it (appears not to have noted or "heard"), dismisses it, or tries to "force" the patient back to a "collaboration" – then the therapeutic relationship is likely to become problematic and the therapeutic process hampered.

The main cause for attachment–caregiving interactions between patient and therapist becoming insecure (provided therapists have learnt to recognize in themselves and to control a possible dysfunctional caregiving attitude) is the activation in the patient of an insecure IWM constructed on the basis of previous unhealthy attachment relationships. It should be emphasized that if the therapist's reply to the manifestation of the patient's insecure IWM within the attachment relationship confirms the patient's negative expectations about attachment–caregiving interactions, then a therapeutic stalemate or even a worsening of the patient's psychopathological symptoms is likely to occur. The rationale for this assertion can be inferred by the notion that the development of many emotional disorders stems from insecure attachments, so that the basic cognitive–emotional structure of symptoms is intertwined with the IWM (Bowlby, 1979; Dozier, Stovall & Albus, 1999; Greenberg, 1999; Guidano & Liotti, 1983).

This chapter will discuss how psychotherapists deal with a patient's insecure IWM in the therapeutic relationship, so that they can avoid confirming it and possibly foster corrective relational experiences while trying to regain a cooperative working alliance. In order to introduce this discussion, a brief reminder of the main types of IWM is mandatory.

Types of internal working model

The IWM is a cognitive–emotive structure based on memories of previous careseeking–caregiving relationships, conveying expectations about the meaning, value and outcome of ongoing or future interactions involving the attachment motivational system. Secure IWMs convey positive expectations that others will generally be helpful and sympathetic, while insecure ones convey expectations that one's attachment needs will be met with rejecting, intrusive, fearful or violently aggressive responses.

At the beginning of life, the IWM is a structure of implicit memory (Amini *et al.*, 1996), constructed on the basis of actual interactions with the primary caregiver. Once established, the IWM guides both attachment behaviour and the appraisal of attachment emotions in self and others. Gilbert (1989, 2005) suggested that attachment experiences affect both threat and safeness processing systems, such that (for example) neglectful or abusive early attachments can sensitize threat systems that will impact on a person's whole orientation to self, others and the world (i.e., not just attachment relationships; cf. Cortina, 2003, and Grossmann & Grossmann, 1991). In essence, attachment relationships help set the "working tone and threshold activation level" of threat and safeness systems. If the attachment figure has been accessible to the child in real-life situations, the corresponding IWM of the developing child conveys an inner sense of legitimacy of the attachment emotions and of potential accessibility of help and comfort even when the attachment figure is not actually present during distressing experiences. This is the IWM of secure attachments. In contrast, the IWMs of insecure/organized attachments convey negative expectations: that the attachment figure will be bored by and will not be available to requests of help and comfort (avoidant attachment), or that he/she will respond ambivalently and intrusively to such requests (resistant attachment). The IWM of insecure/disorganized attachment differs from that of avoidant and resistant attachments because it not only prefigures negative consequences of asking for help and comfort, it also brings on a dissociated (non-integrated) multiplicity of dramatic and contradictory expectations. Disorganized attachment in infancy is the outcome of unresolved traumas and hostile–helpless, frightened and frightening attitudes in the caregivers. It is often related to further traumas suffered by the child within the attachment relationship, leading to borderline and dissociative disorders (Liotti, 1992, 1999, 2004a, 2004b; Lyons-Ruth, 2003; Main & Morgan, 1996).

In later phases of personality development, part of the formerly implicit IWM may become explicit and enter both into the consciously held meanings attributed to attachment needs and into the narratives of autobiographic memory. Although open to modification because of later attachment experiences, the early IWMs show remarkable stability over time (presumably because the relational style between child and parents also remains stable: Bowlby, 1982, 1988). In adult life, the individual state of mind concerning attachment can be assessed with the Adult Attachment Interview (AAI: Hesse, 1999). States of mind characterized by appraisals of basic attachment emotions as legitimate and normal are linked either to early secure attachments or to security in attachment–caregiving interactions that have been earned through later corrective experiences. Early avoidant IWMs are related to adult states of mind that dismiss the value of attachment-related emotions and interpersonal exchanges. States of mind preoccupied as to the meaning and value of attachment experiences are linked to early resistant IWMs. Early disorganized attachments are related to adult states of mind that are characterized by the tendency to attribute multiple, non-integrated, dramatic meanings to attachment experiences (these states of mind may appear in the AAI as unresolved memories of

Table 7.1 Infant attachment patterns, internal working models and adult
states of mind concerning attachment

Adult states of mind (Adult Attachment Interview; see Hesse, 1999)	Infant pattern (Strange Situation Procedure (SSP); see Ainsworth et al., 1978)	IWM (inferred from AAI and SSP)
Organized attachment		
Free: coherence of thought during the description of attachment experiences	Secure: protests at separation, calms down promptly at reunion	Positive evaluation of attachment emotions in self and others
Dismissing: idealized semantic memories of parents, contradicted by episodic memories; dismisses the value of attachment emotions	Avoidant: does not cry at separation, avoids contact at reunion	Negative evaluation of attachment emotions in self and others
Entangled: ambivalent evaluation of the meaning and value of attachment memories and emotions	Resistant: cries at separation, does not calm down and continues protest at reunion	Ambivalent evaluation of attachment emotions in self and others
Disorganized attachment		
Unresolved as to trauma/ loss (lapses and metacognitive deficits while reporting traumatic attachment memories; leads to frightened/ frightening behaviour towards one's child)	Disorganized: multiple, incompatible responses at separation and/or at reunion	Dramatic, multiple, dissociated representations of self and others within attachment interactions; diffuse emotional dysregulation; experience of fright without solution

attachment-related traumas and losses, and as representations of self and others portraying high degrees of both hostility and helplessness that are reciprocally dissociated (Hesse, 1999; Lyons-Ruth, Melnick, Atwood & Yellin, 2003) (see Table 7.1).

Dealing with an insecure organized IWM within the therapeutic relationship

Patients with an avoidant IWM typically have difficulties in revealing painful emotional information. They have learnt to be fearful of inner cues and affects that suggest unmet needs, because in the past expressing needs often required approach behaviour to a parent, and need-seeking that was punished or shamed. They are often very concise in reporting to the therapist, usually in a matter-of-fact tone of voice, interpersonal experiences (including ongoing ones with the therapist) in which they are likely to have felt the wish to be soothed and helped. They may also dismiss this wish as insignificant (Liotti, 1991). Attachment theory and research suggest that they do so because they expect the therapist (often at an implicit, non-conscious level of cognitive processing) to shame them for the need, and to be annoyed or bored by their suffering should they dwell on it and/or express it non-verbally.

This hypothesis prompts therapists to show immediate, explicitly empathic attitudes (and validating comments: Leahy, 2005) to every, however minor, description or expression of painful emotions. "How did you feel?" is a question that should be frequently asked by therapists in these cases, whenever patients report, in their typical dismissing way, interpersonal episodes likely to imply attachment dynamics. Any comment on the patient's expressed emotion that could be felt as critical and shaming should be carefully avoided. On the contrary, therapists should take pains over showing to the patients that expressing attachment emotions (i.e., fear, pain, discomfort, loneliness, sadness for losses, wish for comfort, joy at reunions after separations, etc.) is welcome, normal to being a human being, not shameful and not annoying the therapist in the least. In other words, therapists should help patients re-code these feelings or felt needs from being threatening to being safe to share and explore.

It should be remarked that such a therapist's attitude in the therapeutic relationship may cause a temporary imbalance in the patient's attachment representations. In the transition from avoidant to secure attachment, ambivalent states of mind reminiscent of resistant attachment (see below) are common. The shift from an avoidant IWM to a less desperate expectation about the consequences of expressing wishes for help and comfort implies ambivalence and doubts during the unfolding of the therapeutic process: will a new person to whom a request for soothing is addressed respond as the therapist does, or will he/she respond with rejecting annoyed attitudes, as the former attachment figures did? Will the therapist consistently respond as he/she had until now, or will he/she finally get irritated by the patient's expressed emotions (that the patient may still perceive as lack of autonomy)? Before security develops, the therapeutic relationship should accommodate this transition by acknowledging both its meaning and the need for repeated experiences of validation of attachment emotions.

Patients coming from histories of avoidant attachment are particularly prone to provide unrealistically positive "semantic" descriptions of their attachment figures while at the same time they are usually unable to report autobiographical memories supporting these descriptions (Hesse, 1999). When they become able to report episodes of actual interactions with their primary caregivers, these reports typically contradict the idealized picture of past attachment relationships the patients may have provided on the semantic level. This de-linking between autobiographical and semantic memories may be usefully explored in the therapeutic relationship. When the patient's attitudes toward the therapist become ambivalent, oscillating between dismissing of attachment emotions and anxious, clinging requests for comfort, time is ripe for an enquiry into the manner of careseeking–caregiving interactions in the patient's childhood. Idealizing semantic memories of these interactions (e.g., "My parents were exceptionally good parents") should be matched by the therapist's detailed, albeit tactful, enquiry on childhood episodes that could illustrate their alleged happiness (e.g., "How did your parents respond to your childhood illnesses? Could you provide a concrete example? How did they soothe you when you were emotionally distressed? You said they were perfect at that. Could you narrate a precise episode that could help me understand what you mean by 'perfect'?"). The aim of such an enquiry is to assist patients in acknowledging that they have *had* reasons for expecting rejecting responses to their requests for help or comfort: these expectations make it understandable both that they at times avoid expressing painful emotions and wishes to be soothed, and that in other moments they express them in a very anxious way.

Patients coming from histories of resistant (ambivalent) attachment present almost opposite types of problem in the therapeutic relationship. They usually express freely and intensely their attachment-related emotions to their therapist, easily develop clinging dependency on the therapist, and dwell on their experience of emotional pain at great length. At the same time, they seem unable to calm down in the face of any attempt the therapist could make at sympathizing with their distressing experiences and worries, or at reassuring them about their fears. Patients with hypochondriac and other anxious worries may be typical examples (Liotti, 1991). Attachment theory and research suggest that people with resistant attachments expect that the positive responses to their requests to be soothed will soon prove to be inconsistent and inept, or will shift towards intrusive attitudes. This hypothesis may prompt therapists to show that they are willing and able to help the patient in a concrete way, rather than merely listening sympathetically to their lamentations or trying to reassure them verbally. A good example of this is therapists who, after having declared that they are willing to reassure their patients from their hypochondriac or obsessive–compulsive fears as long as they ask for, enquire as to whether or not patients believe that such reassurances will prevent them relapsing quite soon in their worries. Since patients usually acknowledge that this is not likely to happen, therapists can thereupon remark that there are ways of helping the patient to achieve inner serenity that are different from mere reassurance. The proposal of a cognitive or behavioural technique aimed at increasing the patient's coping abilities or the patient's mastery over common interpersonal problems is likely to substantiate this assertion. For instance, once they have obtained the patients' agreement on giving up the request for verbal reassurance, therapists may guide patients in acknowledging that a hypertrophic sense of responsibility lies at the ground of their hypochondriac or obsessive–compulsive worries (Salkovskis, 1985). If patients acknowledge that an abnormal sense of responsibility rather than a real impending danger is causing their worries, the therapeutic technique will have provided effective soothing of the patients' fear, while therapists avoided confirming the patients' expectation (linked to their resistant IWM) that the attachment figure's reassurances are inefficient.

Patients with histories of resistant attachment are perhaps those that may benefit from corrective relational experiences, leading to increased attachment security, in the therapeutic relationship with therapists that skilfully use standard cognitive-behavioural techniques. These patients will experience concrete, consistent help rather than a mere empathic listening that would fall short of what is required in order to contain their painful emotions and to correct their expectation of inept, inconsistent responses to their need to be soothed.

The disorganized IWM in the therapeutic relationship

The above description of common problems in the therapeutic relationship illustrates the contribution of attachment theory in understanding their meaning and the underlying cognitive–interpersonal processes. It is, however, the knowledge of attachment disorganization that may contribute to an understanding of more dramatic difficulties and dilemmas in the therapeutic relationship, such as those that should be expected when treating patients in the borderline–dissociative spectrum of complex syndromes related to severe chronic childhood traumas (Liotti, 2004a, 2004b).

When therapists face interpersonal situations where patients assume a controlling–punitive or a seductive attitude, threaten self-harm or premature interruption of treatment, and in any other ways induce in the therapist shifting feelings of solicitude, threat and impotence, the possibility that a disorganized IWM is guiding the patients' appraisal of the therapeutic relationship should be considered (Liotti, 2004a, 2004b).

It has been argued that the IWM of disorganized attachment conveys multiple, reciprocally dissociated and dramatic representations of both self and the attachment figure that can be rendered by the prototypic representations of the omnipotent rescuer, the impotent victim and the malignant abuser/persecutor (Liotti, 1999, 2000, 2004a, 2004b). When the disorganized IWM becomes active within the therapeutic relationship, these three representations may reflect themselves in powerful and multiple, sometimes quickly shifting, transferential–countertransferential reactions. In these multiple transferences–countertransferences, the three roles of persecutor, abuser and victim can appear in both partners and in any particular order or sequence. A common sequence is for the therapist to start out in the role of rescuer (a role to which therapists are inclined), while the patient begins in the role of victim, for example by reporting very traumatic experiences suffered during childhood at the hand of a cruel attachment figure. Inadvertently, therapist may solicitously strive to repair the damage by extending hours, not collecting the fee, taking repeated late-night calls and even hugging the patient. Demands by the patient may escalate until the therapist begins to feel tormented, as though a victim of the patient, who is now viewed as an abuser. The therapist, however, may also feel the risk of becoming the cruel persecutor of the patient should he/she relinquish the care of a deeply suffering victim of childhood attachment-related abuse, rejection and neglect.

The situation is complicated by the fact that, in order to preserve early attachment relationships from the annihilating experience of disorganization, children who have been disorganized in their infant attachments usually develop controlling strategies towards their caregivers (Hesse, Main, Abrams & Rifkin, 2003). The controlling strategies may involve, in situations where the attachment system should motivate the child's behaviour, the activation of the competitive-ranking system (controlling–punitive strategies), the caregiving system (controlling–caregiving strategies that imply inversion of the attachment relationship with parents) and even the sexual system (leading to sexualized interactions with a parent). The early construction of controlling strategies to cope with attachment disorganization explains how patients that are motivated to ask for psychotherapeutic help (attachment motivational system) may quickly activate the competitive or the sexual motivational systems in the therapeutic relationship (or even the caregiving system, leading to rather paradoxical interactions in which patients are preoccupied with the well-being of their therapists, a concealed motivation sometimes betrayed by patients' gifts to the therapist).

Many cases of sexual relations between therapist and patient have followed this model, where the therapist, under the guise of trying to love the patient back to health, surrenders to the patient's sexual seduction and becomes an abuser (Gabbard & Lester, 1995). In such cases therapists are often oblivious to the possibility that they are repeating the same kind of incestuous relationship that might have occurred in the patient's childhood. This is a disaster, for the therapist has failed to contain the confused and confusing desires for safeness that lie behind these interactions. The therapist can become the abusive other to the controlling/disorganized patient in other, less dramatic ways. For example, when facing a patient's controlling–punitive strategy, the therapist may start making sarcastic or sadistic comments, may stop paying attention, may be late at sessions, or may force the patient to relive horrendous childhood experiences (thereby re-traumatizing him/her).

Even when the therapeutic relationship is safeguarded from such deleterious occurrences by a proper therapist's attitude, the activation of a patient's disorganized IWM is a serious challenge to the psychotherapy process. For instance, the therapist may be disoriented by alternating manifestation of clinging dependency (when the therapist is perceived as an omnipotent rescuer) and of "phobia of attachment" (when the patient construes the therapist's behaviour as that of a potential abuser: Steele, Van der Hart & Nijenhuis, 2001). Or therapists may feel paralysed by the relational dilemma they perceive in their disorganized patients: traumatic memories of abuses inflicted by attachment figures must be dissociated in order to safeguard the attachment relationship, while at the same time the need for attachment must be disavowed in order to protect the self from the betrayal of attachment needs implied by the abuse (Blizard, 2001; Freyd, 1997). In short, attachment disorganization creates a specific approach-avoidance dilemma, which must be solved within the therapeutic relationship: searching for meaning in the clinical dialogue potentially increases the patients' sense of security, but at the same time the very words used in such a quest for meaning may arouse terrifying memories of attachment trauma (Holmes, 2004).

Correction of the disorganized IWM at an implicit level

It is unlikely, in the treatment of difficult patients, that therapists successfully deal with the disorganized IWM through the identification of its cognitive components and active reflection upon them. The reason is that the implicit structures of severely disorganized attachment, when they emerge in the therapeutic relationship, seriously hinder the patient's meta-cognitive capacity of reflecting on ongoing interpersonal experiences (see, e.g., Fonagy, Target, Gergely, Allen & Bateman, 2003; Liotti, 2000, 2004a). It is therefore necessary to cope with the disorganized IWM at the implicit, non-verbal, emotional level of clinical exchanges.

Gold (2000) and Liotti (1994, 2000, 2004a) propose to carefully organize the overall therapeutic strategy along the lines of a collaborative relationship implying the careful building and rebuilding of the therapeutic alliance, so that both patient and therapist can perceive themselves and the other as striving on equal grounds towards a shared goal. If such a cooperative interpersonal perception is achieved, then attachment needs (and therefore disorganization) are kept at bay during the clinical dialogues, before one attempts to foster experiences of secure attachment within the therapeutic relationship (see also Gold et al., 2001). Dialectic Behaviour Therapy (DBT: Linehan, 1993), although it is not grounded in attachment theory, provides very useful hints at how this goal – implicit correction of the disorganized IWM in the direction of attachment security – can be pursued in the context of exchanges between therapist and patient that are explicitly based on a cooperative therapeutic alliance.

While DBT is based on the careful contracting of the therapeutic alliance since the beginning of the treatment, by explicit statement of the symmetrical responsibilities that therapist and patient agree to take during the whole therapeutic process (see Chapter 11, this volume), it also suggests that the therapist's attention focuses primarily on a series of targets that are easily related to the patient's attachment needs. These targets are organized according to a hierarchy of priorities. At the top of this hierarchy is the patient's safety. If the patient's life is in danger (for example, because of explicit or subtle threats of committing suicide), then the therapist should immediately suspend, whenever this may happen throughout the treatment, any other therapeutic manoeuvre in order to concentrate on the patient's safety. The second level of the hierarchy of priorities for the therapist's attention concerns the safeguard of the therapeutic relationship. Whenever during the therapeutic process the continuity or the significance of the therapeutic encounter is endangered (not only by threats of premature interruptions of the treatment, but also by the patient's being late to the sessions or coming to the session in an altered state of consciousness because of abusing alcohol or drugs before the session), and provided that no threat to the patent's life is impending (in this case the patient's safety is the priority), the therapist will stop paying attention to anything else in the therapeutic dialogue, however interesting other topics for conversation may appear to be to the patient. The third priority in the hierarchy of therapeutic targets is any behaviour that may hinder the quality of the patient's life (i.e., any habit that may yield untoward results in the patient's search for well-being). The fourth priority is any behaviour that may foster the quality of the patient's life. The fifth is behaviour indicative of the effects of traumatic memories on the patient's ongoing mental process (this usually becomes the focus of the therapist's attention only in the second year of treatment, and when no behaviour of the preceding levels is momentarily present). The sixth is the patient's ability to take care of themselves.

One can imagine how the patient may process, at an implicit level, the interpersonal information conveyed by the therapist's continuing shifts of attention according to such a hierarchy of priorities. The shifts of the therapist's attention implicitly mean:

- first, I firmly want you to stay alive
- second, I want you to spend with me every single minute we have planned to spend together, and each of us to be as lucidly aware of the other's presence as possible
- third, I want you to restrain from harming yourself even with relatively minor injuries to your present well-being and happiness
- fourth, I want you to strive actively for increasing well-being and happiness
- fifth, I am willing to deal extensively with your past traumatic experiences only when each of us knows the other's attitudes well enough, so that you will not perceive me as prone to shaming you or your family,

but rather as willing to understand and share the darkest side of your past experiences

- sixth, I am prepared to accept that you will leave me and be autonomous as soon as you are able to take care of yourself.

These, besides constituting the basis for an experience of compassionate relating within the therapeutic relationship (Gilbert & Irons, 2005), are exactly the attitudes of an attachment figure that can foster attachment security. These therapist's attitudes during the therapeutic process may gradually correct the patient's past IWM, constructed on the basis of memories of interactions in which attachment figures may have directly or indirectly suggested to the patient, through violent deeds or bitter words, that they would prefer that the patient die rather than live, that they would like not having them around because they are an unbearable burden, that they do not care if they harm themselves or develop habits that will yield unhappiness and failure, that they do not even notice if they are shaming their children, and that they may not tolerate their children's autonomy. Such a corrective relational experience does not require verbal exchanges dealing with the attitudes of the patient's primary caregivers or with the patient's state of mind concerning attachment, nor verbal comments or explicit techniques aimed at explaining how to develop secure attachments in the future. All this corrective relational experience may take place at the implicit level of cognitive processing where the shifts of another person's attention, indicative of his/her prevailing interests, can first be registered and elaborated.

At the explicit level of cognitive processing, patients involved in DBT may notice and memorize also other types of relational information that correct their IWM in the direction of earned attachment security: while DBT therapists are busy teaching social and self-regulatory skills, they consistently show a positive, validating interest in the patient's emotional experiences, both painful and happier ones. Validation of painful emotional experience by the therapist (for example, by explicitly acknowledging that the patient's suffering involves a *legitimate* request for soothing) is another main road towards constructing attachment security (Leahy, 2005). Another ingredient of DBT explicitly aimed at fostering attachment security and therefore correcting the disorganized IWM is training in the art of properly asking for help, pursued by requiring phone calls to the therapist whenever the patient is in such serious trouble as to risk self-harming behaviours (Linehan, 1993).

Parallel therapies

The simultaneous engagement in the treatment of two therapists operating in different, parallel settings is perhaps the main aspect of DBT that facilitates coping successfully with the otherwise almost unbearable effects of severe attachment disorganization within the clinical dialogue. Although in DBT the two therapists operate in individual and group sessions (Chapter 11, this volume; Linehan, 1993), the lines of reasoning that explain the advantages of parallel interventions in the treatment of patients with severely disorganized attachments can be generalized to other types of two-therapist models (for example, individual and family interventions, or individual psychotherapy and psychologically informed prescription of drug treatments, conducted by different clinicians: Liotti, 2000, 2004a, 2004b).

If the patients' relational dilemmas and the worsening of their most disturbing experiences of fragmentation are contingent upon the activation of the attachment system and of the corresponding disorganized IWM, then one could expect that such an activation will be more difficult to handle when the patient becomes attached to only one therapist. A good example is provided by what may happen when patients disorganized in their early attachments face the idea of a momentary separation from their therapists, for instance when the therapist's summer holidays are approaching.

In the prospect of separation from their one therapist, often the only reliable source of soothing and support patients can count on, a strong and durable activation of the patient's attachment system is to be expected. If the expected separation from the therapist activates an IWM of disorganized attachment, then the patient's state of mind will be invaded by catastrophic expectations concerning the future of the therapeutic relationship. The patient's consciousness will be obsessed by multiple, dramatic representations of self and the therapist that shift without integration between hostility, helplessness, desperate longing for help, guilt, fear and affect phobia. The patient will also lack the capacity of coping with these representations and affects through adequate metacognitive monitoring, self-reflection and critical reflection on the therapist's possible states of mind, because the exercise of all these mentalizing capacities is hindered by the activation of disorganized attachment.

If, however, the patient is attached to two different therapists, then the prospect of a momentary separation from one of them is less likely to bring on a strong and durable activation of the patient's attachment system. Another source of help and comfort will remain available. When one of the two therapists in a parallel treatment will leave, say, to participate in a conference, the presence of the second will make it less likely that the patient experiences exacerbation of symptoms, the appearance in consciousness of dramatic, multiple and non-integrated representations of self and the therapist, and a simultaneous decay in the exercise of self-reflective, mentalizing capacity. The risk of premature interruption of the treatment – not a rare occurrence in borderline and dissociative patients before and after momentary separations from the therapists – will be correspondingly reduced.

During the psychotherapy with borderline and dissociative patients, multiple transferences, i.e., quick oscillation of attitudes and states of mind towards self and the therapist, are common also in moments in which no separation is expected, but other types of experiences, such as intense mental pain, activate the patient's attachment system. In a short span of time, even within a single session, these patients may dramatically ask for help, look distant and indifferent, state their wish to quit therapy because of the fear of being damaged, express the fear of being dangerous to beloved persons, and make the therapist feel important and loved but also threatened or oppressed (Fonagy, 1999; Liotti, 1995). This quick and dramatic change of attitudes, difficult to handle through transference interpretations also because of the patient's metacognitive deficit, may become overwhelming for both the patient and the therapist.

With the benefit of a second therapy, the patient is often able to experience a full range of contradictory feelings of anger and longing for understanding, without being overwhelmed by the fear of completely destroying the relationship with the first psychotherapist. In the parallel model, these patients are offered a second attachment relationship that attenuates the terror of the "all or nothing" consequences so characteristic of these situations. Since the attachment relationship with the secondary therapist is usually less intense than that with the first therapist, the relational–emotional dilemmas are also less intense within the second therapeutic relationship, and the exercise of mentalizing capacities less hindered by the disorganized IWM. The second therapist, thus, may provide an opportunity to examine each component of the conflict with the first therapist, including fears of abandonment or retaliation. From such a secure base of empathic observation, patients can begin to tease out their own transferential material from the intersubjective context within which they are experiencing it. The second therapist can validate, support, and mirror all the contradictory aspects of the patient's multifaceted subjective experience with the first therapist. The patient can then return to the first therapist, with whom he or she felt in conflict, less terrorized by his/her own feelings. By feeling securely anchored with the second therapist, the patient is now ready to address these previously fragmenting issues, and repair of the disrupted therapeutic alliance can now proceed.

From the point of view of the therapist's countertransferential responses, the assistance of a second therapist may also be instrumental in preventing overwhelming feelings of confusion, helplessness, hostility or fear when facing the patient's multiple, non-integrated and dramatic transferences. Parallel therapy is analogous to a typical family where two parents are available to meet the range of needs and feelings of a difficult child. Let us visualize the child with tears in his/her eyes and rage in his/her voice, contorting on the floor in a desperate attempt to be understood, and at the same time frightened by the parents' possible rejecting or retaliating responses. In such situations, it is relieving if one parent can ask for the help of the other ("Please do something! I can't take this anymore!"). At times, we see our borderline and dissociative patients in a similar developmental state, and we find ourselves as therapists in a state akin to that of the helpless–angry parent in the example. At such times, parallel psychotherapies not only offer the patient the prospect of a second and maybe more promising source of soothing; they also offer the first therapist the second one to turn to for help and support. If the first therapist, being aware of the helping availability of the second one, can contain his/her disappointment, frustration and helplessness, then the situation can be worked through. In the perspective of attachment disorganization, such a structure of the parallel psychotherapies reduces the likelihood that the therapeutic relationship becomes, for the patient, the scenario for the repetition of the original attachment trauma: meeting a confused, helpless, frightened and therefore frightening attachment figure just when the need for a soothing response is most intense. Parallel psychotherapy, thus, helps prevent the risk of re-traumatizing the patient through the repetition of the basic experience of disorganized attachment: increasing fear within the relationship that is expected to reduce fear.

Other ingredients of parallel therapies are also instrumental in correcting the basic deficits of disorders based on early attachment disorganization. Patients who, due to their insecure, chaotic and traumatic interpersonal environments, have rarely witnessed cooperation on equal grounds between their parents, can now learn that this is indeed a possibility in human interactions. By noticing, even if only at an implicit level, that the two therapists share a common attitude towards their problems and thus cooperate in their treatment, they can learn that human communication is not confined to care-seeking and care-giving, to competition for dominance, to punitive attitudes, and to sexual seduction. If a patient witnesses the possibility of cooperating on equal grounds by noticing how his or her two therapists exchange information and opinions concerning the treatment, he or she may also appreciate the benefits of a cooperative therapeutic alliance with each of his or her therapists, instead of shifting to aggressive, dependent or seductive attitudes within the therapeutic relationship.

Central to an attachment-based approach to the treatment of borderline patients is the recognition that two parallel therapies, rather than encouraging splitting, serve to acknowledge and contain painful and overwhelming feelings of fragmentation. Patients learn to observe their own internal experience as well as to observe themselves and the other in relationship, because the second therapy offers a secure base for exploring safely the conflicts that almost inevitably arise in the primary therapeutic relationship. However, if the patient witnesses rivalry and competition among his or her therapists, or their incapacity of dealing with diverging ideas without losing a cooperative and respectful reciprocal attitude, then the risk that a two-professional model instigates splitting in the patient's mental processes becomes high indeed.

In summary: attachment theory suggests reflection on parallel treatments as the source either of re-traumatization within the therapeutic relationships, or of corrective relational experiences. The relationship *between the two therapists* makes the difference, according to whether it is akin or radically diverging from the style of family communications that most often underlies the development of borderline and dissociative disorders in the children: a frightened/frightening attachment figure engaged in conflicting or neglecting (rather than supportive and cooperative) interactions with the other parent.

References

Ainsworth, M.D.S., Blehar, M., Waters, E. & Wall, S. (1978). *Patterns of attachment: A psychological study of the Strange Situation*. Hillsdale, NJ: Lawrence Erlbaum Associates.

Amini, F., Lewis, T., Lannon, R., Louie, A., Baumbacher, G., McGuinnes, T. & Zirker, E. (1996). Affect, attachment, memory: Contributions toward psychobiologic integration. *Psychiatry*, 59, 213–239.

Beck, A.T. & Emery, G. (1985). *Anxiety disorders and phobias: A cognitive perspective*. New York: Basic Books.

Blizard, R.A. (2001). Masochistic and sadistic ego states: Dissociative solutions to the dilemma of attachment to an abusive caregiver. *Journal of Trauma & Dissociation*, 2, 37–58.

Bowlby, J. (1979). *The making and breaking of affectional bonds*. London: Tavistock Publications.

Bowlby, J. (1982). *Attachment and loss. Vol. 1: Attachment* (2nd edition). London: Hogarth Press.

Bowlby, J. (1988). *A secure base*. London: Routledge.

Cortina, M. (2003). Defensive processes, emotions and internal working models: a perspective from attachment theory and contemporary models of the mind. In M. Cortina & M. Marrone (2003). *Attachment theory and the psychoanalytic process* (pp. 307–335). London: Whurr.

Dozier, M., Stovall, K.C. & Albus, K.E. (1999). Attachment and psychopathology in adulthood. In J. Cassidy & P.R. Shaver (eds), *Handbook of attachment* (pp. 497–519). New York: Guilford.

Fonogy, P. (1999). The transgenerational transmission of holocaust trauma: Lessons learned from the analysis of an adolescent with obsessive-compulsive disorder. *Attachment and Human Development*, 1, 92–114.

Fonagy, P., Target, M., Gergely, G., Allen, J.G. & Bateman, A.W. (2003). The developmental roots of borderline personality disorder in early attachment relationships: A theory and some evidence. *Psychoanalytic Inquiry*, 23: 412–459.

Freyd, J.J. (1997). *Betrayal trauma: The logic of forgetting child abuse*. Cambridge, MA: Harvard University Press.

Gabbard, G.O. & Lester, E.P. (1995). *Boundaries and boundary violations in psychoanalysis*. New York: Basic Books.

Gilbert, P. (1989). *Human nature and suffering*. London: Lawrence Erlbaum Associates.

Gilbert, P. (2000). Social mentalities: Internal "social" conflict and the role of inner warmth and compassion in cognitive therapy. In P. Gilbert & K. Bailey (eds), *Genes on the couch: Essays in evolutionary psychotherapy* (pp. 118–150). Hove, UK: Psychology Press.

Gilbert, P. (2004). Evolutionary approaches to psychopathology and cognitive therapy. In P. Gilbert (ed.), *Evolutionary theory and cognitive therapy* (pp. 3–44). New York: Springer.

Gilbert, P. (2005). Compassion and cruelty: A biopsychosocial approach. In P. Gilbert (ed.), *Compassion: Conceptualisations, research and use in psychotherapy* (pp. 9–75). Hove, UK: Brunner-Routledge.

Gilbert, P. & Irons, C. (2005). Focused therapies and compassionate mind training for shame and self-attacking. In P. Gilbert (ed.), *Compassion: Conceptualisations, research and use in psychotherapy* (pp. 263–325). Hove, UK: Brunner-Routledge.

Gold, S.N. (2000). *Not trauma alone: Therapy for child abuse survivors in family and social context*. Philadelphia: Brunner-Routledge.

Gold, S.N., Elhai, J.D., Rea, B.D., Weiss, D., Masino, T., Morris, S.L. & McInich, J. (2001). Contextual treatment of dissociative identity disorder: Three case studies. *Journal of Trauma & Dissociation*, 2, 5–35.

Greenberg, M.T. (1999). Attachment and psychopathology in childhood. In J. Cassidy & P.R. Shaver (eds), *Handbook of attachment* (pp. 469–496). New York: Guilford.

Grossmann, K.E. & Grossmann, K. (1991). Attachment quality as an organizer of emotional and behavioural responses in a longitudinal perspective. In C.M. Parkes, J. Stevenson-Hinde & P. Marris (eds), *Attachment across the life cycle* (pp. 93–114). London: Routledge.

Guidano, V.F. & Liotti, G. (1983). *Cognitive processes and emotional disorders*. New York: Guilford Press.

Hesse, E. (1999). The Adult Attachment Interview: Historical and current perspectives. In J. Cassidy & P.R. Shaver (eds), *Handbook of attachment* (pp. 395–433). New York: Guilford.

Hesse, E., Main, M., Abrams, K.Y. & Rifkin, A. (2003). Unresolved states regarding loss or abuse can have "second-generation" effects: Disorganized, role-inversion and frightening ideation in the offspring of traumatized non-maltreating parents. In D.J. Siegel & M.F. Solomon (eds), *Healing trauma: Attachment, mind, body and brain* (pp. 57–106). New York: Norton.

Holmes, J. (2004). Disorganized attachment and borderline personality disorder: A clinical perspective. *Attachment & Human Development*, 6, 181–190.

Leahy, R.L. (2005). A social-cognitive model of validation. In P. Gilbert (ed.), *Compassion: Conceptualisations, research and use in psychotherapy* (pp. 195–217). Hove, UK: Brunner-Routledge.

Linehan, M.M. (1993). *Cognitive-behavioral treatment for borderline personality disorder*. New York: Guilford Press.

Liotti, G. (1991). Patterns of attachment and the assessment of interpersonal schemata: Understanding and changing difficult patient–therapist relationships in cognitive psychotherapy. *Journal of Cognitive Psychotherapy*, 5, 105–114.

Liotti, G. (1992). Disorganized/disoriented attachment in the etiology of the dissociative disorders. *Dissociation*, 5, 196–204.

Liotti, G. (1994). *La dimensione interpersonale della coscienza [The interpersonal dimension of consciousness]*. Rome: NIS.

Liotti, G. (1995). Disorganized/disoriented attachment in the psychotherapy of the dissociative disorders. In S. Goldberg, R. Muir & J. Kerr (eds), *Attachment theory: Social, developmental and clinical perspectives* (pp. 343–363). Hillsdale, NJ: Analytic Press.

Liotti, G. (1999). Disorganized attachment as a model for the understanding of dissociative psychopathology. In J. Solomon & C. George (eds), *Attachment disorganization* (pp. 291–317). New York: Guilford Press.

Liotti, G. (2000). Disorganized attachment, models of borderline states, and evolutionary psychotherapy. In P. Gilbert & K. Bailey (eds), *Genes on the couch: Essays in evolutionary psychotherapy* (pp. 232–256). Hove, UK: Psychology Press.

Liotti, G. (2004a). The inner schema of borderline states and its correction during psychotherapy: A cognitive–evolutionary approach. In P. Gilbert (ed.), *Evolutionary theory and cognitive therapy* (pp. 137–160). New York: Springer.

Liotti, G. (2004b). Trauma, dissociation and disorganized attachment: Three strands of a single braid. *Psychotherapy: Theory, Research, Practice and Training*, 41, 472–486.

Liotti, G. & Intreccialagli, B. (2003). Disorganized attachment, motivational systems and metacognitive monitoring in the treatment of a patient with borderline syndrome. In M. Cortina & M. Marrone (eds), *Attachment theory and the psychoanalytic process* (pp. 356–381). London: Whurr.

Lyons-Ruth, K. (2003). Dissociation and the parent–infant dialogue: A longitudinal perspective from attachment research. *Journal of the American Psychoanalytic Association*, 51, 883–911.

Lyons-Ruth, K., Yellin, C., Melnick, S. & Atwood, G. (2003). Childhood experiences of trauma and loss have different relations to maternal unresolved and hostile–helpless states of mind on the AAI. *Attachment and Human Development*, 5, 330–352.

Main, M. & Morgan, H. (1996). Disorganization and disorientation in infant Strange Situation behavior: Phenotypic resemblance to dissociative states? In L. Michelson & W. Ray (eds), *Handbook of dissociation* (pp. 107–137). New York: Plenum Press.

Safran, J. & Segal, Z. (1990). *Interpersonal process in cognitive therapy*. New York: Basic Books.

Salkovskis, P.M. (1985). Obsessional–compulsive problems: A cognitive-behavioral analysis. *Behaviour Research and Therapy*, 23, 571–584.

Steele, K., Van der Hart, O. & Nijenhuis, E.R. (2001). Dependency in the treatment of complex posttraumatic stress disorder and dissociative disorders. *Journal of Trauma & Dissociation*, 2, 79–115.

Tomasello, M. (1999). *The cultural origins of human cognition*. Cambridge, MA: Harvard University Press.

Tomasello, M., Carpenter, M., Call, J., Behne, T. & Moll, H. (2005). Understanding and changing intentions: The origins of cultural cognition. *Behavioral and Brain Sciences*, 28, 675–691.

Part II

The therapeutic relationship in specific therapies

Chapter 8

The therapeutic relationship in cognitive therapy with difficult-to-engage clients

Cory F. Newman

Introduction

It almost goes without saying that cognitive therapists have the best chance of forming positive, productive, working relationships with their clients if they manifest and demonstrate the humanistic characteristics of inter-personal warmth, genuineness, and positive regard (cf. Rogers, 1957; Truax & Carkhuff, 1967). Therapists who convey these qualities in session are more likely to help clients feel safe and encouraged enough to disclose painful details about their lives, to explore further aspects of their psychological experience, and to strive to make constructive changes. Though cognitive therapy has developed a positive reputation as being conceptually sophisticated and technically rich, it does in fact pay close attention to the therapeutic relationship as well (Gilbert, 1992; Layden, Newman, Freeman, & Morse, 1993; Leahy, 2001; Raue, Goldfried, & Barkham, 1997). A healthy, collaborative, mutually trusting relationship between therapist and client is a significant boon to treatment, and therefore is a priority.

That being said, the therapist's ability to maintain a positive, mature, caring stance is put to the test when clients express mistrust, criticisms, excessive demands, threats, and other interpersonally harmful behaviors in session or between sessions (e.g., via voicemail). This is where cognitive therapists must strive to be aware of their own potentially dysfunctional thoughts, so that they do not respond in such a way as to feed into a vicious cycle of negative interactions (Layden *et al.*, 1993; Leahy, 2001; Safran & Segal, 1996). Instead, the therapists must conceptualize the clients' noxious behaviors so as to gain a compassionate understanding of the clients' vulnerabilities and compensatory strategies that the latter unfortunately express in maladaptive ways (see J.S. Beck, 2005; Leahy, 2001). Therapists then can choose an opportune moment to offer hypotheses about the problems that are occurring in the therapeutic relationship, humbly asking for corrective feedback along the way, while making it clear that the goal is to facilitate a helpful relationship. Ideally, this process becomes the model for what the clients can do in their everyday life, so that they engage in thoughtful reflection with benevolent intent, rather than impulsive counter-attacking with self-defensive intent.

Cognitive therapists also utilize their humanistic qualities and conceptualization skills to become more adept at introducing, teaching, and mentoring their clients in the difficult but necessary process of learning the competencies of cognitive-behavioral self-help, the likes of which are vital not only for symptom improvement, but for long-term relapse-prevention as well (Strunk, Chiu, Cronquist, & DeRubeis, 2006). First, cognitive therapists have to be good role-models, showing that they are willing to do the nuts and bolts work of therapy (for example, assigning and reviewing homework, teaching and practicing the techniques) with grace, enthusiasm, and optimism. In other words, cognitive therapists must demonstrate a strong work ethic, a positive sense of urgency in helping the clients make improvements and experience relief from suffering, and a knack for remembering both critical and trivial details of the client's life and course of treatment to date.

For example, cognitive therapists demonstrate their commitment and diligence by performing a thorough assessment, gaining a developmental, longitudinal understanding of the client's life, family situation, and treatment history, utilizing structured diagnostic methods and client self-report inventories, and taking good session notes that translate to continuity of focus and understanding across sessions. Further, cognitive therapists endeavor to get the most out of any given session, to give thoughtful replies to reasonable questions from the clients, to devise relevant homework assignments which they then review the following session, to demonstrate the various techniques (for example, finding the best ways to benefit from filling out Dysfunctional Thought Records; see J.S. Beck, 1995), and to contribute energy and expressions of hope to each session. By doing the above, therapists *invest* in their clients' well being, and *model* how clients can conduct their lives with self-efficacy and interpersonal skill. Most clients will ascertain this, will appreciate it, and will gradually reciprocate by increasing their willingness to trust and to work. Those clients who have difficulties recognizing or reciprocating their cognitive therapist's best efforts will at least provide the therapist with opportunities to conceptualize the problem, and to hone their professional skills in managing refractory cases.

Clients' success and improvement as part of the therapeutic relationship

There is an impressive body of empirical literature that supports a consistent relation between the quality of the therapeutic alliance and outcomes across a range of treatment orientations (e.g., Horvath & Bedi, 2002; Horvath & Symonds, 1991; Klein *et al.*, 2003; Martin, Garkse, & Davis,

2000). However, a similarly compelling line of research has emerged which supports an alternative hypothesis – namely, that when temporal confounds are methodologically addressed, the data (in studies of cognitive therapy for depression) indicate that symptom reduction causes improvements in the therapeutic alliance, and not vice versa (DeRubeis, Brotman, & Gibbons, 2005; DeRubeis & Feeley, 1990; Feeley, DeRubeis, & Gelfand, 1999). Further studies have suggested that when depressed clients experience a "sudden gain" in treatment, as indicated by markedly improved Beck Depression Inventory scores (Beck, Ward, Mendelson, Mock, & Erbaugh, 1961) from one session to the next, this phenomenon is often followed by substantial improvements in the helping alliance (Tang, Beberman, DeRubeis, & Pham, 2005; Tang & DeRubeis, 1999). These "sudden gains" were often preceded by especially productive therapy sessions, in which clients confirmed significant changes in their previously maladaptive beliefs about themselves and their world. Taken together, the above data support the contention that theory-specific aspects of cognitive therapy are keys in reducing depressive symptoms, which in turn are relevant to the boosting of the quality of the therapeutic alliance.

At the same time, there may be reason to believe that there is a reciprocal (and perhaps synergistic) effect between the technical and relational aspects of cognitive therapy, such that positive changes in one may spur positive changes in the other (Rector, Zuroff, & Segal, 1999), provided that the therapist faithfully delivers the technical components of the treatment, and provided that the clients are not too chronically impaired in their interpersonal functioning (as they might be in cases of severe personality disorders; see Connolly Gibbons, Crits-Christoph, de la Cruz, Barber, Siqueland, & Gladis, 2003). Additionally, the client's learning of the technical self-help skills of cognitive therapy has been shown to be related to maintenance of positive gains at follow-up (Strunk et al., 2006). This finding has important theoretical and practical implications, in that it provides evidence that the termination of the therapeutic relationship does not have to lead to an increase in client vulnerability to relapse, as it might if the relationship alone were causally responsible for positive outcomes.

In light of these data on the importance of the therapeutic relationship, along with the role that symptom improvement and skill-building play in facilitating the short-term outcomes and long-term benefits of cognitive therapy, we should examine the therapeutic relationship in cognitive therapy in the context of the full treatment package. An overarching goal would be to optimize the degrees to which cognitive therapists and their clients feel a positive connection, sharing in the work of exploration, conceptualization, intervention, and maintenance practice. If each party has positive feelings toward the other, and both parties invest sufficient time, energy, and attention to the therapeutic tasks at hand, it is reasonable to predict that the positive results of cognitive therapy will be magnified and sustained (see Hardy, Cahill, & Barkham, Chapter 2, this volume; Katzow & Safran, Chapter 5, this volume).

Let us now take a brief definitional look at the "connectedness" and "competence" factors in cognitive therapy, both in clients and in therapists (for a total of four categories). When all categories have a positive valence, therapy should proceed smoothly. However, let us consider some of the challenges that pertain to each of these areas, as summarized below.

Therapists' interpersonal connectedness

Effective therapists are skilled communicators. They are able to give feedback to their clients – both positive and negative – in a thoughtful, constructive, well-mannered way. Such therapists are invested in helping their clients seek and find relief from their psychological suffering, and in teaching them the cognitive, behavioral, and affect-regulating skills necessary to improve both their current condition and their long-term prospects for wellness. Therapists who can connect with their clients in this way are also adept at handling potentially difficult, tense moments with clients. They do not respond with the sort of fight or flight reactions to the clients' high expressed emotion (e.g., anger, suicide threats) that may be typical of the people in the clients' everyday life. Instead, therapists with good interpersonal skills remain calm, express care and concern, maintain a professional stance (for example, formulating a treatment plan, maintaining proper boundaries), and do not summarily terminate treatment except in extreme circumstances. Arguably, the mark of a therapist's interpersonal mettle is not as much about his or her acts of genuineness and warmth when things are proceeding routinely as it is about an ability to stay constructively connected in the face of aversive client behaviors. Therapists inspire trust and confidence in their clients when they show grace and poise under pressure, maintain a high standard of interpersonal behavior, and do not take punitive or rejecting actions against clients. Instead, they do their utmost to conceptualize the reasons for the alliance rupture, to repair it, and to move forward with hope and optimism. Part of this skill is tied to the therapists' own familiarity and facility with self-monitoring their dysfunctional automatic thoughts, and in quickly, silently generating rational responses that keep them focused on feeling positive and pursuing constructive solutions. As a bonus, therapists who succeed in this manner also add to their cachet as role-models for their clients.

For example, a client angrily tossed his Beck Hopelessness Scale (Beck, Weissman, Lester, & Trexler, 1974) onto the therapist's desk at the start of a session. Through tears and with an angry tone, the client said the following: "How am I supposed to answer these questions about the future? My father is *dying*. These questions just rub it in my face. I was *fine* all day until I saw this questionnaire, and now I'm ticked off." The therapist was a bit stunned, having no clue that the client would react this way to a routine questionnaire, and not realizing that the client's father's health had apparently taken a precipitous turn for the worse. The therapist tuned into his automatic thoughts, which were, "Oh no," "My client thinks I'm an insensitive clod," and "Now the session is going to be unpleasant and unproductive." The therapist gathered himself while he silently formulated some rational responses intended to lower his arousal, stay calm, repair the apparent rupture in the therapeutic relationship, and salvage the session. Some of the therapist's rational responses were, "Imagine how you would feel if your father were dying – be compassionate and let him vent if he wants to," "The Beck Hopelessness Scale is not important right now, so put it aside and focus on the client's anticipatory grief about his father," "This is not about you, so don't take it personally," and "Remember that this client comes from a family where demonstrations of 'weak emotions' are shunned, so he's likely feeling ashamed to be crying in front of you and possibly wants to reassert some control by expressing anger." These rational responses enabled the therapist to engage with the client in a non-defensive way, and to carefully, calmly manage the session.

Therapists' competence in conducting cognitive therapy

As anyone who has trained to become a fully fledged cognitive therapist can attest, it is hard work! A glance at the Cognitive Therapy Rating Scale (CTRS: Young & Beck, 1980) – the measure that is widely used to assess the competency of cognitive therapists in their work with a particular client in a single session – shows that many of the 11 key criterion items are procedural, such as setting an agenda, asking guided discovery questions, focusing on key cognitions and behaviors, applying cognitive-behavioral techniques, and reviewing and assignment homework. This does not mean that the interpersonal aspect of the therapeutic alliance is overlooked by the CTRS. There are items that specifically assess the therapist's interpersonal skills, such as those labeled "understanding," "interpersonal effectiveness," and "collaboration." Further, the procedural items often are rated more highly to the degree that they are done with interpersonal aplomb, which itself is often tied into concepts such as timing, pacing, and tone. The point is as follows – according to the CTRS, *interpersonal skill is necessary but not sufficient* for the therapist to produce a cognitive therapy session that is up to standard. If the therapist does not utilize the procedural components of cognitive therapy, the treatment will be watered down, the client will not learn the requisite self-monitoring and self-modification skills that presage good outcome and maintenance, and the treatment will not pass muster as cognitive therapy. At the same time, one may argue that part of the therapist's competence lies in the ability to stay focused on the important tasks of conceptualizing the case and enacting appropriate interventions, even while simultaneously fielding the client's expressions of fear, anger, and/or apathy about engaging in these procedures.

Clients' interpersonal connectedness

Many clients who do not evince signs of personality disorders (or other serious conditions such as active addictions) are positively responsive to their therapist's genuine demonstrations of concern, professionalism, and optimism. If it is clear that the therapist is friendly and invested in the process of helping the client recover (from depression, anxiety, etc.), such clients will feel encouraged, and will be more inclined to make a good-faith effort to collaborate in the therapeutic venture. When this favorable scenario occurs, there is typically little stress and strain in the therapeutic relationship, and the two parties can put their focus squarely on the skills acquisition and maintenance components of the treatment.

However, some clients (who often meet criteria for moderate to severe personality disorders) manifest many of their problems in the interpersonal sphere, which they then bring to bear in their interactions with their therapists (Beck, Davis, & Freeman, 2004; Connolly Gibbons *et al.*, 2003). Examples are plentiful, including clients being prone to misinterpret their therapist's comments and intentions in negative ways (i.e., maintaining their mistrust schema), holding prejudicial assumptions about the therapist's personal qualities in relation to the client (for example, "This therapist isn't the sort of person who could possibly understand or help me"), expressing hostility and evincing a sense of entitlement (for example, a client who demands excessive between-sessions phone contact, and then complains that, "If you can't be there for your clients when they need you, then you should get out of the profession!"), showing an apathetic passivity in session and often missing appointments, and many other maladaptive ways of relating. The degree of severity of these problems can be assessed by taking into account the frequency, intensity, and duration of the sorts of behaviors described above, while determining whether the clients also are capable of displaying contrasting, positive interpersonal behavior.

Yet another yardstick to measure the clients' difficulties in connecting with the therapist is their responsivity to the therapist's sincere, skilled attempts to make repairs (Safran, Muran, Samstag, & Stevens, 2001). When therapists can use their interpersonal skills to help smooth over a misunderstanding with a client, or to address and alleviate tension between the two parties, the therapists feel a sense of efficacy, the situation seems controllable, and the atmosphere can be made more conducive to the work of cognitive therapy. However, when the therapist's best efforts to address and correct the problem in the therapeutic relationship fail to improve matters, it can create a sense of mutual helplessness, especially if this phenomenon occurs session after session. One way to conceptualize this problem is to hypothesize that the clients in such situations erroneously believe that the establishment of a positive therapeutic relationship is entirely the responsibility of the therapist (see Bedi, Davis, & Williams, 2005), as the clients fail to appreciate the vital role they themselves play in getting along with others (including therapists). The following dialogue illustrates a cognitive therapist's efforts to address this point with a client who complained bitterly that he wasn't "seeing any progress" in therapy.

Therapist: I agree that it's a concern that your depression and family problems have not diminished, and I want to assure you that I am very motivated to work with you to make better progress. To be frank, I need more of your participation.

Client: I don't know what you mean by that. Here I am, week after week. Why can't you help me?

Therapist: Showing up for therapy sessions is a good start, but we're missing a sense of teamwork, and we really need that spirit of collaboration. I welcome the opportunity to work on Thought Records with you to address your thoughts of hopelessness, to do role-play exercises with you to work on interpersonal issues, and to put our heads together to come up with potentially fruitful homework assignments. Usually, when I suggest that we do any of these things, you think I'm being demanding and unkind, and you scold me for putting an undue burden on you. So I've tried to scale back these parts of the treatment out of respect for your wishes, but this holds us back a bit.

Client: I just don't see any progress.

Therapist: I acknowledge what you're saying, though I'm adding another message as well, and I hope you will give this your fullest attention. When you say that you don't "see" any progress, it sounds as though you're *observing*, rather than *participating*. We need to take ownership of this worthy endeavor together, working collaboratively. This is not about what "I am doing for you," but rather what "*we* are doing together" to overcome the problems that brought you here.

When the client's interpersonal behaviors in session continue to be noxious and inappropriate irrespective of the therapist's earnest attempts to ameliorate the situation calmly, we may infer that the client is acting abusively toward the therapist (Newman, 1997). In extreme cases in which the therapists feel personally threatened they are ethically permitted to put their own safety first, rather than believe that they are obligated to continue meeting with the client (Thompson, 1990). Fortunately, such occurrences are rare in outpatient practice, but they highlight the folly of taking the extreme view that a competent cognitive therapist should be able to establish and maintain a therapeutic alliance with *every* client who enters the office, under *all* conditions. All-or-none thinking is contraindicated in cognitive therapists the same as with their clients.

Clients' competence in learning and practicing cognitive therapy skills

Many clients view the therapist's office as a place where they can discuss their concerns freely, without judgment or real-life consequences, and perhaps where they can obtain validation and direction. This is all well and good, but cognitive therapy aims to provide this and much more – namely, the imparting of valuable psychological skills that clients can incorporate into their coping and interpersonal repertoires. By learning and practicing skills such as objective self-monitoring, responding rationally to maladaptive patterns in thinking, scheduling and using their time more effectively, communicating with more clarity and tact, approaching and solving problems rather than avoiding them, and thinking more constructively and optimistically as a new default mode (among other skills), clients can improve their self-confidence and make durable gains in functioning (Strunk *et al.*, 2006).

However, for one reason or another, clients sometimes have difficulties with this *work* aspect of therapy. They may erroneously believe that therapy is exclusively about feeling comforted, and therefore bristle at the idea that they need to make changes, or to learn competencies to effect such changes. Other clients may comprehend that being active and working toward change may be desirable in therapy, but believe that they are incapable of achieving this (for example, in the case of schemas of incompetence or dependence), or that they will be punished or tossed out of treatment by their therapists for performing poorly on homework assignments (for example, in the case of schemas of defectiveness, mistrust, or abandonment). Thus, for clients such as these, conflicts may arise in the therapeutic relationship when the therapist gently persists in structuring the sessions, asks the clients challenging questions, tries to utilize techniques such as role-playing, and assigns homework involving writing or behavioral experimentation.

In response to this problem, therapists can try to institute techniques in small increments, allow the clients more time in session to emote, and occasionally check on the clients' thoughts about trying some skill-building methods. In giving a rationale for the benefits of doing the *work* of therapy, one therapist said, "Sometimes therapy is like one of those classes where the teacher seems excessively demanding, but later you realize that you learned a lot, and you stretched yourself to new levels of achievement." More will be said about this problem area in the next section.

The interaction of the alliance and techniques in problematic clinical situations

Many clients enter treatment feeling depleted, downtrodden, misunderstood, helpless, and hopeless. Thus, when they ascertain that cognitive therapy will be an active treatment involving such directive elements as guided discovery questions and homework assignments, clients sometimes respond by feeling *worse*. They may take umbrage at their therapist's attempts to set an agenda, to question their cognitive interpretations of situations, and to ask for summary statements and substantive feedback. Between-sessions self-monitoring and behavioral experiments may seem utterly out of the question, and may therefore become a source of friction between therapist and client. Without some sort of productive response to solve the impasse, the therapy enterprise will be in danger of breaking down, assuming it even gets started.

Stay close to the middle ground

So what is a cognitive therapist to do? The dysfunctional "all or none" approach would be to continue to insist on following the full cognitive therapy protocol without flexibility (at one extreme), or to completely abandon the structured, well-validated methods of cognitive therapy in the supposed interest of the therapeutic alliance (at the other extreme). Clearly, the spirit of cognitive therapy requires a middle-ground, empirical approach, whereby the therapist evaluates progress on the go, makes adjustments, negotiates mutual accommodations, takes the client's complaints seriously and conceptualizes them, and introduces techniques such as behavioral experiments and graded tasks in trying to gradually implement the methods of cognitive therapy. All the while, the therapist invites the client to examine how things are going in therapy as objectively as possible, reinforcing the methods that are helping the client to improve, and modifying those methods that are not.

As some clients enter therapy with an all-or-none mindset (part and parcel of their psychological dysfunction), they may have some trouble in adjusting to the "happy medium" approach espoused above. Viewing themselves as being thoroughly incapable of coping with demands of any sort, they sometimes maintain that they simply cannot do the work of cognitive therapy, period. In response to this expression of helplessness, the cognitive therapist can explain the following important points.

1   It is a sign of respect that the therapist assumes that the client's level of functioning can be improved, even if the client believes otherwise.
2   The client's feelings are valid as feelings (and therefore warrant attention and empathy), but the cognitive underpinnings of these feelings may be deeply flawed, much to the client's disadvantage, and it is

the therapist's responsibility to help clients assess and modify such cognitive flaws.

3   Cognitive therapy does not focus exclusively on the client's deficits and problems, but also seeks to find and raise the client's "ceiling of functioning," which will necessarily involve an ambitious focus on building strengths.

As one may deduce from the above, the process of cognitive therapy with clients who have difficulties in interpersonal relating (such as those with moderate to severe personality disorders) requires deft, sensitive handling. Tensions will arise from time to time, such as when the therapist gently insists on staying focused in session, tries to institute techniques such as role-playing, constructively critiques the client's problematic coping strategies, gives homework assignments, and takes other therapeutic risks that place demands on the clients.

There is evidence that a moderate degree of such tension is in fact optimal for favorable outcomes in cognitive therapy with clients who have avoidant and obsessive–compulsive personality disorders. A study by Strauss *et al.* (2006) found evidence of a "V-shaped" relationship between therapeutic alliance ratings and response to cognitive therapy, implying that there may be an optimal zone of "stress" in the therapeutic relationship – involving moderate alliance strains and prompt repairs – that bodes well for outcome with these populations. Too little tension may mean that the treatment is largely supportive, but lacking in constructive interventions and related skill-building that improve the chances for change. Too much conflict may reflect a breakdown of collaboration and good will, increasing the likelihood of early drop-out from therapy.

One may hypothesize that the healthy middle ground is composed of a mindful balance of validation and change, support and confrontation, work and rest, to go along with a thoughtful hybridization of the respective opinions, methods, and goals of the therapist and the client. Therapists, by dint of their professional position, bear the lion's share of the responsibility to create, teach, and nurture such a balance. However, in the end, we hope that the balance of power can be transferred to the clients, so that they benefit from improved moods, hopefulness, and self-efficacy for the long run, independent of regular meetings with their therapist.

Be mindful of the client's ongoing choice to stay or leave

As noted above, a particularly definitive manifestation of a breakdown in the therapeutic relationship is the client's abruptly dropping out of treatment. The data in the field of cognitive therapy for personality disorders seems to indicate that retention of clients with personality disorders for a full course of treatment is difficult, yet quite important for success (see

Newman & Fingerhut, 2005). For example, Persons, Burns, & Perloff (1988) found that patients with an Axis-II disorder were significantly more likely to drop out of their treatment outcome study than their non-personality-disordered counterparts. However, those Axis-II clients who succeeded in staying in treatment until completion of the protocol demonstrated clinical gains that were statistically equivalent to the group that did not have personality disorders. Sanderson, Beck, & McGinn (1994) reported strikingly similar findings. In their treatment sample of clients with generalized anxiety disorder, those clients who had concomitant personality disorders tended to leave treatment early. However, those Axis-II clients who remained long enough to receive a reasonable course of short-term therapy showed a significant decrease in both anxiety and depressive symptoms.

The upshot of the above is that cognitive therapists may have to be especially mindful of their difficult-to-engage clients' ambivalence about attending and remaining in therapy. Special attention is needed in order to establish and maintain a connection with such clients. For example, following an emotionally evocative session, therapists may want to contact their clients by phone, just to say that they appreciated the clients' hard work, and look forward to making more progress together in the next session (Newman & Fingerhut, 2005). In essence, this is an invitation to continue with treatment at a time when the clients may be tempted to bolt. Similarly, when therapists feel that they have been stymied in trying to repair damage to the therapeutic relationship in session, they may choose to write a thoughtful letter between sessions in an effort to re-engage the client. The beauty of a letter is that the therapist can speak to the client without interruption, and can model a benevolent, problem-solving approach in addressing the strain in their relationship. The letter should ideally end with a welcoming statement that affirms the therapist's positive spirit of collaboration in anticipation of the next session.

Modify techniques to improve the therapeutic relationship

In addition to the between-sessions communications described above, therapists may need to modify some of their standard in-session behaviors with the difficult-to-engage client. The following is a non-exhaustive sampling of adjustments that cognitive therapists can consider making in order to firm up a solid, working relationship with otherwise hard-to-reach or hard-to-keep clients (for additional points, see Newman, 1998).

1. Watch out for clients' adverse reactions to excessive expressions of optimism

While it is generally true that cognitive therapists endeavor to instill hope in their clients, and while the data show that it is appropriate and necessary to be active in combating the clients' sense of hopelessness (Beck, Brown, Berchick, Stewart, & Steer, 1990), some clients will interpret their therapist's expressions of optimism as a sign that they "don't get it." Instead of responding favorably to the therapist's "can do" attitude, such clients may be apt to feel invalidated, reasoning to themselves that if the therapist *really* understood what they were going through, he or she would acknowledge the clients' misery and despair as being beyond their control. This issue is reflected in Leahy's model of "validation resistance" (Leahy, 2001; Leahy, Chapter 11, this volume).

When cognitive therapists sense (for example, through the client's non-verbal cues) that this may be happening, they can enact one of the key procedural tasks of the treatment model – namely, to ask for feedback. For example, a therapist might say, "I noticed that you were glumly shaking your head 'no' as I talked about the ways that you might be able to improve your life situation, and I wonder what your thoughts are about this important matter." The client might then say, "I've tried everything, and nothing works, so I don't really think you can help me." The therapist's job at this point is not to exhort or persuade the client to come around to a more hopeful position on the spot. Rather, the therapist has to find a way to strike a balance between learning more about the way the client is thinking, and actively illustrating how this process in and of itself might be a significant first step in treatment. The therapist listens to and reflects the client's position, while also expressing concern and empathy regarding how they feel. For good measure (in the interest of educating the client about the cognitive model of psychotherapy), the therapist can explain that treatment does not teach clients merely to engage in idle, positive thinking (Newman & Haaga, 1995). To the contrary, it is important to identify and acknowledge real-life problems, while also learning how to keep them in perspective, simultaneously keeping an open mind about ways to improve things, perhaps in small, gradual steps over time. In sum, therapists do not abandon all expressions of optimism and enthusiasm in order to play "misery loves company" with clients, but they may need to give the clients more room to vent than they might need to give to higher-functioning clients, and they may similarly need to provide more overt expressions of validation before proceeding with technical interventions.

2. Do not identify and test every dysfunctional thought, to the point of micro-managing the client's thinking

Being an involved, active cognitive therapist does not necessitate the relentless pursuit of each and every client thought that may be causing undue distress. In fact, such "hyperactivity" on the part of the therapist may actually be detrimental to the therapeutic relationship, as the spirit of collaborative empiricism is potentially replaced by a litany of perceived interruptions and corrections. It is much more in the spirit of a positive working relationship (not to mention more productive) for the therapists to listen and mentally "gather" (or perhaps write down) key comments from their clients, in the search for patterns and themes that may be addressed collectively and parsimoniously.

When clients are reticent, unclear, vague, or otherwise have difficulty in articulating key thoughts behind their emotional distress, therapists can gently ask for more information, while refraining from immediately testing each response for functionality. In other words, when clients struggle to produce relevant material to work on in session, therapists need to take advantage of every opportunity in which clients do in fact speak up, without distracting them with premature interventions. For example, a therapist may allow for five minutes of client monologue, interspersed only by the therapist's facilitative questions to gain more information, following by his or her saying to the client, "I can hear that you're saying all of this with a heavy heart, about how you feel so alone. I noticed that you mentioned a few situations in which people in your life tried to communicate with you, but your interpretations were along the lines of, 'They pity me,' or 'They think I'm a burden,' or 'They hope I'll decline their obligatory invitations to get together,' and so on. I am concerned about this pattern in your thinking, in which you dismiss or negate the meaning of people in your life expressing care and involvement. Can we examine this further and see if we can look at it from another angle or two?" This sort of summary potentially accomplishes a great deal in terms of both solidifying the alliance, and moving the work of therapy forward.

3. Be alert to a sense of competitiveness or power struggle in session

Clients who are particularly sensitive to issues surrounding autonomy and control may not be optimally receptive to the therapist's implication that they need to change the way they think. This sentiment may be summed up as: "I may not be a happy person, but I know what I know, and don't try to tell me otherwise!" A good management of the therapeutic alliance in such cases necessitates the therapist's averting the escalating of a power struggle over "who is right and who is wrong."

Instead, therapists can carefully, gradually express the view that each participant in therapy brings certain strengths and vulnerabilities to the process. For example, the client brings a wealth of first-hand life experience to the table, along with a tendency to be subjective in evaluating these experiences. By contrast, the therapist is not privy to all of the client's life experiences, but rather brings a great deal of knowledge about psychological functioning to the discussion, along with a vantage point that supports greater objectivity. Taken together, the strengths of the client's and therapist's perspectives may synergize to create a clearer, broader, more constructive perspective on the client's life. This process works best if the two participants work in a spirit of cooperation and active inquiry, without concern for who is in control, who knows best, or whose agenda will prevail. Cognitive therapists can emphasize their own responsibility in this respect by overtly noting that their views about the client are *hypotheses to be tested*, rather than pat interpretations that are inviolable.

4. Deal sensitively with clients' beliefs about "not being ready" to change or to do homework

At times, clients feel rushed into doing therapeutic tasks they believe they are not "ready" to do. Examples include engaging in role-play exercises, trying a behavioral experiment, thinking about upcoming life events in a hopeful way, doing any number of homework assignments (for example, daily thought records), and making psychological changes in general. When therapists nonetheless persist in presenting these interventions, it may put a strain on the alliance. However, to abandon the presentation and pursuit of tasks and skills represents the opposite extreme, and is not the optimal solution, even if it immediately helps the client to feel comfortable in session. As usual, the goal is to find the happy medium, which admittedly is a narrower zone when clients are less well functioning.

Therapists must tune into the client's fears, concerns, and misapprehensions with compassion and understanding, thus making these the focal points of the therapeutic discussion. Therapists also can give the rationale that they are trying to give the clients the "full package" of treatment, and to test their ceiling of functioning in order to achieve the greatest degree of positive change in the most reasonable amount of time. At the same time, therapists can acknowledge that they will ultimately respect the limits that clients set, as the two parties go through their benevolent negotiation process about where therapy is headed, and how they will get there (Safran & Muran, 2000).

5. Handle termination as a "transfer of power," but acknowledge the clients' sense of loss, and/or apprehension about being on their own

An overarching goal of cognitive therapy is to increase the client's sense of self-efficacy. The therapist's use of collaborative empiricism, implementation of homework, and focus on being time-effective are all geared toward the goal of facilitating the client's sense of autonomy. Ideally, therapy continues if there is evidence that the clients are benefiting, and/or if important goals are being pursued actively. Sometimes, treatment serves as relatively more of a caretaking or witness-bearing role when clients are especially vulnerable, such as when they are recovering from trauma or grief. Nevertheless, even in these instances, cognitive therapists are mindful of minimizing the risk that the clients will come to feel dependent on and helpless without their therapists. Thus, therapists continue to bring up the topic of goal-setting, to teach self-help skills, and to allude to a time when the clients will have "graduated from regular sessions." A reduction in frequency of sessions and/or the implementation of periodic booster sessions are means by which to transition clients from a period of intensive therapy to a time where clients are largely expected to practice being their own therapists in everyday life.

The above process often occurs quite smoothly, but there are times when clients have resurgent fears and doubts, perhaps along with a sense of anticipatory loss, when faced with the prospect of the end of treatment. Without a doubt, therapists need to be empathic at such times, and to acknowledge that separation from a supportive person can be daunting. The client's concerns can be dealt with as any other set of thoughts and feelings that have been assessed over the course of therapy, and at times therapists can judiciously share their own thoughts and feelings as well. For example, when a therapist and client openly shed a few tears upon saying farewell at the end of a course of therapy, the therapist said, "This reminds me of high school graduation day, when teachers and students are crying because they're going to miss each other, but it's such a great accomplishment, and the future looks so bright." Another therapist said, "You know that saying, 'When one door closes, another one opens?' Well, in this case, my door is still open to you in the future, but if you come back I'll want to hear all about the new door you've entered toward your improved life and healthier self."

Culture and ethnicity as variables of interest in the therapeutic relationship

Although beyond the scope of this chapter to discuss in depth, it is important to add that culture and ethnicity are important considerations in the therapeutic alliance. In order to be collaborative in a culturally sensitive and effective manner, it behooves cognitive therapists to take every reasonable opportunity to educate themselves about working with clients from minority or foreign backgrounds (see Gilbert, Gilbert, & Sanghera, 2004). At the risk of grossly oversimplifying this most important matter, the following are some brief examples of how an understanding of and respect for the client's heritage can facilitate the therapeutic bond.

1   In working with a Hispanic client, the concept of *personalismo* is important to understand (Organista, 2000). Here, the client is more apt to place value on and trust in the therapeutic relationship if the therapists are willing to share a little bit of personal information about themselves, and are similarly willing to accept small favors or token

gifts from their clients. Naturally, therapists must not stretch their normal, professional boundaries too far, but some added flexibility with some Hispanic clients may be indicated.

2 A Caucasian therapist working with a person of African origin or ancestry needs to be mindful of the client's potential concerns about receiving prejudicial treatment (Mayo, 2004). In order to be accurately empathic, therapists need to be most tolerant and understanding of their client's mistrust, and may need to go the extra mile to earn the client's confidence. This may be especially true in cases of treatment research trials, where (for example) African-American clients may be all too familiar with horror stories from the past such as the Tuskegee experiment, where African-American subjects were deliberately and deceptively not treated for their medical conditions, thus egregiously allowing their health to deteriorate toward death without intervention (Jones, 1993).

3 It is important to respect the traditional family systems and roles of certain Asian clients, for whom respect for parents (filial piety) may be of paramount importance, even when the therapist believes that it would be in the best interest of the client to individuate and become more independent (Chen & Davenport, 2005). Similarly, therapists may need to be more accepting of the Asian client's reticence in revealing information that could be seen as shaming of his or her family. Rather than seeing such clients as being resistant or avoidant, it may be more appropriate for therapists to view them as being understandably dutiful to the honor of their families (Gilbert et al., 2004).

It would be interesting to study the effects of "matching" therapists and clients in terms of shared ethnic heritage, in terms of both its benefits for the therapeutic alliance and its impact on the building of client competencies and the prediction of positive outcome. For example, does the therapist's personal knowledge of the religious rituals and/or the details of the country of birth (or ancestral legacy) of the client facilitate "connectedness" and "competency" in the therapeutic alliance? Likewise, if both the therapist and client are from minorities living within a dominant culture at large, does this improve trust, as well as a sense of a shared mission within the parameters of the same societal obstacles? On the lighter side, does a similar sense of humor, based on a shared ethnic tradition, boost the therapeutic relationship? These are intriguing questions for any orientation of psychotherapy.

Concluding points

As a brief overview, the following points should be emphasized.

- The therapeutic relationship and the technical aspects of skill-building in cognitive therapy likely interact in mutually reinforcing ways. The learning of cognitive-behavioral skills gives a boost to the therapeutic relationship ("Nothing succeeds like success"), while a healthy, collaborative, resilient therapeutic relationship serves to create a climate that is most congenial to exploration and change. Although the data on depressed clients indicates that positive changes brought about by cognitive therapy lead to improvements in the therapeutic alliance, it may be that the therapeutic relationship will be shown to have more primary causal significance in populations whose interpersonal problems are more prominent (for example, severe personality disorders).
- The therapeutic relationship does not always have to be smooth in order for cognitive therapy to proceed. There is evidence that a modicum of strain – perhaps induced by the work demands of the treatment – followed by skilled handling and repairing of the interpersonal conflict may be particularly facilitative of positive outcome with more difficult clients.
- Premature drop-out is a significant risk in working with clients who suffer from personality disorders (among other challenging diagnostic problems). Thus, special attention to the establishment and maintenance of a therapeutic bond early in treatment is imperative. Some degree of concrete improvement in the client's condition and cognitive-behavioral skills development can go a long way toward making this positive alliance occur.
- Performing cognitive therapy competently requires therapists to be interpersonally sensitive and adroit, as well as technically facile in the application of the model and implementation of the techniques of cognitive therapy.
- Technical skill requires flexibility. Therapists can adapt the working aspects of the treatment to the needs and capabilities of a given client at a given time. While cognitive therapy is a time-effective treatment, the delivery of the treatment cannot be artificially rushed without risking a diminishment of the outcome, especially with more challenging clients.
- Therapists do well to stay close to the middle ground, being neither heavy-handed nor passively supportive, but rather actively trying to engage the clients in a constructive endeavor involving objective self-monitoring, the practicing of techniques (both in session and for homework), and striving toward a ceiling of functioning.
- Cultural factors are important to consider in facilitating the therapeutic alliance. While it may not be necessary for therapists to be of the same ethnicity as their clients in order to bond and work well together, a healthy appreciation of (and active interest in learning about) the mores and belief systems of the client's ancestral heritage may be of vital significance in overcoming differences.

- It is a dysfunctional belief to maintain that cognitive therapists should always have the interpersonal, conceptual, and technical skills to work with all clients under all conditions. When clients act abusively toward therapists, and their behaviors do not abate even in the face of repeated, appropriate interventions from therapists, the clinician has the right to disengage unilaterally. Therapists are not obliged to put themselves in harm's way, and their ability to take proper care of themselves in this way is part of appropriate role-modeling for the vast majority of their clients.

References

Beck, A.T., Brown, G., Berchick, R.J., Stewart, B.L. & Steer, R.A. (1990). Relationship between hopelessness and eventual suicide: A replication with psychiatric outpatients. *American Journal of Psychiatry*, 147, 190–195.

Beck, A.T., Davis, D.D. & Freeman, A. (2004). *Cognitive therapy of personality disorders* (2nd edition). New York: Guilford Press.

Beck, A.T., Ward, C., Mendelson, M., Mock, J. & Erbaugh, J. (1961). An inventory for measuring depression. *Archives of General Psychiatry*, 4, 53–63.

Beck, A.T., Weissman, A., Lester, D. & Trexler, L. (1974). The measurement of pessimism: The Hopelessness Scale. *Journal of Consulting and Clinical Psychology*, 42(6), 861–865.

Beck, J.S. (1995). *Cognitive therapy: Basics and beyond.* New York: Guilford Press.

Beck, J.S. (2005). *Cognitive therapy for challenging problems: What to do when basics don't work.* New York: Guilford Press.

Bedi, R.P., Davis, M.D. & Williams, M. (2005). Critical incidents in the formation of the therapeutic alliance from the patient's perspective. *Psychotherapy: Theory, Research, Practice, Training*, 42(3), 311–323.

Chen, S.W. & Davenport, D.S. (2005). Cognitive-behavioral therapy with Chinese-American clients: Cautions and modifications. *Psychotherapy: Theory, Research, Practice, Training*, 42(1), 101–110.

Connolly Gibbons, M.B., Crits-Christoph, P., de la Cruz, C., Barber, J.P., Siqueland, L. & Gladis, M. (2003). Pretreatment expectations, interpersonal functioning and symptoms in the prediction of the therapeutic alliance across supportive–expressive psychotherapy and cognitive therapy. *Psychotherapy Research*, 13, 59–76.

DeRubeis, R.J., Brotman, M.A. & Gibbons, C.J. (2005). A conceptual and methodological analysis of the nonspecifics argument. *Clinical Psychology: Science and Practice*, 12(2), 174–183.

DeRubeis, R.J. & Feeley, M. (1990). Determinants of change in cognitive therapy for depression. *Cognitive Therapy and Research*, 14, 469–482.

Feeley, M., DeRubeis, R.J. & Gelfand, L.A. (1999). The temporal relation of adherence and alliance to symptom change in cognitive therapy for depression. *Journal of Consulting and Clinical Psychology*, 67, 578–582.

Gilbert, P. (1992). *Counselling for depression.* Thousand Oaks, CA: Sage Publications.

Gilbert, P., Gilbert, J. & Sanghera, J. (2004). A focus group exploration of the impact of izzat, shame, and subordinate entrapment on mental health and service use in South Asian women. *Mental Health, Religion & Culture*, 7(2), 109–130.

Horvath, A.O. & Bedi, R.P. (2002). The alliance. In J.C. Norcross (ed.), *Psychotherapy relationships that work: Therapist contributions and responsiveness to patient needs* (pp. 37–69). London: Oxford University Press.

Horvath, A.O. & Symonds, B.D. (1991). Relation between working alliance and outcome in psychotherapy: A meta-analysis. *Journal of Counseling Psychology*, 38, 139–149.

Jones, J.H. (1993). *Bad blood: The Tuskegee syphilis experiment* (revised edition). New York: Free Press.

Klein, D.N., Schwartz, J.E., Santiago, N.J., Vivian, D., Vocisano, C., Castonguay, L.G., Arnow, B.A., Blalock, J.A., Markowitz, J.C., Rothbaum, B.O. & McCullough, J.P., Jr (2003). Therapeutic alliance in depression treatment: Controlling for prior change and patient characteristics. *Journal of Consulting and Clinical Psychology*, 71, 997–1006.

Layden, M.A., Newman, C.F., Freeman, A. & Morse, S.B. (1993). *Cognitive therapy of borderline personality disorder*. Needham Heights, MA: Allyn & Bacon.

Leahy, R.L. (2001). *Overcoming resistance in cognitive therapy*. New York: Guilford Press.

Martin, D.J., Garske, J.P. & Davis, M.K. (2000). Relation of therapeutic alliance with outcome and other variables: A meta-analytic review. *Journal of Consulting and Clinical Psychology*, 68, 438–450.

Mayo, J.A. (2004). Psychotherapy with African American populations: Modification of traditional approaches. *Annals of the American Psychotherapy Association*, 7(1), 10–13.

Newman, C.F. (1997). Maintaining professionalism in the face of emotional abuse from clients. *Cognitive and Behavioral Practice*, 4(1), 1–29.

Newman, C.F. (1998). The therapeutic relationship and alliance in short-term cognitive therapy. In J. Safran & J.C. Muran (eds), *The therapeutic alliance in brief psychotherapy* (pp. 95–122). Washington, DC: American Psychological Association.

Newman, C.F. & Fingerhut, R. (2005). Psychotherapy for avoidant personality disorder. In G. Gabbard, J.S. Beck & J. Holmes (eds), *Concise Oxford textbook of psychotherapy* (pp. 311–319). Oxford: Oxford University Press.

Newman, C.F. & Haaga, D.A.F. (1995). Cognitive skills training. In W. O'Donohue & L. Krasner (eds), *Handbook of psychological skills training* (pp. 119–143). Needham Heights, MA: Allyn & Bacon.

Organista, K.C. (2000). Latinos. In J.R. White & A.S. Freeman (eds), *Cognitive-behavioral group therapy: For specific problems and populations* (pp. 281–303). Washington, DC: American Psychological Association.

Persons, J.B., Burns, D.D. & Perloff, J.M. (1988). Predictors of dropout and outcome in cognitive therapy for depression in a private practice setting. *Cognitive Therapy and Research*, 12(6), 557–575.

Raue, P.J., Goldfried, M.R. & Barkham, M. (1997). The therapeutic alliance in psychodynamic–interpersonal, cognitive-behavioral therapy. *Journal of Consulting and Clinical Psychology*, 4, 582–587.

Rector, N.A., Zuroff, D.C. & Segal, Z.V. (1999). Cognitive change and the therapeutic alliance: The role of technical and non-technical factors in cognitive therapy. *Psychotherapy: Theory, Research, Practice, Training*, 36(4), 320–328.

Rogers, C.R. (1957). The necessary and sufficient conditions of therapeutic personality change. *Journal of Consulting Psychology*, 21, 95–103.

Safran, J.S. & Muran, J.C. (2000). *Negotiating the therapeutic alliance: A relational treatment guide*. New York: Guilford Press.

Safran, J.D., Muran, J.C., Samstag, L.W. & Stevens, C. (2001). Repairing alliance ruptures. *Psychotherapy: Theory, Research, Practice, Training*, 38(4), 406–412.

Safran, J.D. & Segal, Z.V. (1996). *Interpersonal process in cognitive therapy* (2nd edition). Northvale, NJ: Jason Aronson.

Sanderson, W.C., Beck, A.T. & McGinn, L.K. (1994). Cognitive therapy for generalized anxiety disorder: Significance of comorbid personality disorders. *Journal of Cognitive Psychotherapy*, 8, 13–18.

Strauss, J.L., Hayes, A.M., Johnson, S.L., Newman, C.F., Brown, G.K., Barber, J.P., Laurenceau, J.P. & Beck, A.T. (2006). Early alliance, alliance ruptures, and symptom change in a non-randomized trial of cognitive therapy for avoidant and obsessive–compulsive personality disorders. *Journal of Consulting and Clinical Psychology*, 74(2), 337–345.

Strunk, D.R., Chiu, A.W., Cronquist, J. & DeRubeis, R.J. (2006). Components of cognitive therapy for depression: Patients' competencies and risk for relapse following treatment. Manuscript under review.

Tang, T.Z., Beberman, R., DeRubeis, R.J. & Pham, T. (2005). Cognitive changes, critical sessions, and sudden gains in cognitive-behavioral therapy for depression. *Journal of Consulting and Clinical Psychology*, 73(1), 168–172.

Tang, T.Z. & DeRubeis, R.J. (1999). Sudden gains and critical sessions in cognitive-behavioral therapy for depression. *Journal of Consulting and Clinical Psychology*, 67, 894–904.

Thompson, A. (1990). *Guide to ethical practice in psychotherapy*. New York: Wiley-Interscience.

Truax, R. & Carkhuff, R.R. (1967). *Toward effective counseling and psychotherapy*. Chicago: Aldine.

Young, J. & Beck, A.T. (1980). Cognitive Therapy Rating Scale manual. Unpublished manuscript. University of Pennsylvania, Philadelphia, PA.

Chapter 9

The therapy relationship in dialectical behaviour therapy

Michaela A. Swales and Heidi L. Heard

Introduction

Dialectical behaviour therapy (DBT) is a multi-function, multi-modal integrative psychotherapy that was initially developed for the treatment of adult women with a diagnosis of borderline personality disorder (BPD) and a history of chronic parasuicidal behaviour (Linehan, 1993a, 1993b). Since the initial treatment trial (Linehan, Armstrong, Suarez, Allmon, & Heard, 1991) the treatment has been adapted for use with clients with other diagnoses and other problematic impulsive behaviours (e.g., Linehan & Dimeff, 1997; Miller, Rathus, Linehan, Wetzler, & Leigh, 1997; Wiser & Telch, 1999). There have been several randomized controlled trials of the efficacy of the treatment (Koons *et al.*, 2001; Linehan *et al.*, 1991; Linehan, Schmidt, Dimeff, Craft, Kanter, & Comtois, 1999; Linehan *et al.*, 2002; Lynch, Morse, Mendelson, & Robins, 2003; Telch, Agras, & Linehan, 2001; Verheul, Van Den Bosch, Koeter, De Ridder, Stijnen, & Van den Brink, 2003).

DBT is primarily a cognitive-behavioural psychotherapy that has integrated a range of principles, strategies and techniques from acceptance-based approaches, such as Zen Buddhism (Heard & Linehan, 1994, 2005). The application of a dialectical philosophy facilitates the integration of these contrasting approaches. Linehan based the development of DBT on a capability/motivational deficit model of BPD that emphasizes a fundamental impairment of the affect regulation system. These key principles are a common thread uniting the different client populations for which the treatment has been adapted. As a response to the complex difficulties presented by individuals with a BPD diagnosis, Linehan identified certain key tasks or functions of the treatment and developed a variety of integrated modalities to address these functions. As the consideration of the therapy relationship within DBT necessitates some understanding of the dialectical philosophy and the treatment we will consider these issues in the introduction. The main body of the chapter will consider developing, working within, maintaining and ending the relationship within the individual psychotherapy component of the treatment. The chapter will end with a discussion of aspects of the therapy relationship within other modalities of the treatment.

The dialectical relationship

Dialectics as both a world view and a method of persuasion permeates the treatment. For a full discussion of the influence of dialectics on the treatment as a whole, see Heard & Linehan (1994). Dialectical philosophy in DBT emphasizes three key principles: inter-relatedness and wholeness, opposition and polarity, and continual change. These three principles are key in the conceptualization of the therapy relationship in DBT.

The principle of inter-relatedness emphasizes a systems perspective of reality at a number of levels. Most relevant to the therapy relationship, the client and the therapist together form a system in which they reciprocally influence each other. This recognition of the therapy dyad as a system in its own right is made explicit in some of the core assumptions about the therapy (Linehan, 1993a). The therapy relationship is assumed to be a "real" relationship. In some therapeutic approaches it is considered that the therapy relationship is primarily a reflection of past experiences in relationships and the weight of a client's past (presumed to be iatrogenic) experiences in early relationships determines primarily the content and process of the therapy relationship. In contrast, in DBT, while the influence of past relationships on both the client and therapist is acknowledged, the primary focus is on the current experience of the relationship and the recognition that this relationship is a genuine relationship and that each party relates to the other primarily as one human being to another, within the confines of the therapy context. A further assumption relevant to the dialectical nature of the relationship is that the principles of behaviour are universal, and affect therapists as well as clients. Just as the therapist seeks to shape the client into changing his or her behaviour, the client can also (although not always with either intention or awareness) differentially reinforce the therapist for engaging in ineffective therapy behaviours or punish the therapist for engaging in effective therapy behaviours. In DBT these current contingencies are as salient in therapy as any past learning history of the client or therapist.

The second dialectical principle, of opposition and polarity, emphasizes that reality is not static but consists of opposing forces in tension, the thesis and antithesis. It is the synthesis of these opposing forces from which new sets of opposing forces develop. This view recognizes the crucial role of conflict and its resolution in all processes of change, including therapeutic change. The central engine of change within DBT is between the two opposing forces of acceptance and change. Cognitive-behavioural therapies are traditionally technologies of change that focus exclusively on helping clients to modify and alter unacceptable patterns of thought, emotion or behaviour. In the development of DBT, Linehan, the treatment developer, observed that this focus on change was often experienced as invalidating by the client and led to difficulties in engagement in therapy, on retaining a clear therapeutic focus and on ensuring progress within the therapy. As a consequence of these difficulties, other key strategies and concepts from acceptance-based traditions, primarily from Zen Buddhism, were brought into the treatment. The therapeutic task in any given moment is to accept the client as he or she is in such a way that the client is enabled to change in the next moment. This constant interweaving of acceptance and change moves the therapy along. So in any given therapeutic interaction the therapist is balancing acceptance and change, in terms of both the content of the therapy (the primary content of the therapy is in a dialectical balance between problem-solving and validation) and the style (reciprocal communication on the one hand and irreverent communication on the other – more of which later). This constant movement between acceptance and change in terms of content and style is what generates the flow of therapy, through which the process of dialectical change is enabled.

Within DBT, acceptance strategies, whether they relate to the content of the treatment (validation strategies) or the style of the interaction between therapist and client (reciprocal communication strategies), can be utilized in one of two ways. First, acceptance strategies when employed often enable the client to change. In this sense acceptance strategies are utilized in a similar way to other forms of acceptance-based psychotherapies, for example Rogerian psychotherapy (Rogers, 1951). In DBT, however, acceptance strategies are also employed to promote an attitude of acceptance itself: to enable the client to accept himself or herself as they are in this moment, the problems they are experiencing in this moment and also to assist the therapist to fully accept the client as they are in this moment. In this second use of acceptance there is a paradox at the heart of the treatment. To fully accept oneself and one's circumstances as they are is often to have fundamentally changed.

A natural consequence of the first two principles of interconnectedness and opposition is that change is continual. Acceptance of the inevitability of change is a key part of therapy and the therapy relationship. Consequently, a striving for uniformity and consistency within the therapeutic context and within the therapy relationship across time and between therapy relationships is not sought. Though arbitrary change is not introduced, change that occurs naturally is encouraged and embraced. For example, if the therapist and client are developing a good working alliance, the therapist may extend the hours during which he or she will take phone calls from the client to provide skills coaching. Equally, if the client engages in multiple therapy-interfering behaviours while using the telephone, the therapist may contract limits for access. Alternatively, changes in the therapist's private life – a new baby, a sick relative to care for, a new course to complete – may necessitate a constriction in limits. The therapist acknowledges that all such changes are difficult and helps the client to manage these changes. This provides another example in which the therapy relationship is a real relationship, as the therapist strives to mirror common processes of relationships rather than impose arbitrary "therapy rules".

Functions of the therapy relationship

Within the various schools of psychotherapy, there are, broadly speaking, two different stances on the function of the therapy relationship. The first stance emphasizes the inherently healing effect of the therapy relationship in itself. A common conceptual corollary of this stance is that it is the hypothesized reparative nature of this relationship in contrast to earlier relationships that provides the healing effects. It is as a direct consequence of this assumption that the therapy relationship is "a proxy" for all other relationships rather than a "real" relationship in its own right. In contrast, in the second stance, the function of the therapeutic relationship is to provide a supportive and collaborative context in which certain key therapeutic techniques are delivered. For example, within cognitive-behavioural approaches generally, a high-quality, collaborative therapy relationship is considered a necessary condition for effective therapy but the relationship itself is the vehicle for change rather than the cause of change – the techniques and strategies of the therapy fulfil this function. More recently, however, there has been more of an explicit focus on the therapeutic relationship in CBT (indeed, this volume is an example of the change in the *Zeitgeist* in CBT). DBT takes something of a dialectical position in regard to these two perspectives on the function of the therapeutic relationship. It recognizes, like other CBT approaches, that the content of the therapy is crucial in helping clients to move. Clients do experience problematic thoughts and affects that need to be changed or managed and they do engage in behaviours that may need to decrease, and need to learn new behaviours that are absent. Clients also need to learn to cultivate a greater degree of acceptance towards themselves and their difficulties. The alternative perspective, that the relationship in itself is the healing process, is also present, however. The explicit focus on the resolution of therapy-interfering behaviours of both therapist and client (see below) as a means of learning about solving other similar problems outside of therapy is an example of this, as is the use of the therapist themselves as a motivator for change. It is the very embodiment of the treatment, and all its strategies, by the therapist within each interaction with the client that provides the synthesis here.

An overview of the treatment

While a thorough discussion of the biosocial theory that underpins the treatment is beyond the scope of this chapter (the interested reader is referred to Linehan, 1993a), a brief orientation to the conceptual understanding of personality disorder is relevant to what follows. DBT takes a behavioural and developmental approach to the problems presented by individuals who meet criteria for BPD. That is to say, the diagnostic criteria can be re-described as either overt or covert behaviours (thoughts and emotions), with either themselves or the individual's responses to them being amenable to modification. Also, many of the difficulties presented by individuals who meet diagnostic criteria for BPD have occurred as a result of a transaction during development between a biologically based emotional vulnerability and the experience of environments (invalidating environments) that do not recognize this vulnerability or help the developing individual to cope with it. In many cases, indeed, the environment itself plays a major role in the genesis of the emotional vulnerability in the first instance. DBT as a treatment is directed at helping individuals with a BPD diagnosis overcome or more effectively manage the behaviours (both overt and covert) that lead to the diagnosis. Changing these behaviours, in essence, removes the diagnosis, since in behavioural terms there is nothing more to the diagnosis than the experience and expression of a series of behaviours.

Structure: Functions and modalities

As described above, DBT proposes a capability/motivational deficit model of BPD. Based on this model, Linehan designed a multi-modal treatment programme that addresses five discrete treatment tasks or functions:

- capability enhancement
- motivational enhancement
- generalization
- structuring the environment
- enhancement of therapist capabilities and motivation.

Though all five functions or tasks are necessary for a DBT programme, each function can be delivered by a variety of modalities, depending on service context and client population. Capability enhancement is traditionally provided in the context of psycho-educational skills groups that follow the curriculum originally devised by Linehan (1993b), while motivational enhancement is primarily delivered via individual psychotherapy, within which major problem behaviours are targeted. The individual psychotherapist assists the client in identifying the variables (particularly those related to motivation) that control the occurrence and maintenance of problem behaviours, and devising and implementing solutions to overcome these variables. In standard outpatient DBT, the generalization of skilful behaviour from treatment to the natural environment is provided by telephone contact between the individual therapist and client. Structuring the environment facilitates change, in part, by directly involving the client's natural environment. For example, in DBT with adolescents, working with the family to change problematic contingencies around behaviour is key to success, so family involvement in skills groups or in Family DBT sessions is part of this function (Miller, Glinski, Woodberry, Mitchell, & Indik, 2002; Miller *et al.*, 1997; Woodberry, Miller, Glinski, Indik, & Mitchell, 2002). Finally, to ensure the delivery of effective therapy, the treatment addresses the motivation and capability of the therapists. This occurs primarily within the therapist consultation team meeting, a forum within which therapists learn how to solve specific problems that arise in therapy and treat their own motivational issues, primarily by applying the therapy to themselves.

Structure: Stages and targets

DBT is a staged treatment that suggests that overcoming complex and severe behaviours associated with multiple diagnoses takes time and is best accomplished in a series of stages, each with its own goals. Standard DBT begins with a pre-treatment phase, followed by Stage 1. Pre-treatment is discussed in detail below, as it has important implications for the development of the therapy relationship. Stage 1, as described by Linehan, focuses on helping clients with multiple impulsive behaviours regain some control over their behaviour, reduce their level of risk and develop more effective working alliances with treatment systems. Once these goals are achieved most clients will require additional stages, but those are beyond the scope of this chapter (Linehan, 1999).

Within Stage 1 a key aspect of the treatment structure is the use of hierarchical targets within each modality of therapy. This target hierarchy focuses the work of the therapist and the client within any interaction in any given modality. Within individual therapy, the target hierarchy is as follows.

- *Life-threatening behaviours:* decreasing suicidal, parasuicidal or homicidal behaviours, and threats, urges or ideation related to suicidal, parasuicidal or homicidal behaviours.
- *Therapy-interfering behaviours:* decreasing behaviours engaged in by either the therapist or the patient that interfere significantly with the effectiveness of the therapy.
- *Quality-of-life-interfering behaviours:* decreasing behaviours that have a significant risk to or destabilizing effect on the client's life, for example behaviours associated with other Axis I diagnoses, or forensic behaviours.
- *Enhancement of behavioural skills:* increasing new or infrequently engaged in skilful behaviours. Skills taught within the therapy are

dialectically arranged. Mindfulness and distress tolerance are acceptance-based skills, whereas interpersonal effectiveness and emotional regulation are change-based.

Identified behaviours within this target hierarchy form the overarching treatment plan for the contracted period of the therapy and also structure the agenda for each session. The client keeps a record of identified target behaviours between sessions and the content of the session is determined by which high-priority behaviours have occurred between sessions. These behaviours form the focus for the behavioural and solution analyses conducted within the therapy session.

Developing the relationship: Pre-treatment

During pre-treatment, the individual psychotherapist focuses on identifying the client's treatment goals and assessing the corresponding problems, orienting the client to DBT and developing the client's commitment to participating in DBT. Rather than simply discussing each topic, the therapist tends to interweave a variety of DBT strategies from the beginning. For example, if a client had difficulty identifying treatment goals, the therapist might analyse the variables contributing to this difficulty. If the difficulty arose from a fear of failure, the therapist might use various problem-solving strategies (e.g., mindfulness, cognitive restructuring, exposure) to help the client decrease or better manage the fear while identifying treatment goals. In another example, a client left a previous treatment following an unmet demand for more therapeutic time and believed that the therapist refused the demand as a result of not understanding the client's needs. Based on this information, the DBT therapist could clarify the contingencies in DBT that could lead to more time (or less), to help the client to generate alternative interpretations of the former therapist's refusal and/or rehearse how the client could most effectively let the DBT therapist know about any urges to terminate treatment.

As in any other therapy, the therapy relationship also begins to develop at this time. The client's motivation to participate in the therapy is enhanced by a number of strategies that continue throughout the treatment, but perhaps the most important are the validation strategies. Linehan (1993a) describes validation as occurring when "the therapist communicates to the patient that her responses make sense and are understandable within her current life context or situation" (pp. 222–223). Her theoretical development of validation has been strongly influenced by research (Linehan, 1997b; Swann, Stein-Seroussi, & Giesler, 1992) that suggests that humans are more motivated to be with others who validate their self-constructs. The evidence from a recent randomized controlled trial of DBT (Linehan et al., 2002) for substance misuse supports this hypothesis. Trial participants, adult women who met diagnostic criteria for BPD and substance dependence, received either DBT or a comparison treatment called comprehensive validation treatment (CVT). Though DBT had better outcomes with respect to substance abuse, CVT proved more effective than DBT at retaining the women in treatment (64% retention for DBT and 100% for CVT). DBT (Linehan, 1997a) includes six levels of validation, including (1) listening and observing, (2) accurately reflecting, (3) articulating the unverbalized and (4) validating in terms of biological dysfunction or past learning history. Level 5 validation requires the therapist to communicate how a client's response makes sense, is functional or is normal in terms of the current context, rather than in terms of the client's psychiatric disorder or learning history. For example, in a response to a new client who indicates some anxiety about trusting a therapist, the therapist might say, "It makes sense that you have difficulty trusting me, considering that we have just met and you don't know me well." Level 6 requires the therapist to interact with the client simply as a fellow human being, rather than as a particularly fragile or volatile individual. Therapists deliver validation in two forms: verbal (what the therapist says) and functional (what the therapist does). For example, a therapist may verbally validate a target behaviour ("Yes, it makes sense that you want to stop feeling so angry, and cutting is very effective at immediately decreasing your anger.") and then functionally validate *and* problem-solve by suggesting alternative skills to achieve the same function ("We must find more effective ways to help you decrease your anger").

Though validation may prove necessary in the development of the therapy relationship, it is not sufficient in the application of the treatment as a whole. DBT therapists in training, however, sometimes struggle with how to simultaneously apply the treatment fully and develop the relationship. Usually this occurs because they assume that the acceptance strategies, such as validation in general and reflective listening in particular, will enhance the relationship, while change strategies, such as problem-solving and confrontation, will harm it. Such an approach creates two important problems. First, the client will not be able to make an informed commitment to the treatment if they have not had the opportunity to experience some of the change strategies during pre-treatment. Such a situation would resemble the bait-and-switch problem that arises in marketing products. Second, delaying the use of problem-solving strategies until after the development of the therapy relationship also delays the assistance that the client needs to decrease their emotional suffering and achieve their goals. Often, the most validating thing that a therapist can do is to help a client solve the problem(s) leading to the suffering, rather than simply empathizing with the suffering. In most professional relationships, individuals are more likely to maintain relationships with those professionals that help them solve problems effectively. For example, the average car owner wants a mechanic that will fix his car, in addition to treating him nicely.

Finally, the emphasis on the reciprocal nature of the therapy relationship suggests that the therapist must also attend to enhancing his or her motivation to treat the client. This requires the therapist to remain mindful in responding to the client, by developing a non-judgemental stance towards the client and by focusing on what would be effective in the present moment. In addition, the therapist may seek empathic or validating inter-pretations of the client's behaviour. For example, rather than assuming that the client's lack of accurate disclosure results from the client trying to sabotage the treatment, the therapist might generate alternative hypotheses, such as the client is ashamed of a behaviour and wants to hide it and/or the client fears how the therapist will respond to the full facts. If the therapist continues to have low motivation to treat the client, he or she should raise the issue with the consultation team. The team would first help the therapist to increase his or her motivation, but failing that would help the therapist to determine whether the client would benefit from another DBT individual psychotherapist or from another treatment.

Working in the relationship

Within any therapeutic approach there are many aspects to the therapeutic relationship. Only those aspects of the working alliance that have been addressed in other chapters of this volume, for example, non-verbal com-munication, management of affect, limit setting and rupture repair, will be discussed in this section and the next. First, however, some discussion of the general position that DBT takes to the therapeutic relationship is warranted.

As highlighted in the introduction, DBT takes a dialectical position in regard to the therapy relationship. It is neither solely a mechanism for change nor just a vehicle for delivering the mechanisms of change. It is appropriate to ask in this context, "What is the therapy relationship?" Essentially, the therapy relationship is the label that we give to a series of "relating" behaviours that occur over time within a particular context which vary in terms of their levels of effectiveness in promoting change within the client. This focus on a series of interconnected relating behaviours enables the therapist to remain focused on how his or her response in any given moment either promotes or inhibits the desired change and ensures atten-tion to the effectiveness of the response. Overvaluation of the therapy relationship as an object in itself can lead to therapy-interfering behaviours on the part of the therapist. For example, if the therapist believes that confronting the client about parasuicidal behaviour will "damage" the therapy relationship, the therapist will avoid challenging the client on this behaviour. In contrast, a more behavioural focus on the impact of such acceptance on the client's parasuicidal behaviour is more likely to lead to an effective intervention. In these moments, DBT focuses more on applying functional validation (helping the client solve problems and reach goals) than on verbal validation of the reasons for the behaviour.

This focus on the moment-by-moment construction of the relationship enables the therapist to utilize himself or herself as a prime motivator for change and to be fully aware of the importance of his or her responses in any given interaction. Objectifying the relationship can lead to inattentiveness not just to the client's behaviour but also to the impact of that behaviour on the therapist. Such attention or awareness is key to managing burnout in the therapist. Within DBT, therapists observe and monitor their own personal limits both around the structure of the work (for example, number of clients, frequency of sessions) and in terms of the content (for example, identifying behaviours that cross their limits and may lead to burnout). DBT, therefore, favours therapists observing whatever limits are most effective for them in the conduct of therapy rather than the setting of arbitrary boundaries. One common example of this occurs in the use of the telephone for generalization. Some therapists on a team may have phone limits such that they will not take phone calls after 8 p.m., as to do so would run the risk of burnout. Other therapists on the team may prefer to have 24-hour access because, while being disturbed in the middle of the night may affect their sleep marginally, they prefer to deal with a minor crisis at that point rather than a more significant one if the client has to wait till morning to call. Therapists will also have different levels of tolerance for a variety of client behaviours such as risky behaviours, abusive language, hostile voice tone or passivity in sessions. Once a therapist identifies a limit, he or she then orients the client to it and helps the client learn how to live within the limit. The individual therapist also helps the client adjust to different limits of other DBT team members, such as skills trainers. In this sense, the therapy relationship generalizes to non-therapy relationships in which different people have different levels of tolerance for certain behaviours.

Remaining fully present within the relationship in any given moment requires the therapist to be mindful. Though a full description of mindfulness within the therapy is beyond the scope of this chapter, some consideration is relevant (for a fuller description of mindfulness in the treatment, see Williams & Swales, 2004). Mindfulness functions to enhance awareness of one's internal experiences, one's environment and the relationship between the two (see Katzow & Safran, Chapter 5, this volume). Mindfulness also increases attentional control, decreases the impact of cognitive "delusions" or distortions and enables one to experience strong emotions without being controlled by them. DBT therapists learn mindfulness in order to apply it to themselves, as well as to teach it to clients. The mindful therapist endeavours to remain awake to much in the session, including his or her judgements and interpretations, emotional responses to the client, urges to avoid potentially effective interventions and becoming unfocused or drifting away from the main topic. The therapist notices the client's judgements, subtle shifts in the client's mood and how the client responds to the therapist's strategies. Being fully awake or present in any moment with the client enables the therapist to focus on being maximally effective in that moment.

Strategies

As in any therapy, non-verbal communication on both sides is important. For many BPD clients, a history of persistent invalidation of emotional communication has often led to an inaccuracy of non-verbal communication, to a mismatch between internal experiences of emotion and external communication of those emotions and to a lack of awareness of the impact of their communication style on others. Consequently, many of the lower level validation strategies function to help the client gain a better understanding both of their own internal experience of emotions and of the way in which they communicate them to others. As a further consequence of the early experience of invalidation, many clients are highly attuned to non-verbal communications by others, including the therapist. The therapist needs, therefore, to reflect on his or her internal experiences and to describe these to the client in a mindful and non-judgemental way to facilitate the understanding of the client in the moment and the overall learning process. Radical genuineness and self-involving self-disclosure (where the therapist describes to the client his or her responses to the client's behaviour directly) are the relevant strategies to employ here.

The main focus of DBT is problem-solving of identified target problem behaviours. Problem-solving follows the standard procedure observed in the majority of cognitive-behavioural therapies. The first step is to conduct a functional, behavioural analysis of a target behaviour (as identified by reviewing the diary card). This involves a momentary analysis of all the relevant environmental events that may have triggered the start of the chain of events leading up to the problem behaviour and all the intervening events, both external and internal to the client, that culminated in the occurrence of the problem behaviour and followed it. From this analysis the therapist endeavours to identify relevant controlling variables that affect the occurrence of the behaviour, namely a functional analysis. Hence a comprehensive solution analysis is constructed that involves identifying problematic links in the chain and relevant solutions to each link. Possible solutions are drawn from a wide range of cognitive-behavioural procedures. The four primary change strategies are: skills training; exposure; cognitive modification; and contingency management. In this sense DBT does differ from other CBT therapies that have tended to be developed in the context of a single disorder and thus focus primarily on one aspect of these change procedures. As clients with a diagnosis of BPD have a wider range of disorders, a more encompassing range of solutions is required. If a client is also presenting with a comorbid Axis I disorder for which there is a current evidence-based cognitive-behavioural treatment, then the appropriate protocol for that disorder would be incorporated into the DBT treatment programme. A full discussion of the modifications to this standard CBT procedure within DBT is beyond the scope of this chapter. For more information on this aspect of the treatment the interested reader is referred to Linehan (1993a).

A significant proportion of therapeutic effort is directed towards understanding and managing the client's affect. This is a key issue for patients who are troubled by the intensity and complexity of their affect and whose problem behaviours either stem directly from a high level of affect or are attempts to regulate it. For therapists, then, assisting clients in managing affect is important for two reasons. First, it is often high on the list of client goals. Second, high levels of affect within the therapy session present a major management problem either because the affect is directed at the therapist or because the affect is blocking progress on solving the identified problem within the session. The major strategy for managing these challenges is to apply the problem-solving aspect of the treatment to them. In the first case, unwarranted strong affect directed at the therapist is likely to be a therapy-interfering behaviour and is dealt with as described in the next section. In the latter case, the therapist identifies that the affect is present and assists the client in identifying the nature of the affect and the sequence of events that has led to its occurrence, before working with the client on generating solutions to manage the problem. There are two choices here; the first is to help the client reduce the level of the affect in order to continue with the session. The second is to help the client to tolerate the presence of the strong affect and continue to work in the session despite the presence of the affect. Which strategy is opted for will vary according to the intensity of the emotional response, the function of the response and the preference of the client. For example, if the client becomes overwhelmed by shame relating to an aspect of his or her targeted behaviour, they can be guided in how to tolerate shame to a degree in order to analyse the behaviour to develop a solution analysis. In this case, the therapist might invite the client to practise self-validating statements that acknowledge the normative nature of shame in response to behaviours one would rather not engage in or cheerleading statements; for example, that it will be worth surviving the momentary pain in order to get a solution in the long run. If the client is experiencing very intense shame, which is precluding working on the problem, the therapist will work with the client to get a reduction in shame to a level that can be tolerated to enable the analysis to proceed. This may involve, for example, helping the client to restate negative self-judgements in a more descriptive way or modifying body posture such that the shame experience is not amplified by actions in keeping with emotion.

Similar issues can arise for this client group in terms of the occurrence and management of painful memories, as many clients who meet diagnostic criteria for BPD have a history of trauma. The management of such memories in DBT is dependent on the stage of treatment that the client is currently in. For clients in Stage 1 of treatment (for which DBT was primarily developed), when problematic memories or flashbacks occur the therapist, first, assists the client in how to remain mindful in the presence of distressing past content appearing in the present, and to become reconnected or grounded in the present moment – perhaps by mindfully describing the therapy room. Second, by conducting a behavioural analysis of what led up to the occurrence of the memories or flashbacks, the therapist helps the client understand the variables that trigger these responses. The therapist, with the client, identifies opportunities to modify triggering events and rehearses solutions for both managing the occurrence of the memories or flashbacks and reducing the likelihood that they will occur. The therapist will also actively plan with the client how to utilize these strategies outside the therapy session to manage the same behaviour when it occurs. This movement between in-session and out-of-session behaviours is another hallmark of the therapy that creates the movement and flow within the therapy.

Maintaining the relationship: Targeting therapy-interfering behaviour

As within any system, tensions will arise between the therapist and client. Examples of such tensions are (a) the client's position that only hospitalization will prevent suicide now and the therapist's position that hospitalization in response to suicidal threats may increase the probability of a future suicide, (b) the client's wish for more contact with the therapist and the therapist's wish to say no to requests that exceed his or her limits, and (c) the client's belief that drinking large quantities of alcohol is the solution and the therapist's belief that it is the problem. To resolve such conflicts the therapy searches for syntheses. The most effective syntheses are generally those that validate some aspect of both sides of the debate and move toward more effective behaviour. For example, if a client considers alcohol as a solution because it decreases overwhelming anxiety, the therapy may achieve a synthesis by identifying anxiety reduction as a valid therapy goal. With this as the accepted goal, alcohol would no longer be a valid solution, as it will tend, directly and indirectly, to increase, not decrease, anxiety in the long term. The therapy would instead focus on the client developing more skilful means to prevent and manage anxiety. When therapy tensions have not been successfully resolved, they often result in therapy-interfering behaviours. For example, if a therapist simply confronted a client about the use of drugs but never offered alternative solutions that could achieve the client's goal of regulating affect, the client might begin to lie to the therapist about drug use.

Whether as the result of a specific conflict with the therapist or of more general psychological factors, borderline clients frequently engage in therapy-interfering behaviour. Therapy-interfering behaviours include those that directly interfere with the application of the treatment (for example, not attending the session, arriving drunk at a skills training group, leaving sessions early, not completing diary cards) and those that decrease the therapist's motivation to apply the treatment (for example, constantly criticizing the therapist, pushing the therapist's limits, repeatedly responding with "that won't work" without considering the therapist's suggestion). DBT does not consider therapy-interfering behaviours simply as obstacles to avoid or overcome so that therapy can proceed. Instead, it treats them as examples of the behaviours that occur in clients' lives outside of therapy and as the most immediate opportunities to change those behaviours. In the case of the client who arrives drunk at a session, the parallel between the therapy-interfering behaviour and a possible quality-of-life-interfering behaviour appears obvious. More subtly, an analysis of not completing the diary cards may reveal that the client experiences intense shame when acknowledging behaviours on the card, and thus avoids the card. If a similar pattern of shame and avoidance appeared in the analysis of para-suicide, then treating the shame leading to avoiding the diary card might also help to decrease parasuicide.

When therapy-interfering behaviours occur, the therapist applies the standard DBT strategies, with a particular emphasis on the problem-solving strategies. Generally, the therapist would begin to treat the behaviour by describing the behaviour, without judgement or inferring intent, to the client. For example, a therapist would say "You just threatened to harm yourself if I don't extend the session" rather than "You're trying to mani-pulate me"; or "I've noticed that you seldom complete your homework" rather than "I think that you're sabotaging the therapy." The therapist may then try to increase the client's motivation to change the behaviour by highlighting the aversive consequences of the behaviour (including the impact on the therapist) and linking a change in the behaviour to the client's ultimate goals. For example, the therapist might say "When you phone me inappropriately it makes me want to stop all phone contact. You have also said that many of your friends have withdrawn from you because you have pushed their limits. Maybe if we solve the problem in therapy, you can use the same skills with your friends." The therapist would then conduct a behavioural and solution analysis of the behaviour and immediately implement solutions to change the behaviour. In the case of unwarranted shame leading to the avoidance of the diary card, the therapist would primarily apply exposure with the support of mindfulness and perhaps other CBT solutions. In the case of a client who responds with "that won't work" to the therapist's suggestion of a new skill, a behavioural analysis might reveal that the skill won't work because the client has misunderstood the skill or because the client's environment would punish the skill (for example, practising assertion skills). Alternatively, the skill may work, but the client has a bias towards assuming the worst or has other cognitions (for example, "I don't deserve to do pleasant things for myself") or emotions that interfere. Finally, the skill may work and the client may know it, but the client wants to change the topic and believes that they can derail the therapist with this response. After identifying the controlling variables, the therapist would match solutions to the variables. For example, if the function of the behaviour is to change the topic, the therapist may decrease the behaviour by managing the contingencies, changing topics only after the client has stopped the therapy-interfering behaviour and practised new skills.

Like clients, therapists also engage in therapy-interfering behaviours. These behaviours include becoming judgemental of the client, unmindfully making assumptions, avoiding the use of effective strategies because they may upset the client or reinforcing suicidal behaviour. Though the behaviours may arise from the therapist's own issues or lack of skilfulness, they often occur as a result of interactions in therapy. For example, the client's therapy-interfering behaviour may elicit anger from the therapist and at that point the therapist may start judging the client. Just as the therapist shapes the client's behaviour, so the client shapes the therapist's behaviour. With difficult clients, in particular, the transaction between client and therapist may be such that the client punishes therapeutic behaviour and rewards iatrogenic behaviour. For example, one can easily imagine that if a client became verbally aggressive every time the therapist tried to address a presenting problem, the therapist might become less likely to target that problem. Therapists can often notice their own therapy-interfering behaviours and correct the behaviours themselves by applying the treatment to themselves. Also, many clients will happily assist their therapists in this endeavour. Frequently, however, the therapist will require the intervention of the consultation team.

Ending the relationship

In ending the relationship, both the DBT structure and its strategies remain relevant. The structure of DBT as a staged treatment assists in the ending process by clarifying from the outset that the treatment programme is time-limited (albeit quite a long time). Despite this clarity, the process of ending presents a number of significant challenges for therapist and client alike. To assist in this process, we would suggest the development of a clear target hierarchy, such as the following, for this phase as well.

1   Decrease suicidal and life-threatening behaviours related to the end of the therapy relationship; for example, increased suicidal urges when client thinks about future without the therapist.
2   Decrease therapy-interfering behaviours related to ending; for example, increased frequency of asking for therapist support, repeating the statement "I won't be able to cope without you."
3   Increase independent problem-solving.
4   Increase connection in other effective relationships (professional and/or non-professional).

Within sessions the therapist will follow the hierarchy above but will require the client to take a more active part in determining the session agenda and to perform behavioural and solution analysis strategies more independently. Both will have to work on changing the balance within the relationship from the therapist as the primary source of external validation and problem-solving to the client more actively obtaining such external support from others, as well as from himself or herself. In particular, the therapist must attend to fading out as the primary reinforcer of skilful behaviour by helping the client identify other potential reinforcers within the environment and by strengthening the client's own efforts in self-reinforcement. Ideally these processes occur gradually throughout the course of therapy and are assisted by the case management strategy of consultation-to-the-patient. They may become explicit targets, however, if the client is intensely attached to the therapist. Such a client may also need help in "mourning" the pending loss of the therapist. The therapist likewise may have behaviours to targets, such as decreasing their attachment to the client and/or reducing their sense of ownership over the work and transition to the role of ex-therapist.

For many BPD clients, the endings of previous relationships have been fraught with difficulty and may never have been emotionally processed. Such a history tends to exacerbate the emotional intensity of ending DBT as well. The DBT therapist strives to assist the client in remaining mindful of this current ending and in being non-judgemental towards both the ending and the responses evoked by the ending. In addition, the therapist facilitates the client to express and experience the emotional response to the ending and coaches the client in how to manage the thoughts, emotions and behaviours that the imminent ending elicits. As in many relationships, the therapist and client may also plan other meaningful ways to say goodbye and to mark the transition from client and therapist to ex-client and ex-therapist.

DBT therapists also review the types of potential contact between ex-therapists and ex-clients to clarify for the client the circumstances under which it would be appropriate to contact the therapist (for example, for brief refresher coaching, to receive some cheerleading or feedback or just to inform the therapist of any progress). The type and frequency of appropriate contact will depend on the therapist's limits, the long-term impact on the client and the limits of any other system with which the client is engaged. For example, a new non-DBT therapist may have strong views against contact with an ex-therapist. Together, the client and therapist would generate solutions for managing the various known or expected limitations.

Relating to others

As a consequence of the treatment's multi-modal nature, the individual psychotherapist and client each have relationships with other healthcare providers and sometimes with non-professionals that will have an impact on the therapy relationship. The client will have a relationship with the DBT skills trainer, perhaps with a DBT back-up therapist and probably with a non-DBT case manager and a psychiatrist who provides medication. The DBT psychotherapists and skills trainers will have relationships with their DBT consultation team members, with non-DBT professionals and perhaps with the client's family members or friends.

Within DBT, the complex web of relationships is primarily managed through the application of the consultation-to-the-patient strategies. When applying these strategies, the therapist consults with the client about how the client can effectively interact with the environment, including other therapists. The therapist does not dictate to others, including other DBT therapists, about how to interact with the client. For example, if the client has problems with her skills trainer, the individual therapist will not complain to the skills trainer but may teach the client how to use skills to "shape up" the skills trainer or apply other CBT interventions to enhance the client's motivation to use existing skills. Though originally designed to counteract the often passive yet demanding problem-solving style of clients who meet criteria for BPD, the consultation-to-the-patient strategy also appears to decrease the likelihood of "splitting" among professionals, possibly because such splitting tends to occur when professionals try to tell each other how to treat a client. When a situation absolutely requires the direct interventions of the therapist in the environment (for example, regulations requiring therapist reports, an environment that remains iatrogenic despite the client's skilful effort), the therapist still interweaves consulting to the client as much as possible. For example, when writing a required report about the client, the therapist would discuss the content of the report with the client.

The relationship among DBT consultation team members may prove as critical as that between therapists and clients. As emphasized above, the consultation team primarily functions to treat the therapist by enhancing

DBT capabilities and motivation, and thus enhancing adherence to the model. To facilitate this process, team members practise the skills themselves (for example, be mindful of judgements and interpretations, act opposite to emotion, validate the other person) and commit to a set of consultation agreements, such as the consultation-to-the-patient agreement. The dialectical agreement reminds the team to apply the dialectical philosophy, in which absolute truths do not exist. The fallibility agreement explicitly states that all therapists are fallible. This changes the contingency existing in some systems that reinforces therapists for hiding or minimizing problems, as the team already assumes that all the therapists have made mistakes and need consultation.

A properly functioning consultation team usually enhances the therapist's overall sense of safety in working with these clients. The consultation from multiple therapists decreases the therapist's sense of vulnerability that results from working alone with high-risk clients. The emphasis on applying the model adherently also provides the therapist with support. The mindful practising of skills and commitment to the agreements minimizes the likelihood of unproductive conflicts. Finally, when conflicts do arise, the dialectical philosophy will guide the team towards finding an effective synthesis.

Conclusion

The dialectical nature of DBT means that there is an explicit focus on the transactional nature of the relationship between therapist and client throughout the treatment. This emphasis is highlighted both theoretically in the assumptions of the treatment and also practically in the identification of targets for treatment that focus directly on maximizing the effectiveness of the therapeutic relationship. This chapter has described some of the outworking of this approach at different stages in the therapeutic process. Working on in-session behaviours that occur between client and therapist is a crucial part of the learning for clients who, as part of their difficulties, struggle to initiate and maintain sustaining interpersonal relationships.

References

Heard, H.L. & Linehan, M.M. (1994). Dialectical behavior therapy: An integrative approach to the treatment of borderline personality disorder. *Journal of Psychotherapy Integration*, 4, 55–82.

Heard, H.L. & Linehan, M.M. (2005). Integrative therapy for borderline personality disorder. In J.C. Norcross & M.R. Goldfried (eds), *Handbook of psychotherapy integration*, (pp. 299–320). Oxford: Oxford University Press.

Koons, C.R., Robins, C.J., Tweed, J.L., Lynch, T.R., Gonzalez, A.M., Morse, J.Q., Bishop, G.K., Butterfield, M.I. & Bastian, L.A. (2001). Efficacy of dialectical behavior therapy in women veterans with borderline personality disorder. *Behavior Therapy*, 32, 371–390.

Linehan, M.M. (1993a). *Cognitive-behavioral treatment of borderline personality disorder*. New York: Guilford.

Linehan, M.M. (1993b). *Skills training manual for treating borderline personality disorder*. New York: Guilford.

Linehan, M.M. (1997a). Validation and psychotherapy. In A. Bohart & L. Greenberg (eds), *Empathy reconsidered: New directions in psychotherapy*. Washington, DC: American Psychological Association.

Linehan, M.M. (1997b). Self-verification and drug abusers: Implications for treatment. *Psychological Scientist*, 8, 181–184.

Linehan, M.M. (1999). Development, evaluation, and dissemination of effective psychosocial treatments: Stages of disorder, levels of care, and stages of treatment research. In M.G. Glantz & C.R. Hartel (eds), *Drug abuse: Origins and interventions*. Washington, DC: American Psychological Association.

Linehan, M.M., Armstrong, H.E., Suarez, A., Allmon, D. & Heard H.L. (1991). Cognitive-behavior treatment of chronically parasuicidal borderline patients. *Archives of General Psychiatry*, 48, 1060–1064.

Linehan, M.M. & Dimeff, L.A. (1997). *Dialectical behavior therapy manual of treatment interventions for drug abusers with borderline personality disorder*. Seattle, WA: University of Washington.

Linehan, M.M., Dimeff, L.A., Reynolds, S.K., Comtois, K.A., Shaw Welch, S., Heagerty, P. & Kivlanhan, D.R. (2002). Dialectical behavior therapy versus comprehensive validation plus 12-step for the treatment of opioid dependent women meeting criteria for borderline personality disorder. *Drug and Alcohol Dependence*, 67, 13–26.

Linehan, M.M., Schmidt, H., Dimeff, L.A., Craft, J.C., Kanter, J. & Comtois, K.A. (1999). Dialectical behavior therapy for patients with borderline personality disorder and drug-dependence. *American Journal on Addiction*, 8, 279–292.

Lynch, T.R., Morse, J.Q., Mendelson, T. & Robins, C.J. (2003). Dialectical behavior therapy for depressed older adults: A randomized pilot study. *American Journal of Geriatric Psychiatry*, 11, 1–13.

Miller, A.L., Glinski, J., Woodberry, K.A., Mitchell, A.G. & Indik, J. (2002). Family therapy and dialectical behavior therapy with adolescents: Part I, Proposing a clinical synthesis. *American Journal of Psychotherapy*, 56(4), 568–584.

Miller, A., Rathus, J.H., Linehan, M.M., Wetzler, S. & Leigh, E. (1997). Dialectical behavior therapy adapted for suicidal adolescents. *Journal of Practical Psychiatry & Behavioral Health*, 3, 78–86.

Rogers, C.R. (1951). *Client-centred therapy*. London: Constable.

Swann, W.B., Stein-Seroussi, A. & Giesler, R.B. (1992). Why people self-verify. *Journal of Personality and Social Psychology*, 62, 392–401.

Telch, C.F., Agras, W.S. & Linehan, M.M. (2001). Dialectical behavior therapy for binge eating disorder. *Journal of Consulting and Clinical Psychology*, 69(6), 1061–1065.

Verheul, R., Van Den Bosch, L.M.C., Koeter, M.W.J., De Ridder, M.A.J., Stijnen, T. & Van den Brink, W. (2003). Dialectical behaviour therapy for women with borderline personality disorder: 12 month randomised clinical trial in the Netherlands. *British Journal of Psychiatry*, 182, 135–140.

Williams, J.M.G. & Swales, M.A. (2004). The use of mindfulness-based approaches for suicidal patients. *Archives of Suicide Research*, 8, 315–329.

Wiser, S. & Telch, C.F. (1999). Dialectical behavior therapy for binge-eating disorder. *Journal of Clinical Psychology*, 55, 755–768.

Woodberry, K.A., Miller, A.L., Glinski, J., Indik, J. & Mitchell, A.G. (2002). Family therapy and dialectical behavior therapy with adolescents: Part II, A theoretical review. *American Journal of Psychotherapy*, 56(4), 585–602.

Chapter 10

Using acceptance and commitment therapy to empower the therapeutic relationship

Heather Pierson and Steven C. Hayes

Introduction

It is commonplace to emphasize the importance of the therapeutic relationship in clinical interventions. That connection is especially supported by a large body of mainly correlational evidence between outcomes and measures of the therapeutic alliance (Horvath, 2001) and a somewhat smaller body of evidence showing that relationship-focused treatment can be helpful (e.g., Kohlenberg, Kanter, Bolling, Parker, & Tsai, 2002). What is often not provided, however, is a workable model for *how* to empower the therapeutic relationship in therapy more generally.

Acceptance and commitment therapy (ACT, said as a single word, not initials; Hayes, Wilson, & Strosahl, 1999) is a mindfulness, acceptance, and values-focused approach to clinical intervention. ACT, in a relatively short period of time, has shown a surprising breadth of impact, from diabetes management to coping with psychosis, from work stress to smoking (see Hayes, Luoma, Bond, Masuda, & Lillis (2006) for a recent meta-analysis of ACT process and outcome data). We believe that this same model provides a clear guide for the development of more empowering therapeutic relationships.

In this chapter we will outline the ACT model of psychological flexibility and its basic foundations. We will show how the model seems to specify functional components of the therapeutic relationship that can be applied to the conduct of many types of therapy. This chapter will not go into great detail about how to establish these processes, since ACT has already been applied in controlled studies to both therapists and clients, and the technology for the two is quite similar. Book-length sources on ACT technology are readily available (e.g., Eifert & Forsyth, 2005; Hayes *et al.*, 1999; Hayes & Strosahl, 2004).

Acceptance and commitment therapy

Intellectual context

ACT is part of the so-called third generation of cognitive behavior therapy (CBT) interventions (Hayes, 2004). Along with therapies such as dialectical behavior therapy (Linehan, 1993), mindfulness-based cognitive therapy (Segal, Williams, & Teasdale, 2001), and functional analytic psychotherapy (Kohlenberg & Tsai, 1991), these technologies have created new alternatives within empirical clinical psychology. Third-generation CBT treatments tend to be contextual, experiential, repertoire building, and relevant to therapists themselves (Hayes, 2004). All of these features make these approaches ideally suited to empowering the therapeutic relationship.

In this section we will describe the underlying philosophy, basic theory, model of human suffering, and model of intervention that is in ACT. The reader will need to be patient, since it is only after all of this is described that we will be in a position to attempt to show that this model provides an innovative way of thinking about the therapeutic relationship itself.

Philosophy of science

ACT embraces a specific philosophy of science: functional contextualism (Hayes, 1993). Functional contextualism is a type of pragmatism. As with all forms of pragmatism, the "truth" of a theory is dependent on its ability to meet specified goals. Most of the features of contextualism can be derived from this approach to truth. For one thing, the whole must be assumed and the parts then derived for pragmatists. Differences among elements cannot be assumed. In psychology this holistic emphasis means that the historical and situational context of behavior cannot be fully separated from the behavior being analyzed. Another implication of a pragmatic truth criterion is that there can be different truths depending on one's specific goals. Goals are what distinguish functional contextualism from more descriptive forms of contextualism such as dramaturgy, narrative psychology, hermeneutics, or constructivism. The goals of functional contextualism are prediction and influence, with precision, scope, and depth (Biglan & Hayes, 1996). Since the truth of a theory will thus be measured not only by how well it predicts events but also by how well it lends itself to changing those events, the analyses that result are necessarily contextually focused. This turns out to have positive benefits for the linkage between philosophy, basic science, and applied science since clinicians are inherently part of the context in which clients' behavior occurs, and both prediction and influence are usually important to applied work.

Basic science

ACT is the only modern form of CBT with its own comprehensive experimental analysis of human language and cognition, relational frame theory (RFT; Hayes, Barnes-Holmes, & Roche, 2001). RFT takes the view that learning to form arbitrary relations between events is at the core of human verbal and cognitive behavior. There is a growing amount of supporting evidence for RFT, but it is beyond the scope of this chapter. For a more detailed review of the data on RFT, see Hayes *et al.* (2001).

For practical purposes, we can focus on four important findings in RFT research: human language and cognition are bidirectional, arbitrary, historical, and controlled by a functional context.

Bidirectionality means that the functions of language depend on a mutual relationship between symbols and events. This bidirectionality means that words can pull the functions of the events they are related to into the present. Normal adults can remember, predict, and compare things through the use of symbols, whether or not the events referred to are present. This allows verbal problem-solving but it also means that human beings are always only a cognitive instant away from pain – since through memory, prediction, or comparison humans have the capacity for psychological pain at any time and in any situation.

According to RFT, human language and cognition are in principle arbitrary – what we relate is not necessarily dictated by form. Kick a dog and he will yelp in pain – that reaction is dictated by form in that everything causing the pain is present in the dog's current environment. Conversely, a person who has just had someone very near and dear die may cry when seeing a beautiful sunset, wishing the lost loved one could be here to see it. The crying is not dictated by form – even intense beauty can create sadness precisely because it is beautiful. This arbitrary quality of human language and cognition is both a blessing and a curse. A human child who learns that a dime is "bigger than" a nickel is on the way to being able to believe that, say, hard work is better than laziness. That same ability, however, will enable tears at sunsets or, say, thoughts that it would be better to be dead than alive.

RFT researchers have shown that these relational abilities are learned (e.g., Berens & Hayes, in press). They are historical. Behavioral principles themselves suggest that historical processes are not fully reversible (even extinction is a matter of inhibition, not elimination). As this applies to language it means that a person cannot fully get rid of anything in his history. For example, a person who, say, thinks "I'm bad" and then changes it to "I'm good" is not now a person who thinks "I'm good," but a person who thinks "I'm bad. No, I'm good." Where humans start from is never fully erased – because humans are historical creatures. Deliberate attempts to get rid of history and its echoes – the automatic thoughts and feelings that emerge from our past – often only amplify these processes. In part this is because it makes these events even more central. The same often holds true with emotions if they become verbally entangled. For example, a person who tries to get rid of anxiety because otherwise bad things will happen has now related anxiety to impending bad things. But anxiety is the natural response to bad things so this formulation will very likely increase anxiety. Deliberate control efforts focused on anxiety tend to evoke anxiety for this reason, defeating our purpose.

Fortunately, RFT shows a way out of this conundrum. The contextual events that cause us to relate one thing to another are different than the events that give these relations functional properties. Thus, according to RFT it is possible to change the functions of thoughts and feelings, even if their form or frequency does not change. So the person that thinks "I'm bad" may still have that thought as frequently as before, but the thought "I'm bad" will no longer lead to the same reactions. This is why it is not necessary from an ACT perspective to change the client's thinking – what is more important is to change the behavioral functions of the client's thinking. How this is done will become clearer later.

Model of human struggle

The model of psychopathology and human struggle offered by RFT can be summed up by the term psychological inflexibility, which has several inter-related components. The first component is *cognitive fusion*, which refers to verbal processes that excessively regulate behavior or regulate it in unhelpful ways due to the failure to notice the *process* of thinking over the *products* of thinking. Normal humans often become overly attached to a verbal formulation of events (i.e., rules) and as a result will fail to distinguish a verbally constructed world from the process of constructing it. This in turn will lead to a failure to contact the environment in flexible ways. For example, a person believing that she cannot attend social events because she will be anxious may avoid such settings, producing a more restricted life.

Cognitive fusion supports another component of psychological inflexibility, *experiential avoidance*, which is the attempt to change the form, frequency, or contextual sensitivity of private reactions even when doing so causes harm (Hayes, Wilson, Gifford, Follette, & Strosahl, 1996). Experiential avoidance is particularly based on temporal and comparative relations – the relational ability to predict and evaluate emotions or thoughts as undesirable and then avoid them. Many "undesirable" emotions are natural reactions, based on the person's history, to normal life events. When these reactions are avoided, their salience and importance is increased, which means that even situations that only brought up small levels of the undesirable reaction must now be avoided. This narrows the behaviors that a person can participate in if she is to effectively avoid those reactions. The social verbal community contributes to experiential avoidance by promoting a "feel good" culture in which undesirable emotions are supposed to be avoided and controlled.

Cognitive fusion also supports a loss of contact with the present moment and attachment to beliefs about one's self, both of which further increase psychological inflexibility. The verbal construction of the self, the past, and the future gain more control over other behaviors, thus taking the person away from the consequences that are present in the current environment. For example, if a person is highly attached to his understanding of himself or the past (for example, as someone who has been deeply wronged), he may defend that conception with the cost of not engaging in behaviors that would move him toward valued ends (for example, spending so much time proving that the person wronged him that he does not spend time having meaningful interactions with others). As a result, values, or long-term desired ways of being, become less important (as measured by one's overt behavior) than more immediate consequences such as being right, receiving approval from others, and feeling "good." This lack of clarity regarding one's values is another component of psychological inflexibility.

The ACT treatment model

The six main components of ACT are inter-related and address the above problems by targeting psychological inflexibility. Figure 10.1 depicts the hexagonal ACT treatment model. *Acceptance* increases flexibility by bringing the individual into contact with previously avoided experiences in a safer context. *Cognitive defusion* decreases the behavioral regulatory effect of thoughts by increasing contact with the process of thinking instead of the products of thinking. For example, the thought "I'm worthless" is no longer seen as literally true, but instead is seen as simply a thought that is occurring in the present. This is similar to the cognitive therapy concept of distancing, but it is more radical, since it is applied in ACT to *all* thought, regardless of the strength of evidence for or against it. The point is not to note and correct unhealthy thoughts, but to change one's relationship to thinking itself. Training in *contact with the present moment* increases and enriches the person's awareness of external and internal events. Strengthening a transcendent sense of self (what is generally called *self-as-context* in ACT) decreases attachment to a conceptualized self, or one's story about who one is. This sense of self is argued to be a consistent perspective or point of view from which experiences are reported verbally: namely, I, Here, Now. It is transcendent because its limits cannot be contacted consciously (one cannot consciously note when consciousness is not there). Becoming more aware of a transcendent sense of the self empowers acceptance and defusion as the person embraces experiences without excessively judging or evaluating, firm in that the content of experience is not

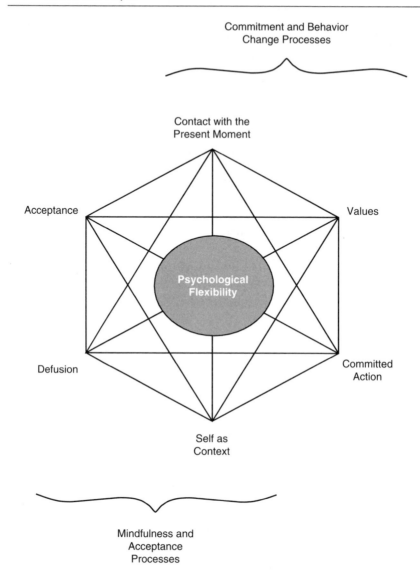

Figure 10.1 The ACT model.

psychologically threatening to this deepest sense of self. The self-as-context is usually experienced only in brief moments; however, those moments serve as examples of detachment from thoughts while still staying present with them. *Values* are chosen qualities of unfolding patterns of action. Values are continuously present from the moment they are chosen, but they are never obtained as concrete objects. For example, being loving is never finished, but once chosen is potentially continuously present as a value. The final component of ACT is *committed action*. Committed action means building larger and larger patterns of effective behavior, linked to chosen values. In all ACT protocols, a variety of behavior change procedures are included, often drawn from the behavior therapy literature.

As is shown in Figure 10.1, the model can be chunked into acceptance and mindfulness components (acceptance, defusion, the present moment, and a transcendent sense of self), and commitment and behavior change components (values, committed action, the present moment, and a transcendent sense of self). These six processes together are argued to lead to *psychological flexibility*, which is the ability to contact the present moment fully as a conscious person (as it is and not as what it says it is), and based on what the situation affords, to persist or change behavior in the service of chosen values.

ACT thus can be simply defined as an approach that uses acceptance and mindfulness processes, and commitment and behavior change processes, to produce psychological flexibility. ACT contains myriad techniques focused on each of its component areas, but it is the model, not the technology, that most defines ACT. Any protocol that accords with the model can be called ACT, whether or not the techniques have been generated by ACT researchers and clinicians.

Brief overview of ACT data

ACT has a growing amount of empirical support with a variety of populations, including depression (Zettle & Hayes, 1986; Zettle & Raines, 1989), worksite stress (Bond & Bunce, 2000), psychosis (Bach & Hayes, 2002; Gaudiano & Herbert, 2005), social phobia (Block, 2002), substance abuse (Hayes *et al.*, 2004b), smoking (Gifford *et al.*, 2004), diabetes management (Gregg, 2004), epilepsy (Lundgren & Dahl, 2005), chronic pain (McCracken, Vowles, & Eccleston, 2005), and borderline personality disorder (Gratz & Gunderson, 2006), among other problems. Some of the studies above include active therapeutic comparisons, as where others are compared to inert control conditions. A recent meta-analysis found large effect sizes for ACT as compared to wait lists or placebos, and medium effect sizes as compared to existing treatments (Hayes *et al.*, 2006); several studies showed good mediational effects for processes specified by the ACT model.

The therapeutic relationship from an ACT model

Thus far we have spent time laying out the underpinnings of an ACT model, and some of the evidence in support of it, so that we can be in a position to examine the therapeutic relationship from this point of view. In summary, an ACT model claims that psychological inflexibility makes it difficult for human beings to learn effectively from experience and to take advantage of opportunities afforded by situations. It is proposed that psychological inflexibility emerges in part from the over-reaching and poorly targeted effects of human language that creates excessive, restrictive, and improperly targeted forms of rule-following and high levels of experiential avoidance. Greater psychological flexibility and effectiveness is said to result from reining in these repertoire-narrowing processes and instead engaging in committed action linked to chosen values.

As a shorthand you can distill this model into seven words: acceptance, defusion, self, now, values, commitment, and flexibility. Although it can readily be applied to psychopathology, the model is not one of abnormal behavior *per se* but of human effectiveness and ineffectiveness. Given that expansive purpose, if this model is correct, it should provide guidance for the establishment of powerful therapeutic relationships. Note that we are not just speaking here of the therapeutic relationship in ACT as a treatment modality. Rather, to the extent that the model focuses on key processes, an ACT approach to therapeutic relationships should be able to be applied to more forms of therapy, provided there is not a fundamental conflict between the models. For that reason, in this section of the chapter we will not attempt to link this analysis to specific ACT techniques or components of therapy. When applied in ACT, however, all of the elements do come together in a unique way, as we will discuss later.

The seven-element ACT model we have described can be applied to the therapeutic relationship at three levels. The first level is the psychological stance of the therapist with regard to his or her own psychological events that is then brought into the moment-to-moment interaction of the therapist and client. In addition to their technical skills, therapists need to have personal psychological skills that they bring into the therapeutic relationship. The ACT model specifies those psychological skills: acceptance, defusion, self, now, values, commitment, and flexibility.

The second level is the level of therapeutic process. By that we mean the qualities of therapeutic interactions. The ACT model suggests qualities that are empowering, whether or not ACT is the treatment modality. These qualities are also acceptance, defusion, self, now, values, commitment, and flexibility.

The final level involves the client's psychological processes that are targeted. This is the usual domain of therapeutic writing, and has been an extensive focus of ACT books and articles. These targets are part of the therapeutic relationship in the same way that such skills on the part of the therapist enter into the therapeutic relationship.

In other words, we are arguing that the ACT model itself is a model of a powerful therapeutic relationship, when examined at the level of the therapist, therapeutic process, and the client. In the following sections we will consider each of the core ACT elements and consider at each of these three levels whether they are a necessary or at least a very helpful psychological aspect of powerful and effective therapeutic relationships.

Acceptance

ACT targets experiential avoidance: the attempt to escape or avoid the form, frequency, or situational sensitivity of private events, even when doing so creates psychological harm. The alternative skill that is taught is acceptance: making undefended contact with such events in the service of chosen values. This domain is relevant to the therapeutic relationship at all three levels we have described: the therapist, therapy processes, and client psychological targets.

Therapist

Experiential avoidance on the part of the therapist is a potent barrier to an open, effective, and empowering relationship. An avoidant therapist may fail to explore certain client topics if they touch on personally difficult material, or may change the topic when they emerge, or even fail to acknowledge their presence at all. For example, a therapist who avoids feelings of anger may not recognize a client's anger, may fail to follow up on it when it emerges in session, or may fail to ask about it and its roots when anger outside of session is described. An emotionally avoidant therapist may fail to notice his or her own feelings that emerge in session, thus losing one of the most important sources of clinical information about subtle events occurring in the moment. An avoidant therapist may fail to see what a client is thinking if those thoughts are disturbing, reducing the richness of understanding that is critical to clinical work.

The therapeutic relationship that is established by an experientially avoidant therapist can take on a fake or manipulative quality for no other reason than that the therapist is avoidant. There is a reason for this: avoidance itself is fake and manipulative. The fact that it is *self*-fakery and *self*-manipulation does not alter that fundamental truth. For example, suppose a therapist is unsure what to do in session and does not feel confident. The experientially avoidant therapist might attempt to escape from these feelings by a show of bravado and certainty, or may withdraw into fear-based inactivity disguised as a therapeutic style, such as validation or Rogerian reflective listening. Either of these reactions, as a method of avoidance, is *designed* to be a false communication. A therapist making a display of bravado and certainty in response to a lack of certainty, for example, is attempting to fool and bully the client into thinking that he or she is confident and sure-footed. Even if the client does not overtly detect the deception, few will fail to notice that the relationship seems disconnected rather than engaged. Meanwhile, the therapist will have a hard time fully focusing on the client while simultaneously attempting to play a role to cover up the true state of affairs. Verbal content, verbal tone, and even facial expressions will need to be carefully monitored, which will quickly reduce the capacity to attend to the client or even to remember what was said (Richards & Gross, in press).

Experiential avoidance need not be based on content-specific therapist issues to be harmful. Fairly generic reasons will do. For example, suppose a clinician has a difficult time seeing another human being in pain, as most humans do. If that feeling cannot be embraced, the clinician has a wide variety of unhealthy steps to take to reduce the pain. The clinician can reassure the client whether or not that is clinically called for, ignore asking more about the client's pain when it appears, or communicate the message that the client should say things are fine even if they are not. In so doing, the focus shifts from dealing effectively with the client's reality to the need for manipulating the therapist's reactions, and an opportunity for clinical progress is squandered.

Conversely, if a clinician has good acceptance skills and is willing to use them in session, a much broader range of flexible alternatives is clinically available. The issue shifts from tracking and avoiding what pushes the therapist's buttons to tracking and approaching what is helpful to the client. Issues the client is dealing with can be more readily allowed into therapy, and the therapist has a richer set of private reactions available to provide subtle information about such issues as the impact the client may be having on others outside of therapy, the current psychological state of the client, or the functional classes that lurk below the readily accessible topographical features of client statements or behavioral reactions.

Quite apart from the utility of acceptance-based clinical work, the secondary impact of therapists' avoidance can be large. When the client senses these avoidant processes, the client may believe that she is inherently unacceptable or loathsome, so much so that even a therapist cannot look unblinkingly at her situation. The client may begin to worry more about protecting the therapist than about therapeutic progress, and may put on a show to rescue the therapist from discomfort. Seeing experiential avoidance being modeled, the client may attempt to adopt this approach and apply it to her own problems. The client may subtly be shaped into avoiding certain clinically important content areas, without even being aware of that process, thus reducing contact with needed information.

In a broader sense, avoidant relationships are inherently invalidating. Part of this sense of invalidation comes because such relationships are not genuine. The client will sense that something else is in the room, but will not know what it is, or even that it is an issue with the therapist and not themselves. In order to stay avoidant the therapist may fail to notice what is actually occurring or may be unwilling to acknowledge it once seen, which makes a sense of the lack of genuineness difficult to describe and correct. The client is put in a "crazy-making" situation, but may be unable to detect where the source of the problem lies, and due to the power differential in therapy, may be particularly unlikely to see the true source of the difficulties.

Process

An eyes-closed exercise commonly done in ACT workshops consists of a process in which individuals return in imagination to their childhood homes. At one point late in the exercise they are asked to be the adult they are now and to meet the child they were then. They are asked to look into the eyes of that child and see what it was that was most wanted. Many answers come up, some of which (e.g., "safety") are extremely poignant, but the most common answer is some form of "love and acceptance."

Humans carry a deep need for acceptance in social relationships. Acceptance does not mean approval. It means looking, seeing, acknowledging, feeling, and thinking. It means being willing to see the client's world from within, without letting judgments and evaluations overwhelm that process.

Concretely, acceptance involves taking in what the client is saying and doing; exploring these events fully when clinically relevant; being fully open to the client's history and the feelings and thoughts it produces; and standing with the wholeness and consciousness of the person. Acceptance does not mean approval or compliance, and it does not mean that change is irrelevant. Especially in domains that can be changed readily, such as overt behavior, or dangerous situations, change is often targeted in ACT. But the therapist is open to all thoughts, feelings, bodily sensations, and memories expressed by the client as valid experiences in and of themselves. They do not necessarily mean what they "say they mean" by their form. Furthermore, the reverse is also true – the therapist is willing to express thoughts, feelings, bodily sensations, and memories when it is appropriate and models acceptance of these events, while simultaneously engaging in valued actions.

Client

When a client is being avoidant in session, it can be manifested in several ways. The client may change the subject when a certain topic comes up, become disengaged or stop interacting with the therapist, become defensive and/or aggressive toward the therapist if a topic is pursued, or may "play along" even though not emotionally contacting the material. All of these reactions can interfere with the therapeutic relationship, especially if the therapist responds in avoidant or cognitively fused ways, such as pretending that nothing is happening or working frantically as if the responsibility for change is entirely with the therapist. Conversely, as the client becomes more accepting, the client is better able to bring difficult private events into the present moment. The positive impact of the acceptance abilities of the therapist and the acceptance process in the treatment sessions is amplified as the client is better able to express difficult psychological material and stay in contact with these events during sessions.

The impact on qualities of a therapeutic relationship

It is not by accident that clients will say that what they most needed as children was "love and acceptance." Acceptance *is* a kind of love – the "agape" kind, brought into a specific moment. In that sense, from an ACT point of view the core of a powerful therapeutic relationship is a loving relationship.

Defusion

Language is a tool. It has evolved because of its utility to human beings. But part of the illusion of language is that symbolic events *are what they say they are* regardless of whether they are useful. This is the core process underlying cognitive fusion. For example, if a therapist thinks "I am bad," the "truth value" of that statement is seemingly to be found in determining whether or not it corresponds with the therapist's competence level. If it corresponds, it is "true," whether or not it is useful.

From an ACT perspective, conversely, effective action *is* truth. Workability is the truth criterion. It is not possible to treat language that way, however, if languaging is allowed to go on entirely in a normal context. The normal context must itself be changed.

In a normal context (a context of literal meaning, reason-giving, prediction, evaluation, and so on) words mean what they say they mean. If a person thinks "I'm bad," it is as if their own badness has somehow been contacted or discovered and then simply described. Said more simply, it is as if the "badness" is in the event (in this case, the person). But evaluations are not primary properties of events – they are in the interaction between the evaluator and the evaluated. Awkward though it is, to be more technically correct about what is happening one would have to say "Right now I'm badding about me," instead of "I'm bad." No one would adopt such an awkward way of speaking for very long, and even if they did the illusion of language would still be a threat, because now this *new* way of speaking could be taken literally. It is the essence of this posture (a detachment from literal language), which we call defusion, that is the goal – precisely so that workability may now move to center stage as a truth criterion. Defusion is the process of altering the automatic behavior regulatory effects of language by noticing the ongoing process of relating events. If the verbal formulation is helpful, it can still be followed. If no behavior change is called for, the person may simply notice what came up. Defusion allows for more behavioral flexibility: one can take what is useful about thoughts and judgments without being compelled to follow verbal rules that may arise if it does not work to do so.

Therapist

Defusion is a powerful ally to the development of a therapeutic relationship, and fusion is a powerful block to that process. When a therapist has become fused with thoughts in session, the behavioral options immediately narrow because only behavioral options that are implied by the adopted verbal formulation are now "logical" or "sensible."

Fusion can come in many forms. The therapist may become fused with the client's stories and support them even if that is unhelpful. This superficially can feel validating ("you poor dear – it is awful to be victimized like that") but it does not have the desired effects of true validation. The client will usually feel supported, but with a sense of righteous entanglement, not a sense of liberation. The creativity possible in a more genuine relationship is diminished since the client intuitively knows that these stories and reasons are old, predictable, and well-explored.

The therapist can become fused with judgments and interpretations about the client, rather than allowing them to be one of many possibilities. It can then become important to be right about these judgments and interpretations, and the client begins to feel as though he is not known but is merely a kind of pawn in a cognitive game being played by the therapist. As fusion takes hold, the therapist may find herself arguing with the client or trying to convince the client of something, which will immediately undermine the therapeutic relationship.

In one of the more destructive forms of fusion, the therapist can become fused with self-focused thoughts. As worries and self-evaluations come up, if they are taken literally the client in essence disappears while the therapist becomes absorbed into a booming monody heard by an audience of one.

Defusion allows a different, more flexible dance on the part of the therapist. All thoughts are eligible to be noticed and considered, from random associations to full-blown formulations. There is nothing to be right about in any of this – rather, thoughts are viewed only as tools for making a difference. Because there is nothing to be right about there is nothing to defend – all formulations are held lightly, not because there is not enough evidence or because they might be wrong. They are held lightly because language itself works better when held lightly: by so doing, one can have the benefits of verbal rules without their costs in the form of psychological rigidity.

Process

By adopting a defused approach, the therapist immediately leaves the mountaintop of defended expertise for a more equal, horizontal, and vulnerable position in the relationship. Every statement, whether by the therapist or by the client, is a possibility that points to opportunities for action, not a dungeon of rightness and wrongness. Differences, and inconsistencies – between and within each party of the relationship – can be noticed without fear, opening up new territory to explore. If an accepting relationship is loving, a defused relationship is playful, flexible, and creative.

When therapeutic interactions are defused they can produce a sense of ambiguity or confusion, almost by definition, but they also lead to a sense of openness, creativity, and genuine interest in the moment that empowers the therapeutic relationship. The benefits are much more easily accomplished as fusion and acceptance are successfully targeted in the client, since the sense of ambiguity or confusion can be a source of struggle on the part of the client when these skills are absent. For that reason, the degree to which the interactions in therapy are obviously defused needs to be titrated to fit the client and the client's current acceptance and mindfulness skills. A little overt defusion can go a long way. Further, some forms of therapy push for much less defused forms of interaction as a matter of technique – cognitive disputation or examining the evidence in support of a thought, for example – and these can be difficult to integrate with a defused approach if they become too dominant clinically.

Client

If the therapist adopts a defused stance, and brings it into the therapy interaction, the client's level of fusion will necessarily be targeted. Fusion emerges from a social/verbal context, and it "takes two to tango." Modeling defusion can help the client see the effects of defusing from thoughts *in vivo*, which may make it more likely that the client will be able to implement it into practice.

When a client is fused with certain content, that attachment will be manifested in his reluctance to consider alternative possibilities, his resistance to letting go of certain explanations, and/or a high level of believability in certain thoughts. The client may become argumentative and defensive or otherwise resistant to suggestions. He may argue specifically that something does not fit in with his self-conceptualization and express that he feels invalidated. Usually the story people have of themselves is too narrow and leaves out other aspects that also make up who they are. Psychological inflexibility is the handmaiden of cognitive fusion. The objective when using the ACT model is to move away from right and wrong and literal truth or falsity, to workability.

The impact on qualities of a therapeutic relationship

When a defused stance is adopted, the therapeutic relationship becomes more playful, creative, and effective. It feels collaborative, horizontal, and connected. Language is now no longer a trap – it is grist for a process of empowerment.

A transcendent sense of self

Attachment to the conceptualized self is a type of fusion that deals with the story of who one is, and thus fusion is an enemy to transcendence. Contact with a transcendent sense of self involves looking at external and internal events from a consistent perspective or point of view, often referred to as the "observer self." We are not speaking of a *literal* point of view but of a locus or a context: I/Here/Now.

Language enables self-awareness: it enables one to see that one sees. But certain aspects of language enable one to see that one sees *from* a perspective. One sees from here; one sees now; and that is very much what ones means when one says, "I see."

This insight was a starting point for both ACT and RFT. In an article entitled "Making sense of spirituality" (Hayes, 1984) it was argued that a transcendent sense of self was a side-effect of what we now call deictic relations, such as I/You, Here/There, and Now/Then. Deictic relations must be taught by demonstration (thus the name, which means "by demonstration") since they are with reference to a point of view. Unlike, say, big and little, here and there have no formal referent. What is "here" to me is "there" to you. As a side-effect of such training a consistent "locus" is produced, which is at the core of a transcendent sense of self.

Seeing from a perspective is inherently transcendent and spiritual for reasons laid out in that article: once a sense of perspective arises it is not possible to be fully conscious without it. You cannot know, consciously, the temporal or spatial limits of "I" in the sense of "I/Here/Now." But the only events without temporal or spatial limits are everything and nothing – the very label Eastern thinkers apply to the spiritual dimension. What is "spiritual" is not thing-like – as we say, not material (the very word "material" means "the stuff of which things are made").

While this started as a theoretical idea more than 20 years ago (Hayes, 1984), we now know that deictic relations are indeed central to perspective-taking skills, and that they can be trained in children who do not have them (Barnes-Holmes, McHugh, and Barnes-Holmes, 2004; McHugh, Barnes-Holmes, & Barnes-Holmes, 2004). There is a deep philosophical meaning in the data coming from the RFT labs. Like all relational frames, deictic frames are mutual and bi-directional. And it is here that the deep philosophical meaning arises: one cannot learn "I" in a deictic frame sense of the term except by also learning "you." The same applied to Here and There, or Now and Then. Said in another way, I do not get to show up as a conscious human being except in the context of you showing up in that same way. If I cannot begin to see the world through *your* eyes, I cannot see the world through *my* eyes. Said in another way, consciousness and empathy are two aspects of the same process. For that reason, contact with a transcendent sense of self supports a particular kind of relating, as we will show.

Therapist

A strong transcendent sense of self, and loosened connection to a conceptualized self, is a powerful skill for therapists. The negative effects of a strong attachment to a conceptualized self can be seen in session. For example, if a therapist is attached to seeing herself as a competent and confident individual, she may avoid trying new things because she feels less confident about her abilities in that area.

Connecting with a sense of self-as-context greatly reduces this process. In a deep and entirely positive sense of the term, "I" am nothing (in the sense of not being a thing – indeed, nothing was originally written "no thing"). There is no need to defend nothing or to be right about nothing – and thus a transcendent sense of self supports acceptance and defusion. It also supports connection, since the no-thing that is "I/Here/Now" for me is in some important way indistinguishable from the no-thing that is "I/Here/Now" for you. Said in another way, at a deep level human consciousness itself is one. There can be no greater sense of sharing and connection than that.

Process

When this sense of oneness and transcendence is part of the therapy process, the work is compassionate and conscious, with a sense of a calmness, humility, and sobriety. It is "in the room" that the therapist and client are more than their roles, and more alike than different. Neither the client nor the therapist is an object – they are conscious human beings mindfully attending to the reality of living.

This sense is profoundly beneficial to the therapeutic relationship. The therapist can more easily be mindful of reactions as information about what is happening in session. Because the client's behavior in session is likely similar to her behavior in other situations in her life, the therapist who is watching her reactions without attachment to them is in a better position to help the client with problematic interpersonal behavior. When the therapist is willing to let go of her attachment to her conceptualized self, she both models self-acceptance for the client and is more able to accept the client and her struggles.

Client

Helping a client contact their own spirituality provides a sense of peace, wholeness, and inherent adequacy. It greatly empowers acceptance and defusion, amplifying the work done in other areas.

The impact on qualities of a therapeutic relationship

This quality of a therapeutic relationship from an ACT point of view linked to a sense of transcendence is connected, conscious, and spiritual.

Contact with the present moment

When the conceptualization of the past and/or the fear of the future dominate the client's or the therapist's attention, it leads to a loss of contact with the present moment. When the client is not in the present moment, he may be actively struggling, daydreaming, or otherwise not engaged with the therapist. This is problematic because life only happens in the present moment. This is true as well of the therapeutic relationship. They are not fully connected to each other and therefore, not fully connected to the work being done.

Therapist

When the therapist is focused on the past or future, it is easy to miss both the connection with the client and certain functions that the client's in-session behaviors are serving. Ways that the therapist can be pulled away from contact with the present moment include thinking about what to do next in session, thinking about what has already happened, or evaluating her performance. Being able to come back to the present grounds clinical work in the moment-to-moment reality of a therapist and a client working together. Now.

Process

When sessions get "mindy" they lose their punch. This can occur if either party to the therapeutic interaction psychologically drifts away to other times and places. Usually simply acknowledging that fact (which is, after all, itself occurring in the present moment) can shift the process in a healthy direction. Consciously saying or doing things that are present-focused, such as taking a deep breath together with the client, or taking a moment to notice (in the present moment) that they are two human beings that have come together for a single purpose, can situate therapy work in the here and now.

It is often necessary to do work in session that is about other times and places. Clients are asked about their lives; problems about to be faced are addressed. But even as that work is being done, it is being done here and now, between two people. Noticing that situates such work in the present even if it is "about" the past.

Often, however, the real work can be done by focusing on the present therapy process. There is no need to *talk about* experiential avoidance or cognitive fusion, for example, when it is usually quite easy to find it then and there . . . in the room . . . in the relationship.

Clients are sometimes disconcerted by this approach. A person struggling with anxiety will not necessarily see the immediate relevance of working on, say, the discomfort of being known in therapy. But from a behavioral perspective larger functional classes are better targeted when they are targeted in a number of ways. It promotes healthy forms of generalization, for example, for an anxiety disordered client to see that experiential avoidance is not merely a matter of avoiding panic attacks. By dancing back and forth between processes occurring in the moment and functionally similar processes occurring in other settings, the present can become a kind of tangible laboratory to unravel functional patterns and to learn new ones, while also making obvious to the client that this is highly relevant to other times and places.

Client

Life goes on now, not then. And life is about many things, not just a few. The repertoire-narrowing effects of fusion and avoidance are resisted by the repertoire-broadening effects of what is afforded by the here and now.

The impact on qualities of a therapeutic relationship

This applies to the therapeutic relationship especially. Building the skills to contact the present moment automatically strengthens the possibility of a more powerful therapeutic relationship for that reason. A powerful therapeutic relationship is alive, vital, and in the present.

Values

The pain of psychopathology has two sources. The smaller source is the one usually focused on: the pain of struggling with symptoms. The larger source is often not mentioned: the pain of a life not being lived. Values are choices of desired life directions. Values are a way of speaking about where to go from a life not being lived. They are what therapy is really about – or should be.

Therapist

What is being a therapist really about? There are no set answers to this question – each therapist can generate their own. What is important about

ACT as it applies to the therapeutic relationship is that it asks this question, and invites the therapist to place the answer into the heart and soul of their clinical work. Most of the barriers to an intense therapeutic relationship are orthogonal or contradictory to therapists' values. Their own psychology may push therapists to want to look good, be confident, be right, not be hurt, be the expert, avoid guilt, make a lot of money, and so on, but it is rare that any of these are chosen values. Therapists usually value such things as wanting to serve others, to alleviate suffering, to be genuine, and to make a difference. All of these values can empower a genuine therapeutic relationship and can help therapists be mindful of the cost that can come from putting on a therapeutic clown suit and acting out their role.

Process

Values work enables the therapeutic relationship to be grounded in what the therapist and client most care about. Each and every moment in therapy should be able to be linked to these values, from the simplest question to the most demanding homework exercises. If the client and therapist are clear about what is at stake, the mundane is vitalized, the painful is dignified, and the confrontational is made coherent. The qualities of therapy are *about* something, and they are about what the client most deeply desires.

Client

Helping clients to realize what they really want as qualities of life and distinguishing this from specific, concrete goals along that path, serves as a profound motivator for taking needed but difficult steps in life. That includes the steps that lead to a meaningful relationship. It is values that make all of the other elements in the ACT model make sense. Acceptance, defusion, and the like are not ends in themselves – they are means to living a more vital and values-based life. Thus, client work on values is directly supportive of the application of the entire model we have presented to the therapeutic relationship.

The impact on qualities of a therapeutic relationship

Thus, the purpose of a therapeutic relationship is not just a concrete goal, but a direction or quality of living. In a sense, if a therapeutic relationship is values-based, the process is the outcome. A therapist doing what there is to be done in the service of the client is modeling an approach to others and to life, one that is dignified by human purpose.

Committed action

The bottom line in therapy is what we *do*; what the client *does*. Committed action is about overt behavior change. While working on committed action (when behavior change is actually taking place) all the other components (acceptance, defusion, values, etc.) are revisited because people become re-stuck. All the other ACT processes are in the service of this behavior change or change in ways of living.

The therapeutic relationship fosters committed action in that it provides an accepting, open, creative environment for trying new ways of living. When the client and therapist are working on committed action, the relationship is enhanced through their common purpose.

Therapist

A therapist living out a valued life in their work is much more powerful in that she is more active, vitalized, and less prone to burnout. It is through the therapist's committed actions that all the other parts of ACT are carried out. From this place the therapist can do what needs to be done to be effective with her clients.

Process

Work on committed action includes finding barriers to the client's moving forward in a personally meaningful life. This process unites the client and therapist in a common purpose. The therapist can be supportive and instructive in the accepting, open, and creative relationship that has already been established through the other ACT processes.

Client

Committed action is about actually living out one's values, or said another way building larger patterns of behavior that work toward valued living. Often clients become stuck again in old patterns. Working with the therapist to identify these barriers and find new ways to act in these situations supports both the client's life and the therapeutic relationship.

The impact on qualities of a therapeutic relationship

Thus, a therapeutic relationship is active and action focused. It is not just about living – it is living.

A psychologically flexible relationship

Putting these all together, an empowering therapeutic relationship, from an ACT perspective, is an accepting, loving, compassionate, mindful, and creative relationship between two conscious and transcendent human beings, who are working together to foster more committed and creative ways of moving toward valued ends. It avoids unnecessary hierarchy and gravitates toward humility over pretense; effectiveness over self-righteousness. Said more simply, powerful therapeutic relationships are psychologically flexible as ACT defines the term.

How is this different than the therapeutic relationship from any other perspective? It is different in several ways: it is not merely a matter of being supportive, or positive, or empathetic – it is a matter of being present, open, and effective. Some parts of this model may be difficult. Applying the model requires substantial psychological work on the part of the therapist – it is not a mere matter of therapy technique. To the extent that the model is correct there is no fundamental distinction between the therapist and the client at the level of the processes that need to be learned. The targets and processes relevant for the client are those relevant to the therapist and those relevant to the relationship between them. This suggests that it should be possible to use ACT with therapists, and indeed ACT is one of the few psychotherapies that is vigorously exploring that very idea in research.

In one recent randomized study (Hayes *et al.*, 2004a), ACT was shown to reduce therapists' entanglement with negative thoughts about their most difficult clients, and that in turn considerably reduced their sense of job burnout. While the impact on the therapeutic alliance was not assessed, it seems quite likely that entanglement with negative thoughts about clients would be harmful.

Several other such studies have been conducted but not yet published. So far we have found that ACT helps therapists learn other new clinical procedures, to produce good outcomes even when they are not feeling confident, and to reduce the believability and impact of thoughts about barriers to using empirically supported treatments.

ACT training usually focuses not just on technique but also on the therapist, and on processes of change. Thus, the research finding that training in ACT makes generally more effective clinicians (Strosahl, Hayes, Bergan, & Romano, 1998) may in part be because training in ACT includes applying an ACT model to the therapist.

While it is early, it appears as though an ACT model does describe processes of relevance to therapists and their relationships with clients. Explicit tests of this idea will await future research, but, as the present chapter shows, the model readily leads to several ideas about how to create curative relationships.

Conclusion

It not uncommon for cognitive behavior therapists to underline the importance of the therapeutic relationship, but in general these efforts have been technological. The therapeutic relationship is a powerful engine of change, and deeply connected relationships empower clinical work of all kinds, but this chapter has attempted to go one step beyond that agreed-upon point. We are arguing that ACT contains within it a model of an empowering therapeutic relationship itself: what it is, why it works, and how to create it. In so doing, a circle is closed that draws the client and therapist into one coherent system. Therapist and client are both in the circle, and for a very basic reason. They are both human beings, each struggling with their own experiences, and yet bound together to accomplish a common purpose that each one values. In this view, therapist, client, and process are all part of one common set of issues that originates from the human condition itself.

References

Bach, P. & Hayes, S.C. (2002). The use of acceptance and commitment therapy to prevent the rehospitalization of psychotic patients: A randomized controlled trial. *Journal of Consulting and Clinical Psychology*, 70, 1129–1139.

Barnes-Holmes, Y., McHugh, L. & Barnes-Holmes, D. (2004). Perspective-taking and Theory of Mind: A relational frame account. *The Behavior Analyst Today*, 5, 15–25.

Berens, N.M. & Hayes, S.C. (in press). Arbitrarily applicable comparative relations: Experimental evidence for a relational operant. *Journal of Applied Behavior Analysis*.

Biglan, A. & Hayes, S.C. (1996). Should the behavioral sciences become more pragmatic? The case for functional contextualism in research on human behavior. *Applied and Preventive Psychology: Current Scientific Perspectives*, 5, 47–57.

Block, J.A. (2002). Acceptance or change of private experiences: A comparative analysis in college students with public speaking anxiety. Unpublished doctoral dissertation, State University of New York, Albany.

Bond, F.W. & Bunce, D. (2000). Mediators of change in emotion-focused and problem-focused worksite stress management interventions. *Journal of Occupational Health Psychology*, 5, 156–163.

Eifert, G. & Forsyth, J. (2005). *Acceptance and commitment therapy for anxiety disorders*. Oakland, CA: New Harbinger.

Gaudiano, B.A. & Herbert, J.D. (2005). Acute treatment of inpatients with psychotic symptoms using acceptance and commitment therapy: Pilot results. *Behavior Research and Therapy*, 41(4), 403–411.

Gaudiano, B.A. & Herbert, J.D. (in press). Believability of hallucinations as a potential mediator of their frequency and associated distress in psychotic inpatients. *Behavioural and Cognitive Psychotherapy*.

Gifford, E.V., Kohlenberg, B.S., Hayes, S.C., Antonuccio, D.O., Piasecki, M.M.,

Rasmussen-Hall, M.L. & Palm, K.M. (2004). Applying a functional acceptance based model to smoking cessation: An initial trial of acceptance and commitment therapy. *Behavior Therapy*, 35, 689–705.

Gratz, K.L. & Gunderson, J.G. (2006). Preliminary data on an acceptance-based emotion regulation group intervention for deliberate self-harm among women with borderline personality disorder. *Behavior Therapy*, 37, 25–35.

Gregg, J.A. (2004). A randomized controlled effectiveness trial comparing patient education with and without acceptance and commitment therapy. Unpublished doctoral dissertation, University of Nevada, Reno.

Hayes, S.C. (1984). Making sense of spirituality. *Behaviorism*, 12, 99–110.

Hayes, S.C. (1993). Analytic goals and the varieties of scientific contextualism. In S.C. Hayes, L.J. Hayes, H.W. Reese & T.R. Sarbin (eds), *Varieties of scientific contextualism* (pp. 11–27). Reno, NV: Context Press.

Hayes, S.C. (2004). Acceptance and commitment therapy, relational frame theory, and the third wave of behavioral and cognitive therapies. *Behavior Therapy*, 35, 639–665.

Hayes, S.C., Barnes-Holmes, D. & Roche, B. (eds) (2001). *Relational frame theory: A post-Skinnerian account of human language and cognition.* New York: Plenum Press.

Hayes, S.C., Bissett, R., Roget, N., Padilla, M., Kohlenberg, B.S., Fisher, G., Masuda, A., Pistorello, J., Rye, A.K., Berry, K. & Niccolls, R. (2004a). The impact of acceptance and commitment training on stigmatizing attitudes and professional burnout of substance abuse counselors. *Behavior Therapy*, 35, 821–836.

Hayes, S.C., Luoma, J., Bond, F., Masuda, A. & Lillis, J. (2006). Acceptance and commitment therapy: Model, processes, and outcomes. *Behaviour Research and Therapy*, 44, 1–25.

Hayes, S.C. & Strosahl, K.D. (eds) (2004). *A practical guide to acceptance and commitment therapy.* New York: Springer-Verlag.

Hayes, S.C., Wilson, K.D. & Strosahl, K.D. (1999). *Acceptance and commitment therapy: An experiential approach to behavior change.* New York: Guilford Press.

Hayes, S.C., Wilson, K.G., Gifford, E.V., Bissett, R., Piasecki, M., Batten, S.V., Byrd, M. & Gregg, J. (2004b). A randomized controlled trial of twelve-step facilitation and acceptance and commitment therapy with polysubstance abusing methadone maintained opiate addicts. *Behavior Therapy*, 35, 667–688.

Hayes, S.C., Wilson, K.W., Gifford, E.V., Follette, V.M. & Strosahl, K. (1996). Experiential avoidance and behavioral disorders: A functional dimensional approach to diagnosis and treatment. *Journal of Consulting and Clinical Psychology*, 64, 1152–1168.

Horvath, A.O. (2001). The alliance. *Psychotherapy: Theory, Research, Practice, Training*, 38, 365–372.

Kohlenberg, R.H., Kanter, J.W., Bolling, M.Y., Parker, C. & Tsai, M. (2002). Enhancing cognitive therapy for depression with functional analytic psychotherapy: Treatment guidelines and empirical findings. *Cognitive and Behavioral Practice*, 9, 213–229.

Kohlenberg, R.J. & Tsai, M. (1991). *Functional analytic psychotherapy: A guide for creating intense and curative therapeutic relationships.* New York: Plenum.

Linehan, M.M. (1993). *Cognitive-behavioral treatment of borderline personality disorder*. New York: Guilford Press.

Lundgren, T. & Dahl, J. (2005). *Development and evaluation of an integrative health model in treatment of epilepsy: A randomized controlled trial investigating the effects of a short-term ACT intervention compared to attention control in South Africa.* Paper presented at the Association for Behavior Analysis, Chicago.

McCracken, L.M., Vowles, K.E. & Eccleston, C. (2005). Acceptance-based treatment for persons with complex, long standing chronic pain: a preliminary analysis of treatment outcome in comparison to a waiting phase. *Behavior Research and Therapy*, 43, 1335–1346.

McHugh, L., Barnes-Holmes, Y. & Barnes-Holmes, D. (2004). Perspective-taking as relational responding: A developmental profile. *Psychological Record*, 54, 115–144.

Richards, J.M. & Gross, J.J. (in press). Personality and emotional memory: How regulating emotion impairs memory for emotional events. *Journal of Research in Personality*.

Segal, Z.V., Williams, J.M.G. & Teasdale, J.T. (2001). *Mindfulness-based cognitive therapy for depression: A new approach to preventing relapse*. New York: Guilford Press.

Strosahl, K.D., Hayes, S.C., Bergan, J. & Romano, P. (1998). Assessing the field effectiveness of acceptance and commitment therapy: An example of the manipulated training research method. *Behavior Therapy*, 29, 35–64.

Zettle, R.D. & Hayes, S.C. (1986). Dysfunctional control by client verbal behavior: The context of reason giving. *The Analysis of Verbal Behavior*, 4, 30–38.

Zettle, R.D. & Raines, J.C. (1989). Group cognitive and contextual therapies in treatment of depression. *Journal of Clinical Psychology*, 45, 438–445.

Chapter 11

Schematic mismatch in the therapeutic relationship

A social-cognitive model

Robert L. Leahy

Introduction

In the past decade cognitive-behavioral therapists have recognized the therapeutic relationship as an important component of the process of change (Gilbert, 1992; Gilbert & Irons, 2005; Greenberg, 2001; Leahy, 2001, 2005b; Safran, 1998; Safran & Muran, 2000). Each of these models implies that the current therapeutic relationship is reflective of earlier or current relationships – similar to the psychoanalytic concept of "transference" (Menninger & Holzman, 1973). The transference relationship consists of all personal and interpersonal processes that occur in the relationship between the patient and therapist. These processes include personal schemas about the self (inadequate, special, helpless), interpersonal schemas about others (superior, judgmental, nurturing), intrapsychic processes (repression, denial, displacement), interpersonal strategies (provoking, stonewalling, clinging), and past and present history of relationships that affect how the current therapeutic relationship is experienced.

The transference relationship in therapy also depends on the particular therapeutic modality that is employed: thus, in some psychoanalytic therapies, the patient may be given little direction except to allow various thoughts and feelings to come into consciousness via free association. In contrast, most cognitive-behavioral therapies entail some directive process, such as Socratic questioning and dialogues, with explicit guidelines in the form of session agendas, bibliotherapy, socialization to the model, direct examination and testing of thoughts, and self-help homework assignments (Beck, 1995; Leahy, 2001, 2003a). Although all therapies implicitly promise change that will be facilitated by the therapist, CBT explicitly calls on the patient to actively engage with current thoughts, feelings, relationships, and behavior. As a consequence of these expectations and therapeutic procedures of the CBT model, non-compliance or resistance may take specific forms.

The therapeutic relationship is a co-construction that is shaped via interactional sequences. An interactional sequence occurs when the therapist and patient are reacting moment-to-moment with each other. For example, the therapist points out a type of negative thought but the patient experiences this as a criticism and withdraws. The therapist may react to this withdrawal by backing away or by being more dominant. In this chapter I will review common dimensions of confusion, disappointment, conflict, and resistance in the therapeutic relationship that emerge from these sequences. Of specific focus in this chapter are the personal schemas and emotional schemas that both patient and therapist bring to the relationship, and how these individual schemas can create mismatches and thus disrupt interactions that can interfere with treatment. I utilize a game metaphor that suggests that patient and therapist follow their own implicit rules as interactional sequences unfold that may result in self-fulfilling prophecies about their own personal schemas. Finally, I will identify some interventions that may be useful in overcoming these potential roadblocks in treatment.

Dimensions of resistance in the relationship

Non-compliance, resistance, or lack of progress in therapy can be understood, to some extent, as a result of strategies and roles that the patient activates to affirm personal schemas, avoid further loss, and defend themselves (Leahy, 2001, 2003a). The assumption here is that patients are trying to protect themselves from further loss, disappointment, or criticism or that they are seeking desired outcomes (for example, validation, legitimacy, moral sanction) from the therapist. I have identified seven common patterns of resistance that interfere with progress, as follows.

1   *Validation resistance.* The patient gets stuck by demanding that the focus is exclusively on validating pain. The patient may view suggestions for alternative action or thought as invalidating: "You don't understand how bad it feels." Failures in validation lead to escalation of complaints and suffering until validation is obtained. Patients may have unique and self-defeating "rules" for validation, such as "You can only validate me if you agree that it is hopeless." Potential conflicts between the therapist and patient may arise when the therapist becomes task-oriented and views validation as interfering with valued goals. Interventions for validation resistance include recognizing the need for validation, and asserting to the patient that therapy involves a dilemma – both validating the pain and encouraging change – and that the patient may be using self-defeating strategies to elicit validation (for example, complaining, catastrophizing, or withdrawing) (Leahy, 2001).

2   *Victim resistance.* Here the patient believes that his identity is defined only by being a victim, and that he can do nothing to make things change, because he was not the cause of his problem. The person stuck in this role will have specific rules for how change has to come about:

"Other people will have to apologize and make compensation. That's how I can get better." Attempts to move the patient toward individual change only lead the patient to view the therapist as another malicious victimizer. Interventions that are useful include acknowledging the legitimacy of the patient's complaint that he is in fact a victim, but that he can also empower himself by focusing on personal goals and the current resources available (Leahy, 2001).

3   *Moral resistance.* In this situation the patient believes that change would run the risk of violating one's own moral or ethical standards. This is especially the case in obsessive–compulsive or perfectionistic patients who believe that their inflated sense of responsibility and fear of making a mistake are based on a moral code. Thus, the therapist who encourages the patient to abandon demanding standards of perfection may be viewed as facilitating irresponsible and reprehensible qualities in the patient. While recognizing that there are legitimate "shoulds" that guide behavior, the therapist can help the patient recognize that his absolutistic, perfectionistic "shoulds" violate a universal moral code of enhancing human dignity and assuring fairness. Thus, the therapist need not reject "moral resistance," but rather can assert a more "rational" and "reasonable" moral code that recognizes human differences and needs (Leahy, 2001; Nussbaum, 2005; Rawls, 2001).

4   *Schematic resistance.* In this role, the patient's personal schemas limit change, since the patient has a confirmatory bias in viewing past, present and future as evidence that maladaptive personal schemas are valid. For example, the patient who views the self as "helpless" selectively recalls past evidence of ineptitude and failure, views current life primarily in terms of inertia, and predicts that the future will be just as barren, thus "justifying" avoidance and procrastination. The patient's response to suggestions is, "You don't realize. I *really am* helpless." (This can be similar to the patient's underlying fear of becoming more powerful and less helpless (Gilbert & Irons, 2005).) In this case the therapist can utilize techniques to modify persistent schemas, such as examining the origin of schemas, developing alternative adaptive schemas, and experimenting with acting against the schema (Leahy, 2001; Leahy, Beck, & Beck, 2005; Young, Klosko, & Weishaar, 2003).

5   *Self-consistency.* All of us like to believe that there is some predictability in life – which is one reason why schemas are "conservative" in nature. A particular kind of self-consistency in resistance is the tendency to justify past failed decisions – a process known as "sunk costs." In this situation, the patient claims that he cannot walk away from a string of bad commitments because he has already invested too much (in his failure). "I can't leave, because I've already put too much time into this." Since the therapist does not have past mistakes to justify, it may be difficult for her/him to understand how difficult it is

for the patient to abandon a prior commitment that has only proved to be a lost sunk cost. Interventions to modify commitment to sunk costs include consideration of rejecting a commitment as an opportunity for new rewards, stepping away from one's own commitment by considering the advice one would give a friend, and considering if one would take on the commitment if one could start over (Leahy, 2001, 2004a).

6   *Risk-aversion.* All change involves an increase in uncertainty, since what is not known is expected to have greater variability than what is known. Resistant individuals often engage a risk-averse strategy of decision-making. This includes high information demands, selective focus on likelihood and magnitude of negative outcomes, high focus on regret, and low value and estimation of positive utility: "I really need to know more because it could very likely be really terrible if it did not work out and I would blame myself. And, for what? How much would I really enjoy it if it did happen the way you suggest?" Individuals with risk-averse strategies are more likely to be depressed, anxious, worried, or to score higher on the Millon Multiaxial Scale on avoidant, dependent, or borderline personality disorder (Leahy, 2002, 2003a, 2005a; Leahy & Napolitano, 2005). These individuals utilize strategies of reassurance-seeking, waiting, stopping-out quickly, quitting "while ahead," and devaluing positive change to avoid their "expectations getting ahead of them." The therapist and patient may face conflicts when the therapist's suggestions for behavioral activation and change are viewed as presenting unacceptable risks to the patient, who believes he has already lost enough. Interventions include evaluation of alternative and more flexible views of calculating reasonable risks and opportunities for change and to avoid "stopping-out" or quitting too early (Leahy, 2001, 2004a). As noted above, what is key is exploring the "fear of change," and to see these kinds of resistances in terms of safety strategies (Gilbert, Chapter 6, this volume).

7   *Self-handicapping.* Some patients come to therapy with the apparent abilities to be successful, but with a history of limited and self-sabotaging behavior. Often labeled "masochistic" or "self-defeating," these patients either openly resist attempts to change or make half-hearted efforts that are doomed to fail. In some cases, this strategy may reflect an attempt to obscure being evaluated at one's best behavior. It is better to fail with limited effort, since one can always claim "I didn't really care" or "I didn't really try," thus preserving some self-esteem based on what one could do under the *best conditions*. The therapist can assist the patient in examining the patterns of self-handicapping, evaluating the global and shame-based ideas of "failure," and help the patient make slow progress to avoid "getting ahead of myself" (Leahy, 2001).

We shall keep these seven dimensions of resistance in mind as we later explore schematic mismatches in therapy. For example, the patient with validation and victim resistance issues will feel especially frustrated with a therapist with demanding standards who views some emotions as "whining" or "self-indulgent." Thus, certain dimensions of resistance may be augmented by the therapist's counter-transference. We will examine this later in this chapter.

Schematic model of personality

The schematic processing model has been extended to an understanding of personality disorders (Beck *et al.*, 2003; Leahy *et al.*, 2005; McGinn & Young, 1996; Pretzer & Beck, 2004; Young *et al.*, 2003). Influenced by the ego analysts – such as Alfred Adler (1924/1964), Karen Horney (1945, 1950), Harry Stack Sullivan (1956), and Victor Frankl (1992) – the cognitive model of personality stresses the importance of how thinking is organized to influence and be influenced by affect, behavior and interpersonal relationships. Various dimensions of personality that are linked to vulnerabilities to psychopathologies can be understood in terms of specific schemas (for example, feeling helpless and needing others is linked to dependent personality). In contrast, seeing self as unique and superior is linked to narcissism. Various strategies flow from these self–other schematic representations – for example, the dependent patient is deferential and clinging, while the narcissistic patient is exploitative and confrontational.

Specific personality "disorders" operate differently in the transference relationship. For example, the dependent patient, fearing abandonment and isolated helplessness, may seek considerable reassurance from the therapist. In contrast, the narcissistic patient, viewing therapy as a potential humiliation, may devalue the therapist and provoke her in order to test his "power." These role-enactments in therapy also reflect the social relational systems described by Gilbert (1989, 2000, 2005b; Chapter 6, this volume) as well as the interpersonal schemas elaborated by Safran and his colleagues (Muran & Safran, 1998; Safran, 1998; Safran & Greenberg, 1988, 1989, 1991; Safran & Muran, 1993) and the relational schemas identified by Baldwin & Dandeneau (2005). I have listed some of the common personality schemas in the transference in Table 11.1.

These schemas can be seen as dimensions that are not mutually exclusive, and different therapists may "pull on" them in different ways. For example, one therapist may stimulate hostility or (say) dependency easily in patients in a way another therapist may not. One therapist may find a particular patient very hard to work with while another therapist may not. One reason for this is that the therapeutic relationship is a co-construction and therefore the therapist's schemas are also key to the co-constructions. Therapists will also have various degrees of these schema vulnerabilities.

Table 11.1 Patient personal schemas in therapy

Schema	Example
Incompetent (avoidant)	Avoids difficult topics and emotions. Appears vague. Looks for signs that the therapist will reject her. Believes that therapist will criticize her for not doing homework well enough. Reluctant to do behavioral exposure homework assignments.
Helpless (dependent)	Seeks reassurance. Does not have an agenda of problems to solve. Frequently complains about "feelings." Calls frequently between sessions. Wants to prolong sessions. Does not think he can do the homework or believes that homework will not work. Upset when therapist takes vacations.
Vulnerable to control (passive–aggressive)	Comes late to or misses sessions. Views cognitive "challenges" as controlling. Reluctant to express dissatisfaction directly. Vague about goals, feelings, and thoughts – especially as related to therapist and therapy. "Forgets" to do homework or pay bills.
Responsible (obsessive–compulsive)	Feels emotions are "messy" and "irrational." Criticizes himself for being irrational and disorganized. Wants to see immediate results and expresses skepticism about therapy. Views homework as a test to be done perfectly or not at all.
Superior (narcissistic)	Comes late or misses sessions. "Forgets" to pay for sessions. Devalues therapy and the therapist. Expects special arrangements. Feels humiliated to have to talk about problems. Believes that therapy will not work since the problem resides in other people.
Glamorous (histrionic)	Focuses on expressing emotions, alternating rapidly from crying to laughing to anger. Tries to impress therapist with appearance, feelings, or problems. Rejects the rational approach and demands validation.

Source: Leahy, 2001.

Emotional schemas and experiential avoidance

Although schematic processing models have largely been focused on personal and interpersonal content, Beck and his colleagues have proposed that schemas are formed for a variety of functions, including physical, emotional, and interpersonal content (Beck *et al.*, 2003). In the cognitive model of psychopathology emotions are implicitly and explicitly identified as important, including emotions as a consequence of cognitive content ("I am helpless" – sad), as necessary in the activation of fear schemas for exposure to be effective, and as important for priming in activating latent schematic content (Beck, Emery, & Greenberg, 1985; Foa & Kozak, 1986;

Ingram, Miranda, & Segal, 1997; Miranda, Gross, Persons, & Hahn, 1998; Riskind, 1989). Emotions are, of course, the primary reason that people seek out help, but individuals differ as to their conceptualization and strategies that are employed when painful or unpleasant emotions are activated.

In recent years there has been increasing emphasis on *experiential avoidance* as an important transdiagnostic component in a variety of disorders (Harvey, Watkins, Mansell, & Shafran, 2004; Hayes, Luoma, Bond, Masuda, & Lillis, 2006; Roemer & Orsillo, 2002). If unpleasant experiences are avoided, however, then opportunities for habituation, extinction, and disconfirmation are decreased. Thus, the individual who avoids social interactions where he might feel anxious cannot experience a decrease in anxiety (habituation) with repeated exposure, which would lead to extinction of escape behavior and disconfirmation of the belief that "I can't stand to be uncomfortable in social situations" or "I will get rejected if I stay longer" (Foa & Kozak, 1986). Moreover, experiential and emotional avoidance maintains dysfunctional beliefs about emotions, such as "painful emotions will overwhelm me or last indefinitely" (Leahy, 2004b). Experiential (or emotional) avoidance has been implicated in a variety of problems, including generalized anxiety disorder, posttraumatic stress disorder, substance abuse, and depression (Hayes *et al.*, 2006). The question here is to what extent the therapeutic relationship facilitates more experiential avoidance. I suggest that the patient's own conceptualization of emotions and the therapist's parallel conceptions will either hinder or facilitate emotional processing.

Greenberg's emotion-focused model proposes that emotions contain the content of other schemas and that individuals may often activate one emotion to hide another emotion (see Greenberg, Chapter 3, this volume; Greenberg & Paivio, 1997; Greenberg & Safran, 1987). Greenberg refers to these as "emotional schemas" – that is, the schemas that are contained within the emotion. My model of emotional schemas draws upon Greenberg's work, but in my model I propose that the individual has a "schema" *about emotion*. I have proposed that individuals differ in their conceptualization and strategies for unpleasant or painful affect (Leahy, 2002). In our work we have identified 14 dimensions. These include the view that one's emotions are unacceptable and cannot be expressed or validated, that they will last a long time, are out of control, are shameful, don't make sense, are similar to the emotions of others; experiences of numbness, rumination, blaming, and intolerance for conflicting feelings; the demand that one should always be rational or that emotions point to higher values. We have found that patients with negative emotional schemas are more likely to be depressed, anxious, worried, more risk-averse in general, and more likely to score higher on dependent, avoidant, or borderline personality disorder (Leahy, 2002, 2005a, 2005b; Leahy & Napolitano, 2005). In contrast to the negative schemas of internalizing disorders, we have found that individuals scoring higher for narcissistic or histrionic personality disorder on the Millon Multiaxial Inventory have more positive views of their emotions (Leahy & Napolitano, 2005). Thus, emotional schemas appear to be a core factor in a range of psychological disorders.

Gottman and his colleagues have pointed out that individuals also differ as to their underlying philosophies about responding to others' painful emotions (Gottman, Katz, & Hooven, 1996). Some people may view the painful feelings of others as an opportunity to get closer and to matter more, while other people view painful feelings in others as a waste of time, as dangerous or as risking activating negative and unwanted feelings in the self. Gottman's emotional philosophies are often reflected in the emotional schemas that the patient may endorse ("My emotions are boring to others" or "My emotions are disgusting") and the emotional philosophies of some therapists ("Emotions get in the way of getting our work done" or "The patient's intense emotions will overwhelm me"). We may view these emotional schemas and philosophies as constituting a set of rules that are often rigidly followed, regardless of the immediate outcome.

Psychopathology as rule-governed behavior

A significant contribution of the cognitive model of psychopathology is that it demystifies the nature of psychopathology. For example, one can write a "rule" that describes the regularity of schematic information processing: "Look for examples that I am helpless" (confirmation bias) or "Discount evidence that I am competent." Similarly, one can view automatic thought distortions as rule-governed: "Use my emotions as evidence that something is true" (emotional reasoning) or "Take one example of a negative and treat it as if it represents who I really am" (labeling). To say that these are rules does not imply that one is consciously aware of the rule, much less aware that one is "following" the rule. But rule-governed behavior and thought has a long history in psychology, most notably in the field of linguistics (Chomsky, 1969; Pinker, 2002). Indeed, the idea that "rules" govern behavior has found a place in neo-Skinnerian models, such as that advanced by Hayes et al. (2006).

Let us assume that a visitor from another planet – let us say, Mars – has descended into our book-lined study. This non-gender specific individual does not know our human ways of neurosis and character-pathology, but being the good psychologists that we claim to be, we will assist him. The Martian (hereinafter arbitrarily assigned the gender, "male" and the name, Martin) asks, "How can I learn to be a neurotic human?"

To entertain our own fantasy and new theory about personality disorders, we have devised a rulebook for him. The specific personality disorder that we will give him is "avoidant personality" (AP). Having looked up the requisite requirements, we note that to qualify as AP one must have low self-esteem, be sensitive to rejection, and look for guarantees before entering a relationship. What rules will help Martin accomplish this promising role?

- Assume that these rules will protect you from devastating and surprising losses.
- Assume that you are inferior to all humans.
- Assume that other people are judgmental and rejecting.
- Look for any signs of rejection from other people.
- Don't disclose anything personal about yourself until you have a guarantee that you are unconditionally accepted.
- Rehearse in your mind different ways that you can be rejected and humiliated.
- Treat these rehearsals as if they are perfect predictions of what could really happen.
- Avoid any uncomfortable emotions.
- If you are uncomfortable in any situation, quickly leave.
- Whenever you can, escape into fantasy that is safer and more comfortable for you.
- Conclude that if you experience any criticism or discomfort it's because you haven't been observant in following these rules.

Now, should Martin prove to be a good student of character pathology, he will quickly adopt the role of being an avoidant personality. Assuming that he is skilled enough to obtain a physical disguise that makes him "look human," he might be able to "pass" in interactions, while still harboring his low self-esteem thoughts of being an inadequate and inferior Martian – that is, literally "fooling" humankind with his act. Indeed, Martin may never get rejected by well-meaning humans, but he will harbor the belief that the only thing that has protected him is his strategy of avoidance and hypervigilance. If Martin is a patient in cognitive-behavioral therapy, and he follows his avoidant personality rules, then it is likely that he will encounter a therapist with another set of rules – which may be in conflict with his rulebook.

Personality disorders as self-fulfilling prophecies

I have suggested that personality disorders may be characterized as rulebooks for dealing with other people and for experiencing the self (e.g., self-awareness, emotional schemas). I now propose that individuals who follow a rulebook elicit behavior in other people that confirms the validity of the rulebook. For example, the avoidant personality appears to other people as inhibited, shy, aloof, and often unemotional. This style is likely to elicit caution, aloofness, and tentativeness in other people – which, in turn, will suggest to the avoidant personality that other people are "holding back something" – perhaps their criticism. Indeed, this may actually be the case, since avoidant personalities are often perceived as unfriendly and, at times, conceited. If the avoidant individual is not "rejected," then he can conclude that his rules are working. If he is rejected, he then concludes that he should be more cautious and hypervigilant.

Similarly, the narcissistic individual follows rules of advertising his grandiosity, devaluing others, and expecting special treatment. He fears devaluation and does not trust others – "I will devalue you before you devalue me." I have noted that therapists, when discussing their narcissistic patients, both fear them and devalue them – "He thinks he's superior – that the rules don't apply to him." Or, "He thinks he is up there but really he is a turkey." Note how the therapist can get pulled into thinking in rank terms of one up and one down and competing for position/dominance. It is quite common for therapists to indicate to me, "I would never want to have someone like that in my life." Let's assume that the narcissist is aware of how others experience him – that is, that others want to distance and devalue him or try to outrank and overpower him if he does not grab top position. Perhaps, from his perspective, it makes sense to exploit people who may be viewed as exploiting the self. Thus, the narcissist may have "good reasons" for distancing and devaluing – although he does not recognize that it is his strategy of dominating, devaluing, and overvaluing himself that leads others to fulfill his predictions.

Using this game metaphor of self-fulfilling prophecies, we might conclude that individuals with personality disorders seldom understand how *they* elicit the very behavior in other people that supports their personality disorder. Taking this one step further, we can look at the therapeutic relationship as two individuals following their own rulebooks (determined by their personality styles or disorders), without awareness that their own style may elicit behavior in the other person. By analyzing the schematic mismatches that may ensue from this, we can determine how problems may arise or be averted in the therapeutic relationship. We turn now to examining how this may occur in the counter-transference.

A social-cognitive model of counter-transference

Although therapists would ideally like to believe that they can work effectively with a wide range of people, clinical experience suggests that each of us has our own difficulties with specific groups of patients. The therapist is similar to the patient in holding certain personal and inter-personal schemas. I have listed a number of these in Table 11.2.

The therapist can ask herself, "What issues concern me most? Which patients are most troubling to me? Are there certain patients I feel *too comfortable* with? How do I feel about telling patients things that might

Table 11.2 Therapist schemas in the therapeutic relationship

Schema	Assumptions
Demanding standards	I have to cure all my patients. I must always meet the highest standards. My patients should do an excellent job. We should never waste time.
Special, superior person	I am entitled to be successful. My patients should appreciate all that I do for them. I shouldn't feel bored when doing therapy. Patients try to humiliate me.
Rejection sensitive	Conflicts are upsetting. I shouldn't raise issues that will bother the patient.
Abandonment	If my patient is bothered with therapy, they might leave. It's upsetting when patients terminate. I might end up with no patients.
Autonomy	I feel controlled by the patient. My movements, feelings or what I say are limited. I should be able to do or say what I wish. Sometimes I wonder if I will lose myself in the relationship.
Control	I have to control my surroundings or the people around me.
Judgmental	Some people are basically bad people. People should be punished if they do wrong things.
Persecution	I often feel provoked. The patient is trying to get to me. I have to guard against being taken advantage of or hurt. You usually can't trust people.
Need approval	I want to be liked by the patient. If the patient isn't happy with me, then it means I'm doing something wrong.
Need to like others	It's important that I like the patient. It bothers me if I don't like a patient. We should get along – almost like friends.
Withholding	I want to withhold thoughts and feelings from the patient. I don't want to give them what they want. I feel I am withdrawing emotionally during the session.
Helplessness	I feel I don't know what to do. I fear I'll make mistakes. I wonder if I'm really competent. Sometimes I feel like giving up.
Goal inhibition	The patient is blocking me from achieving my goals. I feel like I'm wasting time. I should be able to achieve my goals in sessions without the patient's interference.
Self-sacrifice	I should meet the patient's needs. I should make them feel better. The patient's needs often take precedence over my needs. I sometimes believe that I would do almost anything to meet their needs.
Emotional inhibition	I feel frustrated when I'm with this patient because I can't express the way I really feel. I find it hard to suppress my feelings. I can't be myself.

Source: Leahy, 2001.

disturb them?" For example, some therapists are more concerned about the nature of the relationship, others are concerned about the expression of emotion, and others about encouraging the patient to become more active. While some therapists are intimidated by narcissistic patients, others prefer patients who are self-effacing, while other therapists have difficulty with intense emotional experiences. The therapist can note which patients and issues "push his buttons," and what automatic thoughts and personal schemas are activated: "If the patient is disappointed in me it must be because I am an inadequate therapist."

Problems in the relationship can arise when "things are going well." Feeling especially "comfortable" with a patient may make it difficult to identify and address problematic behavior such as alcohol abuse, lack of financial responsibility, or self-defeating patterns. Some therapists are reluctant to confront a patient with "disturbing" information, fearing that the patient may get angry, become sad, or leave therapy. This threat of the termination of therapy may activate the therapist's schemas about abandonment, loss of reputation, or being controlled by the patient.These perceptions of relationship are reflected in the counter-transference schemas held by the therapist. These include demanding standards, fears of abandonment, need for approval, viewing the self as rescuer, or self-sacrifice (see Table 11.2).

In addition, therapists have different *emotional philosophies*, reflecting their belief that painful and difficult emotions either can provide an opportunity to deepen the relationship or should be eliminated or avoided. As noted earlier, Gottman's model of emotional philosophies provides a valuable taxonomy for identifying the shared emotional philosophy within the therapeutic relationship (see Gottman *et al.*, 1996; Katz *et al.*, 1996) – including dismissive, critical, overwhelmed, and facilitative. Of particular interest is the "emotional coaching" style that reflects the therapist's authentic and non-judgmental interest in all emotions, while encouraging the patient to differentiate and explore these emotions, and to consider ways in which self-soothing can be facilitated. This style is similar to the empathic and supportive style advocated by Rogers (1965), Greenberg (2002; Chapter 3, this volume) and by Gilbert in his discussion of compassion as a complex set of abilities that can help the therapeutic relationship (Gilbert, 2005a; Chapter 6, this volume). Some therapists, who view painful emotions as distracting or self-indulgent, may communicate a dismissive attitude ("We need to get back to the agenda") or they may take a critical approach, such as that reflected in Ellis's sarcastic comments about patients who whine (Ellis, 1994). Sometimes patients need to "be with" their feelings, to become familiar with them and learn to tolerate them. However, therapists who are uncomfortable "being with" feeling may constantly ask the patient about his/her thoughts or intrude and inadvertently model emotional avoidance. In psychodynamic approaches the idea is that the patient feels their emotions "can be contained;" that they do not threaten the therapist or the therapy. In this way the patient learns that their emotions are understandable, acceptable, tolerable, and meaningful – but also can change.

The therapist's emotional philosophy – and the strategies that are implemented – will have a significant impact on the patient's own emotional schemas (Leahy, 2005b). For example, the therapist who takes the dismissive approach ("Let's get back to the agenda") conveys the unsympathetic message that "Your emotions are not interesting to me," "Emotions are a waste of time," and "You are indulging yourself." As a consequence of a dismissive or critical stand by the therapist, the patient may conclude, "My emotions don't make sense," "No one cares about them," "I should feel ashamed or guilty for having these feelings," and "Focusing on my emotions won't help me." As the patient dutifully follows the lead of the agenda-setting therapist, emotions become secondary to compliance with an agenda that may never really address the very reason the patient sought out help – that is, help with his feelings.

Crucially, interpersonal styles differ among therapists – some are distancing, are overly attached, engage in rigid boundary-setting, appear deferent, are dominating, soothing, or reassuring. Therapists who view emotions as a waste of time may appear somewhat distancing (aloof and condescending), deferential (intellectualized), boundary-setting ("That's not on our agenda" or "We don't have time for that today"), or dominating ("This is cognitive therapy and we try to focus only on your thoughts and on getting things done"). Other therapists – also viewing painful emotions as intolerable – may be quick to rescue the patient from his feelings ("Oh, you'll be OK – don't worry – it will work out"), may directly tell the patient to stop crying ("Don't cry. Things will be OK"), or may be quick to soothe ("You'll be fine in a while"). The implicit message from these well-meaning interactions is that "Your painful emotions need to be eliminated (as soon as possible)." Thus, rather than share, differentiate, explore, and clarify these emotional experiences (as one would do with emotional coaching or in emotional-focused therapy), the therapist may communicate through rescue and support that painful emotions do not have a place in this relationship and that the patient is too vulnerable to deal with his own emotions. Rescuing someone from painful emotions confirms the belief that experiential avoidance is a desirable coping strategy.

Patient–therapist schema mismatch

Games and self-fulfilling prophecies

Game models have been used extensively in biology, economics, military strategy, negotiation theory, and evolutionary theory (Axelrod & Dion,

1988; Buss & Schmitt, 1993; Dugatkin & Wilson, 1991; Maynard-Smith, 1982). Games may be single-player (such as a lottery) or may be two-person games that are competitive or cooperative. Here I will outline some aspects of a *two-person game* that will be applied to personality, transference, and counter-transference. The assumption guiding this discussion is that personality disorders are "interpersonal games" that are self-fulfilling prophecies and strategies that may play themselves out in the therapeutic relationship.

Games are *systemic* – they will continue until the final move is made. Each participant seeks a "payoff" (von Neumann & Morgenstern, 1944) – which, for individuals with personality disorders, might include escape from negative evaluation (avoidant personality), protective support from a strong individual (dependent personality), or tribute and recognition that one is a superior person (narcissistic personality). Since games are self-contained or systemic – people get stuck within the game – participants may be unable to take the perspective of the game as one of many alternatives (von Bertalanffy, 1976). Thus, the avoidant personality is "stuck" within his rulebook of hesitation, avoidance, and vigilance, leading to a confirmation bias that he is "defective" and others will judge him. The therapist with demanding standards is stuck within the game of compelling others to conform to his agenda.

Games involve *reciprocal causation* – that is, game-players evaluate feedback and the "moves" made by others. Two-person games – such as that reflected in the therapeutic relationship – involve *iterative moves* such that a move by the patient leads to a counter-move by the therapist that then elicits another move by the patient. Theoretically, game-players can anticipate the counter-moves by opponents and adapt their strategies accordingly, as a good chess player might do. However, in real interaction we generally attribute our own behavior to the situation and the other person's behavior to their personality traits. Thus, you may attribute your annoyance with me to the "fact" that I am "boring" rather than to the possibility that you are intolerant of other people. It is the other person who has the trait, while we view our own behavior as determined by the situation (Jones & Nisbett, 1972). Moreover, our explanations tend to be based on the recent prior event, such that we explain our current behavior by what just occurred previously.

Patients (and therapists) with negative schemas may view the therapeutic relationship as a "competitive game" – that is, a *zero-sum game* in which one side loses and the other side wins. This is in contrast to the "ideal" therapeutic relationship where both sides "get what they want" – that is, a facilitative relationship leading to a rapid improvement for the patient. Pessimistic patients may be more focused on avoiding further loss, and may employ hypervigilant strategies to look for rejection, judgment, or lack of interest in the therapist. These patients will "stop-out" quickly, viewing the small loss (frustration) as the beginning of a cascade of other losses. Patients from this perspective cut their losses early, in a manner that seems "rational." This "minimax" strategy – minimizing maximum losses – is also based on the view that losses are suffered more than gains are enjoyed. Indeed, from the patient's perspective, gains seem unlikely, transient, and are not really "enjoyed" that much. Moreover, the pessimistic view of the patient may suggest that a "gain" (increase of feeling good or feeling close to the therapist) may be a *false signal* and may tempt the patient to take further risks of exposure. As things begin "feeling better" the cautious patient may think, "This is an aberration. The axe will fall soon. Better to get out now" (Allen & Badcock, 2003; Leahy, 1997).

If the patient's negative schemas about relationships suggest that he will be abandoned or rejected by the therapist, then the patient may consider himself to be in a "prisoner's dilemma." Thus, from the pessimistic patient's perspective, if he anticipates rejection from the therapist if he does not meet the therapist's "expectations," then it "makes sense" from a game model to quit earlier than later. From game theory the patient believes that the therapist will "defect" (that is, give up the supportive role and reject the patient). Research on prisoner's dilemma shows a general tendency to defect early if the "prisoner" (patient) anticipates that the other side sees a benefit in defecting (rejecting him). Moreover, individuals who view a relationship as competitive are more likely to withhold information that reduces the possibility of any cooperation (Steinel & De Dreu, 2004). Thus, patients with negative schemas – who anticipate negative schemas in the therapist – will terminate early.

Lack of recursive and systemic role-taking

Why aren't patients and therapists "smarter"? Why is it so difficult to be "objective" about the therapeutic relationship? The reason for myopia and egocentrism is that we may be inclined toward snap-shot views through our schemas, rather than a moving picture extended across time (an "evolutionary or unfolding model" of the relationship developing over time). Real interactions between people in a relationship involve "iterative moves" such that I repeat moves in response to a sequence of moves on your part. Thus, real relationships operate in real time. In order for me to figure out what to do in response to your recent move, I might also want to figure out how you will respond to my next move – that is, will you see me as having a strategy? If I think that you have guessed my strategy, then I might want to block your move by doing what you think I won't do. Yet, in order to do this, I must take your perspective of the prior moves, how you see my strategy unfolding, and how you might try to outguess me. Indeed, studies of behavioral economics examining game models find a general limit to anticipating iterations. Our interactions are usually engulfed by one or two moves – it is hard to "play chess" in everyday interactions.

This anticipation of how others might respond to our future moves entails both recursive and systemic role-taking and the elaboration of a *theory of mind*. Recursive role-taking requires the ability to stand back and *view one's own thinking and emotions* (or the thinking and emotions of the other). Systemic role-taking involves the ability to observe the *relationship* across time, and how each participant affects the other (Selman, 1980; Selman, Beardslee, Schultz, Krupa, & Podorefsky, 1986). Insight within the trans-ference relationship entails the awareness of the other's behavior, inference of motive, seeing the other as provocation or elicitor, self as object of other's experience, and self–other role-taking (systemic relationship perspective) within the current interaction, other relationships with similar patterns, and past relationships. As the reader has likely noted, this systemic role-taking – involving anticipation of moves in response to others' moves – is an ability rarely manifested in everyday interactions. Moreover, our own thinking about how others see events or ourselves is often anchored by our own perspective, as if we believe that others respond more like us than like a stranger (Epley, Keysar, Van Boven, & Gilovich, 2004). Indeed, we often use our own mind (the "self") as a best guess as to what the other person is thinking (Nickerson, 1999). Thus, if the patient believes that he is a loser, he will conclude that the therapist can see through his transparent self to the loser underneath. Our views of others' views are anchored in ourselves.

These evaluative or cognitive constraints have important implications in the transference–counter-transference: (1) patient and therapist both have difficulty seeing the "larger picture;" (2) the other person's behavior is attributed to unchangeable traits; (3) the other person's behavior is person-alized; (4) since one is "locked" within one's own rule-book, it is hard to get information that runs counter to one's expectations; and (5) the roles enacted lead to confirmation bias and self-fulfilling prophecies. Needless to say, the ability to view the relationship (in and out of therapy) is more complicated than simply identifying a "distorted automatic thought." The game model extends the cognitive model to address a series of feedback interactions that are similar to the interpersonal reality of everyday life.

Patient–therapist mismatch

What happens when the patient's personality disorder conflicts with the therapist's schema or core belief? Imagine the following: the patient has an avoidant personality – his goal is to keep people from knowing him so that he cannot get rejected. He is cautious, since he does not want to take any chances of getting rejected or failing. Consequently, he is reluctant to carry out self-help assignments, he seldom has an agenda (since he either does not have direct access to his emotions – as he has avoided emotions – or does not want to "make a stand" in therapy). In contrast to this avoidant personality, consider the possibility that the therapist has demanding standards – expecting patients to conform to his agenda and treatment plans. In this interaction, the therapist has little tolerance for "vague complaints," "procrastination," or lack of clear goals.

Each participant – patient and therapist – is following a rulebook determined by their schematic dispositions and their personality disorder. The rulebooks are based on attempts by each to "make sense" of the other and to modify the other's behavior. For example, the patient is trying to find out if the therapist can be trusted, thus, the patient hesitates, remains vague, and waits to see how the therapist reacts. These are passive probes in the patient's rulebook. Any behavior on the part of the therapist is attributed either to dispositions or traits that the therapist has ("He is critical") or to defects in the self ("I am a loser"). (The patient does not recognize the situational game-like quality – "When I hesitate some people will either probe or withdraw from me".) Similarly, the therapist with demanding standards will activate probes, controls, criticisms, and exhortations if the patient is "non-compliant." The therapist will attribute his own behavior to the patient's "non-compliance," not recognizing that this kind of controlling and demanding behavior creates a self-fulfilling prophecy: When the therapist demands, the patient withdraws. This confirms the schematic perception of the patient as non-compliant (see Figure 11.1).

Utilizing the strategic game model outlined above, we can see that the therapeutic relationship is characterized by *reciprocal causation*. Specifically, therapists will often utilize interpersonal strategies to compensate or avoid the schematic issues raised by the patient. Consider the case of a dependent patient (with fears of abandonment and beliefs about personal helplessness) and a therapist who also is dependent and fears abandonment by patients.

Compensatory or avoidant strategies by therapist

Dependent patient, dependent therapist

- Avoidant strategy
    - Therapist does not bring up difficult topics, avoids discussing patient's dependent behavior, does not set limits on patient
    - Therapist avoids using exposure techniques
    - Patient's experience
        - My emotions must be overwhelming to other people. Doing new things will be risky and terrifying
        - My therapist must think I am incapable of doing things on my own
        - I should avoid independent behavior

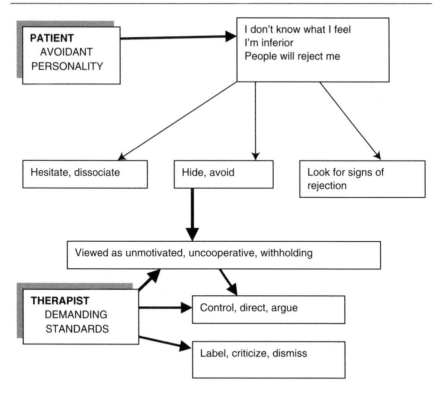

Figure 11.1 Patient–therapist mismatch.

- Compensatory strategy
  - Constantly reassures patient
  - Prolongs sessions, apologizes for absence
  - Patient's experience
    - I need to rely on others to solve my problems
    - I must be incompetent
    - I can't get better on my own
    - The only way to get better is to find someone to take care of me and protect me

Or consider the schematic mismatch that arises for the dependent patient whose therapist has demanding standards. This mismatch is outlined below.

- Helpless (dependent) patient
  - Seeks reassurance. Does not have an agenda of problems to solve. Frequently complains about "feelings." Calls frequently between sessions. Wants to prolong sessions. Does not think he can do the homework or believes that homework will not work. Upset when therapist takes vacations

- Demanding standards therapist
  - I have to cure all my patients
  - I must always meet the highest standards
  - My patients should do an excellent job
  - We should never waste time

The therapist may adopt either a demanding-coercive or an avoidant strategy.

- Demanding-coercive strategy
  - Views patient's lack of progress as "personal" resistance
  - Demands agenda and task compliance
  - Critical of lack of progress
  - Labels patient as "dependent"
  - Patient's experience
    - I can't count on my therapist
    - I will be abandoned if I don't improve
    - My emotions are not important to my therapist
    - I am a failure in therapy
    - I can't solve any problems
- Avoidant strategy
  - Loses interest in the patient
  - Does not explore patient's need for validation and emotional expression
  - Terminates patient for "non-compliance"
  - Patient's experience
    - I must be boring
    - My therapist has no interest in me
    - Therefore, my therapist will leave me

Using the counter-transference

The therapist is not a neutral object onto which internal dynamics are projected. Rather, the therapist is a dynamic part of the patient's inter-personal world. The therapist with "demanding standards" can recognize *his own resistance to the patient* in his tendency to impose his agenda onto the patient, coerce him into changing, or withdraw from the patient with indifference. Indeed, if the therapist acts and feels this way, then the patient may be eliciting these responses from other "demanding" people. Three questions can be posed: (1) How does the patient respond when other demanding people interact with him? (2) What are the typical personality characteristics of the people in the patient's life? and (3) What is the developmental history of relationships and dysfunctional strategies?

I had recognized a number of years ago that I often had "demanding standards" with patients – trying to impose agendas, homework, task-orientation, and techniques. This was motivated by my desire to "get the job done," but I realized that it was annoying and dismissive for patients. Although I use cognitive therapy techniques and agendas, I place a greater emphasis now on exploring the patient's emotional schemas, and how others in the patient's life have responded to these needs. This particular contrast between "demanding standards" and "emotional schemas" presented itself to me with a patient who had previously seen a hard-driving, agenda-setting, "rational" therapist who took a didactic stand.

The patient was a married woman, with long-standing relationship problems, characterized by feeling she was not heard, did not feel emotionally or physically in touch with her husband, and who felt guilty. She responded to the homework "demands" in therapy with statements of her own help-lessness and inadequacy, complaining that her problem resided in her controlling and narcissistic husband. In this context, I recognized my own demanding standards coming up again. These would have led me to set strict agendas, "challenge" her automatic thoughts, suggest alternatives, and help lay out some problem-solving strategies. Unfortunately, as I quickly realized, this would replicate the domineering, dismissive, and emotionally empty experiences that she had with other people in her life, from her parents to her husband. I then decided to back away from imposing home-work on the patient in order to examine her pattern of deferring to other people in intimate relationships. In fact, her deference to others – based on her view that she did not know her own needs and that she did not have a right to have needs – resulted in others "taking charge" or taking the lead. This reinforced her view that she was secondary in relationships, although she hoped that a strong, determined man "who knew what he wanted" would be able to satisfy her. Just as she deferred in her relationship in therapy, she also deferred in family and intimate relationships.

Prior to seeing me, she had seen an argumentative "rational" therapist who lectured to her. She indicated that this prior therapy reminded her of her father and mother who would tell her how to feel and how to act, but who never appeared to validate her individuality. She experienced the prior therapist as dismissive, critical, and condescending – experiences that she complained of with her husband.

While recognizing the importance of change, we focused on her emo-tional schemas. I indicated that "the most important thing in our relation-ship is for both of us to understand and respect your emotions; it's what you feel that counts the most." She had difficulty labeling her emotions, often suddenly crying "for no reason" (as she would say). She believed that her emotions made no sense, that no one could understand her emotions, and that she had no right to feel upset since she had a lucrative job and a husband who loved her. She believed that she needed to control her

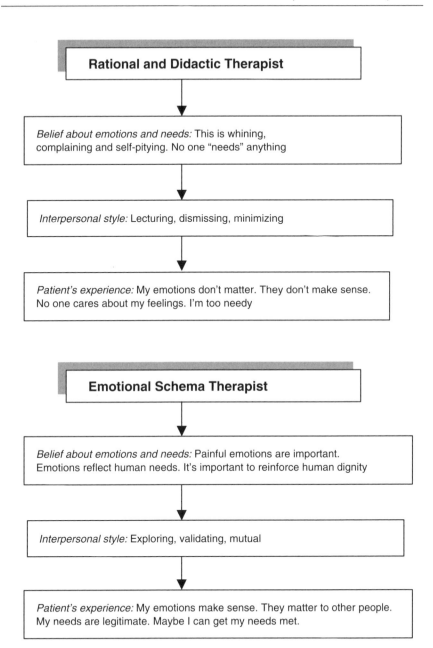

Figure 11.2 Therapist schemas.

emotions in order to prevent them from "going out of control." The emotional philosophies of her mother and father were that her emotions were self-indulgent, manipulative, and unwarranted. In fact, she observed that much of her life around her father was focused on trying to "put out" his emotional tirades. There was no room for her emotions in their lives – or in the life of her husband.

We decided to view her pain and suffering as a window into her needs and values – that her painful emotions needed to be heard and respected. This new "emotional schema" included the following: "It's important to recognize a wide range of my emotions," "My emotions come from human needs for love, closeness, and sensuality," "I have a human need for validation, warmth, and acceptance," and "I want to seek this out in a new relationship." Although she had come for "cognitive therapy" (with an emphasis on "rationality"), she acknowledged that focusing on her rights to have emotions and needs – and to develop relationships where possible – would be worth pursuing.

Let's review the different therapeutic styles that she experienced. With the demanding and anti-emotional didactic therapist, the "coercive" and "intellectual" style reflected the belief that she was whining, had too many "shoulds," and had low frustration tolerance. The message was "get over it" and "it shouldn't matter that much." The therapist appeared to her to be condescending, out of touch, and critical of her feelings. This confirmed her belief with him that her feelings didn't make sense, she was self-indulgent, and she had too many needs: "I must be too needy." In contrast, in taking an emotional schema approach in treatment with me, she was able to recognize and differentiate her various emotions, experiment with expressing emotions and getting validation, explore how her emotions were linked to important needs that were unmet, and recognize that while she was good at supporting and validating others, she would need to direct this nurturant and compassionate mind toward herself.

Conclusions

Cognitive models of psychopathology can be enhanced by incorporating the roles of both emotional processing and social interaction in understanding the therapeutic relationship. I have outlined a model of personality disorders – initially based on the schematic processing model – that stresses several points: (1) Personality disorders follow a rulebook that directs the individual in understanding the self and in interacting with others; (2) Individuals with personality disorders follow confirmation biases in eliciting the very behavior in other people that will confirm their own schemas; (3) Individuals in interaction may have different views of how emotions in others are handled and these differences may reaffirm the underlying schemas of both parties; (4) Participants in the therapeutic relationship are egocentrically biased toward viewing the other's behavior as due to stable traits, but to viewing one's own behavior as situational or goal-directed; (5) It is difficult for participants to distance themselves and take a systemic role-taking perspective; and (6) A systemic perspective is possible by identifying the therapist's and patient's rulebooks and schemas and examining how the confirmation biases are fulfilled.

Taking this systemic game perspective allows both the therapist and the patient to find regularities in the patient's past relationships that continue to play out in the current relationship. The therapist and patient can use cognitive, experiential, emotion-focused, emotional schema, and compassionate mind techniques to modify the rulebook that the patient has been using and that maintains his problems even though the patient has come to believe that the rulebook has protected him from worse problems arising.

References

Adler, A. (1924/1964). *Social interest: A challenge to mankind*. New York: Capricorn Books.

Allen, N.B. & Badcock, P.B.T. (2003). The social risk hypothesis of depressed mood: Evolutionary, psychosocial, and neurobiological perspectives. *Psychological Bulletin*, 129(6), 887–913.

Axelrod, R. & Dion, D. (1988). The further evolution of cooperation. *Science*, 242(4884), 1385–1390.

Baldwin, M.W. & Dandeneau, S.D. (2005). Understanding and modifying the relational schemas underlying insecurity. In M.W. Baldwin (ed.), *Interpersonal cognition* (pp. 33–61). New York: Guilford.

Beck, A.T., Emery, G. & Greenberg, R.L. (1985). *Anxiety disorders and phobias: A cognitive perspective*. New York: Basic Books.

Beck, A.T., Freeman, A., Davis, D.D., Pretzer, J., Fleming, B., Arntz, A., Butler, A., Fusco, G., Simon, K., Padesky, C.A., Meyer, J. & Trexler, L. (2003). *Cognitive therapy of personality disorders* (2nd edition). New York: Guilford Press.

Beck, J.S. (1995). *Cognitive therapy: Basics and beyond*. New York: Guilford.

Buss, D.M. & Schmitt, D.P. (1993). Sexual strategies theory: An evolutionary perspective on human mating. *Psychological Review*, 100(2), 204–232.

Chomsky, N. (1969). *Aspects of the theory of syntax*. Cambridge, MA: MIT Press.

Dugatkin, L.A. & Wilson, D.S. (1991). Rover: A strategy for exploiting cooperators in a patchy environment. *American Naturalist*, 138, 687–701.

Ellis, A. (1994). *Reason and emotion in psychotherapy* (2nd edition). Secaucus, NJ: Carol Publishing Company.

Epley, N., Keysar, B., Van Boven, L. & Gilovich, T. (2004). Perspective taking as egocentric anchoring and adjustment. *Journal of Personality and Social Psychology*, 87(3), 327–339.

Foa, E.B. & Kozak, M.J. (1986). Emotional processing of fear: Exposure to corrective information. *Psychological Bulletin*, 99, 20–35.

Frankl, V.E. (1992). *Man's search for meaning: An introduction to logotherapy* (4th edition). Boston: Beacon Press.

Gilbert, P. (1989). *Human nature and suffering*. Hove, UK: Lawrence Erlbaum Associates.

Gilbert, P. (1992). *Counseling for depression*. London: Sage.

Gilbert, P. (2000). Social mentalities: Internal 'social' conflicts and the role of inner warmth and compassion in cognitive therapy. In P. Gilbert & K.G. Bailey (eds), *Genes on the couch: Explorations in evolutionary psychotherapy* (pp. 118–150). Hove, UK: Brunner-Routledge.

Gilbert, P. (ed.) (2005a). *Compassion: Conceptualisations, research and use in psychotherapy*. Hove, UK: Brunner-Routledge.

Gilbert, P. (2005b). Social mentalities: A biopsychosocial and evolutionary approach to social relationships. In M.W. Baldwin (ed.), *Interpersonal cognition* (pp. 299–333). New York: Guilford Press.

Gilbert, P. & Irons, C. (2005). Focused therapies and compassionate mind training for shame and self-attacking. In P. Gilbert (ed.), *Compassion: Conceptualisations, research and use in psychotherapy* (pp. 263–325). Hove, UK: Brunner-Routledge.

Gottman, J.M., Katz, L.F. & Hooven, C. (1996). Parental meta-emotion philosophy and the emotional life of families: Theoretical models and preliminary data. *Journal of Family Psychology*, 10(3), 243–268.

Greenberg, L.S. (2001). Toward an integrated affective, behavioral, cognitive psychotherapy for the new millennium (Paper presented at meeting of the Society for the Exploration of Psychotherapy Integration).

Greenberg, L.S. (2002). *Emotion-focused therapy: Coaching clients to work through their feelings*. Washington, DC: American Psychological Association.

Greenberg, L.S. & Paivio, S. (1997). *Working with emotions*. New York: Guilford.

Greenberg, L.S. & Safran, J.D. (1987). *Emotion in psychotherapy: Affect, cognition, and the process of change*. New York: Guilford.

Harvey, A., Watkins, E., Mansell, W. & Shafran, R. (2004). *Cognitive behavioural processes across psychological disorders: A transdiagnostic approach to research and treatment*. New York: Oxford University Press.

Hayes, S.C., Luoma, J.B., Bond, F.W., Masuda, A. & Lillis, J. (2006). Acceptance and commitment therapy: Model, processes and outcomes. *Behaviour Research and Therapy*, 44(1), 1–25.

Horney, K. (1945). *Our inner conflicts*. New York: Norton.

Horney, K. (1950). *Neurosis and human growth*. New York: Norton.

Ingram, R.E., Miranda, J. & Segal, Z.V. (1997). *Cognitive vulnerability to depression*. New York: Guilford.

Jones, E.E. & Nisbett, R.E. (1972). The actor and the observer: Divergent perceptions of the causes of the behavior. In E.E. Jones, D.E. Kanouse, H.H. Kelley, R.E. Nisbett, S. Valins & B. Weiner (eds), *Attribution: Perceiving the causes of behavior* (pp. 79–94). Morristown, NJ: General Learning Press.

Katz, L.F., Gottman, J.M. & Hooven, C. (1996). Meta-emotion philosophy and family functioning: Reply to Cowan (1996) and Eisenberg (1996). *Journal of Family Psychology*, 10(3), 284–291.

Leahy, R.L. (1997). An investment model of depressive resistance. *Journal of Cognitive Psychotherapy*, 11, 3–19.

Leahy, R.L. (2001). *Overcoming resistance in cognitive therapy*. New York: Guilford.

Leahy, R.L. (2002). A model of emotional schemas. *Cognitive and Behavioral Practice*, 9(3), 177–190.

Leahy, R.L. (2003a). Emotional schemas and resistance. In R.L. Leahy (ed.), *Roadblocks in cognitive-behavioral therapy: Transforming challenges into opportunities for change* (pp. 91–115). New York: Guilford Press.

Leahy, R.L. (ed.) (2003b). *Roadblocks in cognitive-behavioral therapy: Transforming challenges into opportunities for change.* New York: Guilford Press.

Leahy, R.L. (2004a). Decision making and psychopathology. In R.L. Leahy (ed.), *Contemporary cognitive therapy: Theory, research, and practice* (pp. 116–138). New York: Guilford Press.

Leahy, R.L. (2004b). Panic, agoraphobia and generalized anxiety. In N. Kazantzis, F.P. Deane, K.R. Ronan & L. L'Abate (eds), *Using homework assignments in cognitive behavior therapy* (pp. 195–221). New York: Routledge.

Leahy, R.L. (2005a, November 18–21). Meta-cognitive factors of worry and decision-making style. Paper presented at the Association for the Advancement of Behavior Therapy, Washington, DC.

Leahy, R.L. (2005b). A social cognitive model of validation. In P. Gilbert (ed.), *Compassion: Conceptualisations, research and use in psychotherapy.* Hove, UK: Brunner-Routledge.

Leahy, R.L., Beck, A.T. & Beck, J.S. (2005). Cognitive therapy of personality disorders. In S. Strack (ed.), *Handbook of Personology and Psychopathology* (pp. 442–461). New York: Wiley.

Leahy, R.L. & Napolitano, L. (2005, November 18–21). What are the emotional schema predictors of personality disorders? Paper presented at the Association for the Advancement of Behavior Therapy, Washington, DC.

McGinn, L.K. & Young, J.E. (1996). Schema-focused therapy. In P.M. Salkovskis (ed.), *Frontiers of cognitive therapy* (pp. 182–207). New York: Guilford.

Maynard-Smith, J. (1982). *Evolution and the theory of games.* Cambridge: Cambridge University Press.

Menninger, K.A. & Holzman, P.S. (1973). *Theory of psychoanalytic technique* (2nd edition). New York: Basic Books.

Miranda, J., Gross, J.J., Persons, J.B. & Hahn, J. (1998). Mood matters: Negative mood induction activates dysfunctional attitudes in women vulnerable to depression. *Cognitive Therapy & Research*, 22(4), 363–376.

Muran, J.C. & Safran, J.D. (eds) (1998). Negotiating the therapeutic alliance in brief psychotherapy: An introduction. In J.D. Safran & J.C. Muran (eds), *The therapeutic alliance in brief psychotherapy.* Washington, DC: American Psychological Association.

Nickerson, R.S. (1999). How we know – and sometimes misjudge – what others know: Imputing one's knowledge to others. *Psychological Bulletin*, 125, 737–759.

Nussbaum, M. (2005). *Frontiers of justice: Disability, nationality, species membership.* Cambridge: Belknap Press.

Pinker, S. (2002). *The blank slate: The modern denial of human nature.* New York: Viking.

Pretzer, J. & Beck, A.T. (2004). Cognitive therapy of personality disorders. In J.J. Magnavita (ed.), *Handbook of personality disorders: Theory and practice.* New York: Wiley.

Rawls, J. (2001). *Justice as fairness: A restatement.* Cambridge: Belknap Press.

Riskind, J.H. (1989). The mediating mechanisms in mood and memory: A cognitive-priming formulation. *Journal of Social Behavior and Personality*, 4, 173–184.

Roemer, L. & Orsillo, S.M. (2002). Expanding our conceptualization of and treatment for generalized anxiety disorder: Integrating mindfulness/acceptance-based approaches with existing cognitive-behavioral models. *Clinical Psychology: Science & Practice*, 9(1), 54–68.

Rogers, C. (1965). *Client centered therapy: Its current practice, implications and theory*. Boston: Houghton-Mifflin.

Safran, J.D. (1998). *Widening the scope of cognitive therapy: The therapeutic relationship, emotion and the process of change*. Northvale, NJ: Aronson.

Safran, J.D. & Greenberg, L.S. (1988). Feeling, thinking, and acting: A cognitive framework for psychotherapy integration. *Journal of Cognitive Psychotherapy*, 2(2), 109–131.

Safran, J.D. & Greenberg, L.S. (1989). The treatment of anxiety and depression: The process of affective change. In P. Kendall & D. Watson (eds), *Anxiety and depression: Distinctive and overlapping features*. San Diego, CA: Academic Press.

Safran, J.D. & Greenberg, L.S. (eds) (1991). *Emotion, psychotherapy, and change*. New York: Guilford.

Safran, J.D. & Muran, J.C. (1993). Emotional and interpersonal considerations in cognitive therapy. In K. Kuehlwein & H. Rosen (eds), *Cognitive therapies in action: Evolving innovative practice* (pp. 185–212). San Francisco: Jossey-Bass.

Safran, J.D. & Muran, J. (2000). Resolving therapeutic alliance ruptures: Diversity and integration. *Journal of Clinical Psychology*, 56(2), 233–243.

Selman, R.L. (1980). *The growth of interpersonal understanding*. New York: Academic Press.

Selman, R.L., Beardslee, W., Schultz, L., Krupa, M. & Podorefsky, D. (1986). Assessing adolescent interpersonal negotiation strategies: Toward the integration of structural and functional models. *Developmental Psychology*, 22(4), 450–459.

Steinel, W. & De Dreu, C.K.W. (2004). Motives and strategic misrepresentation in social decision making. *Journal of Personality and Social Psychology*, 86(3), 419–434.

Sullivan, H.S. (1956). *Clinical studies in psychiatry*. New York: Norton.

von Bertalanffy, L. (1976). *General system theory: Foundations, development, applications*. New York: George Braziller Publishers.

von Neumann, J. & Morgenstern, O. (1944). *Theory of games and economic behavior*. Princeton, NJ: Princeton University Press.

Young, J.E., Klosko, J.S. & Weishaar, M. (2003). *Schema therapy: A practioner's guide*. New York: Guilford.

Chapter 12

Self and self-reflection in the therapeutic relationship

A conceptual map and practical strategies for the training, supervision and self-supervision of interpersonal skills

James Bennett-Levy and Richard Thwaites

Introduction

Many contributors to this volume have described the importance of the therapeutic relationship to outcome, and the complexities involved in developing and maintaining a therapeutic relationship. This chapter focuses on issues of training and supervision and asks: what training, supervision and self-supervision strategies may best facilitate the development and refinement of cognitive therapists' interpersonal skills? We approach these questions through the framework of a new cognitive model of therapist skill development, the declarative–procedural–reflective (DPR) model (Bennett-Levy, 2006), which:

1 enables therapists, trainers and supervisors to consider a variety of interpersonal factors and processes that go towards developing a positive, helpful therapeutic relationship
2 provides a conceptual map to pinpoint the particular area(s) of difficulty that may be causing a therapeutic relationship to deteriorate
3 identifies key learning processes and training strategies to enhance interpersonal skills and thereby refine therapeutic relationships.

Within this context, it is a further aim of the chapter to provide a coherent account that explains why interpersonal skill development differs from other forms of skill development (e.g., conceptual, technical) in cognitive therapy; and why *specific* training and supervision strategies are required to develop the interpersonal skills of cognitive therapists to best advantage. Much of the chapter focuses on these strategies; examples are provided.

The chapter is divided into six major sections. The first section outlines the DPR model of therapist skill development. The second section places the focus more specifically on the interpersonal skill components within the model. The third section describes the special role of the self, and self-reflection, in the refinement of interpersonal skills. The fourth section emphasizes the necessity of creating positive, supportive supervisory and training relationships, and attending to process issues, if the trainees are to have sufficient confidence to address their therapeutic relationship issues in these contexts. The fifth section presents a six-stage process model for addressing therapeutic relationship difficulties, which we believe has wide application. The sixth section focuses on three learning contexts (training, supervision and self-supervision), and suggests which kinds of learning strategies (role-playing, didactic teaching, reflective practice, etc.) may be most appropriate for which types of interpersonal difficulty (perceptual skills, therapist attitude, etc.). We end by drawing the conclusion that if cognitive therapists wish to develop their therapeutic expertise and in particular their interpersonal skills across a range of client problems, then willingness to self-reflect and to develop the personal as well as the professional self is a prerequisite.

The declarative–procedural–reflective (DPR) model

The aim of the DPR model is to provide a comprehensive model of therapist skill development (of any orientation) from an information-processing perspective. The model identifies and maps different elements of therapist skill and their relationship to one another, and suggests that different learning strategies are needed for different skills. Figure 12.1 illustrates the DPR model, and highlights those components particularly related to interpersonal skills.

In this section, the DPR conceptual framework is outlined (for a full description, see Bennett-Levy, 2006). We describe the three main information-processing systems (declarative, procedural and reflective), and focus on the key distinction between the self-schema and self-as-therapist schema. In the following two sections, we turn the spotlight more specifically onto the interpersonal elements of the model.

The declarative, procedural and reflective systems

The *declarative system* contains the verbal propositional knowledge base for therapy. This is knowledge that we might write about, talk about or read about. Declarative knowledge is distinguished from procedural skills (see below), because at the declarative level, knowledge may be purely abstract; for example, the novice therapist who has read about cognitive-behavioural treatment for depression, but has not utilized the skills in practice. The model posits three basic kinds of knowledge within the declarative system: interpersonal, conceptual, and technical. For example, the *interpersonal knowledge* base about cognitive therapy might contain information about the value of the collaborative relationship; more advanced interpersonal knowledge might include understanding about therapeutic rupture markers (Safran & Muran, 2000).

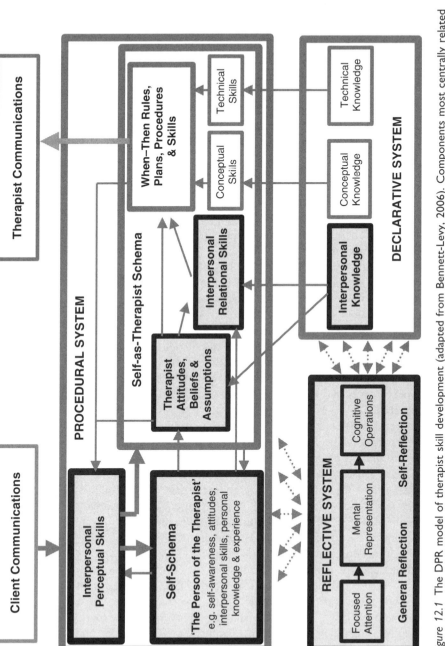

Figure 12.1 The DPR model of therapist skill development (adapted from Bennett-Levy, 2006). Components most centrally related to the acquisition and development of interpersonal skills, and to the therapeutic relationship, are highlighted.

The *procedural system* contains the often implicit storehouse of skills that are the manifestation of our declarative knowledge in practice. There are various procedural skill sub-components, some specifically oriented towards interpersonal skills (*interpersonal perceptual skills; therapist attitudes, beliefs and assumptions; interpersonal relational skills; self-schema*) – see next two sections – and some towards therapy-specific skills (*conceptual skills; technical skills*). Over time, skilled therapists are able to combine these sub-components into a largely automatized, implicit set of *when–then plans, rules, procedures* and *skills*, which can have an almost seamless appearance. These when–then rules enable us, for example, to decide with which client, at which point in time in therapy, with which kind of problem, it is most appropriate to use what kind of intervention, under what circumstances.

The reflective system is the third major system in the model. Unlike the declarative and procedural systems, the reflective system has no permanent knowledge or skill base and is a purely short-term representational system, which is created and dissolved in response to particular issues that require reflection. There are two broad types of reflection: *self-reflection*, where we reflect on our internal world, and *general reflection* (for example, reflection on technical skills – "did I use the best strategy to test the client's belief?"), which has a more distanced, objective quality. As we shall describe in the third section, self-reflection is particularly important in the creation and maintenance of effective therapeutic relationships.

The reflective system is usually prompted into action by a particular problem that requires attention, by puzzlement or curiosity, or by a mis-match between expectations and reality (for example, the client has been unexpectedly distressed by what was meant to be a therapist compliment). Supervision is, *par excellence*, a time when the reflective system is typically operative.

The reflective system comprises three principal elements: *focused attention* on a particular problem, *mental representation* of that problem (previously termed *autonoetic consciousness*; Bennett-Levy, 2006), and a set of *cognitive operations* to try to resolve the problem. Guided discovery, Socratic questioning, and logical analysis are characteristic of the cognitive operations that supervisors and trainees typically use. The reflective system then "returns" the solution to declarative and/or procedural systems, perhaps leading to modification of declarative knowledge, or of when–then plans, rules, procedures and skills.

In essence, it is the reflective system that provides the ongoing dynamic for therapist skill development. As Schön (1983) and Skovholt (2001) have written, it is this process of reflection that, perhaps more than anything else, can help to move therapists from being average to expert, from being adequate technicians to being sophisticated, flexible and responsive practitioners.

Self-schema and self-as-therapist schema

In the DPR model a distinction, which has important implications for inter-personal skills, is made between the personal (*self-schema*) and professional self (*self-as-therapist schema*) of the therapist. It is assumed that prior to becoming a therapist, we process information about the world through our self-schema. In the model, the self-schema contains our beliefs about ourselves, others and the world; our skills, our experience, our emotional intelligence, our values and so on. (In reality, the size of the self-schema is misrepresented in Figure 12.1 – it should dwarf the self-as-therapist schema and have numerous sub-components). As others have written (Gilbert, Hughes, & Dryden, 1989), and as we shall demonstrate below in the context of the DPR model, the "person of the therapist" exerts a profound influence on therapeutic process, over and above technical and conceptual proficiency.

When we train as therapists, we develop a new identity with some new beliefs and behaviours. This is the *self-as-therapist schema*. For instance, we develop new skills (e.g. *conceptual skills, technical skills*), which we (hope-fully) tend not to use in non-therapy situations with friends or relatives, and we adapt our behaviour so that it is appropriate to the therapy milieu (for example, we do not discuss our own problems and expect the client to help us solve them). However, not all of our behaviours and skills are new. In particular, we carry with us our interpersonal skills, and some of the attitudes and values that may have been instrumental in our choice of profession (for example, compassion for people in distress) (Dryden & Spurling, 1989). Some therapists appear to start with an intrinsic advantage – people who have a "naturally" warm, empathic, compassionate stance (*therapist attitudes, beliefs and assumptions*), who can easily tune into where the client is at and pick up subtle nonverbal signals (*interpersonal perceptual skills*), and can communicate their empathy and concern in a collaborative – "let's work on this together" – way (*interpersonal relational skills*). Other therapists may not have such natural advantages.

As various authors have noted (e.g. Bateman & Fonagy, 2004; Gilbert, 2005), social information processing is highly specialized. In the context of therapist skill development, the DPR model suggests that therapists' inter-personal skills are distinguished from technical and conceptual cognitive therapy skills in several ways: first, by their recruitment of different infor-mation processing systems – specifically, their dependence on the *self-schema* and *self-reflection* (see the third section); and second, because they require specific training strategies (see the sixth section).

A specific focus on interpersonal skills

Since this chapter is concerned with the development and refinement of interpersonal skills, we shall focus on the interpersonal skill components of the model in more detail. Key elements here are: *interpersonal perceptual skills, therapist attitude, interpersonal relational skills,* and *interpersonal knowledge* (see Figure 12.1).

Interpersonal perceptual skills

Interpersonal perceptual skills function as a filter that determines what information we pick up from the client and what we miss. They allow us to attune to the client's "in process" state (Greenberg & Goldman, 1988), as well as to focus on verbal and nonverbal indicators that enable us to create and gather evidence for our formulation.

Bennett-Levy (2006) suggested that perceptual skills comprise at least three partially overlapping skills: empathy, mindfulness, and reflection-in-action. Empathic attunement enables us to represent the client's experience internally within our own self-schema system, so that we can understand the nature and extent of the client's distress from the inside. Mindfulness enables us to engage in a form of double consciousness (Gabbard & Wilkinson, 1994) where we can attend to both the client's experience and our own (Katzow & Safran, Chapter 5, this volume; Safran & Muran, 2000). Reflection-in-action represents a level of skill which is sufficiently sophisticated that we are taking complex decisions about where to focus our attention, and what to do next, often out of conscious awareness.

Perceptual skills have received very little attention from cognitive therapists, possibly because these skills are difficult to measure. Yet arguably they are one of the most crucial elements of effective therapy (Greenberg & Goldman, 1988). Deficits or problems with perceptual skills can come from a variety of sources: for instance, novice therapists often do not have the attentional resource to focus on interpersonal skills as well as conceptual/technical skills, and tend to favour the latter; some may lack confidence and, like clients with social anxiety, focus their attention internally. Other therapists are simply "over-technical" (a commonly reported issue with cognitive therapists in former times) or lack capacity for empathic representation. Sometimes, where therapeutic ruptures occur, therapists may be hijacked by their own powerful countertransference reactions (Leahy, 2001; Safran & Muran, 2000).

Therapist attitudes, beliefs and assumptions

Therapist attitudes, beliefs and assumptions encompass values, beliefs, and assumptions about self, clients, and the therapy process (see Leahy, 2001). Some therapist attitudes/beliefs/assumptions have a general impact on performance (for example, "I must get all my clients better"), and may lead to irritation, sense of failure or burnout. Some attitudinal issues are specific to particular client groups (for example, difficulty working with people who get hostile, or with perpetrators of sexual assault), or to particular elements of the therapy process (for example, "I must be available for all of my clients all the time"). There are, of course, natural variations in therapist attitudes over time, often related to life or work issues (Bennett-Levy & Beedie, 2007). These can be explicitly addressed in supervision, as can the possible need for personal therapy. *Therapist attitudes, beliefs and assumptions* are likely to impact both on *perceptual skills* and on *relational (communication) skills*. As a number of chapters in this volume suggest, the stance of the therapist is fundamental.

Interpersonal relational skills

The distinction within the model between perceptual and relational skills is that whereas the former are *receptive skills* focused on the client's communications, the latter are *active therapist communication skills*, for instance the *expression* of empathy, warmth or compassion. Some relational skills are relatively simple; some undoubtedly complex. For instance, while some novice therapists may from the start have little difficulty in communicating genuineness or warmth, most therapists will require considerable training to acquire the kind of therapeutic rupture repair skills identified by Safran and colleagues (Katzow & Safran, Chapter 5, this volume; Safran & Muran, 2000). Although as indicated above, there are clear links between *relational skills* and *therapist attitudes and beliefs*, there are often disjunctions. Novice therapists sometimes need to learn that *feeling* empathic towards clients is not enough; there are skills that can be practised to *communicate* empathic understanding (Thwaites & Bennett-Levy, submitted for publication).

Interpersonal declarative knowledge

At a declarative level, therapists need a conceptual understanding of the key elements of interpersonal processes; the role they play in successful therapy; and ways to conceptualize interpersonal difficulties. Indeed, the subject matter of this entire book is contemporary declarative understandings of the therapeutic relationship in cognitive therapy, plus a wealth of procedural tips (which remain declarative knowledge until enacted). However, only when these understandings and tips are taken on board and practised do they start to become part of a therapist's procedural skills system.

Attitudinal or relational skill problems at a procedural level are often related to "person of the therapist" issues. However, sometimes they are simply a result of declarative knowledge deficits. For instance, at a basic level, if novice therapists do not understand the centrality of the collaborative approach in cognitive therapy, then they are unlikely to act collaboratively, or recognize the importance of acquiring the requisite technical knowledge and skills (for example, asking for client feedback). At a more advanced level, in order to be able to provide clients with a convincing rationale for compassionate mind training, it may be helpful for therapists to understand social mentality theory and the affect regulation systems model (Gilbert, Chapter 6, this volume).

The particular relevance of the self-schema and self-reflection to interpersonal skill development

In this section, we point to the particular contribution of the self-schema and self-reflection in the development of interpersonal skills, and suggest that it is this contribution that distinguishes interpersonal skills training from conceptual or technical skills.

The self-schema

The DPR model suggests that the self-schema is directly linked to *interpersonal perceptual skills, therapist attitude* and *interpersonal relational skills* (see Figure 12.1). As noted above, interpersonal skills and beliefs are part of who we are in everyday life, and predate therapist training, so almost inevitably there is a significant carry-over into therapist interpersonal skills and beliefs. In this sense, the relationship of therapists' interpersonal skills to the self-schema is rather different from the relationship of conceptual and technical skills to the self-schema; conceptual and technical skills are almost entirely learned *de novo*.

The proposition that personal (self-schema) development is intrinsically related to therapists' interpersonal skills gains support from a number of studies (Bennett-Levy, Turner, Beaty, Smith, Paterson, & Farmer, 2001; Bennett-Levy, Lee, Travers, Pohlman, & Hamernik, 2003; Jennings & Skovholt, 1999; Laireiter & Willutzki, 2005; Machado, Beutler, & Greenberg, 1999; Rennie, Brewster, & Toukmanian, 1985). For instance, Machado *et al.* (1999) found that therapists' personal awareness of their own emotions had a positive impact on the accuracy of identifying the emotions of a videotaped client; and Jennings & Skovholt (1999) reported that master therapists had exceptional relational skills and at a personal (self-schema) level were highly self-aware, reflective, non-defensive, and mentally healthy and mature. At times, therapists may avoid personally experiencing certain emotions (e.g. grief), which pose a threat to their self-schema (for example, from their own unresolved experiences of loss), thus limiting the processing of particular types of information (Gilbert *et al.*, 1989; Safran & Greenberg, 1998). This can block communication around significant issues and therefore constitute a threat to the working relationship between therapist and client.

Of course from a clinical perspective, it makes sense that personal (self-schema) development is highly related to therapists' interpersonal skills and attitudes, since issues such as lack of confidence (Bennett-Levy & Beedie, 2007) and the triggering of countertransference reactions (Leahy, 2001) are, of necessity, based in the therapist's personal (self-schema) experience.

Self-reflection

The other system that has particular importance in the context of inter-personal skill development is the reflective system, comprising two broad types of reflection, *general reflection* and *self-reflection*. While a number of writers point to the importance of *general reflective* capability in the development of therapist skills, including interpersonal skills (Bennett-Levy, 2006; Bennett-Levy & Padesky, submitted for publication; Milne & James, 2002; Skovholt, 2001), here it is suggested that the capacity to *self-reflect* is one of the key elements that distinguishes the learning of sophisticated interpersonal skills from the learning of technical or conceptual skills.

The distinction between these two forms of reflection, and modes of processing, is important because some clients – and therapists – may be quite adept at reflecting in one mode (for example, reflecting on a conceptual issue), and quite avoidant or unskilled in the other (for example, reflecting on a personal, emotional issue). We propose that while both general reflective skills and self-reflection are important for interpersonal skill development, deficits in each have quite different implications for the supervision or training of therapist interpersonal skills (see "Learning strategies and types of interpersonal skill problem" below).

As discussed above, interpersonal skills may in large part derive from the self-schema and are usually tacit and highly automatized. Therapists may often be unaware of some of the subtler aspects of their nonverbal communication. If personal issues or interpersonal skill difficulties of which the therapist is either unaware or only partially aware are implicated in a therapeutic rupture, then self-reflection is a prime requirement. For some supervisees who are emotionally avoidant, or have little skill at taking an observer position on their own behaviour (Ladany, Friedlander, & Nelson, 2005), this may be deeply challenging. For example, we know of supervisees with rigid technical styles who have baulked at the prospect of engaging in self-reflective practice.

The implications for training and supervision of interpersonal skills are quite apparent. A focus on the personal as well as the professional self, and a capacity and willingness to self-reflect, are central aspects of therapist skill development. While other training strategies (observational learning, role-play, lectures, reading, etc.) and learning modes (role-play, general reflection) are as applicable to the development of technical or conceptual skills as to interpersonal skills, the particular focus on self-schema and self-reflection in interpersonal skill development is both central and unique.

Interpersonal process issues in the supervisory/training relationship

In the following sections, we shall be addressing training and supervision strategies for developing and refining interpersonal skills. However, careful conceptualization of interpersonal problems and useful remediation strategies on their own are not enough. Training or supervision initiatives will be hindered unless trainees feel safe enough to discuss their therapeutic relationship difficulties. Ladany *et al.*'s (2005) suggestion about process in supervision is: "Do unto others as you would have them do unto others" (p. 215). Nowhere is this truer than when we are working with interpersonal skills.

Because perceptual or relational skill difficulties, and therapist attitudes, beliefs and assumptions, are more intrinsically tied to the self-schema than technical or conceptual skills, challenges in this domain are more emotionally sensitive, more personally felt. Furthermore, because we may experience interpersonal issues as just a vague sense of "something wrong" without a rudimentary hint of conceptualization, or because we may find ourselves tripped up time and again by an acknowledged difficulty (for example, staying calm in the face of anger), we can easily experience a feeling of foolishness, or a sense of embarrassment or shame.

The interpersonal process between the supervisor or trainer and the trainee is fundamental to effective interpersonal skills training. To create an environment in which such issues can be helpfully addressed, supervisors and trainers must model the process effectively, or trainees are likely to self-censor (Neufeldt, 1999). A sense of safeness (Gilbert, Chapter 6, this volume), non-judgemental acceptance, affirmation, empathy, care, warmth and encouragement to explore are prime requirements (Worthen & McNeill, 1996). Trainers and supervisors can assist trainees by normalizing interpersonal issues as something all therapists encounter, empathizing with the difficulty of acting effectively when emotions are aroused, acknowledging and validating their attempts to deal with the issue, and disclosing similar experiences of their own when appropriate (Worthen & McNeill, 1996). The sense of safeness is also enhanced by being clear about boundaries (for example, in supervision how to address interpersonal or personal issues, and when not to), confidentiality agreements (for example, on a training course when doing pairs work on interpersonal problems, who says what in a group discussion) and by the provision of a rationale for the focus on the experiential rather than purely the conceptual (Safran & Muran, 2000). Supervisors should model respect by seeking permission before addressing potentially sensitive self-schema issues, and openness by welcoming feedback from supervisees, in particular when things do not feel right.

These requirements underpin the discussion of training and supervision strategies below. For instance, trainees are unlikely to engage fully in an experiential training programme where they practise cognitive therapy techniques on themselves unless their doubts are welcomed and addressed, the conditions are collaboratively negotiated, and confidentiality agreements are clear (Bennett-Levy *et al.*, 2001). Similarly, supervisees who feel that they may be negatively judged are likely to be reluctant to raise interpersonal difficulties with their supervisor (Ladany *et al.*, 2005). Further suggestions about process issues are contained in Table 12.1.

A six-stage process model for addressing therapeutic relationship difficulties

In Figure 12.2, we present a six-stage model for addressing therapeutic relationship difficulties developed from examples in the literature, consultation with colleagues, and our own practice. We suggest that the model has particular applicability for supervision, and may also be used in self-supervision and training contexts.

The six stages are mapped out in Figure 12.2. The supervisee arrives for a supervision session, having recently experienced an interpersonal problem with a client. The issue may be quite clear, or it may be felt as a vague sense of unease in need of clarification. At Stage 1 (*focused attention* – first part of the reflective system; see Figure 12.1), the problem is raised and becomes a focus for reflection in the session.

At Stage 2 (*mental representation*), the issue is brought to mind. Here the supervisor helps the supervisee to evoke a direct experiential awareness of the feelings, thoughts and behaviours activated at the time of the session. This typically takes one of two forms. In the first procedure, the supervisor helps the supervisee to reconstruct his/her experience in the therapist's chair; it is often helpful to use role-play or imagery to bring the feelings back to life. A second procedure – especially useful when there is a strong countertransference reaction and the supervisee appears blind to the client's experience – is for the supervisee to use his/her self-schema reaction to process the situation as if in the client's chair. Here, the supervisor role-plays the therapist, and the supervisee the client.

At Stage 3 (*cognitive operations: clarify experience*), the supervisor helps the supervisee reflect on the experience in the therapist's or client's chair, still in a subjective, experiential, how-it-felt mode. Here the purpose is to clarify their understanding of the emotions and cognitions they experienced; to move from vagueness to clarity, or from knee-jerk reaction to experiencing the underlying feelings.

At Stage 4 (*cognitive operations: conceptualize using declarative system*), there is a shift in mode of processing from the primarily subjective, experiential mode of Stage 3 to a more objectifying conceptual–analytic stance. The Reflective System (Stage 4a) engages with the declarative system (Stage 4b) to create a "reflective bridge", using the enhanced experiential

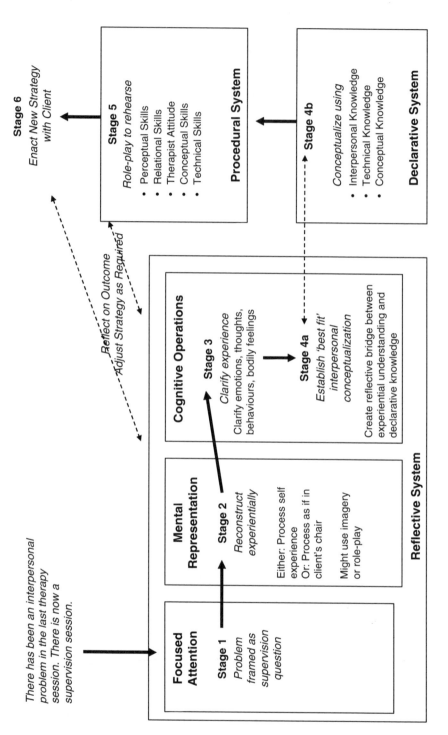

Figure 12.2 The six-stage process model for addressing therapeutic relationship difficulties (solid arrows indicate progression through the stages; broken arrows are reflective processes).

understanding together with declarative knowledge to create an inter-personal conceptualization of the difficult interaction. Movement from Stage 3 to Stage 4 is what Safran & Muran (2000) term "disembedding" from the experience, adopting a metacognitive perspective. Due to the emotion aroused by the difficult therapy session, and the subjective mode of processing in Stages 2 and 3, the supervisor is often particularly helpful in helping to shift modes of processing between Stages 3 and 4.

Once the situation has been conceptualized, using interpersonal and conceptual knowledge, the situation can be role-played to put the appropriate procedural skills into practice (Stage 5). When these have been adequately refined, they can be tried out with the client (Stage 6). At Stages 5 and 6, supervisee and supervisor reflect on the experience of the role-play or on the actual experience with the client, and adjust procedural skills accordingly.

To bring the model to life, below we give a specific example from a supervision session.

Stage 1: Focus on and frame the problem

Terry, the supervisee, came to his supervision session concerned that his depressed client, Mary, was not making the progress that might have been expected. Listening to an audiotape of a recent session, it became clear to Terry and his supervisor Jane that as soon as Mary started crying, he moved hastily into problem-solving mode. Terry said this often occurred in their sessions.

Stage 2: Evoke mental representation of the experience

Jane suggested a reverse role-play, where she role-played Terry in his problem-solving mode and Terry moved into the client's chair as Mary.

Stage 3: Clarify the experience

When Terry experienced the rush into problem-solving mode for himself, he reflected that he found it hurtful and invalidating, and withdrew emotionally.

Stage 4: Conceptualize the experience

Jane and Terry were now able to use this experience to derive an inter-personal formulation that identified the particular behaviours that Mary's crying "pulled" from Terry; the impact of the rush to problem-solving on Mary's sense of being heard and validated; her emotional withdrawal; and the effect on the relationship, collaboration and homework compliance.

They used the formulation, and other interpersonal and technical knowledge, to identify more helpful procedural skills that Terry could try out.

Stage 5: Practise procedural skills

Terry and Jane now did several role-plays. With Terry in the therapist's chair, and Jane role-playing Mary, Terry practised first responding empathically and validating Mary's distress before moving into a collaborative formulation and problem-solving mode. Jane gave Terry feedback about her experience in the client's chair after each role-play, and they discussed what adjustments might enhance Terry's skills further.

Stage 6: Try out new strategy

Terry tried the new strategy with Mary with immediate positive results.

At all stages, reflection was intrinsic to the process, as identified by the broken arrows in Figure 12.2. It is also worth noting that the process continued beyond Stage 6.

Beyond Stage 6

Terry confided to Jane that he tended to rush into problem-solving mode with other clients as well. Jane asked what could be behind this thinking. Terry said that for as long as he could remember, he'd felt uncomfortable when people were upset (*self-schema* emotional activation). He had implicit rules that he was there to help people, not to cause pain (*self-schema* rule, now translated into a *therapist attitude/belief*), and as a therapist that it might be dangerous to his clients to stick with upsetting things (*therapist attitude/belief*). Jane suggested that for Terry to change these feelings and rules, it might be useful for him to explore their derivation in his personal history (*self-schema*), and consider how he would like to feel instead. He might then develop and test out some more adaptive rules (further reflection on *self-schema*, develop new rules, behavioural experiments with new rules).

This example demonstrates the close links between interpersonal difficulties and the self-schema, and why there is often a need for therapists to self-reflect and engage in further self-schema work to address interpersonal problems, using strategies such as self-practice/self-reflection or personal therapy (see next section).

Learning strategies and types of interpersonal skill problem

In this section, we highlight some of the strategies that cognitive therapists currently use to develop and refine their interpersonal skills, which are crucial to the therapeutic relationship, and point to some new possibilities. We suggest that some strategies (for example, emotion recognition training) are particularly appropriate for certain types of interpersonal skill problem (for example, interpersonal perceptual skills), and less so for others (for example, general reflection deficit); however, other learning strategies (for example, reflective practice) may have broad applicability.

Table 12.1 links strategies to types of problem, and provides the framework for the following discussion. It contains many suggestions, some empirically supported, some more speculative. A detailed discussion of each element is beyond the scope of the chapter. In this section, we focus on the three key strategies that we believe impact significantly at *most* levels of interpersonal skill: reflective practice, self-practice/self-reflection and role-playing. We then briefly discuss the value of other common training strategies (didactic presentations, demonstrations/observational learning) and aids to supervision (use of videotapes and audiotapes). For perceptual skills training, we speculate that there may be useful training strategies specific to these skills. Finally we highlight the fact that interpersonal skills may be significantly impaired when clinicians have personal (self-schema) problems or deficits in reflective function.

Reflective practice

Within the context of the DPR model, we use the term "reflective practice" to refer to the activity of reflecting on clinical experience, including our personal reactions, attitudes and beliefs, with the purpose of enhancing our declarative knowledge and procedural skills. Reflective practice is the self-supervision cornerstone of our day-to-day development as therapists. It is also the quintessential characteristic of good supervision, with the added advantage that the supervisor can ask Socratic questions, provide declarative information and stimulate reflection that is beyond the internal frame of reference of the supervisee. As noted in the first and third sections, and Table 12.1, reflection is a particularly important component in the refinement of interpersonal skills.

Reflective practice requires certain practitioner qualities, as well as an understanding of its rationale: "The ability to reflect upon one's own practice requires self-awareness, honesty and insight into one's values and attitudes, and an understanding of what it is that one is trying to achieve. To then utilize such reflection in the development of one's clinical practice requires flexibility, adaptability and a willingness to accept that the work one is doing

Table 12.1 Problem areas and some suggested self-supervision, supervision and training strategies: declarative knowledge and perceptual skills

	DECLARATIVE KNOWLEDGE	PERCEPTUAL SKILLS
Examples of markers of the problem	**Tape observation** • e.g. Therapist does not appear to understand role of collaboration in CBT **Therapist report** • Therapist is aware of, but unable to conceptualise interpersonal problems e.g. "*I can't understand why I feel so angry with this client*" e.g. "*Something about the sessions just doesn't feel right*"	**Client feedback** • Feeling not heard or understood **Tape observation** • Therapist not picking up on emotional states of client (e.g. unacknowledged shame) • Nonverbal behaviour of client (e.g. emotional withdrawal) • Inappropriate use of relational skills or deficits may indicate problems at a perceptual skill level
Self-supervision strategies	**Reflective practice** • e.g. Theory-based conceptualisation **Self-directed reading** • Basic interpersonal knowledge, e.g. role of collaboration • Complex interpersonal knowledge, e.g. Safran & Segal (1990) model of interpersonal process	**Reflective practice** • Including review of tapes of own sessions, focusing on client's emotional state moment-to-moment **Mindfulness practice**
Supervision strategies	**Supervisor-directed reading** **Didactic teaching** **Role playing** • Supervisor role plays client then supervisee formulates	**Tape review** • With appropriate reflection on client communications (including nonverbal) • Practice recognition of emotional state of client **6-Stage process model** **Interpersonal process recall**
Training strategies	**Didactic teaching** **Role playing** **Modelling/observational learning** **Problem-based learning**	**Emotion and nonverbal communication recognition training** **Role playing** **Self-practice/self-reflection** **Modelling/observational learning**
Relevant process issues	**Sensitive/non-shaming questioning to identify knowledge deficits** • Bringing to awareness • Build on current declarative knowledge	**Sensitivity** **Explicit agreement/contracting** • Confidentiality • Implications for joint/group supervision

Table 12.1 (continued) Problem areas and some suggested self-supervision, supervision and training strategies: therapist attitude and relational skills

	ATTITUDES/BELIEFS/ASSUMPTIONS	RELATIONAL SKILLS
Examples of markers of the problem	**Client feedback** • In-session feedback (e.g. "*It feels as if you don't care about my problems*") • Formal complaints **Tape observation** • Could be identified by verbal content, tone of voice, nonverbal communication **Therapist report** • Awareness of a difficulty in empathising with a particular client **Rigid gender- or culture-based assumptions**	**Tape observation** • Absence of, or poor skills in, establishing or maintaining a therapeutic relationship **Client behaviour** • Early termination of therapy • Resistance to procedure (e.g. not completing homework)
Self-supervision strategies	**Reflective practice** • Emotion as a guide **CBT techniques to identify and test therapist beliefs/rules** • Automatic thought records • Behavioural experiments • Self-Socratic questioning	**Reflective practice** • Including review of tapes of own sessions focusing on therapist's relational skills • Imaginal work – being in the client's chair
Supervision strategies	**Identify type of attitudinal difficulty** • Therapist belief questionnaires • Distinguish between general attitude, problem-specific (e.g. depressed clients) or client-specific • Distinguish between temporary problem (e.g. life issue) vs. personality problem **6-Stage process model**	**Tape review** • With feedback and reflection **Role playing** **Supervisory relationship** **Modelling** **6-Stage process model** **Interpersonal process recall**
Training strategies	**Self-practice/self-reflection** **Role playing** **Modelling/observational learning**	**Role playing** • Microcounselling training **Self-practice/self-reflection** **Modelling/observational learning**
Relevant process issues	**Particularly sensitive as may be closely related to self-schema** **Boundaries** • e.g. Regarding which personal issues are discussed in supervision and which require personal therapy	**Supervisor aware of own assumptions regarding supervisee relational skills** • e.g. General training issue or quality control for exceptions? **Overcoming therapist resistance to role plays within supervision** • Normalise anxiety • Provide rationale • Self-disclosure • Supervisor initially model therapist role

Table 12.1 (continued) Problem areas and some suggested self-supervision, supervision and training strategies: general reflection and self-reflection

	GENERAL REFLECTION	SELF-REFLECTION
Examples of markers of the problem	**Curiosity not aroused by therapeutic anomalies** **Difficulty bringing to mind therapeutic incidents** **Absence of self-Socratic questioning** **Problems with conceptual or abstract thinking**	**Difficulty or unwillingness to reflect on own beliefs, feelings or contribution to the therapeutic relationship** • e.g. Emotional avoidance • Difficulty tolerating own emotions • Inexperienced therapist with high levels of anxiety • External attributions regarding therapeutic process
Self-supervision strategies	**Reflective practice** • Reflective writing, e.g. session review • Self-evaluation of tapes of sessions • Actively seeking client feedback • Putting oneself in the client's shoes • Identifying gaps in knowledge **Mindfulness practice**	**Reflective practice** • Reflective writing about own feelings, thoughts and behaviours **Self-practice/self-reflection** **Mindfulness practice**
Supervision strategies	**Detailed session notes** **Preparation for supervision** (e.g. identify question) **Role playing + reflection** **Attentional shift to arouse curiosity** (e.g. identify one surprising aspect of each session) **Reflective writing**	**Socratic questioning in supervision** **Interpersonal process recall**
Training strategies	**Self-practice/self-reflection** **Problem-based learning** **Reflective work sheets** **Role playing**	**Self-practice/self-reflection** **Reflective worksheets** • To facilitate internalisation of reflective structure **Role playing**
Relevant process issues	**Provide clear rationale/ framework (declarative knowledge)** **Sensitivity/tact** **Explicit agreement/contracting** • Confidentiality and implications for joint/group supervision **Major reflective deficit – consider suitability for profession?**	**Provide clear rationale/framework (declarative knowledge)** **Sensitivity/tact** **Explicit agreement/contracting** • Confidentiality and implications for joint/group supervision **Contextual factors** • Is self-reflection mandatory? • Quality of supervisory relationship • Institutional/service parameters • Personal resources

Table 12.1 (continued) Problem areas and some suggested self-supervision, supervision and training strategies: the self-schema (person of the therapist)

	SELF-SCHEMA
Examples of markers of the problem	**Self-confidence problems**
	Emotional exhaustion/vicarious trauma
	Personality problems
	Counter transference/interpersonal schema activated • Unusual or strong emotional reactions, e.g. attraction to clients, anger, frustration
Self-supervision strategies	**Reflective practice**
	Personal therapy
	Self-practice/self-reflection
	Personal growth strategies (e.g. psychodrama, yoga)
Supervision strategies	**Awareness raising**
	Attentional refocus
	Normalising
	Therapist self-care
	Identify need for personal therapy
	6-Stage process model
Training strategies	**Self-practice/self-reflection**
	Mindfulness practice
Relevant process issues	**Provide clear rationale/framework (declarative knowledge)**
	Sensitivity/tact
	Explicit agreement/contracting • Confidentiality and implications for joint/group supervision
	Awareness of supervisor responsibilities
	Boundaries e.g. Regarding which personal issues are discussed in supervision

may benefit from this process" (Cushway & Gatherer, 2003, p. 9). Possible strategies to enhance reflective practice include: reflective writing, self-evaluation of tapes and sessions, actively seeking and using client feedback, using supervision to maximum effect by preparing well and seeking help with difficult or uncomfortable issues, putting oneself in the client's shoes, continuing to reflect on client conceptualizations between sessions, and seeking out relevant literature when identifying gaps in knowledge and skills.

Reflective writing (Bolton, 2005) soon after sessions, particularly difficult ones, can be an effective practice. As an example, below is an excerpt from Susan's writing after a difficult session with a rigid emotionally controlled client:

> I think I got it wrong this session. It was not collaborative. I took her somewhere she had expressly said she didn't want to go [revisiting the break-up of a past relationship]. I did not respect her wishes. Why did I do it? Because it seemed to me that at some level her continued love for Harry was ridiculous, absurd. Why is she idolizing him? Is it like my experience with Ben? . . . [reflects on similarities and differences of own experience with former partner, and draws the conclusion that problematic self-schema beliefs of her own were activated in a counter-transference reaction to the client's experience] . . .
>
> I think I should start next week with apologising. I think I made a wrong move. It might work out OK in the end, but for now we need to work more gently. She has avoided emotions for many years, so to open them up like this was too much. Let's go for looking at the future, who she was then, and who she might yet become.

Self-practice/self-reflection (SP/SR)

Self-practice/self-reflection (SP/SR) refers to a structured training experience in which trainees practise cognitive therapy techniques on themselves (SP), and then do written reflections (SR) focused on (i) their experience, (ii) its implications for their clinical practice, and (iii) the implications for cognitive theory (Bennett-Levy et al., 2001, 2003). Two forms of SP/SR have been developed: one where trainees practise on their own via a structured workbook, and one where they engage in a limited "co-therapy" relationship, typically over four to six sessions each way.

Participants report a wide range of changes in the declarative understandings and procedural skills of cognitive therapy (Bennett-Levy et al., 2001), and in their self-concept (e.g. confidence as therapist). More specifically, with regard to the present chapter, it has been suggested that the *prime* impact of SP/SR is on interpersonal skills (Bennett-Levy, 2005). For example, an experienced therapist who recently participated in an SP/SR course reflected: "I feel I have taken away so many important things, but having experienced therapy has deepened my understanding of the importance of a good therapeutic alliance, collaboration, interest, trust, acceptance, compassion, etc."

Bennett-Levy (2005) has argued that the enhanced interpersonal skills (e.g. perceptual, relational) infuse other more cognitive therapy-specific skills (e.g. the technical skills of setting up a behavioural experiment) with greater interpersonal sensitivity; the end result is greater "professional artistry" (Schön, 1983), or, in terms of the DPR model, more seamless when–then skills. The fact that SP/SR also impacts on two other major contributors to interpersonal skills, the self-schema (Bennett-Levy et al., 2001) and self-reflection (Bennett-Levy et al., 2003), further suggests its particular relevance to interpersonal skill training. Though the value of self-experiential and reflective strategies still awaits empirical verification using behavioural skill measures rather than self-report, a growing empirical base and an increasingly coherent theory of therapist skill development suggest that cognitive therapists need to seriously consider taking on board self-practice and self-reflection as frontline training strategies (Laireiter & Willutzki, 2005).

Role-playing

Role-playing is the key way in training workshops to develop procedural skills without using personal material, which for a number of reasons is often not appropriate; for example, confidentiality, safety, type of issue or type of client group. It also became a prominent part of interpersonal skills training with the development of the microcounselling training model (Daniels, Rigazio-Digilio, & Ivey, 1997). There is a sound evidential base for its effectiveness (Alberts & Edelstein, 1990; Daniels et al., 1997), especially when appropriate feedback is provided. For supervisors, role-playing provides a live opportunity to see strengths and limitations, and coach microskills.

Other strategies such as didactic learning or live or videotaped demonstrations may provide the conceptual background and guidance for procedural learning, but it is only by enacting the skills in practice that trainees can gauge what works and what does not, and where the gaps in their skills lie (Padesky, 1996). Furthermore, there is evidence that procedural skills are encoded and stored differently in memory from declarative learning, and require enactive strategies for effective learning (Engelkamp, 1998).

Other common training strategies: Didactic teaching and modelling/demonstrations

It is our perception that the value of didactic teaching is frequently over-rated by cognitive therapy trainers. Trainers who spend the greater proportion of day-long workshops in lecture mode – we have seen many examples of this – may be doing trainees a disservice if the purpose of training is the acquisition or refinement of procedural skills. Certainly, didactic learning is a useful method, but not the only one (others being, for example, reading, video demonstrations) for acquiring declarative knowledge (Padesky, 1996). As Binder (1999) has so cogently observed, there is a danger that declarative knowledge becomes "inert" unless practised.

Video or live demonstrations can be very helpful, especially with appropriate orientation and reflection questions (Padesky, 1996). We can, and should, ask trainees to focus their attention on specific elements of demonstrations according to need: content or process, verbal or nonverbal communication, therapist attitude, perceptual skills, relational skills, declarative theory – or even reflective skills. For instance, Safran and Muran (2000) suggest a strategy where supervisors model the reflective process by role-playing the therapist while "thinking aloud", thus illustrating their internal reflections on their emotional state, thoughts and when–then rules.

At best, demonstrations can provide a powerful bridge between declarative knowledge and procedural skills. A colleague recently remarked that a video demonstration by a therapist calmly and effectively dealing with a very hostile client taught her more than hundreds of hours of reading could ever do. However, as microskills trainers have so effectively demonstrated, it is not enough just to tell and show (Alberts & Edelstein, 1990; Baker *et al.*, 1990). Practice, feedback and reflection are necessary to maximize acquisition of interpersonal skills.

Use of videotape and audiotape in supervision

We cannot rely on self-report if we want to assess interpersonal skills. Trainees may simply not notice problems because these skills are so intrinsic to the self-schema and automatized; or they may feel embarrassed about skills deficits, and unwilling to report them; or they may attribute difficulties to client factors rather than the relationship. Videotapes or audiotapes of trainees' clinical sessions provide essential information unavailable by other means. Videotape has the advantage over audiotape of providing considerably more information about nonverbal interpersonal behaviours.

Perceptual skills training

We are specifically addressing perceptual skills training here because the understanding of interpersonal skills within cognitive therapy has lagged behind that of conceptual and technical skills, and cognitive therapists have rarely identified perceptual skills as a separate identifiable category. Writers from other psychotherapeutic traditions (e.g. Greenberg & Goldman, 1988) have highlighted their importance. Since the recognition of nonverbal signals and complex emotions is such an important feature of perceptual skill, we would suggest the specific value of emotion recognition training (Machado *et al.*, 1999), and nonverbal skills sensitivity training (Grace, Kivlighan, & Kunce, 1995), especially for novice cognitive therapists without previous therapy experience.

An alternative method for using session tapes specifically to focus on perceptual skills has been described by Safran and Muran (2000). Here the supervisor stops the tape at key interpersonal points and asks the supervisee to reconstruct their reaction at the time. The aim of this strategy (similar to interpersonal process recall; Kagan & Kagan, 1997) is for supervisees to become more attuned to their internal processes by recalling thoughts, feelings and goals whenever they come to mind.

Deficits in reflection

We have suggested that reflection, and in particular self-reflection, is central to the development and refinement of interpersonal skill, and have identified two kinds of reflection deficits: general and self-reflection deficits. We believe the identification of these two kinds of deficit to be important to the conceptualization of interpersonal skills problems. At this stage, while our suggestions for remediation in Table 12.1 are largely speculative, we have recent evidence from trainees' self-report that reflection worksheets promote procedural skills (Bennett-Levy & Padesky, submitted for publication).

Self-schema problems

Figure 12.1 indicates that self-schema problems may directly impact on interpersonal skills. Ladany *et al.* (2005) suggest that three kinds of self-schema problem may affect therapeutic efficacy: self-confidence problems, emotional exhaustion or vicarious traumatization, and major characterological deficits. Clearly ways of addressing each vary considerably. In addition, of course, countertransference reactions resulting from self-schema emotional activation are central to interpersonal problems, as various chapters in this book (e.g. Leahy, Chapter 11; Newman, Chapter 8) have indicated. The six-stage process model has been suggested as an appropriate strategy here.

The traditional path for addressing self-schema problems has been personal therapy. Cognitive therapists apparently seek therapy less than other therapists (Orlinsky, Botermans, Rønnestad & the SPR Network, 2001). When they do, they tend to choose therapists from other therapy traditions. Full discussion of the value of personal therapy and therapy orientation is beyond the scope of the present chapter. However, we concur with Laireiter and Willutzki's (2005) suggestion that, early in their career, it makes sense for cognitive therapy trainees choosing a personal therapy path to experience cognitive therapy for themselves. Later, they may choose other orientations for personal reasons, and/or to broaden and enrich their style.

Mindfulness training has also been suggested as an appropriate strategy for the personal and professional development of therapists (Safran & Muran, 2000). Again, though data on its impact on therapists is lacking, the suggestion is certainly consistent with the need for therapists to develop mindfulness of inner states (Safran & Muran, 2000; Bennett-Levy, 2006). At a personal level, there is plenty of data to suggest that mindfulness also has beneficial effects on mental health.

Finally, both Mahoney (2000) and Skovholt (2001) have emphasized the importance of therapist self-care for both personal and professional reasons. Being a therapist is a demanding task; treating ourselves with the care and respect that we would want for our clients may be just as important for their health as for ours.

Concluding remarks

It has been our aim in this chapter to present a model of therapist skill development that conceptualizes interpersonal skill problems in therapists within an information-processing context. The model identifies different types of interpersonal difficulty (for example, perceptual, relational), derived from different sources (for example, declarative knowledge problems, self-schema, general reflection deficit), and suggests a variety of developmental strategies for different contexts (training, supervision, self-supervision). We have emphasized that if we are to engage trainees to change their behaviours in this most sensitive of areas, supervisors and trainers must be particularly mindful of their own communications in the supervisory relationship.

Our analysis, derived from the DPR model, leads to the inescapable conclusion that interpersonal skills are intimately related to our personal (self-schema) development and capacity to reflect on our experience. We suggest that cognitive therapists should no longer avoid the implications of this conclusion. What does this mean for training? How can we incorporate and balance personal and professional development within our courses? What kind of personal development is most appropriate? Clearly there are many questions to be addressed, and considerable need for research. We believe that we are now at the point where there is sufficient empirical and theoretical rationale to canvass these issues. Enough of avoidance! Time for cognitive therapy to engage in this kind of reflection on itself.

Acknowledgements

We are grateful to Heather Balleny, Melanie Fennell and Kate Frost for providing examples for this chapter.

References

Alberts, G. & Edelstein, B. (1990). Therapist training: A critical review of skill training studies. *Clinical Psychology Review*, 10, 497–511.

Baker, S.D., Daniels, T.G. & Greeley, A.T. (19900. Systematic training of graduate-level counselors: Narrative and meta-analytic reviews of three major programmes. *The Counseling Psychologist*, 18, 355–421.

Bateman, A. & Fonagy, P. (2004). *Psychotherapy for borderline personality disorder*. Oxford: Oxford University Press.

Bennett-Levy, J. (2005). What role does the "person of the therapist" play in therapist skill development? Empirical and theoretical perspectives. In M. Jackson & G. Murphy (eds), *Theory and practice in contemporary Australian cognitive and behaviour therapy: Proceedings of the 28th National AACBT Conference* (pp. 32–37). Melbourne: Australian Association for Cognitive and Behaviour Therapy.

Bennett-Levy, J. (2006). Therapist skills: A cognitive model of their acquisition and refinement. *Behavioural and Cognitive Psychotherapy*, 34, 57–78.

Bennett-Levy, J. & Beedie, A. (2007). The ups and downs of cognitive therapy training: What happens to trainees' perception of their competence during a cognitive therapy training course? *Behavioural and Cognitive Psychotherapy*, in press.

Bennett-Levy, J., Lee, N., Travers, K., Pohlman, S. & Hamernik, E. (2003). Cognitive therapy from the inside: Enhancing therapist skills through practising what we preach. *Behavioural and Cognitive Psychotherapy*, 31, 145–163.

Bennett-Levy, J. & Padesky, C.A. (submitted for publication). Learning therapist skills: Reflection *is* important.

Bennett-Levy, J., Turner, F., Beaty, T., Smith, M., Paterson, B. & Farmer, S. (2001). The value of self-practice of cognitive therapy techniques and self-reflection in the training of cognitive therapists. *Behavioural and Cognitive Psychotherapy*, 29, 203–220.

Binder, J.L. (1999). Issues in teaching and learning time-limited psychodynamic psychotherapy. *Clinical Psychology Review*, 19, 705–719.

Bolton, G. (2005). Reflective practice (2nd edition). London: Sage.

Cushway, D. & Gatherer, A. (2003). Reflecting on reflection. *Clinical Psychology*, July, 6–10.

Daniels, T.G., Rigazio-Digilio, S.A. & Ivey, A.E. (1997). Microcounseling: A training and supervision model for the helping professions. In C.E. Watkins (ed.), *Handbook of psychotherapy supervision* (pp. 277–295). New York: Wiley.

Dryden, W. & Spurling, L. (eds) (1989). *On becoming a therapist*. London: Routledge.

Engelkamp, J. (1998). *Memory for actions*. Hove, UK: Psychology Press.

Epstein, S. (1994). Integration of the cognitive and the psychodynamic unconscious. *American Psychologist*, 49, 709–724.

Gabbard, G.O. & Wilkinson, S.M. (1994). *Management of countertransference with borderline patients*. Washington, DC: American Psychiatric Press.

Gilbert, P. (2005). Compassion and cruelty: A biopsychosocial approach. In P. Gilbert (ed.), *Compassion: Conceptualisations, research and use in psychotherapy* (pp. 9–74). Hove, UK: Brunner-Routledge.

Gilbert, P., Hughes, W. & Dryden, W. (1989). The therapist as a crucial variable in psychotherapy. In W. Dryden & L. Spurling (eds), *On becoming a therapist* (pp. 3–13). London: Routledge.

Grace, M., Kivlighan, D.M. & Kunce, J. (1995). The effect of nonverbal skills training on counselor trainee nonverbal sensitivity and responsiveness and on session impact and working alliance ratings. *Journal of Counseling and Development*, 73, 547–552.

Greenberg, L.S. & Goldman, R.L. (1988). Training in experiential therapy. *Journal of Consulting and Clinical Psychology*, 56, 696–702.

Jennings, L. & Skovholt, T.M. (1999). The cognitive, emotional, and relational characteristics of master therapists. *Journal of Counseling Psychology*, 46, 3–11.

Kagan, H. & Kagan, N.I. (1997). Interpersonal process recall: Influencing human interaction. In C.E. Watkins (ed.), *Handbook of psychotherapy supervision* (pp. 296–309). New York: Wiley.

Ladany, N., Friedlander, M.L. & Nelson, M.L. (2005). *Critical events in psychotherapy supervision*. Washington, DC: American Psychological Association.

Laireiter, A.-R. & Willutzki, U. (2005). Personal therapy in cognitive-behavioural therapy: Tradition and current practice. In J.D. Geller, J.C. Norcross & D.E. Orlinsky (eds), *The psychotherapist's own psychotherapy: Patient and clinician perspectives* (pp. 41–51). Oxford: Oxford University Press.

Leahy, R. (2001). *Overcoming resistance in cognitive therapy*. New York: Guilford Press.

Machado, P.P.P., Beutler, L.E. & Greenberg, L.S. (1999). Emotional recognition in psychotherapy: Impact of therapist level of experience and emotional awareness. *Journal of Clinical Psychology*, 55, 39–57.

Macran, S. & Shapiro, D. (1998). The role of personal therapy for therapists: A review. *British Journal of Medical Psychology*, 71, 13–25.

Mahoney, M.J. (2000). Training future psychotherapists. In C.R. Snyder & R.E. Ingram (eds), *Handbook of psychological change* (pp. 727–735). New York: Wiley.

Milne, D.L. & James, I.A. (2002). The observed impact of training on competence in clinical supervision. *British Journal of Clinical Psychology*, 41, 55–72.

Neufeldt, S.A. (1999). *Supervision strategies for the first practicum* (2nd edition). Alexandria, VA: American Counseling Association.

Orlinsky, D.E., Botermans, J.-F., Rønnestad, M.H. & the SPR Network (2001). Towards an empirically grounded model of psychotherapy training: Four thousand therapists rate influences on their development. *Australian Psychologist*, 36, 139–148.

Padesky, C.A. (1996). Developing cognitive therapist competency: Teaching and supervision models. In P.M. Salkovskis (ed.), *Frontiers of cognitive therapy* (pp. 266–292). New York: Guilford Press.

Rennie, D.L., Brewster, L.J. & Toukmanian, S.G. (1985). The counsellor trainee as client: Client process as predictor of counselling skill acquisition. *Canadian Journal of Behavior Science*, 17, 16–28.

Safran, J.D. & Greenberg, L.S. (1998). Affect and the unconscious: a cognitive perspective. In J.D. Safran (ed.), *Widening the scope of cognitive therapy* (pp. 145–169). Northvale, NJ: Aronson.

Safran, J.D. & Muran, J.C. (2000). *Negotiating the therapeutic alliance: A relational treatment guide*. New York: Guilford.

Schön, D.A. (1983). *The reflective practitioner*. New York: Basic Books.

Skovholt, T.M. (2001). *The resilient practitioner: Burnout prevention and self-care strategies for counselors, therapists, teachers, and health professionals*. Boston: Allyn & Bacon.

Thwaites, R. & Bennett-Levy, J. (submitted for publication). Making the implicit explicit: Conceptualising empathy in cognitive therapy.

Worthen, V. & McNeill, B.W. (1996). A phenomenological investigation of "good" supervision events. *Journal of Counseling Psychology*, 43, 25–34.

Index